THE
COMPLETE
GUIDE
TO
EVERYDAY
KANJI

THE
COMPLETE
GUIDE
TO
EVERYDAY
KANJI

Yaeko S. Habein
Instructor, University of Hawaii at Manoa

Gerald B. Mathias
Associate Professor, University of Hawaii at Manoa

KODANSHA INTERNATIONAL
Tokyo • New York • London

Publication of this book has been assisted by a grant from the Japan Foundation.

Distributed in the United States by Kodansha America, Inc., 114 Fifth Avenue, New York, N.Y. 10011, and in the United Kingdom and continental Europe by Kodansha Europe, Ltd., Gillingham House, 38-44 Gillingham Street, London SW1V 1HU.

Published by Kodansha International Ltd., 17-14 Otowa 1-chome, Bunkyo-ku, Tokyo 112, and Kodansha America, Inc.

ISBN 4-7700-1509-7 (in Japan)

First edition, 1991
91 92 93 94 10 9 8 7 6 5 4 3 2 1

Library of Congress Cataloging-in-Publication Data

Habein, Yaeko Sato.
   Complete guide to everyday Kanji / by Yaeko S. Habein, Gerald Barton Mathias.—1st ed.
     p.   cm.
   Includes bibliographical references and index.
   ISBN 0-87011-793-9 (U.S.)
   1. Chinese characters—Japan. 2. Japanese language—Glossaries, vocabularies, etc. I. Mathias; Gerald Barton. II. Title.
PL528.H23 1990
496.6'11—dc20
90-44026
CIP

CONTENTS

Preface

This book is for the student of modern written Japanese. Its purpose is to provide information on the structure of both individual kanji (Chinese characters) and kanji compounds, to enable the student to study kanji systematically. We have limited ourselves to the 1,945 Jōyō Kanji (a list of "common use" characters selected by the Japanese Ministry of Education in 1981), feeling that a mastery of these would provide a strong background in the subject.

The book has been designed, not as a textbook in the strict sense, but rather as a reference book for students just beginning to study kanji and for more advanced students who feel they need to review systematically what they have learned. The nature of the content precluded ordering the presentatioin of kanji from most to least common, or in any such way as to coincide with the student's acquisition of vocabulary. The book can, however, be used as a text if complemented by appropriate materials.

The manuscript of this book was prepared under a grant from the University of Hawaii Japan Studies Endowment, funded by a grant from the Japanese government. We wish to express here our sincere appreciation for this assistance. We are also greatly indebted to the Japan Foundation for its financial support of the book's publication, and to the editors at Kodansha International, for all that they have contributed to the realization of this book.

Introduction

It is no easy task to learn the 2,000 or so kanji needed to read newspapers and magazines in Japanese. A good deal of memorization is required, and adult learners of Japanese are at a disadvantage compared to Japanese children embarking on their study of kanji: Adults cannot afford to spend the nine school years that Japanese children take to learn the Jōyō Kanji, and they have to learn the vocabulary as they go along.

No matter how enthusiastically one may begin the study, one is likely to reach sooner or later a frustrating plateau where groups of kanji begin to look alike. It may be easy to learn 暮 (ボ/くらす nightfall, end; live) in isolation, but then along comb 墓 (ボ/はか grave), 募 (ボ/つのる raise [funds], advertise for), 幕 (マク/バク curtain), and 慕 (ボ/したう yearn for), almost certain to bring confusion. One soon realizes, too, that contrary to common belief, not many kanji originated as pictographs, and they hardly look like pictures today.

Readings of Kanji

Learning the forms of kanji and their approximate meanings is one thing, but one must also learn the multifarious ways of *reading* the kanji.

There are two basic kinds of kanji readings in Japanese.

1. *On-yomi* 音読み (reading by sound). *On-yomi* are readings that are based on historical Chinese pronunciations of the character and that have been modified by Japanese pronunciation and natural language change over the centuries. Many kanji with a common element have identical or similar *on-yomi* (e.g., 暮, 墓, 募, 慕 listed above, all have the *on-yomi* ボ), a phenomenon that will prove very helpful in learning the readings of kanji.
2. *Kun-yomi* 訓読み. These are native Japanese reading of kanji. *Kun-yomi* bear no relation to the forms or origins of the kanji; rather they are native Japanese words that were "assigned" to their kanji based on meaning. There is therefore no form-reading shortcut as there is with *on-yomi*.

A kanji may have only one reading, but most have several. Multiple *on-yomi* are the result of their having been introduced to Japan at various periods of history. Also, more than one *kun-yomi* may be assigned to a kanji, if the kanji has more than one meaning or has developed extended meanings.

9

Grouping of the Kanji

The goal of this book is to make the kanji learner's task a little easier by clarifying two fundamental relationships: the form-meaning relationship of a kanji, and form-*on-yomi* relationships of kanji. Toward this end, special care has been taken with regard to the order of presentation. After a brief chapter on the stroke order of kanji, the complete set of 1,945 Jōyō Kanji, the "common use" characters listed by the Japanese Ministry of Education in 1981, will be introduced in three categories, one chapter for each, in the following sequence.

1. Basic-form kanji. These are 152 independent kanji that, having originated in unitary pictures or signs, cannot be analyzed into components. If one becomes familiar with these first, complex kanji that include them will be easier to learn later.
2. Semantic compound kanji. These are kanji made up of some combination of two or more basic forms or components that would have been basic forms had they not lost their status as independent kanji (at least as far as the Jōyō Kanji are concerned). The 483 kanji in this chapter are made of components that together suggest the meaning of the kanji (although a few of them also have characteristics of the third, phonetic, category). The emphasis of this chapter is thus on the association of meanings with forms.
3. Phonetic compound kanji. These are kanji that can be analyzed into a meaning-representing (or semantic) component and a sound-representing (or phonetic) component. Although most of the phonetic components have, or at least had, their own semantic significance as well, this chapter emphasizes the relationship between the phonetic components and the *on-yomi* of the 1,310 kanji listed.

Within the chapters on semantic and phonetic compound kanji, the characters are presented in an order that builds upon kanji and components previously introduced.

Whenever possible, we list the surmised earliest meanings of the kanji. Among the later variations on the meanings, we concentrate on those that are relevant to modern Japanese. Occasionally it is noted that a meaning applies only to Japanese, particularly when a peculiar usage in Japanese seems unrelated to the Chinese history of the kanji.

Modern Forms

The first kanji were created more than three thousand years ago. Their forms, their meanings, and their readings have frequently changed since their birth in China, as they continue to do in both China and Japan today. Our classificatory scheme is based roughly on the traditional one established nearly 2,000 years ago by Xu Shen (ca. 58—147) in his *Shuo Wen Jie Zi* (説文解字), a book analyzing and explaining Chinese characters and referred to in English as "the *Shuo Wen*." We have also relied heavily on the recent work of Japanese scholars, especially that of Morohashi Tetsuji (1883—1982), Katō Jōken (1894—1978), and Tōdō Akiyasu (1915—1985), whose writings are listed at the end of this Introduction. When the authorities disagree, we often choose the theory that seems most likely to be useful to beginners in their studies. The forms of the kanji used in this book are the *shin-jitai*, or "new kanji forms," prescribed by the Ministry of Education in 1949. Some Jōyō Kanji are radically simplified from the old forms, so whenever the earlier forms are necessary to the discussion of the kanji, they are shown.

Format of the Kanji Presentations

In the kanji listings in each chapter, the readings are those prescribed by the Ministry of Education. The order of the readings is *on-yomi* first, in *katakana*, then *kun-yomi*, in *hiragana*. Readings are separated by a diagonal slash. If a kanji has more than one *on-yomi*, the readings are listed in the order of frequency of use, the most frequent reading first.

Kun-yomi are also listed in order of frequency of use. One example of the *okurigana* (an inflectional or other word ending written in *kana*, not kanji) that may follow a given *kun-yomi* is provided after a raised dot, for example, 閉（と・じる/し・める）. In standard Japanese writing, the syllables before the dot are written with the kanji, those after the dot in *kana*, for example, 閉じる, 閉じます; 閉める, 閉めない, 閉めます; etc.

We do not follow the dictionary practice of listing all *okurigana*. For example, we give the readings of 広 as （コウ/ひろ・い）rather than as （コウ/ひろ・い/ひろ・まる/ひろ・める/ひろ・がる/ひろ・げる）.

Also not listed are *rendaku* readings (readings whose initial sound is voiced in compound words). For example, the reading ビャクof 百 in 三百 （サン・ビャク three hundred) is not listed separately, but is treated as a variant of its proper reading, ヒャク. Likewise, we follow standard Japanese practice in not treating readings that are result of *sokuonbin* as separate readings. For example, the reading ハッ of 八 in 八百 （ハッ・ピャク eight hundred) is not listed separately, but is treated as a variant of the reading ハチ.

Following the explanation of each kanji, examples of vocabulary are given for each reading. Examples were chosen with frequency of use in mind, tempered by a desire to display the variety of meaning exemplified by the kanji. However, if a kanji with only one listed reading is used independently to write a word, the reading listed at the top of the entry is the example, and there is no separate example below the kanji explanation. English glosses in these examples (as well as elsewhere in the text) are separated by commas if they are closely related in meaning and by semicolons if relatively less related or unrelated in meaning.

Kanji are, of course, combined to form compound words, far too many to list as examples in this book. Chapter 6 describes the ways the kanji in compound words relate to each other and the meaning of the word as a whole.

It is assumed that the reader of this book knows the *hiragana* and *katakana* syllabaries. The Japanese syllabary order, or *gojūon-zu* (table of the fifty sounds), is used to put words, names, kanji readings, and the like in order just as alphabetical order is used in other languages. For reference, the *gojuon-zu* is shown on the front end paper.

List of References

大原信一　漢字のうつりかわり　東方書店　1980
角川書店編　新しい常用漢字の書き表し方　角川書店　1981
加藤常賢他　角川字源辞典（第二版）角川書店　1983

武部良明　漢字の用法　角川書店　1976
第一法規編集部　常用漢字　第一法規出版株式会社　1981
藤堂明保編　学研漢和大字典　学習研究社　1978
中沢希男　漢字・漢語概説　教育出版株式会社　1978
西尾実他　岩波国語辞典（第三版）岩波書店　1979
諸橋轍次　大漢和辞典　大修館書店　1968
山田勝美　漢字の語源　角川書店　1976

Karlgren, Bernhard. *Analytic Dictionary of Chinese and Sino-Japanese.* New York: Dover Publications, Inc., 1974.

O'Neill, P.G. *Japanese Names: A Comprehensive Index by Characters and Readings.* New York and Tokyo: John Weatherhill, Inc., 1972.

Osaka University of Foreign Studies. *The First Step to Kanji.* Part 1. Osaka: Department for Foreign Students, Osaka University of Foreign Studies, 1969.

Osaka University of Foreign Studies. *The Second Step to Kanji.* Part 1. Osaka: Department for Foreign Students, Osaka University of Foreign Studies, 1971.

Chapter 1

Stroke Order of Kanji

It would be extremely difficult to master kanji forms without learning their stroke order. One learns a simple stroke order much like that of kanji when one learns *katakana*, but whereas the majority of *katakana* are written with two or three strokes, the largest number being the six in ボ, the Jōyō Kanji average is between ten and eleven strokes; the kanji with the greatest number of strokes is 鑑. Since complicated kanji are usually combinations of several components, we will place emphasis on the stoke order of the basic forms. To some, it may seem unnecessary to learn stroke order to learn to *read* kanji, but we consider mastering stroke order important for the following reasons :

1. Learning the stroke order leads to learning the forms accurately, essential for distinguishing many similar, but different, kanji.
2. One must be able to count strokes in order to use a kanji dictionary. Thus, learning to write kanji accurately is a foundation for future dictionary use.
3. Knowing how kanji are written by hand from personal experience will be an aid in reading handwritten kanji, which may blur the distinctions between strokes.

The forms of kanji and their individual strokes differ somewhat among typeface styles. The Ming style, which is most commonly used for printing, has more straight lines than the Textbook style, found in the textbooks used in compulsory education, and the handwritten Square style. The Ming style is also distinctive in having its vertical lines thicker than the horizontal ones.

Ming style	人	子	女	手	心	回	前	野	近	雪
Textbook style	人	子	女	手	心	回	前	野	近	雪
Square style	人	子	女	手	心	回	前	野	近	雪

The Textbook style is a "happy medium" between the Ming and Square styles, and for that reason it is the style that will be used in the first four chapters of this book, in which the kanji are presented. (The last two chapters use the Ming style.)

The Basic Strokes

The basic strokes are listed below, with examples of their use in kanji. Except for three cases of "dots" (numbers 23-25 below), in which we have listed two, three, or four dots together to show how they cluster, each item presented is counted as a single stroke, no matter how it may twist and bend, and is written without lifting the pen or brush. For the most part, the length of lines is variable; a few exceptions are noted.

1. A straight line, written vertically downward, (a) with or (b) without a *hane* (hook) at the end.
   (a) 亅 , in 小、 寸、 水.
   (b) 丨 , in 十、 中、 牛.
2. A vertical line written downward, straight but curving slightly to the left at the end.
   丿 , in 月、 川、 舟.
3. A vertical line, bowed slightly to the right, with a *hane*.
   亅 , in 子、 手、 承.
4. A line falling vertically, then curving to the right to become horizontal, (a) with or (b) without a *hane,* or (c) bending sharply.
   (a) 乚 , in 己、 礼、 化.
   (b) 乚 , in 七、 亡、 切.
   (c) 乚 , in 区、 山、 直.
5. A line falling vertically, with a long *hane* to the right.
   乚 , in 良、 氏、 衣.
6. A straight horizontal line from left to right, (a) with or (b) without a downward *hane* at the end.
   (a) ㇇ , in 安、 皮、 欠.
   (b) 一 , in 三、 工、 女.
7. A straight line rising slightly from the horizontal, bending sharply down and leftward, with a *hane*.
   ㇇ , in 他、 池、 地.
8. A straight horizontal line, bending down to straight vertical, (a) with or (b) without a *hane*.
   (a) 丁 , in 内、 司、 門.
   (b) 乛 , in 口、 田、 目.
9. A straight horizontal line, bending down to fall toward the left, with a slight curve, (a) with or (b) without a *hane*.
   (a) 丁 , in 刀、 力、 勺.
   (b) 丿 , in 夕、 又、 神.
10. A straight horizontal line, bending to fall, bowed slightly to the left, curving to the right, and ending with a *hane*.
    乙 , in 九、 乙、 風.

11. A slanting line, written downward to the left.

ノ, in 人, 力, 文.

12. A short line, sloping down to the left.

ノ, in 白, 先, 化.

13. A line sloping downward to the right.

乀, in 入, 木, 父.

14. A short line sloping down to the right.

丶, in 小, 外, 糸.

15. A slightly curved line sloping downward to the right, with a *hane*.

乀, in 代, 民, 戦.

16. A line rising slightly to the right.

一, in 虫, 求, 打.

17. A line falling toward the left, then bending to fall toward the right.

く, in 女, 母, 災.

18. A line falling to the left, then bending to rise slightly to the right.

ㄥ, in 公, 糸, 伝.

19. A vertical stroke, bending sharp right to horizontal, then to vertical again,
    (a) with or (b) without a *hane*.

(a) ㄅ, in 弓, 朽, 考.

(b) ㄥ, in 呉, 娯, 誤.

20. A stroke starting horizontal, bending three times, ending (a) with or (b)
    without a *hane,* or (c) written small.

(a) ㄋ, in 秀, 透, 携.

(b) ㄋ, in 及, 吸, 扱.

(c) ⻌ , in 近, 進, 道.

21. A short downward stroke, curved, with a *hane*.

丶 , in 院, 都, 部.

22. An elongated dot, (a) sloping or (b) vertical.

(a) ⟍, in 主, 寸, 式.

(b) ⟍, in 文, 良, 庫.

23. Two elongated dots(counted as two strokes), sloping in (a) the same direction
    or (b) opposite directions.

(a) ⟍, in 斗, 母, 卵.

(b) ⟍⟍, in 火, 堂, 谷.

24. Three dots (three strokes) (a) in a horizontal line, the first two sloping
    right and the third left, or (b) with the first separate from the other two.

(a) ⟍⟍⟍, in 単, 学, 労.

(b) ⟍⟍⟍, in 心, 必, 念.

25. Four dots (four strokes) (a) in a line or (b) in two pairs.

(a) ⟍⟍⟍⟍, in 鳥, 黒, 馬.

(a) ⟍⟍, ⟍⟍, or ⟍⟍ in 羽, 雨, 兆.

Rules of Stroke Order

The basic rules for stroke order presented below are based on those recommended by the Ministry of Education, although other acceptable variations exist. For the learner, the most important thing is to always use the same stroke order for a given kanji, so that no strokes or dots will be missed. This will also make it easier to count strokes before looking up a kanji in the dictionary.

Here are the basic rules, with examples.

Rule 1. Write from top to bottom.

三 (three): 一 二 三

弓 (bow): フ フ 弓

This rule always applies to kanji that can be divided into top and bottom parts.

音 (sound): 产 + 日

鼻 (nose): 自 + 田 + 廾

Rule 2. Write from left to right.

川 (river): ノ 川 川

行 (go): ノ ク 彳 彳 行 行

This rule always applies to kanji that can be divided into left and right parts.

村 (village): 木 + 寸

柳 (willow): 木 + 夕 + 卩

For any part that can be further divided into top and bottom, Rule 1 applies.

招 (invite): 扌 + 刀 + 口

雑 (miscellaneous): 九 + 木 + 隹

When parts can be further divided into left and right, Rule 2 applies.

露 (dew): 雨 + 𧾷 + 各

懇 (intimate): 豸 + 艮 + 心

Rule 3. When vertical and horizontal lines cross, write the horizontal line first.

十 (ten): 一 十

井 (well): 一 二 井 井

Exceptions : The vertical lines are written first in the following kanji :

田 (rice paddy): 丨 冂 冂 用 田

王 (king): 一 丁 干 王

隹 (bird): ノ 亻 亻 仁 仁 仹 隹 隹

曲 (curve): 丨 冂 曱 曲 曲 曲

Rule 4. Strokes descending left and right starting from or near the same place are written in succession.

八 (eight): ノ 八

金 (gold): ノ 八 人 今 全 全 全 金 金

父 (father): ノ ハ グ 父

The same is true for strokes slanting toward each other.

火 (fire): 丶 丷 火 火

首 (neck): 丶 丷 ナ 产 产 产 首 首 首

Rule 5. When a pair of slanting lines or dots are separated by a central element, write the central element first.

小 (small): 亅 亅 小

赤 (red): 一 十 土 土 亣 亣 赤 赤

Exceptions:

火 (fire): 丶 丷 火 火

米 (rice): 丶 丷 丷 平 米 米

Rule 6. When a slanting line and a horizontal line cross, write the horizontal line first.

左 (left): 一 ナ 广 左 左

大 (large): 一 ナ 大

Exceptions:

右 (right): ノ ナ オ 右 右

有 (have): ノ ナ オ 有 有 有

Rule 7. Write the top and sides of an enclosing element first.

灰 (ashes): 一 厂 厂 灰 灰 灰

羽 (feather): 丁 丌 刁 羽 羽 羽

円 (circle; yen): 丨 冂 冂 円

田 (rice paddy): 丨 冂 冂 用 田

Rule 8. A component extending down the left side and across the bottom is written after the components above it.

直 (direct): 一 十 广 亩 亩 直 直 直

込 (crowded): ノ 入 込 込 込

画 (painting): 一 丁 声 而 雨 由 画 画

区 (section): 一 フ ヌ 区

However, when the left side of the enclosing element is large, the left-to-right rule applies.

起 (get up): 一 十 土 走 走 起 走 起 起 起

Rule 9. A stroke all the way through a kanji is written last.

車 (wheel): 一 厂 厅 盲 盲 車 車

半 (half): 丶 丷 丷 兰 半

母 (mother): 乚 乜 母 母 母

舟 (boat): ノ 丿 力 舟 舟 舟

Exceptions:

里 (village): 丨 冂 日 旦 甲 甲 里

重 (heavy): 一 二 千 亩 亩 盲 重 重 重

Rule 10. A single dot is written as either the first or last stroke of the component to which it belongs: first when it is top center of the component, last otherwise.

文 (writing): ' 亠 ナ 文

犬 (dog): 一 ナ 大 犬

玉 (gem): 一 丁 千 王 玉

Exceptions:

氷 (ice): 丨 刂 氵 氷 氷

丹 (red): 丿 冂 冃 丹

Rule 11. Dots in a line are written left to right or top to bottom.

斗 (*to* 〔18 liters〕): ` ⟩ ⟩一 斗

単 (single): ' ⟩ ⟩⟩ ⟩⟩⟩ 丷 当 単 単 単

雨 (rain): 一 冂 冂 帀 帀 雨 雨 雨

魚 (fish): 丿 ⟩⟩ ⟩⟩⟩ 冎 冎 角 角 魚 魚 魚 魚

It should be noted that individual kanji may have stroke orders that do not exactly reflect the rules.

In this book, stroke order is indicated for basic forms (Chapter 2) and semantic compound kanji that are basic forms with additional strokes (the first section of Chapter 3).

Chapter 2

Basic-Form Kanji

Form-Meaning-Reading Relationships

Each kanji is an association of three elements: its concrete form (forms), at least one meaning, and at least one "reading" (pronunciation). Although the relationships between the elements are complex, we are mainly concerned with the form-meaning relationships and form-*on-yomi* relationships of kanji. As stated in the Introduction, this results for our purposes in three classes of kanji: basic-form kanji, semantic compound kanji, and phonetic compound kanji. Let us look at three related characters, all Jōyō Kanji, to illustrate the relationships and classes: 門, a basic form; 間, a semantic compound kanji; and 閥, a phonetic compound kanji.

The kanji 門 (モン/かど gate) was created three or four thousand years ago in China—it was a picture of a gate. With a kanji such as this, form and meaning are in a sense inseparable: the kanji are pictures of what they mean. (A stylized picture of an ancient Chinese gate, however, will not necessarily look like a gate to a twentieth-century kanji learner. It will always take a measure of imagination and effort to fix in mind the association of picture-derived kanji with what it represents now.)

The kanji 間 (カン/ケン/あいだ/ま space) was created after the establishment of 門. Originating in the combination of 門 and 月 (moon, eventually reduced to 日 for this character), 間 represents a word for "space" by alluding to moonlight shining through an opening (space) between doors of a gate. The character is today associated with extent between two spatial or temporal points. Such a character, based on the combination of meaningful components, is a semantic compound kanji. The problems involved with learning semantic compound kanji are much like those involved with the basic forms: one needs to keep track of the forms and meanings of the various components.

Other semantic compound Jōyō Kanji using 門 are 開 (open: gate+a picture of two hands opening it), 閉 (shut: gate+a kanji meaning "block off"), and 閑 (quiet; leisure time: gate+a kanji meaning "tree; wood"). Although the first two combinations make sense in terms of the components of which they are made, a character such as 閑 introduces a difficulty. The combination of "gate"+"tree; wood" hardly brings to mind the meanings of "quiet; leisure time." Actually, the word originally represented by 閑 referred to a gate bar to keep domestic animals from getting out; in modern Japan, however, the use of 閑 is restricted to the meanings mentioned above. Students of kanji should keep in mind that many of the kanji in use today are not used for their original meanings. There is not always a consensus, or even a hypothesis, among scholars as to how a particular kanji came to be used for a totally new meaning, although it can often be ascribed to confusion between characters of similar form or reading.

The kanji 閥, our third example, was put together on an entirely different principle. The ancient Chinese had a word that meant "prestigious family," the sort whose home would have an impressive gate. The word was pronounced with the ancient Chinese predecessor of the Japanese バツ. To represent this word with a character, the ancient Chinese chose 門 as one component, for its meaning, and 伐 (also pronounced with the Chinese predecessor of バツ) as the other component, for its phonetic value. The result was 閥. Combining two components in this manner—one representing a word semantically related to the "new" word, the other pronounced the same or nearly the same as it—was a frequently used method of creating new kanji. In modern Japanese terms, such kanji have the same, or similar, *on-yomi*. (Incidentally, in modern Japanese, the word 閥 means "clique.")

The ancient Chinese were probably often able to recognize on first seeing a character the word it was meant to represent, if they were familiar with the components of it. The kanji 閥 would be pronounced like 伐 and would have something to do with gates. Modern students of kanji do not already know a spoken language to associate the kanji with and thus cannot learn the kanji in this fashion. But with a little experience, one comes to recognize the phonetic components of kanji. If one knows the *on-yomi* of 伐 (バツ chop), one can guess that 閥 (clique) might also be read バツ, even if there is no real clue to its meaning.

Other phonetic compound Jōyō Kanji that include 門 as their semantic component are 閣 (カク tall building: originally meaning "a stake to hold a gate open"), 閲 (エツ inspect: originally "an inspection of troops in front of a gate"), and 関 (カン/せき bolt; checkpoint: originally meaning "to lock a gate"). The components inside the 門 are the phonetic components, each of which has at least one *on-yomi* identical to that of the respective compound character. One other Jōyō Kanji appears to use 門 as its phonetic component: 闘 (トウ/たたか・う fight). However, the semantic component of this kanji is actually 鬥 (fight), which was "merged" with 門 for the Jōyō Kanji. 闘 thus has nothing to do with gates. In this book, such altered forms will be treated in the groups to which their new forms assign them.

The component 門 was also used phonetically, that is, for its *on-yomi*, モン. Two Jōyō Kanji include 門 as their phonetic component: 問 (モン/と・う ask, with 口 "mouth" as the semantic component) and 聞 (ブン/モン/き・く hear, with 耳 "ear" as the semantic component).

Unfortunately for the learner, there can be considerable variation in the current readings of characters with the same phonetic component. The 兌 of 閲 is a case in point, as the readings of the following characters containing this component illustrate: 閲 (エツ), 鋭 (エイ), 税 (ゼイ), 説 (セツ/ゼイ), 脱 (ダツ). Such instances are usually the result of irregular sound changes that took place during the long history of the Chinese language or variations among its many dialects. Sometimes they result from misreadings, for reasons not now understood, on the part of Japanese of earlier periods.

Compound kanji were themselves used as phonetic components in kanji created later. One such Jōyō Kanji involving 門 is 簡 (カン bamboo tablet; concise: 間［カン］ as phonetic component＋竹 [bamboo] as semantic component). Complex compound kanji were usually created in this manner, that is, with a semantic component added to an established compound kanji serving as the phonetic component.

Characteristics of Basic Forms

The basic-form kanji used in this book have the following characteristics:

1. (a) Basic forms are essentially pictographic and not analyzable into parts corresponding to elements of meaning.
   (b) They may have more than one form. Whereas 門 has only one form, the kanji 水 (スイ/みず water), for example, is replaced by the variant form 氵 in the majority of compound kanji with "water"-associated meanings, and sometimes by the other variants.
2. (a) Basic forms have been used as semantic components in the creation of later kanji.
   (b) A basic form may have more than one meaning, since the basic forms are simplified and stylized pictographic characters. For example, 田 (デン/た) originated in a picture of a field, but the same graphic form in 果 (カ/は・ たす fruit; result) represents fruit in a tree, and in 胃 (イ stomach) it represents food in a stomach.
3. (a) Many basic forms have been used as phonetic components.
   (b) Many phonetic components have a variety of readings, as we saw above in the example of 兄.
4. Most basic forms began as independent kanji. However, the independent use of many of them was abandoned early on. The number of basic forms included as independent kanji in the Jōyō Kanji is further limited to those used with high frequency. Thus, for practical purpose, basic forms will often be encountered only as phonetic or semantic components of compound characters.

Another point to be noted about basic forms and other kanji is that some characters were "borrowed" to represent a word usually pronounced (in ancient Chinese) the same as the word it originally represented; such kanji thus have a meaning totally different from their original one and may no longer represent that meaning at all. For example, there was a word pronounced with the ancient Chinese predecessor of the Japanese トウ that meant "dish with tall base"; this word was written 豆. There was also a homophonous word that meant "bean." For whatever reason, the ancient Chinese "borrowed" the character 豆 to write "bean." Eventually 豆 came to be used exclusively for "bean," and no longer represented "dish with tall base" at all. (Sometimes, however, the original meaning of such "borrowed" characters remains in compound kanji using them).

In order to learn to associate the forms of kanji with their meanings and *on-yomi* with maximum efficiency, those basic forms that are most frequently used should be studied first. As we saw in the case of 門, knowing its meaning allows us to associate seven other kanji, 開, 間, 閉, 閣, 閥, 関, and 関 with that meaning. Knowing the *on-yomi* of 門 makes it possible to guess the *on-yomi* of two other kanji, 問 and 聞, and certainly makes it easier to remember their *on-yomi*. In the remainder of this chapter we introduce basic forms to establish the relationship of form and meaning first.

List of Basic Forms

The kanji derived from actual pictorial representations should be the easiest to learn, being in principle pictures. In fact, some of them are easy to associate with the things they are images of, but others are more difficult, particularly when they depict ancient Chinese things that no longer exist.

Such kanji are considered to be the oldest of all, though we do not know just how old they are. They are significant in that they furnish the elements of later kanji forms. The oldest kanji known are those called *kōkotsubun* (甲骨文) and *kinbun* (金文) by the Japanese. The former were written on turtle shells or animal bones for divination purposes from approximately 1400 B.C. to 1000 B.C., and the latter were written on items of bronzeware in the period from roughly 1400 B.C. to 500 B.C. Implements of divination excavated in the area where it is believed that the capital city was located during the Yin dynasty (1400–1066 B.C.) preserve some four thousand, of which a thousand have been deciphered and another five hundred have debated interpretations.

Even these kanji do not represent quite the most primitive stage of development, however, for there are compound characters among them and instances of characters being used for their sound value alone, a secondary development. Nonetheless, they are much closer to being pictures than later kanji are, and they represent a stage when many characters had variant forms and were not yet fully conventionalized.

Four thousand characters are a lot. Apparently the divine will was consulted on all sorts of occasions and about a wide variety of matters. Nearly every aspect of ancient Chinese life is represented by one or another of these kanji.

One other early style is called, in Japanese, *tenbun* (篆文). These characters were written during the Qin dynasty (221–106 B.C.) when Emperor Shi Huang Di attempted to establish a standardized set of kanji forms. The modern squarish handwriting style originated in this *tenbun* style, which abstracted and stylized the earlier rather free-form characters. *Tenbun* kanji are much showier than modern typefaces and so are still used for the characters of a personal seal.

Today's kanji styles, both printed and written, reflect a long history of simplification and standardization. No longer do they look anything like pictures. But when we compare them and their ancestral forms in the *kōkotsubun, kinbun,* and *tenbun* stages, we can recognize the relationships among them, as well as see the resemblance to the original pictures.

	Picture	*Kōkotsubun*	*Kinbun*	*Tenbun*	ModernKanji
(bird)	🐦	𠦝	𠃊	𠃊	鳥
(dog)	🐕	犬	犬	犬	犬
(moon)	🌙	月	月	月	月
(tree)	🌳	木	木	木	木
(woman)	👤	女	女	女	女

The next four sections introduce basic-form kanji that can be traced back to pictographs representing the basic meaning of the kanji. The four categories into which we have grouped the kanji are elements of the environment, people and body parts, necessities of life, and abstract concepts.

Included in these categories are basic-form kanji listed as independent characters in the Jōyō Kanji list. Not included are two groups of basic-form kanji: those used as components of other characters but not independently and characters that are used independently but are not in the Jōyō Kanji. Characters in these categories are mentioned in later chapters, when Jōyō Kanji made up of them are discussed.

The handwritten characters on the first line of each entry in the following sections are the kanji in *kōkotsubun, kinbun, tenbun,* and modern print forms, followed by an illustration of the stroke order used to write the kanji. Italicized English equivalents show the original (now obsolete) meanings of the original character.

The Environment

We can tell what things in the environment the ancient Chinese felt were worth their notice by the pictographic characters they left behind. The sun, the moon, the land, rivers, the rain—these were no doubt crucial elements of their life and civilization as it developed near the Yellow River. Water and fire are of course represented by fundamental characters, as were the tree, bamboo, and a variety of animals used for food, clothing, transportation, and religious sacrifice.

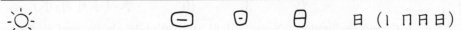

日 (ニチ／ジツ／ひ／か) means "the sun." It has the derived meaning, "day," and is used in naming and counting days.

日曜 (ニチ・ヨウ Sunday), 休日 (キュウ・ジツ holiday), 日 (ひ sun; a day), 十日 (とお・か ten days; the tenth of the month)

月 （ゲツ/ガツ/つき） represented the crescent moon, and means "moon,"; it has the derived sense of "month," which is used in naming and counting months.

月末 （ゲツ・マツ end of month）, 一月 （イチ・ガツ January; ひと・つき one month）

山 （サン/やま） means "mountain." As a suffix, it is used in names of mountains or mountain temples.

山林 （サン・リン mountain forest）, 山 （やま mountain）

丘 （キュウ/おか） was a picture of two mounds of earth and means "hill."

砂丘 （サ・キュウ dune）, 丘 （おか hill）

土 （ド/ト/つち） started as a pile of soil, and means "soil" or "land."

本土 （ホン・ド mainland）, 土地 （ト・チ land）, 土 （つち soil）

石 （セキ/シャク/コク/いし） was a picture of a stone at the bottom of a rocky cliff. It means "rock" or "pebble." Derived senses are "hard" and "worthless." With the reading コク it is a unit of cubic measure and also now a counter for semiconductors.

石油 （セキ・ユ petroleum）, 磁石 （ジ・シャク magnet）, 一石 （イッ・コク *ikkoku* [180 liters] ; イッ・セキ one stone）, 石 （いし stone）

田 （デン/た） was a drawing of fields and broadly means "cultivated land." In Japan, it is all but restricted to "paddy field."

水田 （スイ・デン wet rice field）, 田 （た rice field）

川 （セン/かわ） depicted the flow of a river and means "river."

河川 （カ・セン rivers）, 川 （かわ river）

水 （スイ/みず） means "water." Note that 川, immediately above, and 水 derive from almost identical pictographic characters, but that they are distinct in form, meaning, and usage today.

水害 （スイ・ガイ flood damage）, 水 （みず water）

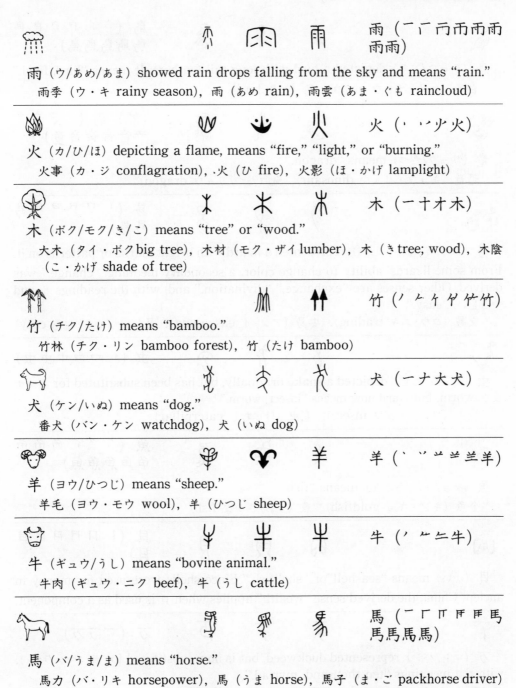

雨（ウ/あめ/あま）showed rain drops falling from the sky and means "rain."
　　雨季（ウ・キ rainy season），雨（あめ rain），雨雲（あま・ぐも raincloud）

火（カ/ひ/ほ）depicting a flame, means "fire," "light," or "burning."
　　火事（カ・ジ conflagration），.火（ひ fire），火影（ほ・かげ lamplight）

木（ボク/モク/き/こ）means "tree" or "wood."
　　大木（タイ・ボク big tree），木材（モク・ザイ lumber），木（き tree; wood），木陰（こ・かげ shade of tree）

竹（チク/たけ）means "bamboo."
　　竹林（チク・リン bamboo forest），竹（たけ bamboo）

犬（ケン/いぬ）means "dog."
　　番犬（バン・ケン watchdog），犬（いぬ dog）

羊（ヨウ/ひつじ）means "sheep."
　　羊毛（ヨウ・モウ wool），羊（ひつじ sheep）

牛（ギュウ/うし）means "bovine animal."
　　牛肉（ギュウ・ニク beef），牛（うし cattle）

馬（バ/うま/ま）means "horse."
　　馬力（バ・リキ horsepower），馬（うま horse），馬子（ま・ご packhorse driver）

象（ショウ/ゾウ），used with the reading ゾウ， means "elephant." The derived
meaning associated with the reading ショウ is "image; to make a model."
　　現象（ゲン・ショウ phenomenon），象（ゾウ elephant）

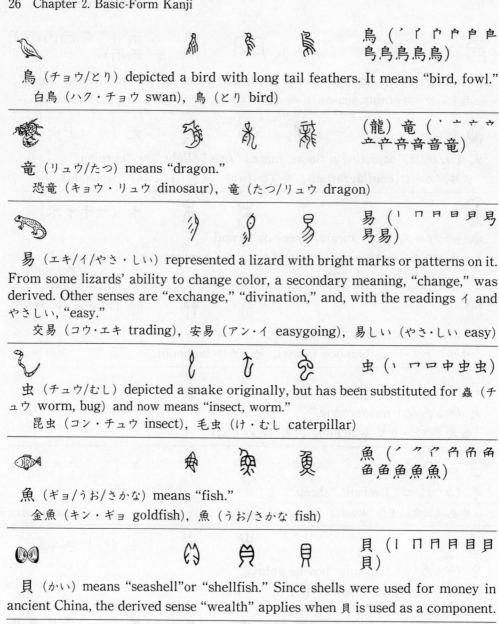

鳥（チョウ/とり）depicted a bird with long tail feathers. It means "bird, fowl."
　白鳥（ハク・チョウ swan）, 鳥（とり bird）

竜（リュウ/たつ）means "dragon."
　恐竜（キョウ・リュウ dinosaur）, 竜（たつ/リュウ dragon）

易（エキ/イ/やさ・しい）represented a lizard with bright marks or patterns on it.
From some lizards' ability to change color, a secondary meaning, "change," was
derived. Other senses are "exchange," "divination," and, with the readings イ and
やさしい, "easy."
　交易（コウ・エキ trading）, 安易（アン・イ easygoing）, 易しい（やさ・しい easy）

虫（チュウ/むし）depicted a snake originally, but has been substituted for 蟲（チ
ュウ worm, bug）and now means "insect, worm."
　昆虫（コン・チュウ insect）, 毛虫（け・むし caterpillar）

魚（ギョ/うお/さかな）means "fish."
　金魚（キン・ギョ goldfish）, 魚（うお/さかな fish）

貝（かい）means "seashell" or "shellfish." Since shells were used for money in
ancient China, the derived sense "wealth" applies when 貝 is used as a component.

万（マン/バン）represented duckweed, but is now substituted for 萬（マン/バン）,
with the meanings "ten thousand, myriad."
　万（マン ten thousand）, 万国（バン・コク all countries）

不（フ/ブ）originally depicting a calyx, was "borrowed" for the homophonous
word "not (do/be)," used to negate a verbal or adjectival kanji following it.
　不足（フ・ソク insufficiency）, 不用心（ブ・ヨウ・ジン unsafe）

Since the kanji used today have been geatly simplified, it is not surprising that there are coincidental similarities among them. In particular, parts of basic kanji may sometimes seem to have other basic kanji, or parts of other basic kanji, within them, but they originally represented quite different things. For instance, the top part of 易 (*lizard*, change) looks like 日 (sun), but does not and never did represent the sun in any way. The following kanji from this section share forms unrelated in meaning:

日 (sun)　　　易 (*lizard*; change)
田 (field)　　　竜 (dragon)
魚 (fish)　　　象 (elephant)
馬 (horse)　　　烏 (bird)

The following kanji are also believed to have derived from pictographic characters: 兎 (hare), 鼠 (rat), 亀 (turtle), 鹿 (deer), 虎 (tiger), 燕 (swallow), 烏 (crow), 辰 (clam), 豕 (pig), and 隹 (short-tailed bird). They are not Jōyō Kanji, although all but the last two are still used as independent kanji. They will be discussed only when they appear as components of certain Jōyō Kanji later.

People and Body Parts

Some basic pictographic characters represented a man, a woman, a child, a mother, and so forth. Others, based on body parts, may have been influenced by their creators' observations of the abundant animals in their environment; they played an extremely important role as components of complex characters.

人 (ジン/ニン/ひと) represents a side view of a standing person and means "person."

人口 (ジン・コウ population), 三人 (サン・ニン three people), 人 (ひと person)

女 (ジョ/ニョ/ニョウ/おんな/め) represents a person with a curvaceous figure and means "woman, female ; daughter."

長女 (チョウ・ジョ eldest daughter), 女体 (ニョ・タイ female body), 女房 (ニョウ・ボウ wife)、女 (おんな woman), 女神 (め・がみ goddess)

子 (シ/ス/こ) means "child, offspring; little one ; very small thing." In China it was used as a title of respect, particularly for established philosophers. With the reading こ it is very often used as the end of girls' given names in Japan.

電子 (デン・シ electron), 扇子 (セン・ス fan), 子 (こ child)

母 （ボ/はは） shows a woman （女） with dots for the breasts; it means "mother." Like "mother" in English, it has a derived sense of "from which one comes or to which one belongs."

母国 （ボ・コク motherland）, 母 （はは mother）

父 （フ/ちち） represented beating something with a stone hatchet; it came to be used for "father; old man."

父母 （フ・ボ parents）, 父 （ちち father）

老 （ロウ/お・いる/ふ・ける） depicted an old, bent, long-haired man with a cane, and means "old person; aged, grow old."

老人 （ロウ・ジン old person）, 老いる （お・いる get old）, 老ける （ふ・ける get old, old-looking）

身 （シン/み） showing a pregnant woman in side view, originally meant "pregnant woman." The character was borrowed to represent "body, flesh; self," its current meanings.

身体 （シン・タイ body）, 脂身 （あぶら・み fatty meat）

士 （シ） depicted a phallus to indicate "grown man." It is used in the derived senses of a man with some official position or rank, and profession. In Japan it has been used for "samurai," from association with 仕 （シ service）.

武士 （ブ・シ warrior）

目 （モク/ボク/め/ま） means "eye," and has a wealth of derived meanings: "see; face; expression; aim; item; small opening." With the reading め as a suffix, 目 is used to form ordinal numbers.

目前 （モク・ゼン just ahead）, 面目 （メン・ボク/メン・モク face, honor）, 目（め eye）, 目の当り （ま・の・あた・り before one's very eyes）

口 （コウ/ク/くち） means "mouth." It has the derived meanings "opening" and "entrance." Read くち, it is used as a counter for mouthfuls and lots（batches）.

河口 （カ・コウ river mouth）, 口調 （ク・チョウ tone of voice）, 口 （くち mouth）

自 （ジ/シ/みずか・ら） represented a nose, but now means only "self; by itself, spontaneously," meanings probably ultimately derived from the custom of touching one's nose to indicate "self."

自信 （ジ・シン self-confidence）, 自然 （シ・ゼン nature: natural）, 自ら （みずか・ら oneself）

耳 （ジ/みみ） means "ear" or "hearing."

耳鼻科 （ジ・ビ・カ otorhinology）, 耳 （みみ ear）

心 （シン/こころ） represented a heart. It is most often used for its derived meanings in the area of "mind, spirit, psyche, feeling; center."

心理 （シン・リ mentality）, 心 （こころ mind, heart）

手 （シュ/て/た） means "hand" or "hand and arm." Derived therefrom are senses of "something done by hand, skill; one who does it."

助手 （ジョ・シュ assistant）, 手 （て hand; skill）, 手綱 （た・づな reins）

又 （また） represented the right, preferred, hand and arm, and still represents a hand when used as a component of a kanji. As an independent kanji, however, it is used only in senses of "and, or, also, again." Note that the original forms of 又 and 手, immediately above, are very similar.

足 （ソク/あし/た・りる） depicting the knee, lower leg, and foot, means "foot, leg," and, derivatively, "walk." It is also used as a counter for pairs of footwear and was borrowed to represent the meanings "suffice; add to."

一足 （イッ・ソク a pair [of footwear]）, 足 （あし foot; leg）, 足りる （た・りる suffice）

止 （シ/と・まる） represented a foot, or perhaps a foot-print. As an independent kanji, it means "stop; stand still." 止 is similar to the lower part of 足, immediately above, with the last two strokes at different angles.

中止 （チュウ・シ cessation）, 止まる （と・まる halt）

毛 (ー ニ 三 毛)

毛 (モウ/け) means "hair, fur; wool." It has derived senses of "very fine, minute; grow like hair."

毛布 (モウ・フ blanket), 毛 (け hair)

肉 (｜ 冂 内 内 肉 肉)

肉 (ニク) depicting a chunk of meat, means "animal flesh"; it also means "flesh" in the metaphorical sense. The meaning of 肉 has been extended to include "flesh of fruit."

角 (ノ ク ク 甬 角 角 角)

角 (カク/かど/つの) depicted the horn of an ox or sheep beginning to grow. "Horn" is the basic meaning, with the derived senses "angle, corner."

角度 (カク・ド angle), 角 (かど corner), 角 (つの animal horn)

羽 (フ コ ヨ 羽 羽 羽)

羽 (ウ/は/はね) originally depicting a bird's wings, means "wing; feather." With the reading は it is used as a counter for birds.

羽毛 (ウ・モウ feather), 羽根 (は・ね fan-blade; shuttlecock), 羽 (はね feather; wing)

卵 (ノ Ľ Ĺ 身 卵 卵 卵)

卵 (ラン/たまご) means "egg"or "roe." A derived sense is "embryonic."

産卵 (サン・ラン egg-laying), 卵 (たまご egg)

革 (ー 十 サ サ 芦 芦 莒 莒 革)

革 (カク/かわ) may have represented the skeleton of a small animal, or, according to another hypothesis, its hide. It is used in the sense of "treated hide, leather,"with the derived meaning "replace, renew."

改革 (カイ・カク reform), 革 (かわ leather)

求 (ー 十 寸 寸 才 求 求)

求 (キュウ/もと・める) depicted a garment made of animal hide, but was borrowed to represent the meaning "seek, solicit."

求人 (キュウ・ジン job offer; help wanted), 求める (もと・める ask for)

The following kanji from this section share forms unrelated in meaning:

目 (eye)   自 (*nose*; self)
                           貝 (shell)
                           耳 (ear)
自 (*nose*; self)   身 (*pregnant woman*; body)
口 (mouth)   石 (stone)
                           足 (leg)
角 (horn)   魚 (fish)
手 (hand)   毛 (hair)
土 (soil)   士 (*phallus*; man)

The characters 牙 (tusk) and 頁 (head) belong to the "people" category, but are treated in later chapters, where they appear as components of other kanji.

Necessities of Life

In this section we introduce pictographic characters representing foods, clothing, shelter, household tools, and implements of war.

皿 (⎟ ⌐ ⊓ ⫪ 皿)

皿 (さら), depicting a serving dish with two handles and a base, now means "dish, plate, platter."

豆 (⎺ ⎕ ⊓ 曰 豆 豆)

豆 (トウ/ズ/まめ) originally represented a vessel in which to offer food to a god. It is now used only in a meaning for which the character was borrowed, "bean, pea." A derived meaning is "small."

豆腐 (トウ・フ tofu), 大豆 (ダイ・ズ soybean), 豆 (まめ bean, pea)

缶 (′ ⎡ 亠 午 缶 缶)

缶 (カン) stems from a drawing of an unglazed lidded water pot; it now means "metal can," having been substituted for 罐 (カン), from which it also gets its reading.

去 (一 十 土 去 去)

去 (キョ/コ/さ・る) originally depicted a container with a cover, and it is hypothesized that the meaning "depart," for which it is now used, relates to the "depressed" shape of the vessel, through the notion of "withdraw." Other current derivative senses are "remove; the past."

去年 (キョ・ネン last year), 過去 (か・こ the past), 去る (さ・る leave; last)

甲 （コウ/カン） depicted a bean sprouting and meant "bean sprout with the seed skin on it; skin of a seed." Derived senses are "hard shell; back [of a hand etc.]; armor." Borrowed to write a Chinese word meaning "the first in a cycle of ten," it is often used to mean "number one; first rank," usually of two or three items now.

甲 （コウ shell）, 甲板 （カン・パン deck）

米（ベイ/マイ/こめ）originally represented millet grains coming out of their husks, but soon came to be used of rice. It means "uncooked rice." Due to its resemblance to 八十八 (eighty-eight) written vertically, it has been given the special sense of "eigty-eight [years old]." Its use for the *me* in "America," once written 亜米利加 （アメリカ）; has led to its use (pronounced ベイ) as a word-element meaning "America." It is also used for "meter [unit of length]," again read ベイ.

米国 （ベイ・コク U.S.A.）, 玄米 （ゲン・マイ unpolished rice）, 米 （こめ rice）

平 （ヘイ/ビョウ/たい・ら/ひら） depicted an edible plant floating on water. It means "flat, level; calm; ordinary."

平野 （ヘイ・ヤa plain）, 平等 （ビョウ・ドウ equality）, 平ら （たい・ら flat）, 手の平 （て・の・ひら the flat of the hand）

白 （ハク/ビャク/しろ/しら） was a picture of an acorn, chosen to represent "white" because the meat of an acorn is white. Derived senses are "blank, clear, pure." The character was borrowed to write a word meaning "report."

白紙 （ハク・シ blank paper）, 黒白 （コク・ビャク/くろ・しろ black and white）, 白い （しろ・い white）, 白魚 （しら・うお whitebait）

来 （ライ/く・る/きた・る） in its old form 來, was originally a drawing of a wheat or barley stalk, but it was borrowed for "come; visit," and 麦 （earlier 麥） replaced it in the sense of "barley" in ancient times. Derived meanings from "come" are "the next, the coming," used of time periods, and "since."

来年 （ライ・ネン next year）, 来る （く・る come）, 来る （きた・る next）

両 （リョウ） depicted a kind of balance. It means "both, the two." In some compounds it is used for "car," particularly "train car," as a substitute for 輌 （リ

ョウ), not a Jōyō Kanji. In Japan it was a monetary unit for which there used to be a gold coin.

両手 (リョウ・て both hands)

   斗 (` ⁼ ⁼-斗)

斗 (ト) was originally a drawing of a ladle for serving alcoholic beverages. It means "ladle, ladle-shaped." As a unit of measure for *sake* or rice, it is approximately equivalent to eighteen liters.

一斗 (イッ・ト 1 *to* [18 liters])

   升 (ʼ ノ 千 升)

升 (ショウ/ます) refers to a box-shaped device for either liquid or dry measure, in which case it is read ます. When read ショウ, it refers to a specific amount, one-tenth of a *to*, the preceding character.

一升 (イッ・ショウ 1 *shō*), 升 (ます box-shaped measure)

  勺 (ノ ク 勺)

勺 (シャク) originally meant "to ladle." It refers to a unit of cubic measure, one-tenth of a *gō*, about 0.018 liters, or in Japan only a unit of area, one one-hundredth of a *tsubo*, about 0.033 square meters.

一勺 (イッ・シャク 1 *shaku* [180 milliliters; 0.033 square meters])

    丁 (一 丁)

丁 (チョウ/テイ) means "strong; man in his prime; servant; polite," probably ultimately derived from an original meaning of "nail." In Japan, it refers to an urban unit of distance of about 109 meters, to an even number on a throw of dice, and to folios of a book. チョウ counts blocks of tofu and servings of food ordered.

一丁 (イッ・チョウ 1 *chō* [109 meters]), 丁重 (テイ・チョウ polite)

   凡 (ノ 几 凡)

凡 (ボン/ハン) began as what seems to be a picture of a large board or piece of cloth covering a wide space. It means "general, ordinary, mediocre."

平凡 (ヘイ・ボン common), 凡例 (ハン・レイ explanatory notes)

辛 (シン/から・い) depicted a tattooing needle. It is associated with the meanings "stinging, painful; hot- or salty-tasting."

辛苦 (シン・ク hardship), 塩辛い (しお・からい salty)

 工 工 工 工 (一 丁 工)

工 (コウ/ク) depicted an adze or hatchet. It is used to mean "construct, manufacture; workman; industry."

工業 (コウ・ギョウ industry), 大工 (ダイ・ク carpenter)

玉 (ギョク/たま) means "jewel; round thing." The dot, not always added when this kanji is used as a component, is an extra stroke to differentiate it from 王 (オウ king).

玉石 (ギョク・セキ gems and stones), 玉 (たま ball)

糸 (シ/いと) represented a skein of raw silk. It means "thread," with derived senses of "thin, fine."

金糸 (キン・シ gold thread), くもの糸 (くもの・いと cobweb)

衣 (イ/ころも) represented the collar of a garment and means "clothing."

衣食 (イ・ショク food and clothing), 衣 (ころも robe)

面 (メン/おも/おもて/つら), showing someone wearing a mask, means "mask; face." Derivative meanings are "surface, flat object; direction; aspect," and it is used to count certain flattish things such as mirrors and *koto*.

面接 (メン・セツ interview), 面影 (おも・かげ visage), 能の面 (のう・の・おもて/メン *no* mask), 面 (おもて/つら face)

冊 (サツ/サク) depicted a bundle of turtle shells with queries written on them for divination and, later, a bundle of inscribed bamboo tablets. It means "book" or "writing paper," and is used as a counter for books and magazines.

一冊 (イッ・サツ one [book]), 短冊 (タン・ザク strip of paper for artistic inscription)

用 (ヨウ/もち・いる) once depicted a fence, but was borrowed for a word now meaning "use, useful for; matters to take care of."

用 (ヨウ errand), 用いる (もち・いる use)

井 (セイ/ショウ/い) means "well," or "square," the shape of a wooden well curb.

油井 (ユ・セイ oil well), 天井 (テン・ジョウ ceiling), 井戸 (い・ど well)

戸 （コ/と） means "door, doorway," and, by synecdoche, "house," and it is also used as a counter for houses.

戸数 （コ・スウ number of houses）, 戸 （と door）

門 （モン/かど） means "gate, gateway." By derivation, it refers to "entrance into an academic field, school of art, or religion; and house; family."

仏門 （ブツ・モン Buddhism）, 門口 （かど・ぐち entrance）

京 （キョウ/ケイ）, depicting a house on top of a hill, meant "sovereign's residence," extended to "capital." It often has reference to Kyoto or Tokyo in current Japanese usage.

京風 （キョウ・フウ Kyoto style）, 京浜 （ケイ・ヒン Tokyo and Yokohama）

車 （シャ/くるま） means "wheel; wheeled vehicle."

車内 （シャ・ナイ in the car）, 車 （くるま wheel, car）

舟 （シュウ/ふね/ふな） depicted a boat or canoe. It means "boat, water craft" and, as in English, where "boat" and "tub" are somewhat interchangeable, it can refer to an open container for liquids, mainly water and *sake*.

舟運（シュウ・ウン shipping by boat）, 舟（ふね boat）, 舟歌（ふな・うた boatmen's song）

干 （カン/ほ・す/ひ・る） comes from a drawing of a weapon made from tree branches. Its original meaning is barely retained in the sense of "meddle" or "violate." It was borrowed for "a shield" and thence "to shield, defend; to make dry, get dry; small amount."

干渉 （カン・ショウ interference）, 干す （ほ・す dry）, 干物 （ひ・もの dried fish）

矢 （シ/や） means "arrow"

一矢を報いる （イッ・シ・を・むく・いる reprisal）, 矢 （や arrow）

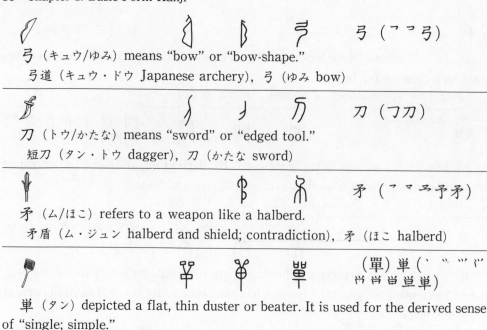

弓 (キュウ/ゆみ) means "bow" or "bow-shape."
弓道 (キュウ・ドウ Japanese archery), 弓 (ゆみ bow)

刀 (トウ/かたな) means "sword" or "edged tool."
短刀 (タン・トウ dagger), 刀 (かたな sword)

矛 (ム/ほこ) refers to a weapon like a halberd.
矛盾 (ム・ジュン halberd and shield; contradiction), 矛 (ほこ halberd)

単 (タン) depicted a flat, thin duster or beater. It is used for the derived sense of "single; simple."
単一 (タン・イツ single)

西 (セイ/サイ/にし) is from a drawing of a basket but was borrowed for "west," and thence its derived meaning of "Western"
西洋 (セイ・ヨウ the West), 東西 (トウ・ザイ east and west; the East and the West), 西 (にし west)

東 (トウ/ひがし) seems to have depicted a bag with a stick through it, tied to the stick at both ends. This was somehow associated with the eastern direction, the character's only known meaning. Derivative uses include the abbreviation of 東京(Tokyo).
東大 (トウ・ダイ Tokyo University), 東 (ひがし east)

由 (ユ/ユウ/ユイ/よし) is from a drawing of a basket or a pot. It is used only for derived senses, namely "source; means; effect; depend on."
由来 (ユ・ライ origin), 自由 (ジ・ユウ freedom), 由緒 (ユイ・ショ lineage), 由 (よし purport)

午 (ゴ) depicted a pounder with which to pound food in a mortar, but as a Jōyō Kanji, it is used only for "noon," derived from another meaning it was borrowed for.

正午 (ショウ・ゴ high noon)

氏 (シ/うじ), originally a spoon, was borrowed to mean "clan." Read シ, 氏 may be suffixed to a family name as an honorific.

氏名 (シ・メイ full name), 氏 (うじ clan)

民 (ミン/たみ) either came from a drawing of a pointed instrument and was borrowed for a word meaning "the people, folk," or represented a needle in an eye, blinding a slave, to represent a word for which the sense "subject people" was derived.

国民 (コク・ミン a people), 民 (たみ the people)

王 (オウ), originally depicting a large ax, was borrowed for a word meaning "sovereign; royal."

方 (ホウ/かた) early lost its sense of "spade tip" when it was borrowed to write a word meaning "direction, way, manner; side; square." The Japanese word かた written with it is used for polite reference to persons, deriving its politeness from indirect, and thus impersonal, reference.

方向 (ホウ・コウ direction), 読み方 (よ・み・かた the way to read)

乙 (オツ) comes from a drawing of a carving knife with two edges, but was very early borrowed to write the word naming the second position in the Chinese cyclical series of ten stems; that is, it means "second [of from two to ten items]." In Japan, it is used to write the root of words meaning "quaint, offbeat but nice."

丙 (ヘイ), a pictograph of a large sacrificial stand, lost that sense early when it was borrowed to write the word meaning "third [in a series of from three to ten items]."

斤 (キン), originally a drawing of an ax, was borrowed to write the name of a unit of weight, about six hundreds grams in Japan.

一斤 (イッ・キン 1 *kin* [600 grams])

六 （ロク/む/むっ・つ/むい） originally depicted a house, or perhaps a cave, but was borrowed to write the word for "six."

六 （ろく six）, 六月 （むつき six months; ロク・ガツ June）, 六つ （むっ・つ six）, 六日 （むい・か six days, the sixth of the month）

十 （ジュウ/ジッ/とお/と） was a symbol of a needle, but was borrowed to write "ten," meaning also "full."

十分 （ジュウ・ブン enough; ジッ・プン ten minutes）, 十日 （とお・か ten days, the tenth of the month）, 十月 （と・つき ten months; ジュウ・ガツ October）

予 （ヨ） represented a shuttle originally, but has been borrowed to write a word meaning "give; previous, beforehand" and, more anciently, "I, me."

予告 （ヨ・コク previous notice）

亜 （ア） was a drawing of the excavation for a building or perhaps of a grave; it is used in the abstract senses of "sub- ; secondary; pseudo-." It has often been used for its sound value ア in transliteration of foreign place names, and is used alone as the abbreviation of one of them, 亜細亜 （アジア Asia）.

亜流 （ア・リュウ epigone）

The following have similar forms and share elements of meaning :

工 (*ax*; construct)   王 (*ax*; King)
由 (*basket*; source)   西 (*basket*; west)
十 (*needle*; ten)   干 (*piercer*; dry)
    辛 (*needle*; painful)

The following kanji from this and earlier sections share forms unrelated in meaning:

矢 (arrow)   缶 (*pot*; can)
王 (*ax*; king)   玉 (gem)
冊 (*bamboo tablets*; book)   用 (*fence*; use)
万 (*duckweed*; ten thousand)   方 (*spade*; direction)
車 (wheel)   東 (*bag*; east)
予 (*wearing shuttle*; previous)   矛 (halbend)
十 (*needle*; ten)   米 (rice)
米 (rice)   来 (*barley*; come)

干 (*piercer*; dry) 午 (*pounder*; noon)

午 (*pounder*; noon) 牛 (ox, cow)

田 (field) 甲 (*bean sprout*; shell)

由 (*basket*; source)

単 (*duster*; single)

口 (mouth) 豆 (*dish with tall base*; bean)

京 (*house on hill*; capital)

日 (sun) 白 (*acorn*; white ; tell)

氏 (*spoon*; clan) 民 (*gimlet*; people)

土 (soil) 去 (*container*; leave)

丙 (*stand*; third) 両 (*balance*; both)

肉 (meat)

The following characters belong to this category, but are treated in later chapters, where they appear as components of other Kanji: 几 (table), 匕 (spoon), 巾 (cloth), 戈 (halberd), 禾 (rice plant), 酉 (liquor cask).

Abstract Concepts

The Chinese who devised early kanji found it necessary to write abstract concepts, including numbers and human activities. It cannot always have been easy to reduce abstract concepts to pictorial characters, but they managed to do so with astonishing ingenuity. Of course, many kanji now representing abstract concepts got those meanings by derivation from concrete meanings or by borrowing kanji with concrete meanings for abstract words, but many kanji were created for abstract meanings from the start.

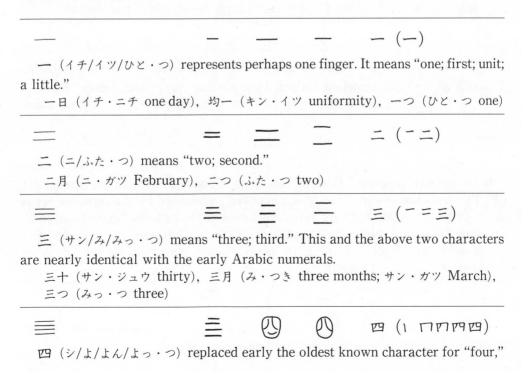

一 (イチ/イツ/ひと・つ) represents perhaps one finger. It means "one; first; unit; a little."

一日 (イチ・ニチ one day), 均一 (キン・イツ uniformity), 一つ (ひと・つ one)

二 (ニ/ふた・つ) means "two; second."

二月 (ニ・ガツ February), 二つ (ふた・つ two)

三 (サン/み/みっ・つ) means "three; third." This and the above two characters are nearly identical with the early Arabic numerals.

三十 (サン・ジュウ thirty), 三月 (み・つき three months; サン・ガツ March), 三つ (みっ・つ three)

四 (シ/よ/よん/よっ・つ) replaced early the oldest known character for "four," which was simply four lines. 四 originally meant "exhale through the mouth," the word for which had the same pronunciation as the word for "four."

四季 (シ・キ the four seasons), 四人 (よ・にん four persons), 四千 (よん・セ ン four thousand), 四つ (よっ・つ four)

五 （ ˉ 丆 万 五 ）

五 (ゴ/いつ・つ) Similarly, "five" was originally written with five lines, but 五, representing a spool, was substituted for it by virtue of homonymy.

五月 (ゴ・ガツ May), 五つ (いつ・つ five)

六 (See p.38)

七 （ 一 七 ）

七 (シチ/なな/なの), a horizontal line cut by a vertical line, is thought nonetheless to have suggested "indivisibility," a characteristic of the integer "seven," which the character represented.

七 (シチ/なな seven), 七日 (なの・か/シチ・ニチ seven days; the seventh of the month)

八 （ ノ 八 ）

八 (ハチ/や/やっ・つ/よう) represents left and right set off against each other, or "divisibility," and thus was suitable to represent the very divisible number "eight." The Japanese word for "eight" had the secondary meaning of "many."

八十 (ハチ・ジュウ eighty), 八百屋 (や・お・や grocery), 八つ (やっ・つ eight), 八日 (よう・か/ハチ・ニチ eight days; the eighth of the month)

九 （ ノ 九 ）

九 (キュウ/ク/ここの・つ) is thought to have depicted an elbow bent as far as it would go, and this somehow reflected the number "nine" and, again, "many."

九十 (キュウ・ジュウ ninety), 九月 (ク・ガツ September), 九つ (ここの・つ nine)

上 （ l ト 上 ）

上 (ジョウ/ショウ/うえ/うわ/かみ/あ・がる/のぼ・る), a mark above a line, means "above, on; top, superior." Derived meanings include "first; from the standpoint of." The verbal senses are "rise, go up; improve"; when used for the Japanese verbs あ・がる/あ・げる, the character may associate with the meaning "come to an end."

上位 (ジョウ・イ upper rank), 身上 (シン・ショウ fortune), 上 (うえ above), 上着 (うわ・ぎ jackat), 川上 (かわ・かみ upstream), 上がる (あ・がる go up), 上る (のぼ・る ascend)

下 （ 一 丁 下 ）

下 (カ/ゲ/した/しも/もと/さ・がる/くだ・る/お・りる), similarly, means "under, down, inferior; last" or as a verb, "get lower; hang down."

地下 (チ・カ underground), 下水 (ゲ・スイ sewage), 下着 (した・ぎ under-wear), 川下 (かわ・しも downstream), 下 (した/しも/もと under), 下がる (さ・がる hang; go down), 下さる (くだ・さる give[me, us]), 下りる (お・りる descend)

中 (ヽ 口 口 中)

中 (チュウ/なか) is thought to have depicted a flag pole centered in a bamboo frame to hold it up; it means "inside; middle." Derived senses include "middling" and "direct hit."

中心 (チュウ・シン center), 中 (なか inside)

大 (一 ナ 大)

大 (ダイ/タイ/おお・きい) was a stick figure of a person standing with arms and legs spread, used to write a word meaning "large, great." A derived sense is "size."

大 (ダイ the large one), 大半 (タイ・ハン majorty), 大きい (おお・きい big)

小 (亅 小 小)

小 (ショウ/ちい・さい/こ/お) seems to have been three small dots that signify "small, trivial." As the first element of some compound words, 小 (read ショウ) gives a sense like "my humble."

大小 (ダイ・ショウ big and small ; size), 小さい (ちい・さい small), 小包 (こ・づつみ parcel), 小川 (お・がわ brook)

甘 (一 十 廿 甘 甘)

甘 (カン/あま・い) shows something in a mouth and was devised to write a word meaning "sweet, tasty." Derived senses include "pleasing; indulgent; seek indulgence."

甘言 (カン・ゲン sweet talk), 甘い (あま・い sweet; indulgent)

長 (｜ 「 「 FＦ 토 툐 長)

長 (チョウ/なが・い) represented an old man with long hair, and means "long, lengthen; older, eldest ; chief."

社長 (シャ・チョウ company president), 長い (なが・い long)

高 (ヽ 亠 亠 古 古 亡 高 高 高 高)

高 (コウ/たか・い), depicting a tower or two-story building, means "high; tall; rise." Other associations include "superior; haughty; exalt; expensive" and, in Japan, "amount."

高価 (コウ・カ high price), 高い (たか・い high)

良 (リョウ/よ・い) signified measuring with a box measure, but was borrowed for "good." An alternate hypothesis is that it depicted a container of washed cereal grain and that the meaning "good" derived from "clean."

良心 (リョウ・シン conscience), 良い (よ・い good)

力 (リョク/リキ/ちから), an arm with muscles straining, is used for words meaning "strength, force; strain, strive."

圧力 (アツ・リョク pressure), 力士 (リキ・シ sumo wrestler), 力 (ちから strength)

文 (ブン/モン/ふみ) showed perhaps left and right collars, perhaps cords, neatly crossed; the word written with it meant "beautiful pattern, design." From that sense derived "written character" and then "sentence; written correspondence or document; literacy." Read モン, 文 was a counter for coins with a hole through them used until the mid-nineteenth century in Japan and is a counter for specifying footwear size.

文化 (ブン・カ culture), 文句 (モン・ク phrase; gripe), 文 (ふみ letter)

才 (サイ) indicated a stream dammed for irrigation. Scholars disagree whether its current meaning, "inborn ability, talent," is derived from an original sense of "dam," or whether the character was borrowed to write the "talent" word. The kanji is also commonly substituted for 歳, a counter for years of age.

才能 (サイ・ノウ talent)

世 (セイ/セ/よ) combined three lines to represent a thirty-year period, regarded as the length of one "generation." It has the derived senses of "era the world of humanity."

二世 (ニ・セイ second generation), 世界 (セ・カイ world), 世 (よ world)

寸 (スン) showed a finger placed across the arm about an inch below the wrist to represent a Japanese unit of length, the *sun* (about three centimeters). Derived senses are "measurement; little."

寸前 (スン・ゼン just before)

尺 (シャク) depicted a hand stretched out in measurement. The character represents a Japanese unit of length corresponding to ten *sun* (寸) (about thirty centimeters). It has derivative senses of "length," especially "short length," and the figurative meaning of "yardstick."

尺八 (シャク・ハチ bamboo flute)

元 (ゲン/ガン/もと), a man with a large head, wrote a word for "chief, leader" that has a derived sense of "first, beginning."

元気 (ゲン・キ vigor), 元日 (ガン・ジツ New Year's Day), 元 (もと origin)

主 (シュ/ス/ぬし/おも), originally a picture of a burning oil lamp, is thought to have represented a word meaning "stay." Its common associations are "primary" and "owner; master," probably as the one who, unlike a visitor, stays.

主人 (シュ・ジン master; husband), 坊主 (ボウ・ズ monk; boy), 主 (ぬし owner; おも main)

互 (ゴ/たが・い) depicted either a tool for twisting fibers into thread or rope, or two sticks notched to hook each other. Its sense is "alternately; mutual."

相互 (ソウ・ゴ mutual), 互い (たが・い each other)

夕 (セキ/ゆう) represented a young crescent moon as a symbol for "evening."

一朝一夕 (イッ・チョウ・イッ・セキ a day), 夕方 (ゆう・がた evening)

古 (コ/ふる・い), thought to represent a skull, was used for a word meaning "old, hard," perhaps like "ossified." It is also used for "of old; the ancient past."

古代 (コ・ダイ ancient times), 古い (ふる・い old)

生 (セイ/ショウ/い・きる/う・まれる/お・う/は・える/き/なま), a mark on a drawing of a grass shoot to symbolize growth, was used to write a word meaning variously "come to life; grow; live," and so also "bear; birth; life." Extended meanings include "come/bring into existence" of inanimate or abstract things, as well as "fresh, raw; pure; creature, being."

生物 (セイ・ブツ animate beings), 一生 (イッ・ショウ lifetime), 生きる (い・きる live), 生まれる (う・まれる be born), 生い立ち (お・い・た・ち breeding), 生える (は・える grow), 生糸 (き・いと raw silk), 生 (なま raw)

立 （リツ/リュウ/た・つ） showed a man standing on the ground and represented a word meaning "stand; erect." "Establish, get established; set in; set out; depart" are among the figurative and idiomatic senses derived from the basic meaning.

立春 （リッ・シュン start of spring）, 建立 （コン・リュウ construction of a Buddhist temple）, 立つ （た・つ stand）

入 （ニュウ/い・る/はい・る）, a drawing of the entrance to a cave or house symbolized "entrance" and "putting in."

入学 （ニュウ・ガク entering school）, 入る （い・る/はい・る enter）

出 （シュツ/スイ/で・る/だ・す）, a foot with a shoe on it, symbolizing the notion of going out, was used to mean "go/come out; put out" and thence "appear; put forth, produce."

出場 （シュツ・ジョウ appearance）, 出納 （スイ・トウ accounts）, 出る （で・る come out）, 出す （だ・す bring out）

行 （コウ/ギョウ/アン/い・く/ゆ・く/おこな・う） depicted a crossroad to write a word meaning "go." Other important meanings associated with it include "line, column (of persons, written characters, etc.); perform, undertake," and the semicursive style of kanji writing, ギョウ.

行動 （コウ・ドウ action）, 行事 （ギョウ・ジ event）, 行脚 （アン・ギャ foot travel）, 行く （い・く/ゆ・く go）, 行う （おこな・う conduct）

欠 （ケツ/か・ける）, a picture of a stooping person yawning widely, was used to write a word meaning both "yawn" and "stoop," but it gets its current readings and meanings, "lacking, missing; broken, defective," by substitution for 缺 （ケツ）.

欠点 （ケッ・テン fault）, 欠ける （か・ける lack）

交 （コウ/まじ・わる/ま・じる/か・う） depicted a person with legs crossed for the meaning "cross, intersect," from which senses of "intermingle, mix; exchange; alternately" have derived.

交互 （コウ・ゴ alternation）, 交わる （まじ・わる mingle）, 交じる （ま・じる mix）, 交わす （か・わす exchange）

示 （ ˉ ニ テ 亓 示 ）

示 (ジ/シ/しめ・す) symbolized a sacrifice to the gods over which purifying liquor was poured. The word it was used to write means "show, indicate," the connection thought to be in that a sign was to be given by the gods to the worshipers at such an event.

指示 (シ・ジ indication), 示唆 (シ・サ implication), 示す (しめ・す show)

曲 （ ｜ 冂 帀 冊 曲 曲 ）

曲 (キョク/ま・がる) depicted a container the sides of which were made by bending thin slats of wood or bamboo; it means "curve, bend." It has the derived meanings "perverse, corrupt; changeful; details; tune." Read キョク, it is used as a counter for pieces of music.

曲目 (キョク・モク title of a piece of music), 曲がる (ま・がる bend)

飛 （ ⺄ ⺅ ⺄ 升 飛 飛 飛 飛 ）

飛 (ヒ/と・ぶ), depicting a bird in flight, means "fly, leap."

飛行機 (ヒ・コウ・キ airplane), 飛ぶ (と・ぶ fly)

申 （ ｜ 冂 日 曰 申 ）

申 (シン/もう・す), a representation of a straight spine and the ribs, meant "stretch; straight."   The character was borrowed to write words meaning "tell, state (humbly)."

申告 (シン・コク report), 申す (もう・す tell)

且 （ ｜ 冂 月 月 且 ）

且 (か・つ)represented stones piled up as a gravemarker or fence and originally meant "pile up."   Now it is used in the probably derived senses of "also, furthermore; at the same time; on the other hand."

臣 （ ˉ 冖 冖 乥 乥 乥 臣 ）

臣 (シン/ジン), an eye straining to see, was used for "vassal, minister"; scholars disagree whether this is a derivation of the character's original meaning or whether the character was borrowed.

忠臣 (チュウ・シン loyal retainer), 大臣 (ダイ・ジン minister of state)

己 （ ⺄ ⺄ 己 ）

己 (コ/キ/おのれ) was either a person getting up or a piece of thread; scholars disagree. It would have meant, originally, either "get up" or "leading end of thread," but it is now used for the meaning of "self."

自己 (ジ・コ self), 知己 (チ・キ acquaintance), 己 (おのれ oneself)

県 （｜ 冂 月 月 目 直 県 県 県）

県 （ケン） depicted a head, probably that of a criminal hung up for display and originally meant "hang." Through an extension of the original sense, it now means "prefecture."

南 （一 十 宁 宁 宁 宁 南 南 南）

南 （ナン／ナ／みなみ） is thought to have been a drawing of either a curtain or a framework to protect plants, either way representing a place of warmth. Its meaning "south" is said to have derived from that. In the case of the reading ナ, the character is used for part of its sound value alone.

南西 （ナン・セイ southwest）, 南無 （ナ・ム Hail! [e.g., in Buddhist prayers]）, 南 （みなみ south）

屯 （一 匸 口 屯）

屯 （トン） depicted a new plant forcing its way out of the earth with difficulty and, it is said, originally represented "trouble getting under way." Its familiar sense of "encamp, encampment" derives from that.

駐屯 （チュウ・トン stationing）

斉 （丶 一 ナ 文 齐 斉 斉 斉）

斉 （セイ） showed several plants shooting up at the same time; it means "altogether" or "equal."

一斉 （イッ・セイ altogether）

兆 （ノ ノ ノ 丬 北 兆）

兆 （チョウ／きざ・し）, a depiction of cracks made in a turtle shell for divination, means "divination" or "omen." It is also used to write a word, homophonous in Chinese, meaning "trillion; a huge number."

兆 （チョウ trillion）, 兆し （きざ・し omen）

比 （一 ヒ ヒ 比）

比 （ヒ／くら・べる）, two persons standing side by side, means "compare."

対比 （タイ・ヒ contrast）, 比べる （くら・べる compare）

北 （一 ナ ヲ 北 北）

北 （ホク／きた）, depicting two persons standing back to back, has perhaps its basic meaning in "oppose, act against." The senses "run away" and, most importantly, "north" derive from that.

敗北 （ハイ・ボク defeat）, 北 （きた north）

北 北 非（ノ ） ゴ ヺ ヺ 非 非
非 非）

非（ヒ）, the open wings of a bird, is said to have symbolized the meanings "turn away; run counter to."   Derived therefrom are "not; wrong; blame."
    非常（ヒ・ジョウ extraordinary)

 弱 弱（ ゛ ゛ ゙ ゙ ゙
ゔ ゙ ゙ 弱 弱 弱）

弱（ジャク/よわ・い）depicted decorative bows or a young bird's wings to suggest "weak; young."
    貧弱（ヒン・ジャク poor, meager), 弱い（よわ・い weak)

 与 （與）与（ ゛ 与 与）

与（ヨ/あた・える）represented gear cogs meshing and meant "meshing."   It has the derived meanings "engage; side with" and has been borrowed to write "give."
    与党（ヨ・トウ party in power), 与える（あた・える give)

The following kanji pairs are based on very similar pictographic elements, but the present-day forms and meanings are very different:

月 (moon) 　　　　　　　　　夕 (evening)
京 (*house on hill*; capital) 　　高 (*tall building*; high)
比 (*two persons facing the same direction*; compare) 　北 (*two persons back to back*; north)
口 (mouth) 　　　　　　　　甘 (sweet)
老 (old man) 　　　　　　　長 (*hairy old man*; long)
大 (*spread-eagle man*; large) 　立 (stand)
目 (eye) 　　　　　　　　　臣 (*big eye*; vassal)
羽 (wings) 　　　　　　　　非 (wrong)
　　　　　　　　　　　　　飛 (fly)

As the number of kanji increases, so does the number of similar forms, making it harder to associate them with what they were originally pictures of.   Here are more on our ever-lengthening list of kanji that share formal elements but are not related in origins and meanings.

四 (four) 　　　　　　　西 (*basket*; west)
八 (eight) 　　　　　　　六 (*house*; six)
上 (above) 　　　　　　　止 (*foot*; stop)
下 (below) 　　　　　　　不 (*calyx*; not)
中 (center) 　　　　　　　虫 (insect; worm)
　　　　　　　　　　　申 (*spine*; tell)

大 (*spread-eagled man*; large) 　犬 (dog)

小 (small)

衣 (*collar*; garment)
長 (*hairy old man*)
子 (child)
刀 (sword)
文 (*collars*; letter)

父 (father)
二 (two)
王 (*ax*; king)

口 (mouth)
十 (*needle*; ten)
立 (stand)

人 (person)
山 (mountain)
由 (*basket*; source)

甲 (*bean sprout*; shell)
目 (eye)

矢 (arrow)
京 (*house on hill*; capital)
県 (*gibbeted head*; prefecture)
示 (*altar*; indicate)
糸 (thread)
長 (*hairy old man*; long)
良 (good)
与 (give)
力 (strength)
交 (crossing)
斉 (altogether)
交 (cross)
元 (*leader*)
玉 (gem)
主 (*lit oil lamp*; master)
古 (old)
古 (old)
竜 (dragon)
辛 (*needle*; painful)
入 (entrance)
出 (go out)
曲 (*wood or bamboo container*; curve)
申 (tell)
申 (tell)
且 (also)
県 (*gibbeted head*; prefecture)

More on the Basic Forms

The examples in the previous sections showed that similar forms do not necessarily have similar meanings, and that similar ancient pictorial characters with similar meanings will not necessarily turn into modern kanji with similar forms. Here is a summary of the simpler basic forms (on the left) and other basic forms that look like they contain the simpler one.

口 (mouth)

日 (sun)

目 (eye)

小 (small)

石 (stone)
足 (leg)
豆 (*dish with tall base*; bean)
京 (*house on hill*; capital)
古 (old)
易 (*lizard*; change)
白 (*acorn*; white)
自 (*nose*; self)
貝 (shell)
且 (also)
県 (*gibbeted head*; prefecture)
京 (*house on hill*; capital)

田 (field)

示 (*altar*; indicate)
糸 (thread)
単 (*duster*; single)
由 (*basket*; source)
甲 (*bean sprout*; shell)
申 (tell)

王 (*ax*; king)

玉 (gem)
主 (*lit oil lamp*; master)

立 (stand)

竜 (dragon)
辛 (*needle*; painful)

刀 (sword)

力 (strength)

中 (center)

虫 (insect; worm)

大 (*spread-eagled man*; large)

犬 (dog)

山 (mountain)

出 (go out)

父 (father)

交 (crossing)

文 (*collars*; letter)

斉 (altogether)

予 (*weaving shuttle*; previous)

矛 (halberd)

土 (soil)

去 (leave)

In the preceding sections were some kanji that can be divided into two similar formal elements with either the same, or opposite orientation.   Listed on the left below are the ones with elements in the same orientation; the ones on the right have a reversed element.

竹 (bamboo)   門 (gate)
羽 (wings)   非 (wrong)
比 (compare)   北 (north)
弱 (weak)   卵 (egg)
行 (go)   兆 (omen; trillion)

Although the individual "halves" may have evolved slightly differently, they originally depicted identical objects.   Kanji such as those above should be differentiated from single kanji repeated to form a compound kanji, such as 林 (woods) and 森 (forest). While the elements of such compound kanji can also be combined with other elements to form new kanji, this is generally not true of the elements of the kanji in the lists above.   Two exceptions are the right side ヒ of 比 (compare) and the left side 彳 of 行 (go), which are used in other kanji as well. (The ヒ in 比[compare], 北[north], and 老[old]represents a person.   Another basic kanji, ヒ [spoon], looks the same, but has a different historical derivation; it is used only as a component.)

Due to the further simplification of kanji that were very simple pictures to start with, a number of kanji are confusingly similar in form.   Here are some of the basic-form kanji that might be easily confused by beginners. (Only one gloss for each is given here.)

人 (man), 入 (enter)
日 (sun), 白 (white), 目 (eye)

目 (eye), 且 (also), 自 (self), 貝 (shell), 耳 (ear)

西 (west), 四 (four), 面 (face), 両 (both)

由 (source), 田 (field), 曲 (curve)

用 (use), 肉 (flesh), 角 (horn), 冊 (volume)

角 (horn), 魚 (fish)

川 (river), 小 (small), 三 (three)

土 (dirt), 士 (man), 工 (construct), 上 (above)

上 (above), 止 (stop)

下 (below), 不 (not), 丁 (*chō*)

丁 (*chō*), 寸 (*sun*), 才 (talent)

王 (king), 生 (live), 玉 (gem), 主 (master)

缶 (can), 生 (live), 出 (go out), 豆 (bean)

立 (stand), 丘 (hill)

干 (dry), 牛 (ox), 午 (noon), 平 (flat)

午 (noon), 矢 (arrow), 牛 (ox)

大 (large), 犬 (dog), 木 (tree)

犬 (dog), 求 (seek)

米 (rice), 来 (come), 水 (water)

毛 (hair), 手 (hand), 屯 (encamp)

中 (center), 虫 (insect)

甲 (shell), 申 (tell), 由 (source), 単 (single)

万 (ten thousand), 方 (direction)

力 (strength), 刀 (sword), 九 (nine)

母 (mother), 舟 (boat)

父 (father), 交 (crossing), 文 (letter)

馬 (horse), 鳥 (bird)

羽 (wings), 弱 (weak)

戸 (door), 尺 (*shaku*)

車 (wheel), 申 (tell), 東 (east)

予 (previous), 矛 (halberd)

氏 (clan), 民 (people)

乙 (second), 己 (self)

長 (long), 良 (good)

元 (leader), 示 (indicate)

比 (compare), 北 (north)

Chapter 3

Semantic Compound Kanji

The kanji in this chapter are made up of a basic form and at least one other component that contributes to the kanji's meaning; in the vast majority of cases neither component serves as a phonetic element indicating the *on-yomi* of the kanji. We have divided this large category into five groups, each treated in a separate section;

1. Basic forms with an additional stroke or strokes. For example, the basic-form kanji 刀 (sword) with an added stroke makes 刃 (edge).
2. Reduplicated forms. For example, two 火 (fire) give 炎 (flame).
3. Combinations of two basic forms (both of which have already been introduced). For example, 米 (rice) and 斗 (ladle) give 料 (measure).
4. Combinations using "classifiers" not introduced previously. For example, 宀 (roof), one the "classifiers," and 女 (woman) give 安 (ease).
5. Combinations of greater complexity. For example, 山 (mountain), 上 (ascend), and 下 (descend) give 峠 (mountain pass).

The kanji in each section are grouped (and headed) by either the basic form or the "classifier." Within sections and groups, kanji are arranged according to increasing number of strokes; when two of more characters have the same number of strokes, they are ordered in the *gojūon* (Japanese syllabary) order, based on the first reading of the kanji.

Basic Forms with Additional Strokes

A number of kanji were put together by adding one or more strokes to a basic form, or, rarely, by removing one or more strokes from such a form. In most cases the shapes of the original basic forms remain unchanged, but in some cases they are different, although their identities are retained. For example, the top part of 介 (mediate) is another form of 人 (man). Such variants are shown in the heading after the standard form.

Occasionally a kanji has an element that is identical to a basic form but that originated in an entirely different pictorial element. We will list such kanji under the apparent basic forms; for example, 弔 (mourn) is here listed under 弓 (bow) even though the 弓 of 弔 had nothing to do with bows. The meaning association for which a semantic component is used in a compound kanji is often not the same

51

as its contemporary meaning as an independent kanji, but an earlier meaning or pictographic value. Such meanings are cited in italics.

2-Stroke Components

九   *(bent arm)*

丸 (ガン/まる) (ノ 九丸) represented someone's bent body, an extension of 九. It means "round; circle," from which a sense of "full, entire" was derived. It is also used in the names of medicines (suffix ガン) and ships (suffix まる).

    弾丸 (ダン・ガン bullet), 丸い (まる・い round)

人;へ   (person)

久 (キュウ/ク/ひさ・しい) (ノ ク久) marked 人 with a line, as if to pull the person from behind, to indicate holding someone back. It is now used in the derived sense "long time."

    永久 (エイ・キュウ forever), 久遠 (ク・オン eternity), 久しく (ひさ・しく for a long time)

千 (セン/ち) (⌐ 二千) is a combination of a line, or 一 (one), and 人. This apparently evoked the meaning "thousand" and, figuratively, "very many."

    千 (セン one thousand), 千草 (ち・ぐさ a great variety of plants)

介 (カイ) (ノ 人个介) combines 人, written へ as the top part of a kanji, and two lines to suggest the idea of being between two things: "in between; mediate; help." Other senses, "shell" and "armor," are perhaps derivative.

    介入 (カイ・ニュウ intervention)

内 (ナイ/ダイ/うち) (丨 冂内内) originally 內, stood for the entrance to a house, perhaps by combining an element meaning "roof" and 入 (enter). It means "inside, inner; private; unofficial."

    内部 (ナイ・ブ inner part), 境内 (ケイ・ダイ precincts), 内(うち inside; home)

年 (ネン/とし) (' ⺧ ⺊ ⺊ ⺧ 年) originally combined 禾 (rice plant) and 人, but neither element remains recognizable. It presumably meant "harvest, harvest time," from which derives its current sense, "year; age."

    一年 (イチ・ネン one year), 年 (とし year; age)

刀   (sword; edged tool)

刃 (ジン/は) (フ刀刃) adds a mark to the blade of 刀 to give the meaning "edged, blade." It has a derived sense of "slash to death."

    自刃 (ジ・ジン suicide by sword), 刃 (は blade)

又   *(hand)*

及 (キュウ/およ・ぶ) (ノ 乃及) combines 人 (man) and 又, as can be seen more clearly in the slightly older form 及, and is said to suggest a hand reaching a running man for the senses of "catch up with, reach; be extended; as well."

及第（キュウ・ダイ passing an examination），及ぶ（およ・ぶ reach）

反（ハン/ホン/タン/そ・る）（一厂万反） is thought to have depicted a hand bending a cloth or a thin board. It means "warp, bend back; reverse," with derived senses of "do over; in opposition to, anti-; oppose." With the reading タン, which it gets by substitution for another kanji, it means a unit of length (approximately ten meters) for measuring kimono material and a unit of area (about 990 square meters) for measuring cultivated fields.

反対（ハン・タイopposition），謀反（ム・ホンrebellion），反物（タン・モノdry goods），反る（そ・るwarp）

友（ユウ/とも）（一ナ方友） shows two hands helping each other. The *on-yomi* ユウ is that of 又 (which has no official Jōyō Kanji *on-yomi*). 友 means "allies, friend."

友好（ユウ・コウ amity），友（とも friend）

支（シ/ささ・える）（一十ㄘ支） depicts a hand holding a branch torn off a bamboo stalk. Its meanings are "branch; prop, support." Another sense, "allot, pay," is thought to be derived, via "divide one's money," from the "branch" sense. Its sense of "obstacle" may come by substitution for another character.

支店（シ・テンbranch shop），支える（ささ・えるsupport）

皮（ヒ/かわ）（一厂广皮皮） is thought to have depicted a hand holding an animal hide; it means "skin, hide," and, by extension, "bark, husk."

樹皮（ジュ・ヒ bark），皮（かわ leather）

史（シ）（丨 口口史史） depicted a hand holding a bamboo tube used as a container for bamboo tablets, the mark of a "scribe," the primary meaning of the character. What the scribe wrote provides the derived and more important meaning, "history."

史跡（シ・セキ historic site）

吏（リ）（一亠亓亘吏吏）, a hand holding a stick with a small flag on it, emblematic of public office, means "government official; civil servant."

官吏（カン・リ public official）

事（ジ/ズ/こと）（一亠亓亘写写写事） may be essentially the same as the preceding, a hand holding a flag, or the hand may have held several bamboo sticks. The meaning, too, may have been a very similar "government service." Its common associations now are in the area of "job, task; person in charge; incident, case, fact; serve."

事情（ジ・ジョウ circumstance），好事家（コウ・ズ・カ dilettante），事（こと fact）

3-Stroke Components

弓 (bow)

弔（チョウ/とむら・う）（㇆コ弓弔） depicted a stake or tree with a vine twined around, drooping, to suggest sympathy. It is used to mean "mourn, pray for the dead."

弔問 （チョウ・モン condolence call）, 弔い （とむら・い funeral service）

引 （イン／ひ・く） （ ﾏ ﾕ 弓 引 ） is a bow with its string drawn back, suggesting the meaning "draw, pull."   Derived and figurative senses include "prolong; lead; quote; deduct, reduce."

引用 （イン・ヨウ quotation）, 引く （ひ・く pull）

弟 （テイ／ダイ／デ／おとうと） （ 丶 丷 丷 兰 肖 弟 弟 ） is thought to have depicted some sort of stake with a piece of string dangling from it and a mark near the bottom to indicate a sense of lower position.   It means "younger brother; cadet; disciple."

師弟 （シ・テイ master and pupil）, 兄弟 （キョウ・ダイ brothers）, 弟子 （デ・シ disciple）, 弟 （おとうと younger brother）

口 (mouth; opening)

可 （カ） （ ﾏ 丆 ﾃﾞ 可 可 ） adds a hook symbol to 口 to suggest the notion of difficulty in speaking.   The senses of "affirmative" and "possible" are thought to derive therefrom.

可能 （カ・ノウ possible）

吉 （キチ／キツ） （ 一 十 士 吉 吉 吉 ） may have depicted either a covered jar or the combination of 才 (block off) and 口; both would mean "filled with food." The current meaning, "good, fortunate" is said to be a derivative of this.

吉 （キチ good omen）, 吉報 （キッ・ポウ good news）

司 （シ） （ 丁 刁 刁 司 司 司 ） depicts someone looking through a hole to mean "to probe a matter," of which extended meanings are "control, manage" and the person or task of "controller, manager."

司会者 （シ・カイ・シャ master of ceremonies）

右 （ユウ／ウ／みぎ） （ ノ ナ ナ 右 右 ） comes from a combination of 又 (*right hand*) and 口.   The hypothesis is that the hand is shielding the mouth, but in effect the compound means "right (not left)" and is close to the original meaning of 又, which had nearly the same pronunciation.   The modern addition of the sense of "political conservatism" is a Western language influence.

左右 （サ・ユウ left and right）, 右派 （ウ・ハ right-wing sect）, 右 （みぎ right）

向 （コウ／む・かう） （ 丶 ｲ 门 向 向 向 ） is said to depict a hole in a roof or a window in a wall as a direction of air flow.   From this it gets its meaning "face, orientate; facing; toward; opposite."

向上 （コウ・ジョウ improvement）, 向かう （む・かう face）

后 （コウ） （ ﾉ 厂 斤 斤 后 后 ）combines 人 (person) and 口 in the sense of "opening" to suggest the anus, the hypothesis goes, to write a word meaning "rear, backside."   Because the emperor's consort or queen lived in the rear of the palace, the word was used to refer to her.

皇后 （コウ・ゴウ empress）

舌 (ゼツ/した) (ノ 二 千 千 舌 舌) showed a tongue sticking out of a mouth and means "tongue," with the derived senses of "speech; language."

弁舌 (ベン・ゼツ eloquence), 舌 (した tongue)

同 (ドウ/おな・じ) (｜ 冂 冂 同 同 同) according to one of various theories, represented a hole through boards by which they could be united. It means "similar, same" and "gather; together; share."

同士 (ドウ・シ one's fellow), 同じ (おな・じ same)

言 (ゲン/ゴン/い・う/こと) (ヽ 一 亠 亖 言 言 言) combines a representation of an edged tool with 口 to symbolize punctuation of utterance. It means "say; speak; word; speech; call."

言語 (ゲン・ゴ language), 言う (い・う say), 一言 (ひと・こと/イチ・ゴン a word)

谷 (コク/たに) (ノ 八 ケ 父 谷 谷 谷) combines two pairs of diverging lines and 口, to indicate water coming out of an opening. It means "ravine, valley," extended figuratively to the chasm that city streets follow between rows of tall buildings.

渓谷 (ケイ・コク gorge), 谷 (たに valley)

音 (オン/イン/おと/ね) (ヽ 亠 亠 立 产 产 音 音 音) comes from nearly the same original pictograph as 言, with line across the mouth (口) which, it is conjectured, indicated muffled voice, or "sound." A special use in Japan is for reference to *on-yomi* (音読み), the Sino-Japanese reading of kanji.

音楽 (オン・ガク music), 母音 (ボ・イン vowel), 音 (おと sound), 音色 (ね・いろ tone color)

工   (*ax*; construct)

巨 (キョ) (一 厂 匚 巨 巨), in one hypothesis, depicted a square or rule for setting things apart at a standard distance; in another hypothesis, it depicted a kind of ax. But the sense it has been used in is that of "enormous."

巨人 (キョ・ジン giant)

左 (サ/ひだり) (一 ナ 左 左 左) stands for a left hand holding a products for the right hand to work on; the basic meaning is "left," from which derives "next in command." It has a sense of "sinister," and the Western "politically radical" has been added. It is sometimes used in place of the cognate 佐(サ) for "help" and in Japan is associated with "tippling."

左遷 (サ・セン relegation), 左 (ひだり left)

子   (child)

了 (リョウ) (フ 了) is variously reconstructed as an armless child or something all tangled up. The sense for which it is actually used is "finish, complete." It also takes the meaning of a homophonous word for "obvious; understand clearly."

完了 (カン・リョウ completion)

小 (small)

少 (ショウ/すく・ない/すこ・し) (ノ 丶 小 少) is an expansion on 小 to write an apparently related word meaning "few, little; decrease."

少年 (ショウ・ネン boy), 少ない (すく・ない few), 少し (すこ・し a little)

川 (river)

州 (シュウ/す) (丶 丿 丿 州 州 州) adds marks to 川 to represent sandbars or river islets and means "sandbar, islet." It has been extended to "land, continent," and is also used to refer to administrative units such as the "states" of the U.S.

州 (シュウ state), 中州 (なか・す sandbar in river)

大 (*spread-eagle man*; large)

太 (タイ/タ/ふと・い) (一 ナ 大 太) adds a mark to 大 that at least some scholars think might have been meant to emphasize it; in any event, 太 is a simple variation representing a probably related word, meaning "very large; thick." Derivative meanings are "very; splendid; noblest."

太鼓 (タイ・コ drum), 丸太 (まる・タ log), 太い (ふと・い thick)

天 (テン/あめ/あま) (一 二 チ 天) has a line across the top of 大, representing either the sky or a head. It means "top; sky, heaven," as well as "divinity; nature; innate."

天気 (テン・キ weather), 天 (テン/あめ sky, heaven), 天の川 (あま・の・がわ Milky Way)

夫 (フ/フウ/おっと) (一 二 チ 夫) shows a man (大) wearing a crown, signifying "adult male." Extensions of that include "husband" and "worker." For reasons not entirely clear, the word 夫人 (フ・ジン), used after a surname in Japan, means "Mrs."

夫妻 (フ・サイ husband and wife), 工夫 (ク・フウ scheme), 夫 (おっと husband)

央 (オウ) (丶 冂 冂 央 央) marks the middle of person (大) with a line for the meaning "center."

中央 (チュウ・オウ center)

土 (soil)

至 (シ/いた・る) (一 工 乙 至 至 至) depicted an arrow coming down onto the ground (土) for the sense of "reach the destination," and from this derive "going all the way; extreme; thorough; every (where)."

至急 (シ・キュウ urgency), 至る (いた・る lead to)

幸 (コウ/さいわ・い/さち/しあわ・せ) (一 十 土 キ 去 去 幸 幸) had nothing to do with 土 originally, but depicted handcuffs and meant "handcuff." Its usage for "good luck; happy" is said to have derived from that.

不幸 (フ・コウ misfortune), 幸い (さいわ・い lucky), 幸 (さち blessing), 幸せ (しあわ・せ happiness)

4-Stroke Components

| 火 | (fire) |

灰 (カイ/はい) (一厂厂厂灰灰), earlier 灰, combines a symbol for "hand" with 火 to represent "ash," perhaps as what can be picked up after burning something.

石灰 (セッ・カイ/いし・ばい lime), 灰 (はい ashes)

| 牛 | (ox) |

半 (ハン/なか・ば) (丶 丶丷半半) adds ハ (*divide*) to 牛 to symbolize division into two, for "half." Further senses are "partial; odd number; mid."

半日 (ハン・ニチ half a day), 半ば (なか・ば halfway)

| 斤 | (*hatchet*) |

斥 (セキ) (一厂厂斤斥) has a mark on 斤 conjectured to signify chopping to pieces. It means "reject" and sometimes "investigate."

排斥 (ハイ・セキ expulsion)

兵 (ヘイ/ヒョウ) (一厂厂斤丘兵兵) originally combined two hands (usually written ハ as the lower part of a kanji) with 斤 (*hatchet*) to symbolize "soldier; military, martial."

兵士 (ヘイ・シ soldier), 兵量 (ヒョウ・リョウ provisions)

| 止 | (*foot*; stop) |

乏 (ボウ/とぼ・しい) (一丶乇乏) is a line over a reversed form of 止, symbolizing an inability to proceed, but it is used for the meaning "scanty; shortage."

欠乏 (ケツ・ボウ shortage), 乏しい (とぼ・しい scarce)

正 (セイ/ショウ/ただ・しい/まさ) (一丁下正正) adds a straight line to 止 (*foot*) to symbolize going straight and means "straight; right, correct; just," with derived associations of "formal; official."

改正 (カイ・セイ revision), 正直 (ショウ・ジキ honest), 正しい (ただ・しい correct), 正に (まさ・に exactly)

| 尺 | (*hand stretched in measurement*; *shaku*) |

丈 (ジョウ/たけ) (一ナ丈) melded 十 (ten) with 尺 to mean *jō*, a unit of length about three meters long, ten times a *shaku*. It also is used in senses of "length; height; tall; strong." Suffixed to an old man's name or, in Japan, to that of a Kabuki actor, it is used as a title of respect.

丈夫 (ジョウ・ブ strong), 丈 (たけ height; length of body)

| 手 | (hand) |

失 (シツ/うしな・う) (丿 ﾉ二失失) adds a line to 手 with the top stroke moved to the left to symbolize something slipping out of one's grip.   It means "lose; let slip."

失言 (シツ・ゲン slip of the tongue), 失う (うしな・う lose)

心 (heart)

必 (ヒツ/かなら・ず) (ノ ソ 义 必 必) does not really include 心; note the stroke order.   Originally it may have depicted a wooden handle tightly wrapped with bamboo; it is used as a component of characters which relate to a sense of tightness or squeezing.   The sense of this character is "certainty, necessity."

必要 (ヒツ・ヨウ necessity), 必ず (かなら・ず necessity)

水 (water)

永 (エイ/なが・い) (丶 寸 寸 永 永) is said to have symbolized a long, meandering watercourse; it signifies "long time; eternity."

永遠 (エイ・エン eternity), 永い (なが・い lengthy)

氷 (ヒョウ/こおり/ひ) (丿 寸 寸 永 氷) adds a mark to 水 to signify "ice; freezing."

氷山 (ヒョウ・ザン iceberg), 氷 (こおり ice), 氷雨 (ひ・さめ hail)

泉 (セン/いずみ) (丶 亻 宀 白 白 阜 身 泉 泉) represented water coming out of a hole in the ground, a "spring."

温泉 (オン・セン hot spring), 泉 (いずみ spring)

井 (well)

丹 (タン) (丿 冂 月 丹) is 井 with a mark in it to suggest cinnabar coming out of a mine shaft.   It is used in the sense of "cinnabar red" and can also mean "medicinal pill" and "sincere."

丹念 (タン・ネン careful)

日 (sun)

旧 (キュウ) (丨 刂 阝 旧 旧) is an abbreviation of 舊, which apparently originally depicted a kind of owl, but both original and abbreviation are used for "old, ancient; of old."

旧友 (キュウ・ユウ old friend)

早 (ソウ/サッ/はや・い) (丨 冂 日 旦 旦 早) depicted the black nut of an alder or oak, it is hypothesized, and meant "dark," but came to be used in the derived sense of "early" through reference to the darkness of early morning.   The meanings "young" and "fast" are derived from "early."

早朝 (ソウ・チョウ early morning), 早速 (サッ・ソク immediately), 早い (early)

月 (moon; meat, flesh)

Although the component 月 may signify a connection with "moon" in a kanji, it is also an important variant of 肉 (meat, flesh).

有 (ユウ/ウ/あ・る) (ノ ナ オ 冇 有 有) combines "hand" with 月 (meat). It means "have, possess; exist."   In Buddhist writings it has been used for "illusion."
　　有力 (ユウ・リョク powerful), 有無 (ウ・ム existence; yes or no), 有る (あ・る exist; possess)

育 (イク/そだ・つ) (` 亠 云 产 育 育 育) combines 子 (child) inverted, to signify a newborn infant, and 肉 to suggest the meanings of "grow; nurture."
　　育児 (イク・ジ child care), 育つ (そだ・つ grow)

文 (letter)

匁 (もんめ) (ノ ク 勺 匁) is a Japanese-made combination of 文, from which it gets part of its reading, and *katakana* メ, to write the word *monme*, a Japanese unit of weight, approximately 3.75 grams.   In the Edo period, the *monme* was also a unit of currency.
　　一匁 (イチ・もんめ one *monme*)

木 (tree; wood)

片 (ヘン/かた) (ノ 丿 ゲ 片) originated as the right half of 木, to signify a piece of wood.   It means "piece of; a small bit; one of what normally come in pairs; out-of-the-way."
　　破片 (ハ・ヘン fragment), 片足 (かた・あし one leg)

本 (ホン/もと) (一 十 オ 木 本) has a mark on the trunk part of 木, signifying "root, base."   From that derives "origin; originally; basic; this particular...."   It is also used as a counter for long cylindrical objects, which once included rolled-up written documents; from this came the current meaning of "book."
　　本土 (ホン・ド mainland), 本 (もと basis; ホン book)

末 (マツ/バツ/すえ) (一 二 キ 丰 末) has a long mark near the top of 木, indicating ends of branches.   It means "far removed from the origin; end, tip." Apparently derived meanings are "of little account; powder."
　　年末 (ネン・マツ year-end), 末弟 (バッ・テイ/マッ・テイ youngest brother), 末 (すえ end)

未 (ミ) (一 二 キ 未 未) expresses the meaning "not yet" by putting a short line on the top of 木 to suggest a tree not yet grown.
　　未来 (ミ・ライ the future)

朱 (シュ) (ノ ゲ 二 牛 牛 朱) started as 木 with a mark across the middle to suggest a tree stump.   It is used for "vermillion," the color of certain fresh stumps.

束 (ソク/たば) (一 戸 戸 吉 束 束 束) adds to 木 a circle, now written rectangularly, to suggest a rope around a bundle of wood.   It means "bundle; tie."
　　約束 (ヤク・ソク promise), 束ねる (たば・ねる tie in bundle)

果 (カ/はた・す) (丨 ロ 曰 甲 旦 甲 界 果) depicts fruit in a tree. It means "fruit," with derived senses of "result; fulfill; end."

果実 (カ・ジツ fruit), 果たす (は・たす fulfill)

乗 (ジョウ/の・る) (ノ 二 ｽ 千 千 乖 乗 乗 乗) depicted someone up high in a tree. It means "ride," and has derived senses of "vehicle; use to one's advantage; power (in math)."

　　乗客 (ジョウ・キャク passenger), 乗る (の・る ride)

桑 (ソウ/くわ) (ワ ヌ ヲ ヌ 叒 叒 叒 桑 桑 桑) depicts a tree with large leaves to mean "mulberry."

　　桑田 (ソウ・デン mulberry patch), 桑 (くわ mulberry)

集 (シュウ/あつ・める/つど・う) (ノ イ イ 仁 竹 仹 隹 隹 隼 集 集 集) puts a bird (隹) in a tree to suggest flocking together. It means "gather, collect."

　　集金 (シュウ・キン bill collecting), 集める (あつ・める assemble), 集い (つど・い gathering)

業 (ギョウ/ゴウ/わざ) (ノ ″ ″ ″ 业 业 业 堂 堂 業 業) is said to have depicted a rack for hanging musical instruments on, consisting of a pole with a notched board across it. It means "skill, forte; act; vocation; business" and represented the word the Chinese selected to translate the Buddhist term "karma," for which the reading ゴウ is used in Japan. The same reading is used for a strictly Japanese sense of "vexation."

　　業者 (ギョウ・シャ tradesman), 業 (ゴウ karma), 神業 (かみ・わざ preternatural act)

楽 (ガク/ラク/たの・しい) (ノ ´ ｆ 白 白 白 泊 泊 渼 渼 楽 楽) earlier 樂, depicted an oak or horse chestnut tree with cocoons on it. It is now used for the meanings of two probably related Chinese words for "music" and for "pleasure; comfort; amusement."

　　楽団 (ガク・ダン orchestra), 楽 (ラク comfort), 楽しい (たの・しい enjoyable, fun)

5-Stroke Components

冊　　　　　　　　　　　　　　　　　　　　　　　(*bamboo tablets*; book)

典 (テン) (ヽ 口 巾 冊 曲 曲 典 典) depicted bamboo tablets on a stand, an "important work of writing, a canon" with derivative meanings "authoritative; immutable; rite."

　　古典 (コ・テン classics)

矢　　　　　　　　　　　　　　　　　　　　　　　　　　(arrow)

黄 (コウ/オウ/き/こ) (一 十 艹 共 共 芾 芇 黄 黄 黄 黄) depicted a fire arrow, giving off the color "yellow."

　　黄葉 (コウ・ヨウ yellow leaves), 黄金 (こ・がね/オウ・ゴン gold), 黄色 (き・いろ yellow color)

皿　　　　　　　　　　　　　　　　　　　　　　　　　　(dish)

　　血 (ケツ/ち) (ノ イ 白 血 血 血) depicted an offering to a deity of blood in a dish, and signifies "blood."

　血圧 （ケツ・アツ blood pressure）, 血 （ち blood）

□田□　　　　　　　　　　　　　　　　　　　　　　　　　　(field)

　里 （リ/さと） （丨 丆 冂 曱 甲 甲 里） combines 田 and 土 (soil) to signity a standardized unit of area for agricultural or residential purposes. It means "village" as well as the Chinese unit of distance, the *li*, the Japanese version of which is the 3.9-kilometer *ri*.

　一里 （イチ・リ one *ri* [3.9 kilometers]）, 里 （さと village, home）

□白□　　　　　　　　　　　　　　　　　　　　　　　　　(*acorn*; white)

　百 （ヒャク） （一 丆 丆 百 百 百） combines 一 (one) with 白, if not an acorn then perhaps a thumb, but means "hundred," both precisely and figuratively.

□母□　　　　　　　　　　　　　　　　　　　　　　　　　　(mother)

　毎（マイ） （丿 𠂊 𠂉 毎 毎 毎） adds two strokes to 母, slightly modified, signifying hair done up, perhaps to indicate status attained in producing one child after another. It now means "each in turn, every."

　毎日 （マイ・ニチ every day）

□目□　　　　　　　　　　　　　　　　　　　　　　　　　　　(eye)

　直 （チョク/ジキ/ただ・ちに/なお・す） （一 十 宀 古 青 直 直 直） was earlier 目 with one straight line added to give the meanings "straight; directly; direct, immediate; straighten out; cure." It also means "price," and it can mean "job shift." The other lines were added later.

　　直接 （チョク・セツ　direct）, 正直 （ショウ・ジキ　honest）, 直ちに （ただ・ち に immediately）, 直す （なお・す straighten out）

　首 （シュ/くび） （丶 丷 亠 丷 产 首 首 首 首） depicted a head with hair, and means "neck, head," with extensions of that sense to "top, highest; leader." Read シュ, 首 counts poems, especially the Japanese *waka*.

　　首席 （シュ・セキ top rank）, 首つり （くび・つり hanging）

　盾（ジュン/たて） （丿 厂 厂 盾 盾 盾 盾 盾 盾） depicts something shielding an eye, and means "shield."

　　矛盾 （ム・ジュン contradiction）, 盾 （たて shield）

　真 （シン/ま） （一 十 宀 古 青 直 直 直 真 真） depicted a spoon （ヒ, seen in the older form 眞） being used to fill a tripod kettle. Its meaning is "true, genuine; exact."

　真実 （シン・ジツ truth）, 真心 （ま・ごころ sincerity）

□由□　　　　　　　　　　　　　　　　　　　　　　　　　(*basket*)

　再 （サイ/サ/ふたた・び） （一 冂 冂 帀 再 再） is, it is suggested, a depiction of a basket or a pile of wood, with a line over it to suggest duplication of the basket or wood. In any event, the character is used to mean "again, a second time."

再会 (サイ・カイ meeting again), 再来年 (サ・ライ・ネン the year after next), 再び (ふたた・び again)

卑 (ヒ/いや・しい) (` 丶 宀 白 由 由 申 卑 卑) represented a hand holding either a wooden spoon or a basket for straining liquor.　Such was the imagery to signify "humble, modest; base; despise."

卑近 (ヒ・キン familiar), 卑しい (いや・しい lowly)

6-Stroke Components

衣 (garment)

卒 (ソツ) (` 亠 广 亣 亣 衣 衣 卒) combines 衣 and 十 (ten) to suggest a squad of uniformed soldiers.　It means "member of the rank and file," but also "finish; die; sudden."

卒業 (ソツ・ギョウ graduation)

表 (ヒョウ/おもて/あらわ・す) (一 十 キ 主 声 表 表 表) adds 毛 (fur) to 衣 to suggest the outside of a garment and signify "front; surface; exterior."　Derivative meanings include "appear, manifest, express; chart, table; document."

表 (ヒョウ chart; おもて surface; front), 表す (あらわ・す express)

衰 (スイ/おとろ・える) (` 亠 亠 亣 亩 声 声 声 衰) involves 衣 in a picture of a drooping straw raincoat, an apt figure to suggest shabbiness.　It means "decay, decline."

衰弱 (スイ・ジャク debility), 衰える (おとろ・える decline)

糸 (thread)

系 (ケイ) (一 亠 乤 乥 卒 系 系) puts a mark on the top of "thread" to indicate, it is presumed, tying pieces of thread together, and it has the senses of "lineage; system."

家系 (カ・ケイ family line)

索 (サク) (一 十 宀 宀 宑 宓 宓 宓 索 索) shows 糸 with hands either braiding the thread or stripping out hemp fibers.　It means "rope," with derived meanings "track down" and "dispersed."

索引 (サク・イン index)

7-Stroke Components

貝 (shell; wealth)

負 (フ/ま・ける/お・う) (丿 ⺈ 俨 冎 冎 台 負 負) adds 人 (person) to 貝 (wealth) to give "carry on the back; bear, suffer; be defeated; minus."

負担 (フ・タン burden), 負ける (ま・ける be defeated), 負う (お・う bear on back)

員 (イン) (丶 冖 冖 ⻏ ⺜ 冃 冒 冒 員 員) has 貝, the simplified form of 鼎, representing a tripod kettle rather than a shell, with a circle, now squared off, over it, to represent "round." The experts tell us the word for "round" was used to count kettles, then to count people, so that the character now means "number (of people); member, personnel."

全員 (ゼン・イン the whole membership)

貫 (カン/つらぬ・く) (乚 口 四 毌 毌 毌 毌 冒 冒 冒 貫 貫) was designed to suggest shells or coins with holes in their centers strung together and means "pass all the way through; pierce."   The *kan* is also a unit of weight, about 3.75 kilograms.
    貫通 (カン・ツウ penetration), 貫く (つらぬ・く penetrate; carry through)

貴 (キ/とうと・い/たっと・ぶ) (丶 口 口 中 虫 串 胄 胄 青 書 貴 貴) combines with 貝 (shell) a symbol suggesting holding a large load in the hands, thus indicating the notion of wealth.   The meaning is "noble; precious; to esteem" and as such it is used as the first member of some Sino-Japanese compound words where it means in effect "your."
    貴社 (キ・シャ your conpany), 貴い (とうと・い noble), 貴ぶ (たっと・ぶ to value)

| 辛 | (*needle*; painful) |

章 (ショウ) (丶 一 十 立 产 音 音 音 章 章) combined a tattooing needle (辛) with a tattoo design, but the basic meaning of the character seems to have had to do with conspicuousness.   It means "make (a matter) conspicuous; badge." It can also refer to such segments of written materials as "sentence" and "chapter."
    紋章 (モン・ショウ family crest)

| 足 | (foot) |

是 (ゼ) (丨 口 月 日 旦 旦 早 早 是 是) was meant either as a very straight kind of spoon, or as a spoon and a foot, to evoke walking straight. It means "right, correct."
    是非 (ゼ・ヒ right or wrong; by all means)

8-Stroke Components

| 京 | (*house on hill*; capital) |

享 (キョウ) (丶 亠 六 古 亨 亨 享) depicted the sort of tall gate building that stood at the south and north entrances to a castle. Its meaning, "receive," is said to be derived from this.
    享楽的 (キョウ・ラク・テキ pleasure-seeking)

| 東 | (*bag*) |

重 (ジュウ/チョウ/え/おも・い/かさ・ねる) (一 二 千 盲 盲 盲 重 重 重) combines elements meaning "person," "bag" (東), and "ground" (土), they say, suggesting someone with a weighty load and signifying "heavy."   Derivations from this sense are "important; grave; pile up; repetition" and the use of 重 as a counter of layers or duplications.
    二重 (ニ・ジュウ/ふた・え double), 尊重 (ソン・チョウ respect), 重い (おも・い heavy), 重ねる (かさ・ねる pile up)

12-Stroke Components

象   (elephant)

為 (イ) (丶 ノ 厂 广 产 为 为 为 為 為) earlier 爲 is said to have combined a variant of "fingers" (爪) and 象 to indicate elephant taming. Whether or not they derive from such an original meaning, the associations of the character relate to "do; do for; carry out; become; use for."

行為 (コウ・イ conduct)

Reduplicated Forms

This section treats kanji created through the combination of two or more of the same basic forms. There are only a few such kanji included among the Jōyō Kanji, but others will be found as components of more complex Jōyō Kanji introduced later.

The type of kanji in this section should not be confused with such kanji introduced earlier as 竹 (bamboo), which can be divided into two similar graphic elements that are not themselves kanji and cannot be used separately either alone or as components of other kanji.

2-Stroke Component

又   *(hand)*

双 (ソウ/ふた), or the words it represents, used to be written 雙, a hand holding a pair of birds, but two 又 is quite adequate to signify "pair of; both; twin."

双方 (ソウ・ホウ both parties), 双子 (ふた・ご twins)

3-Stroke Components

口   (mouth)

品 (ヒン/しな), three squares symbolizing merchandise on display, means "article, goods; a work" and thence "quality (of goods or people); evaluate."

品位 (ヒン・イ dignity), 品物 (しな・もの goods)

夕   (evening)

多 (タ/おお・い) is a reduplication of 夕 or perhaps of 肉 (meat). Either way, it apparently symbolized multiplicity, and the character means "much, many."

多分 (タ・ブン probably; much), 多い (おお・い plentiful)

4-Stroke Components

火   (fire)

炎 (エン/ほのお) stacks two 火 components for "flames," extended metaphorically to scorching weather and inflammation, "-itis."

炎天 (エン・テン scorching sun), 炎 (ほのお flames)

止 (foot; stop)

歩 (ホ/ブ/フ/ある・く/あゆ・む) originally combined a left foot and a right foot, misshapen though one has become. Imagine them alternating, and the meaning "pace, walk" becomes clear. The Japanese use the reading ブ to mean "odds, percentages"; the reading フ is the "pawn" in Asian chess.

歩行 (ホ・コウ walking), 歩合 (ブ・アイ percentage), 歩 (フ pawn), 歩く (あ る・く walk), 歩み (あゆ・み pace, stepping)

日 (sun)

晶 (ショウ) seems to have been intended as three stars rather than suns; it means "clear and glittering," and also "crystal."

水晶 (スイ・ショウ quartz crystal)

木 (tree; wood)

林 (リン/はやし) suggests a bunch of trees for the meaning of "woods, forest," sometimes used figuratively for "collection" of something.

林業 (リン・ギョウ forestry), 林 (はやし woods)

森 (シン/もり) suggests a denser bunch of trees than 林, but still "forest," with overtones of "hushed; awe inspiring."

森林 (シン・リン timberland), 森 (もり forest)

5-Stroke Components

立 (stand)

並 (ヘイ/なみ/なら・べる) originated as 竝, with a subsequent blending of the two pairs of horizontal strokes, to signify "standing side by side; in a line." Derived meanings are "besides; average, like all the others."

並行 (ヘイ・コウ parallel), 並 (なみ ordinary), 並べる (なら・べる line up)

Combinations of Two Basic Forms

This section presents kanji formed by combining two different basic forms, (and occasionally some of the combinations made in the previous two sections). The meaning of each of the two component characters relates to the meaning of the compound kanji.

In most cases the compound characters are easily separated into recognizable parts, such as 名 into 夕 and 口, and 男 into 田 and 力; often the components are squeezed vertically or horizontally, as are 心 in 思 and 木 in 林, respectively. In other cases, one or both of the components have been distorted. For example, it takes some effort to see 赤 as a combination of 大 and 火, or 善 as a blending of 羊 and 言. However, many of the common distortions (e.g., 氵 for 水, and 亻 and 人 for 人) are standardized and will appear as components in a number of kanji. They are listed together with the basic forms.

Sometimes the graphic similarity of a component with a previously introduced kanji is entirely coincidental. The left side of 射, for instance, does not have the same origin as 身 (body), but was a picture of an arrow fixed to a bow.

Each kanji will be listed under one of its components and cross-listed under the other, so that it will be easy to find. When both components of the kanji are equally recognizable, or both difficult to recongnize, the kanji's main listing is under the component with the fewer strokes. If one component element is more recognizable than the other, its main entry is under that component.

2-Stroke Components

| 十 | *(needle*; ten; fill) |

計 (ケイ/はか・る) combines 言 (say) with 十 in its sense of "fullness." The result means "total up," with derived meanings "measure; plan."

計画 (ケイ・カク plan), 計る (はか・る measure)

| 刀; 刂 | (sword; edged tool) |

分 (ハ, p.67)

初 (ショ/はじ・め/はつ/うい/そ・める) combines 刀 and ネ, a standard left-side variant of 衣 (garment). The associations with the meaning of the compound, "start; first; early," are believed to be "cutting the cloth to start making a garment."

初級 (ショ・キュウ beginning class), 初め (はじ・め beginning), 初孫 (はつ・まご/うい・まご first grandchild), 書初め (かき・ぞ・め New Year's calligraphy)

則 (ソク) combines 貝 (not as "shellfish" but as "tripod-kettle") and 刂. Just as a knife is needed to cut the meat in the kettle, the explanation goes, principles are needed to live in society; the meaning of the kanji is "rule, principle."

原則 (ゲン・ソク principle)

| 人; イ; ヘ | (person) |

付 (フ/つ・ける) combines イ with 寸 (*hand*) to suggest someone laying a hand on another. The character means "stick to, attach; accompany; give."

付近 (フ・キン vicinity), 付ける (つ・ける attach)

企 (キ/くわだ・てる) combines ヘ with 止 (*foot*) to evoke someone standing on tiptoe, looking into the distance, or, metaphorically, the future. It means "plan; enterprise."

企業 (キ・ギョウ enterprise), 企てる (くわだ・てる plan)

休 (キュウ/やす・む) combines イ with 木 (tree) to suggest someone at rest under a tree and means "rest, temporarily cease."

休業 (キュウ・ギョウ suspension of business), 休む (やす・む rest)

件 (ケン) combines イ with 牛 (ox). Apparently the basic image is that of someone leading an ox. Oxen seem to have been used to symbolize "things," and this character came to mean "thing; a matter; incident" and is used as a counter of incidents or cases.

事件 (ジ・ケン incident)

伏 (フク/ふ・せる) combines 亻 and 犬 (dog) to suggest the idea of "submission." It is also used for "lie prostrate," as a dog does in submission, and "hide."

伏線 (フク・セン subplot), 伏せる (ふ・せる lay face down)

位 (イ/くらい) combines 亻 with 立 (stand) to suggest "where one stands," that is, "position; rank."   The Japanese word is used in the derived senses of "extent" and "or thereabouts" as a kind of suffix, usually pronounced ぐらい.

地位 (チ・イ status), 十人位 (ジュウ・ニン・ぐらい about ten people)

体 (タイ/テイ/からだ) has lost its original reading and meaning, now being used as a replacement for 體, not a Jōyō Kanji; 體 is a combination of 骨 (bone) and 豊 (arranged neatly).   体 means "body; appearance, style," and is used as a counter for religious statues and the remains of religious figures.

体格 (タイ・カク physique), 体裁 (テイ・サイ appearance), 体 (からだ body; health; タイ figure)

使 (シ/つか・う) combines 亻 with 吏 (civil servant) and has a meaning similar to the latter in "messenger; assign a mission to; employ (things, as well as people)."

使者 (シ・シャ messenger), 使う (つか・う use)

信 (シン) combines 亻 with 言 (say); the basic association seems to be that of "a person's word," because it means "trust, believe."   The sense of "communication," which used to be written with a different character, is also subsumed now under this one.

信じる (シン・じる believe)

二 (two)

次 (欠, p.71)

八 (*divide*; *oppose*)

分 (ブン/フン/ブ/わ・ける) combines 八 with 刀 (sword), both associated with division.   More abstract than just "divide," its senses include "branch, part, separate; differentiate; portion, element; thickness (e.g., of lumber)."   Extensions of "portion" include both "one-tenth" and "one percent," (ブ) as well as "minute (of time)."   The Japanese word わかる written with this character means "understand."

分割 (ブン・カツ division), 五分 (ゴ・フン five minutes; ゴ・ブ five percent; fifty percent), 分かれる (わ・かれる diverge)

尚 (ショウ), which used to be written 尙, combines 八 with 向 (*window; toward*), and is said to have suggested air going through a window and dispersing, leading to the meanings "rise; high"; another sense is "still; as ever."

高尚 (コウ・ショウ lofty)

又 (*hand*)

取 (シュ/と・る) combines 又 and 耳 (ear) to suggest holding (a captive) tightly by the ear and therefore "seize, take."   From the concrete sense of "take" derives the figurative: "interpret, understand as."   In Japan, 取り (とり) used as a prefix to verbs imparts a meaning like "fully, adequately."

取材 (シュ・ザイ collecting material; covering a story), 取る (と・る take)

力 (strength)

加 (カ/くわ・える) combines 力 with 口 (mouth); the experts explain that it originally meant something like "re-emphasize (in speech)," but it is used to mean "add to; join in with." It has long been used to write the syllable *ka* in non-Chinese words; as such, it is used to abbreviate "Canada."

加工 (カ・コウ processing), 加える (くわ・える add)

劣 (レツ/おと・る) combines 少 (few) and 力 to write "weak, inferior."

下劣 (ゲ・レツ churlish), 劣る (おと・る inferior)

男 (ダン/ナン/おとこ) combines 力 with 田 (field) to signify "man" through the notion that men used their strength cultivating, or hunting in, the fields. In certain words where it is read ナン, it means "son."

男女 (ダン・ジョ man and woman), 長男 (チョウ・ナン eldest son), 男 (おとこ man)

勅 (チョク) combining 束 (bundle) and 力, has lost its original meaning; it now means "Imperial message."

勅題 (チョク・ダイ theme of New Year's Imperial poetry competition)

3-Stroke Components

丸 (*bent body*)

執 (シツ/シュウ/と・る), a combination of 幸 (*handcuff*) and 丸, symbolizes putting a person under restraint. It is used to mean "hold tenaciously; take up (a task); transact."

執行 (シッ・コウ execution, performance), 執念 (シュウ・ネン tenacity), 執る (と・る transact)

口 (mouth; opening)

加 (カ, p.68)

名 (メイ/ミョウ/な) combines 夕 (evening) and 口. It becomes necessary to identify oneself by voice in the dusk, so this means "name" and thence "fame."

名人 (メイ・ジン expert), 本名 (ホン・ミョウ real name), あだ名 (あだ・な nickname)

告 (コク/つ・げる), formerly written 告, combines 牛 (ox) and a square that seems to have originally represented not a mouth, but a device for holding an ox still. "Mouth" is now appropriate, however, for it means "tell, announce; sue."

告示 (コク・ジ official notice), 告げる (つ・げる tell)

知 (チ/し・る) is a combination of 矢 (arrow) and 口 "getting straight to the truth of things." It means "know; acquaintance; govern."

知人 (チ・ジン acquaintance), 知る (し・る come to know)

鳴 (メイ/な・く) combines 鳥 (bird) and 口 to suggest the call of a bird and refers to the natural cries of animals and to giving off sound in general, that is, "sing; cry; sound; rumble."

悲鳴 (ヒ・メイ shriek), 鳴る (な・る sound)

| 才 | *(block off)* |

存 (子, p.69)

閉 (ヘイ/と・じる/し・める) is a combination of 門 (gate) and 才 and means "shut, confine."

閉口 (ヘイ・コウ dumbfoundment), 閉じる (と・じる close), 閉める (し・める close)

| 山 | (mountain) |

岳 (ガク/たけ) is a combination of 丘 (hill) and 山 and means "stately mountain." Followed by 父 (father), it means "my wife's (stately) father."

山岳 (サン・ガク mountains), 白馬岳 (しろ・うま・だけ Mt. Shirouma)

岩 (ガン/いわ) combines 石 (stone) with 山 and refers to "rock; crags, rocky places."

岩石 (ガン・セキ rock and stones), 岩 (いわ rock)

| 子 | (child) |

好 (コウ/この・む/す・く) combines 女 (woman) and 子 to symbolize "fond, likable; good-looking; favorable; excel."

好意 (コウ・イ good will), 好み (この・み one's tastes), 好き (す・き like)

存 (ソン/ゾン) is a combination of 才 *(block off)* and 子 and seems to have meant originally "comfort an orphan," but means "live; exist." In Japan, it has picked up the senses "think, know."

存在 (ソン・ザイ existence), 存じる (ゾン・じる I think, I know)

孝 (コウ) combines 耂 (old man) and 子 to express "filial piety."
孝行 (コウ・コウ filial conduct)

孫 (ソン/まご) combines 系 (lineage) and 子 to indicate "grandchild; progeny of the third or greater generation."

子孫 (シ・ソン descendant), 孫 (まご grandchild)

| 勺 | *(ladle)* |

約 (ヤク) is a combination of 糸 (thread) and 勺 and seems to have meant something like "mark a measurement by tying a thread tight." It now means "tight; abbreviate; approximate; promise."

節約 (セツ・ヤク economizing)

| 女 | (woman) |

好 (子, p.69)

妙 (ミョウ) is a combination of 女 and 少 (few), indicating "thin, small woman." It is used for the derived meanings of "young and pretty; exquisite; strange" today.

妙技 (ミョウ・ギ exquisite performance)

要 (ヨウ/い・る) is a combination of what was originally two hands pinching a waist and 女. The combination was used to refer to "waist, hips" of the human body, but through a figurative use like "pivotal" it derived the meaning "essential; need."

要求 (ヨウ・キュウ demand), 要る (い・る be required)

寸 (hand)

付 (人, p.66)

対 (タイ/ツイ), until recently written 對, combines a vastly simplified form of 業(*musical instrument rack*) and 寸 and, it is said, suggested someone arranging a pair of instrument racks. Read ツイ, it means "pair" and is used as a counter for pairs of things; otherwise it means "face to face; toward; against; respond."

対話 (タイ・ワ dialogue), 一対 (イッ・ツイ a pair)

射 (シャ/い・る) is a combination of 身, not "body" this time, but a representation of an arrow fixed to a bow, and 寸; it means "archery; launch an arrow at," expanded in the age of firearms to "fire, discharge."

注射 (チュウ・シャ injection), 射る (い・る shoot)

夕 (evening)

名 (口, p.68)

大 (*spread-eagle person*; large)

赤 (セキ/シャク/あか・い) combines 大 (large) and 火 (fire) to symbolize indirectly "red" via "conflagration." It has derived a sense of "utter(ly)" as well as the translation sense of "communist."

赤貧 (セキ・ヒン destitution), 赤銅 (シャク・ドウ an alloy of copper, gold, and silver), 赤い (あか・い red)

走 (ソウ/はし・る) combines of 大(*spread-eagle person*)and 足 (*leg*) *to symbolize* "*run.*"

逃走 (トウ・ソウ *running away*), 走る (はし・る *run*)

美 (ビ/うつく・しい) *combines* 大 *and* 羊 (*sheep*). *Large sheep must have been a beautiful sight to the sheep-herding Chinese, because the character means "beautiful; glorify" as well as "delectable."*

美術 (ビ・ジュツ *fine arts*), 美しい (うつく・しい *beautiful*)

4-Stroke Components

火; 灬 (fire)

畑 (はたけ/はた) is a made-in-Japan combination of 火 and 田 (field) to stand for a cultivated field that is cleared by burning after the harvest. It means "farm field; garden patch," and figuratively "vocational field."

畑 (はたけ vegetable patch), 田畑 (た・はた field)

黒(コク/くろ), originally 黑, is a combination of a symbol for soot in a chimney and a variant of 火. Originally meaning "soot" or "sooty fire," it is used for a derivative word meaning "black."

黒板 (コク・バン blackboard), 黒い (くろ・い black)

牛 (ox)

件 (人, p.66)

告 (口, p.68)

斤 (hatchet)

折 (セツ/お・る/おり) combines 斤 and 扌, not the common variant of 手 (hand) in this case, but a depiction of a tree or plant cut down, suggesting chopping a tree down. It means "break in two; bend, fold." The Japanese noun form has the derived sense of "occasion, juncture" on the one hand and "chip box" on the other.

右折 (ウ・セツ right turn), 折る (お・る fold), 折 (おり chip box; occasion)

析 (セキ) combines 木 (tree) and 斤 for the notion of chopping up a tree. The meaning is "cut into pieces; analyze."

分析 (ブン・セキ analysis)

欠 (*person yawning*)

次 (ジ/シ/つ・ぐ/つぎ) is a combination of 二 (two) and 欠. One explanation is that this suggests someone resting after having put some things in order. It means "arrange, get ordered; next; second," and as ジ is used as a suffix in ordinal numbers corresponding to those in English ending in "-ary"(primary, secondary, etc.).

次男 (ジ・ナン second son), 次第 (シ・ダイ sequence), 次いで (つ・いで secondly), 次 (つぎ next)

月 (moon; meat; flesh)

青 (セイ/ショウ/あお・い) has, actually, nothing to do with "moon"; it used to be written 靑, where the top is a variant of 生 (*growing grass*) and the bottom a modification of 井, i.e., 丼 (well) with a dot in it representing water. It denotes the range of colors from "green" to "blue," the cool colors of growing things and pure water. Through an ancient Chinese system of philosophical interrelating of things, it also means "young; spring."

青年 (セイ・ネン young man), 紺青 (コン・ジョウ deep blue), 青い (あお・い blue; green)

明 (メイ/ミョウ/あか・るい/あ・ける) combines 日, generally believed to have represented a window rather than the sun, and 月 (moon). The modern interpretation, "sun+moon," works fine, however, for its meaning of "light, bright." 明 also means "clear; wise; dawn," all derivations on the notion of "light."

明白(メイ・ハク obvious), 明日 (ミョウ・ニチ tomorrow), 明るい(あか・るい bright), 明ける (あ・ける dawn)

肯 (止, p.72)

肩 (ケン/かた) is a combination of 月 (flesh) and what looks just like 戸 (door) but is in this case a representation of an arm and shoulder.   It means "shoulder."
　　双肩 (ソウ・ケン one's shoulders), 肩 (かた shoulder)

胃 (イ) combines 田, not "field" here, but a stomach full of food, with 月 (flesh) to indicate that it does indeed have to do with bodily matters; it means "stomach."

犬   (dog)

伏 (人, p.67)

戸   (door)

戻 (レイ/もど・る) is a combination of 戸 and 犬 (dog), written 戾 until the final dot was recently eliminated. They say it symbolized a word originally meaning something like "sneak out," that later came to mean "be contrary, perverse." The Japanese now use it only in the sense of "return to previous location or state."
　　返戻 (ヘン・レイ giving back), 戻る (もど・る go back)

肩 (月, p.71)

扇 (セン/おうぎ) combines of 戸 and 羽 (wing), designed to suggest "fan," apparently as something sharing characteristics of both.
　　扇動 (セン・ドウ agitation), 扇 (おうぎ folding fan)

止   (*foot*; stop)

企 (人, p.66)

走 (大, p.70)

肯 (コウ) is a combination of 止 (stop) and 月, the common variant of 肉 (meat). Whether or not it ever meant, as one expert says, "meat stuck between bones," it now means "nod, affirm."
　　肯定 (コウ・テイ affirmation)

手; 扌   (hand)

折 (斤, p.71)

扱 (あつか・う) is a combination of "hand" in its left-side variant form with 及 (reach), and means "handle, treat, deal."

看 (目, p.76)

損 (ソン/そこ・なう) combines 扌 with 員 (*round tripod kettle*), and is said to have had something to do with hollowing out by hand.   It means "loss; damage."
　　損 (ソン loss), 損なう (そこ・なう damage)

少 (few)

劣 (カ, p.68)

妙 (女, p.69)

省 (セイ/ショウ/かえり・みる/はぶ・く), a combination of 少 and 目 (eye), means "look at things carefully; reflect upon; visit (one's home town)." It is also borrowed for the meanings of "omit; administrative division."

> 帰省 (キ・セイ return to one's home town), 外務省 (ガイ・ム・ショウ Ministry of Foreign Affairs), 省みる (かえり・みる reflect upon), 省く (はぶ・く omit)

心 (heart)

思 (シ/おも・う) combines 田, not "field" but a head, and 心 to suggest "think, imagine."

> 思想 (シ・ソウ thought), 思う (おも・う think)

息 (ソク/いき) combines 自 (*nose*) and 心 to suggest "breathe." Extended meanings, besides "rest, take a breather," include "live (and propagate); propagate; progeny, young."

> 利息 (リ・ソク bank interest), 息 (いき breath)

意 (イ) combines 音 (*muffled sound*) and 心 to suggest "unexpressed thoughts"; it means "intention; meaning."

> 意向 (イ・コウ intention)

水; 氵; 氺 (water)

泣 (キュウ/な・く) is a combination of 氵 and 立 in the sense it has in 粒 (grain) of "granule, drop." In this case, the "water drops" are tears, and the character means "cry, weep."

> 号泣 (ゴウ・キュウ wailing), 泣く (な・く cry)

法 (ホウ/ハッ/ホッ) is now a combination of 氵 and 去 (leave), but the earliest forms of this character had a third element thought to represent a Chinese mythical beast somewhat like a unicorn, while sometimes having a circle around the animal and eliminating 去. The hypothesis is that this symbolized preventing the animal from leaving by surrounding it with water, perhaps a moat. What the character means now is "law, regulations; manners; method" and Buddhist "dharma."

> 方法 (ホウ・ホウ method), 法度 (ハッ・ト ordinance; ban), 法主 (ホッ・ス/ホッ・シュ/ホウ・シュ Buddhist high priest)

益 (エキ/ヤク) combines 益, an irregular variant of 水, and 皿 (dish). From a meaning that a dish full of water might suggest derived "increase; profit; beneficial."

> 利益 (リ・エキ gain), 御利益 (ゴ・リ・ヤク divine favor)

渉 (ショウ), a combination of 氵 and 歩 (walk), means "ford, wade; connect with."

交渉 (コウ・ショウ negotiation)

涼 (リョウ/すず・しい) is a combination of 氵 and 京 (*house on hill*). The top of a hill is a cool place for a house, and water too suggests "cool." Another sense is "desolate."

荒涼 (コウ・リョウ desolate), 涼しい (すず・しい cool)

| 斗 | (*ladle*) |

料 (リョウ) combining 米 (rice) and 斗, suggests "measure," or that which is measured, the "ingredient." It is also used for "charge, fee."

料金 (リョウ・キン charge)

| 日 | (sun) |

昆 (コン), 比 (*two persons in line*) under 日, came to be used, according to one hypothesis, for the meaning "swarm," and took its association with "insects" from that.

昆虫 (コン・チュウ insect)

者 (シャ/もの) had nothing to do with "sun" originally, but depicted a cooking fire in a stove and meant "cook." Borrowed to write an abstract nominalizer, it has derived the sense of "-er, one who (does)," and, in Japan, "person."

学者 (ガク・シャ scholar), 者 (もの person)

明 (月, p.71)

問 (門, p.154)

普 (フ) combines 並 (line up) and 日 to suggest sunlight beaming everywhere. It means "widespread, universal."

普及 (フ・キュウ diffusion)

量 (リョウ/はか・る) is another character with a false "sun"; it is believed 日 stood for grain. The bottom is a slightly disfigured 重 (heavy), so the character suggests weighing grain, with a range of meaning over "weigh, measure ; quantity, capacity."

量 (リョウ quantity), 量る (はか・る measure)

| 比 | (*two persons in line*; compare) |

昆 (日, p.74)

皆 (カイ/みな) is a combination of 比 and either 日 (say), a "sun" look-alike, or 白 (tell). It takes a leap of intuition, but from "two persons in line telling," we get to "everyone, all."

皆勤 (カイ・キン perfect attendance), 皆 (みな/みんな all; everyone)

| 木 | (tree; wood) |

休 (人, p.66)

析 (斤, p.71)

枠 (わく), a Japanese-made kanji, combines 木 and a simplification of 卒 (finish) that was used for "spool" in Japan; the result means "wooden bobbin."   It is now used in senses of "frame; crate; rim; limit."

柔 (ジュウ/ニュウ/やわ・らかい) combines 矛 (halberd) and 木, to suggest the kind of resilient wood used in making halberds.   The meaning is "resilient; soft; gentle; weak."
　　柔道 (ジュウ・ドウ judo), 柔和 (ニュウ・ワ gentle), 柔らかい (やわ・らかい soft)

相 (ソウ/ショウ/あい), a combination of 木 and 目 (eye), has meaning encompassing "face-to-face; mutual; successive; scrutinize features; features" and, with the reading ショウ, "minister (of state)."
　　人相 (ニン・ソウ physiognomy), 首相 (シュ・ショウ Prime Minister), 相手 (あ
　　い・て opponent; partner)

某 (ボウ) combines 甘 (sweet) and 木, to mean "plum tree," originally, but it is used to write an abstract word meaning "a certain (person, place, etc)."
　　某所 (ボウ・ショ a certain place)

閑 (カン) is a combination of 門 (gate) and 木 and originally meant something like "locked." They say it was borrowed to write another word meaning "not busy, quiet; neglect."
　　閑静 (カン・セイ secluded)

5-Stroke Components

甘	(sweet)

　　某 (木, p.75)

丘	(hill)

　　岳 (山, p.69)

去	(leave)

　　法 (水, p.73)

皿	(dish)

　　益 (水, p.73)

矢	(arrow)

短 (タン/みじか・い) combines 矢 and 豆 (*dish with tall base*). The meanings are "short; deficiency."
　　短気 (タン・キ short-tempered), 短い (みじか・い short)

示	(*altar*)

禁 (キン) is a combination of 林 (woods) and 示. The woods around a shrine being a taboo area, the combination can suggest "prohibited place; forbid."
　　禁じる (キン・じる prohibit)

生 *(growing grass)*

　青 （月, p.71）

毒（ドク）, combination of 生, slightly modifield, and 毋, a variant of 母 (mother), indicates, according to one hypothesis, medicinal herbs used for fertility or child-birth. Such drugs may have had severe side effects; the character now means "poison."

石 *(stone)*

　岩 （山, p.69）

斤 *(cut with hatchet)*

　訴（ソ/うった・える）combines 言 (say) and 斤 to indicate a verbal counterattack, "sue; appeal."

　　起訴（キ・ソ indictment）, 訴える （うった・える sue）

田 *(field)*

　男 （カ, p.68）

　胃 （月, p.72）

　思 （心, p.73）

　畑 （火, p.70）

白 *(white; tell)*

　皆 （比, p.74）

習（シュウ/なら・う）is a combination of 羽 (wing) and 白, but originally 自 (self), which one specialist maintains is a sign of a verb, to evoke a young bird practicing its flight. It means "learn, practice; custom."

　　習慣（シュウ・カン habit; custom）, 習う （なら・う learn）

母；毋 *(mother)*

　毒 （生, p.76）

矛 *(halberd)*

　柔 （木, p.75）

目 *(eye)*

　看（カン）is an eye, with a hand （手）shading it, and it means "look (carefully) at; watch, look after; nurse."

　　看病 （カン・ビョウ nursing）

　相 （木, p.75）

　省 （少, p.73）

立 (stand)

位 (人, p.67)

泣 (水, p.73)

6-Stroke Components

羽 (wings)

扇 (戸, p.72)

習 (白, p.76)

衣; ネ (garment)

初 (刀, p.66)

向 (*window*; toward)

尚 (ハ, p.67)

糸 (thread)

約 (勹, p.69)

自 (*nose*; self)

臭 (シュウ/くさ・い) is a combination of 自 (*nose*) and 犬 (dog), from which the final dot has recently been omitted, to suggest sniffing. It means "smell, stench."

悪臭 (アク・シュウ offensive odor), 臭い (くさ・い stinking; suspicious)

息 (心, p.73)

耳 (ear)

取 (又, p.67)

舌 (tongue)

辞 (ジ/や・める) combines 舌 and 辛 (*needle*). Since criminals were tattooed, this combination brought to mind arguments in a court trial. Its derived meanings are "word, phrase, diction; make excuses; decline; resign."

辞典 (ジ・テン dictionary), 辞める (や・める resign)

早 (early)

卓 (タク) is a combination of 人 (person) and 早 meaning "prominent, conspicuous," like someone very early or fast. It also means "table."

食卓 (ショク・タク dining table)

米 (rice)

料 (斗, p.74)

| 吏 | (civil servant) |

使 (人, p.67)

| 老; 耂 | *(old man)* |

孝 (子, p.69)

者 (日, p.74)

| 羊; 羊 | (sheep) |

美 (大, p.70)

善 (ゼン/よ・い) is a combination of 羊 and 言 (say) . Evoking the image of the statement accompanying a sacrifice, it means "good, benevolent."

善意 (ゼン・イ good will), 善い (よ・い good)

鮮 (セン/あざ・やか) combines 魚 (fish) and 羊 (sheep), the meat of both of which must be fresh to be good; it means "fresh" and also "vivid; bright."

鮮魚 (セン・ギョ fresh fish), 鮮やか (あざ・やか vivid)

7-Stroke Components

| 貝 | (shell) |

則 (刀, p.66)

| 系 | (lineage) |

孫 (子, p.69)

| 言 | (say) |

計 (十, p.66)

信 (人, p.67)

訴 (斤, p.76)

| 里 | (village) |

黒 (火, p.71)

| 身 | (body) |

射 (寸, p.70)

| 辛 | (painful) |

辞 (舌, p.77)

| 束 | (bundle) |

勅 (力, p.68)

豆 (bean)

短 (矢, p.75)

8-Stroke Components

京 (capital)

涼 (水, p.74)

幸 (luck)

執 (丸, p.68)

並 (side by side)

普 (日, p.74)

歩 (walk)

渉 (水, p.73)

門 (gate)

閉 (才, p.69)

閑 (木, p.75)

間 (カン/ケン/あいだ/ま) is a combination of 門 and originally 月 (moon), now abbreviated to 日, evoking moonlight shining through the space between doors to signfy "space; opening," and "between, among; interval, period; duration." It sometimes means "room" and, read ま, serves as a counter for rooms; read ケン, it is a unit of length of approximately 1.8 meters.

時間 (ジ・カン time), 人間 (ニン・ゲン human being), 間 (あいだ interval), 間口 (ま・ぐち frontage)

林 (woods)

禁 (示, p.75)

9-Stroke Components

音 (sound)

意 (心, p.73)

重 (heavy)

量 (日, p.74)

11-Stroke Components

魚 (fish)

鮮 (羊, p.78)

鳥   (bird)

鳴 (口, p.68)

These regular variant forms have been introduced in this or the first section:

刂 (刀 sward)	灬 (火 fire)	扌 (手 hand)
氵 (水 water)	主 (生 live)	毋 (母 mother)
衤 (衣 garment)	月 (肉 meat)	耂 (老 old man)
䒑 (羊 sheep)	亻, 入 (人 person)	卆 (卒 finish)

A number of irregular form changes have also occurred here, such as 犬 (dog) becoming 大, identical with 大 (large). The regular variant of 肉 (meat; flesh) is now identical with 月 (moon). Pictographic representations of hands have led to three forms, 又 (*hand*; again) , 寸 (*hand*; sun) and 手 (hand), any of which may be interpreted as "hand" in a given compound character.

Classifiers

This section presents the last of the two-component semantic compound kanji. The kanji in the two subsections below are arranged by components here termed "classifiers." The classifiers, often referred to as "radicals" in English-language Kanji dictionaries, comprise 214 character components, at least one of which was found in every character by Chinese lexicographers. Classifiers provide a convenient means of arranging characters in a dictionary; some kanji dictionaries for non-native speakers use innovative classifiers not part of the original 214.

Many of the kanji presented so far—and their variants—are classifiers. Examples include 人 (person) and its variants亻 and 入, 水 (water) and its common variant 氵, and 手 (hand) and its common variant 扌. Such classifiers which are independent kanji and their variants already introduced make up the first subsection below.

Other classifiers never appear as independent kanji. Examples of these are 冫, which usually imparts some sense related to "ice," and 宀, which suggests association with "roof" or "house." These classifiers, as well as some that are independent kanji but not Jōyō Kanji make up the second subsection. None of these have been introduced yet in this book.

When faced with a kanji one wishes to look up in a character dictionary, one must first determine which part or parts are classifiers and, if there is more than one classifier, which is the one under which the kanji is listed. One of the following will most often apply.

1. If the kanji is an indivisible unit (such as a basic form), the whole kanji may be a classifier. Such is the case with 手 (hand), 魚 (fish), and 山 (mountain). (If the whole kanji is not a classifier, part of it is, based on that part's similarity to another classifier.)

2. If the kanji can be divided into a top and bottom part, either part might be the classifier. For 男 (man), either 田 or 力 could be the classifier (田 is). Classifiers at the top (e.g., 艹 and 宀) are more common than classifiers at the bottom (e.g., 心 and 皿).

3. If the kanji can be divided into a left and right part, either part might be the classifier. For 信 (believe), either 亻 or 言 could be the classifier (亻 is). There

are three times as many left-side classifiers (e.g., 亻 and 氵) as right-side classifiers (e.g., 寸 and 斗).

4. If the kanji can be divided into an enclosure or partial enclosure and an enclosed portion, either part might be the classifier. For 閑, either 門 or 木 could be the classifier (門 is). An enclosure is more commonly a classifier than what is enclosed.

Some classifiers occur in different positions in different kanji. 口, for example, is variously positioned: 鳴, 知, 号, 告, 句. The forms of a given classifier may vary according to position. For 人, 亻 appears on the left and 今 at the top of a kanji.

Many of the classifiers have nicknames. The main elements of these names, which indicate their positions in characters, are as follows:

1. へん (-べん) means "side"; components so named are commonly left-side components.
2. つくり (-づくり) means "maker" and names commonly right-side components.
3. かんむり means "crown," used of components that are usually above and separate from the rest of the character.
4. かしら (-がしら) means "head," at the top but usually connected to the rest of the kanji.
5. あし means "foot," for bottom components.
6. した means "bottom," also usually bottom components.
7. かまえ (-がまえ) means "enclosure," for components that at least partially enclose other components.
8. たれ (-だれ) means "hanger," for components that extend over the top and down the left side.
9. にょう (or にゅう) is used in the names of components that commonly extend down the left side and along the bottom.

The following information appears in the headings in this section: the classifier and its variants, the nickname or nicknames of the classifier, if any; and the general meaning the classifier imparts to the kanji. More specific interpretations of a classifier are sometimes given in the explanatory paragraphs for the kanji. As has been stated before, two or more historically different elements might have merged to the same form, so a given classifier or other component might have two or more entirely different meanings.

The classifiers and components are arranged by increasing stroke count. If a standard form (within the Jōyō Kanji) and variant have different stroke counts (e.g., four for 水 and three for its common variant, 氵), the classifier is listed under the stroke count of the standard form (in this case, four). An exception is 月, a variant of 肉; this is listed as a four-stroke (not a six-stroke) classifier.

When both of the components of a kanji are classifiers, the kanji is listed under the more common classifier, and a cross-reference is given from the other classifier (within each subsection only).

Basic Forms as Classifiers

In this group, the headings are classifiers that have been previously introduced as independent kanji.

1-Stroke Classifier

| 乙; し | *(double-edged knife*; second) |

孔 (子, p.84)

札 (木, p.86)

乱 (ラン/みだ・れる) is a combination of 舌, in this case a simplifying replacement for 𤔔 (hands pulling tangled thread) and し (pin down), to suggest attempting to deal with a tangle. (The 乱 here is probably not related to the character 乙). The word so written means "entanglement," abstracted to "confusion, disorder; violence; war."

乱用 (ラン・ヨウ abuse), 乱れる (みだ・れる fall into disorder)

2-Stroke Classifiers

| 亻 (にんべん) 𠆢 (ひとがしら) | (person) |

化 (カ/ケ/ば・ける) is a combination of 亻 and 匕 (person in a different posture). It means "change, transformation."

変化 (ヘン・カ change), 化粧 (ケ・ショウ make up [cosmetics]), 化ける (ば・ける take the appearance of)

今 (コン/キン/いま) is a combination of a lid (𠆢) and something caught under it, to suggest capturing the present moment in order to evoke the word with the abstract meaning "now."

今月 (コン・ゲツ this month), 今上 (キン・ジョウ reigning Emperor), 今 (いま now)

令 (レイ), a cover (𠆢) over a kneeling person (卩), to represent someone getting a message from a god, means "command, ordinance; fine, honorable," particularly in honorific words referring to someone else's family members.

命令 (メイ・レイ command)

会 (カイ/エ/あ・う) is an abbreviation of 會, which is a combination of 𠆢 (lid) with something which might have suggested a snug fit or else a gathering of people. It means "meet; assemblage, association."

会 (カイ meeting), 会釈 (エ・シャク salutation), 会う (あ・う meet)

合 (口, p.85)

全 (ゼン/まった・く) is a completed piece of work, 工 or perhaps 王 (gem) with a lid (𠆢) over it. It means "complete, whole, all."

全身 (ゼン・シン whole body), 全く (まった・く completely)

伐 (バツ) combines 亻 and 戈 (halberd) to mean "chop" and thence "smite, kill."

伐採 (バッ・サイ lumbering)

余 (ヨ/あま・る) has debated origins, a picture of an umbrella-shaped bower or a combination of an element depicting a shovel and one suggesting dispersion, but it is not used in its original sense anyway. Its meaning of "surplus, remains" comes from another word.

余地 (ヨ・チ room, margin), 余る (あま・る left over)

食 (ショク/ジキ/た・べる/く・う) is a combination of 亼 (lid) and 良 (*grain in a container*), and means "eat; food." It also has derived senses, "eclipse; erosion." 食 (𩙿) is a traditional classifier.

食事 (ショク・ジ a meal), 断食 (ダン・ジキ fast), 食べる (た・べる eat), 食う (く・う eat, feed on)

傘 (サン/かさ) originates from a picture of an open umbrella and means "umbrella."

落下傘 (ラッ・カ・サン parachute), 傘 (かさ umbrella)

| 刂 | (りっとう) | (sword; edged tool) |

列 (レツ) is a combination of 歹 (joints, bones) and 刂. It means "line up; line, row; rank."

行列 (ギョウ・レツ parade)

別 (ベツ/わか・れる) combines 歹 (jointed bones) and 刂 to suggest dismembering. It is used to mean "distinguish, distinction; separate, separation."

別館 (ベッ・カン annex), 別れる (わか・れる part)

制 (セイ) combines 朱 (a tree, felled but with branches intact) and 刂 to mean "trim away excess." It has derived senses of "control; establish; system," as well as the borrowed meaning "make."

制定 (セイ・テイ enactment)

| 又 | (またづくり) | (*hand*) |

収 (シュウ/おさ・める) combines 丩 (twisted threads) and 又 to suggest the act of gathering together. Its usual senses are "collect; take/put in; income."

収穫 (シュウ・カク harvest), 収める (おさ・める take in)

叔 (シュク) combines 尗 (bean-bearing stalk) and 又 to signify small beans, or picking small beans. Now it means "younger sibling of one's parent."

伯叔 (ハク・シュク uncles)

| 力 | (りきづくり) | (strength; power) |

労 (ロウ) combines 𭥴, a simplification of 熒 (firefly), and 力 to suggest burning away energy in work. It is used in the sense of "labor," and as an abbreviation of words meaning "laborer" and "labor union."

過労 (カ・ロウ overwork)

| 八 | (はちがしら) | (*divide; opposition*) |

Besides "dividing, opposition," 八 as a component can indicate two hands, especially when at the bottom of a character.

公 (コウ/おおやけ) combines 八 and 厶 (private) for "not private." It means "public; official, governmental; impartial." As コウ, it is sometimes attached to someone's family name as a title of respect, or to an abbreviation of someone's name as a sign of fondness or of contempt.

公正 (コウ・セイ fair), 公 (おおやけ public)

共 (キョウ/とも) is no longer neatly divisible in terms of its original pictorial elements, something held in two hands. Its meaning now is "both" (from the two hands), and "together; share"; it is also used to abbreviate the word for "communism."

共産党 (キョウ・サン・トウ communist party), 共に (とも・に together)

具 (グ) combines a depiction of a tripod-kettle and two hands to mean "offer a kettle of food." Its derived meanings are "implement; equipment; equip; cooking ingredient."

家具 (カ・グ furniture)

兼 (ケン/か・ねる) originated as two 禾 (rice stalk) and ハ (two hands). It means "serve jointly; dual."

兼業 (ケン・ギョウ dual business), 兼ねる (か・ねる combine)

3-Stroke Classifiers

| 土 | (つちへん) | (earth) |

垂 (スイ/た・れる) is a slight distortion of grain (禾) dangling towards the ground (土), meaning "hang, droop; drop."

垂直 (スイ・チョク vertical), 垂れる (た・れる hang down)

| 女 | (おんなへん) | (woman) |

妥 (ダ) combines ⺍ (fingers), and 女 to suggest carressing a woman, and means "soothe; compromise."

妥協 (ダ・キョウ compromise)

妻 (サイ/つま) joins a hand (ヨ), to suggest working, with a combination of 女 and a mark representing a hair ornament to evoke an adult woman. "The adult woman who does the housework" is the result; it means "wife."

妻子 (サイ・シ wife and children), 妻 (つま wife)

威 (イ) combines 戊 (halberd) and 女 to suggest "threat." It means "aggression; might, mighty."

威力 (イ・リョク might)

婦 (フ) is a combination of 女 and 帚 (broom). It means "housewife, matron."

婦人 (フ・ジン adult woman)

| 子 | (こへん) | (child) |

孔 (コウ) is a combination of 子 and し (pin down), representing its meaning "hole" with the image of a child squirming through one.

鼻孔 (ビ・コウ nostrils)

口 （くちへん）   (mouth; opening)

号 （ゴウ） is a combination of 口 and 丁 and has been interpreted as symbolizing "shout; loud wailing"; it also means "command; sign; name; number."
信号 （シン・ゴウ traffic light)

合 （ゴウ/ガッ/カッ/あ・う） puts a cover （亼） over an opening （口） for the meaning of "fit; combine; join together." It also is used as a unit of about 0.18 liters and for one-tenth of the distance from the foot to the top of a mountain (both ゴウ).
合計 （ゴウ・ケイ total), 合唱 （ガッ・ショウ chorus), 合戦 （カッ・セン battle), 合う （あ・う fit)

呉 （ゴ） is thought to have originated in a pictograph of someone with inclined head and laughing. Its use in Chinese has been as a proper noun, Wu in Mandarin, the name of a dynasty and of an area of China. In Japan it has been extended to "Chinese."
呉服 （ゴ・フク kimono textiles)

吹 （スイ/ふ・く） combines 口 and 欠 (*person with mouth open*). The meaning is "blow, spout."
吹奏 （スイ・ソウ play wind instrument), 吹く （ふ・く blow)

唐 （トウ/から） originally combines 庚, thought to represent stretching something, with 口 for a word meaning "big talk; empty," but its important meaning derives from its use as the name of the Tang dynasty and the further senses, in Japan, of "China; Chinese; foreign."
唐突 （トウ・トツ all of a sudden), 唐紙 （から・かみ Chinese paper; sliding door)

喜 （キ/よろこ・ぶ） combines 壴 (dish of food or drum) and 口, to evoke enjoyment of food or music; it means "joy."
喜劇 （キ・ゲキ comedy), 喜ぶ （よろこ・ぶ rejoice)

士   (male)

声 （セイ/ショウ/こえ/こわ） is the simplified form of 聲, which is a combination of 声 (a musical instrument), 殳 (hand holding a stick), and 耳 (ear) to signify "sound, tone"; its meanings range through "voice" and "fame."
名声 （メイ・セイ renown), 声明 （ショウ・ミョウ Buddhist incantation; セイ・メイ statement), 声 （こえ voice), 声色 （こわ・いろ tone of voice; assumed voice)

寸   (*hand*)

尊 （ソン/たっと・い/とうと・ぶ） combines 酋 (ceremonial decanter) and 寸 to suggest elegance and grace. The character means "valuable, esteemed; revere"; as the first character in certain compounds it is in effect an honorific "your."
尊敬 （ソン・ケイ respect), 尊い （とうと・い/たっと・い valuable), 尊ぶ （とうと・ぶ/たっと・ぶ respect)

4-Stroke Classifiers

| 水;氵 | （さんずい） | (water) |

酒 （シュ/さけ/さか） combines 氵 with 酉 (wine jar) to mean "liquor."
ぶどう酒 （ぶどう・シュ wine）, 酒 （さけ *sake*）, 酒屋 （さか・や liquor shop）

| 手;扌 | （てへん） | (hand) |

拐 （カイ）, 打 and 另 (jointed bones) combined, means "using a crooked method."
誘拐 （ユウ・カイ abduction）

拝 （ハイ/おが・む）, 扌 and the unique element 手, representing an offering, means "pray, worship"; it is often combined with another kanji of a verbal sense to suggest "do...with reverence," as a humble word.
拝見 （ハイ・ケン look at respectfully）, 拝む （おが・む pray）

| 牛;牜 | （うしへん） | (ox) |

牧 （ボク/まき） combines 牛 and 攵 (beating; action) to suggest the character's meaning, "tend a herd; raise cattle."
牧師 （ボク・シ pastor）, 牧場 （ボク・ジョウ/まき・ば pasture）

| 木 | （きへん） | (tree; wood) |

札 （サツ/ふだ） is the combination of 木 and ㇄(*double-edged knife*) and means "inscribed wooden tablet or plate," with derived senses of "tag; card; ticket; banknote; writing."
札 （サツ banknote）, お札 （お・ふだ talisman）

枚 （マイ） is 木 combined with 攵 (beating; action), and meant "whip; stick" and "count one by one."   The latter sense, and its more important use as a counter for thin, flat things, survive in Japan.
田一枚 （た・イチ・マイ one paddy field）

巣 （ソウ/す） has an element depicting a bird's nest on a 木 (tree), and means "nest."
卵巣 （ラン・ソウ ovary）, 巣 （す nest）

| 月 | （つきへん; にくづき） | (moon; meat, flesh) |

As we have seen, the component 月 is an important variant of 肉 (meat) as well as 月 (moon) itself.   It is also a variant of 舟 (boat), as will be noted in the second kanji below.   The variants of the three kanji are identical in form.

骨 （コツ/ほね）, 冎 (bone) combined with 月, is itself one of the traditional classifiers.   It means "bone; skeleton" and, figuratively, "body; character, disposition."   It is also used to refer to "one's ashes, remains after cremation."
骨肉 （コツ・ニク flesh and bones; kinfolk）, 骨 （コツ/ほね bone; ashes）

朕 （チン） was originally a combination of 舟 (boat), rather than 月, and a graphic element signifying holding something up.   The character apparently originally stood for "lift, buoyancy," but was used until the end of World War II for an imperial "I, me."

日 (ひへん) (sun)

昔 (セキ/シャク/むかし) combines 日 and a graphic element interpreted as "laying one thing upon another," meaning "past days, long ago."
　昔日 (セキ・ジツ bygone days), 今昔 (コン・ジャク past and present), 昔 (むかし long ago)

春 (シュン/はる) combines a pictorial element interpreted as "new buds sprouting" with 日 to mean "spring, springtime." A derived sense is "erotic."
　青春 (セイ・シュン youth), 春 (はる spring)

曹 (ソウ) is a combination of an element interpreted as "two bags" or "many things," and 口 (mouth), later replaced by 日; the combination suggests public discussion. Its meaning is something like "court officials; members of military forces."
　法曹界 (ホウ・ソウ・カイ legal circles)

支 (*hand holding branch*)

鼓 (コ/つづみ) combination of 壴 (decorated drum on a stand) and 支, means "drum; beat." The character is one of the traditional classifiers, but no Jōyō Kanji are classified under it.
　鼓動 (コ・ドウ beating), 鼓 (つづみ Japanese hand drum)

心 (したごころ) (heart)

恵 (ケイ/エ/めぐ・み) combines a picture of a spool and 心. It means "mercy; bless" and has the borrowed sense "wise."
　恩恵 (オン・ケイ favor), 知恵 (チ・エ wisdom), 恵む (めぐ・む bless)

止 (*foot*; stop)

武 (ブ) is a combination of 止 (*foot*) and a slightly deformed 戈 (halberd), suggesting an armed advance, and means "military, martial."
　武力 (ブ・リョク military force)

火 (ひへん) 灬 (れっか) (fire)

炊 (スイ/た・く) combines 火 and 欠 (*stooping person with mouth wide open*), to suggest tending a fire. It means "boil, cook."
　自炊 (ジ・スイ cooking for oneself), 炊く (た・く boil)

焦 (ショウ/こ・げる/あせ・る) has 隹 (bird) over 灬. It means "scorch; irritate."
　焦点 (ショウ・テン focal point), 焦げる (こ・げる scorch), 焦る (あせ・る be impatient)

煩 (ハン/ボン/わずら・う) is a combination of 火 and 頁 (head), to suggest a headache. It means "adversity; distressing."
　煩雑 (ハン・ザツ complicated), 煩悩 (ボン・ノウ earthly passions), 煩う (わずら・う be troubled, afflicted)

5-Stroke Classifiers

目   (eye)

見 (ケン/み・る), a combination of 目 and 儿 (person), is itself a traditional classifier and means "look, see; appear."

見地 (ケン・チ point of view), 見る (み・る look at)

具 (ハ, p.84)

示   (*altar*; indicate)

票 (ヒョウ) merges 要 (*narrow waist*) and 示, and has had an association with flying sparks. It is used for "ballot, vote" and as a counter for votes.

投票 (トウ・ヒョウ voting)

田   (field)

番 (バン) is a combination of 釆 (sowing) over 田, perhaps for "sow." Used to number certain things in a series, such as turns at guard duty or bat, it means "number, turn, watch."   In Japanese, it also means "ordinary."

番号 (バン・ゴウ number)

6-Stroke Classifiers

糸 (いとへん)   (thread)

素 (ソ/ス) combines a simplified form of 垂 for the sense of dangling and 糸 for "raw silk," with derived meanings of "raw; bare; white; simple; element."

水素 (スイ・ソ hydrogen), 素顔 (ス・がお face without makeup)

縄 (ジョウ/なわ) combines 黽, which depicted a lizard, with 糸; it means "rope."
縄文 (ジョウ・モン straw-rope pattern), 縄 (なわ rope)

舌 (したへん)   (tongue)

乱 (し, p.82)

⺮ (たけかんむり)   (bamboo)

笑 (ショウ/わら・う/え・む), combination of ⺮ and 夭 (supple), has its original meaning replaced by "laugh, smile."

苦笑 (ク・ショウ wry smile), 笑う (わら・う laugh), 笑む (え・む smile)

筆 (ヒツ/ふで), a combination of ⺮ and 聿 (hand holding a brush), means "writing implement" and, by synecdoche, "writing."

筆記 (ヒッ・キ taking notes), 筆 (ふで brush)

7-Stroke Classifiers

足 (あしへん)   (foot)

跡 (セキ/あと) combines ⻊ and 亦 (armpit), probably to evoke a trail of footprints. It means "footprint; trace; historic remains."

古跡（コ・セキ historic remains）, 跡（あと trace）

| 貝 | (shell; wealth) |

買（バイ/か・う）combines 罒 (net) and 貝 to write words meaning "buy."
買収（バイ・シュウ buying; bribery）, 買う（か・う buy）

8-Stroke Classifiers

| 雨 | （あめかんむり） | (rain) |

雪（セツ/ゆき）combines 雨 and an element that looks like a broom, for "snow."
It is also sometimes used to mean "cleanse."
雪辱（セツ・ジョク vindicate oneself）, 雪（ゆき snow）

雲（ウン/くも）is a combination of 雨 and 云 (misty) meaning "cloud."
雲泥の差（ウン・デイ・の・サ great dissimilarity）, 雲（くも cloud）

需（ジュ）has 雨 and 而 (beard) and originally meant "wet; soft." That
meaning has been replaced by "need, demand."
需給（ジュ・キュウ supply and demand）

| 門 | （もんがまえ） | (gate) |

開（カイ/ひら・く/あ・ける）is a combination of 門 and a sketch of two hands
moving a gate bar; it means "open; begin; cultivate, develop."
開店（カイ・テン store opening）, 開く（ひら・く/あ・く open）

Classifiers Not Yet Introduced

The headings in this group are common classifiers newly introduced in this
section.

2-Stroke Classifiers

| 冫 | （にすい） | (ice) |

冬（トウ/ふゆ）combines 夂, a graph interpreted as "stored food," with 冫 to
suggest "winter."
冬季（トウ・キ winter season）, 冬（ふゆ winter）

| 几 | | (table) |

冗（宀, p.90）

処（夂, p.95）

| 卜 | | (divination) |

占（セン/し・める/うらな・う）combines 卜 with 口, perhaps symbolizing a place.
The character means "to divine" or "to occupy."
占星（セン・セイ astrology）, 占める（し・める occupy）, 占う（うらな・う divine）

比 (person; spoon)

尼 (尸, p.96)

死 (歹, p.98)

旨 (シ/むね) was a combination of ヒ (spoon) and 甘 (tasty) originally and apparently meant "tasty food." It now has the sense of "purport."

主旨 (シュ・シ gist), 旨 (むね purport)

卩; 㔾 (ふしづくり) (person kneeling)

厄 (厂, p.91)

印 (イン/しるし) combines another form for a hand with 卩 and perhaps once meant "press someone to kneel." Its meanings "stamp; sign, mark" may derive from that. It is also used as an abbreviation of the word for India.

印象 (イン・ショウ impression), 印 (しるし sign)

色 (ショク/シキ/いろ) is a combination of a crouching man and 巴 (stooping woman). It means "amorousness, erotic; color; complexion, look; feature."

特色 (トク・ショク feature), 景色 (ケ・シキ scenary), 色 (いろ color)

即 (ソク), earlier 卽 shows food on a table and someone kneeling next to it to symbolize proximity. It means "immediate."

即死 (ソク・シ instantaneous death)

冖 (わかんむり) (cover)

冗 (ジョウ), a combination of 冖 and 儿 (person), suggests relaxation. It means "lax, superfluous."

冗談 (ジョウ・ダン joke)

軍 (グン) combines 勹 (surround), not originally 冖 in this case, and 車 (wheel), perhaps to suggest a military encampment; it means "war, battle; army."

軍人 (グン・ジン military personnel)

儿 (にんにょう) (human body)

兄 (ケイ/キョウ/あに) puts 口 (large head) on 儿; it means "older brother."

父兄 (フ・ケイ guardians), 兄弟 (キョウ・ダイ brothers), 兄 (あに big brother)

光 (コウ/ひか・る/ひかり) has someone holding fire (火). It means "light, glow; glory; fine scenery."

光景 (コウ・ケイ scene), 光る (ひか・る shine), 光 (ひかり light)

先 (セン/さき) combines a variant of 止 (*foot*) and 儿, apparently to evoke toe tips. It means "forepart, tip; previous, ahead; precede" and, in Japan, "destination."

先方 (セン・ポウ the other party), 後先 (あと・さき before and behind)

克 (コク) has 古, taken to be a helmet, on 儿 to suggest enduring. It means "outlast ; overcome."

克服 (コク・フク overcome)

児 (ジ/ニ) combines 旧, a recent simplification of something taken to represent a baby's head, and 儿, for "infant; small child."

児童 (ジ・ドウ child), 小児科 (しょう・に・か pediatrics)

免 (メン/まぬか・れる) seems, in its earliest forms, to depict childbirth. Its meaning now is in the area of "escape, avoid; exemption; permit; discharge (from service)."

免許 (メン・キョ license), 免れる (まぬか・れる escape)

鬼 (キ/おに) developed from a picture of a ghost, or a combination of a big head, 儿, and a mark (厶) of unclear meaning. A traditional classifier in its own right, it means "ghost, goblin; ogre, demon."

鬼才 (キ・サイ genius), 鬼 (おに ogre)

厶   (private)

弁 (艹, p.96)

参 (彡, p.93)

勹 (つつみがまえ)   (wrap; surround)

句 (ク) combines 勹 and 口 (mouth) to give a basic meaning like "phrase." It also means "verse" and, in Japan, can refer to or be used as a counter for the seventeen-syllable haiku.

包 (ホウ/つつ・む) has 勹 around 己 (fetus) to suggest enclosure; it means "wrap." It also sometimes substitutes for 庖 (kitchen).

包丁 (ホウ・チョウ kitchen knife), 包み (つつ・み package)

厂 (がんだれ)   (cliff)

厄 (ヤク) has a kneeling or bent person 己 ander 厂; it means "misfortune."
厄介 (ヤッ・カイ bother)

圧 (アツ) combines 厂 (cover from above) and 土 (dirt); it means "press, pressure."

圧迫 (アッ・パク pressure)

厚 (コウ/あつ・い) has a unique element, interpreted as depicting a pile of dirt, under 厂. It means "thick; cordial; brazen."
厚生 (コウ・セイ welfare), 厚い (あつ・い thick)

原 (ゲン/はら), showing a spring 泉 under 厂, originally meant "spring, source of a stream of river"; the character is used in a derived sense, "origin" and, via an unrelated Chinese homophone, can mean "field." It is also used in compounds as an abbreviation of the first example below.

原子力 (ゲン・シ・リョク nuclear energy), 原 (はら field)

匸 (かくしがまえ; はこがまえ)   (hide)

匸 is an amalgamation of two different forms: 匚 (はこがまえ, meaning "box") and 匸 (かくしがまえ, meaning "hide"). Since there is but one form, 匸, in the Jōyō Kanji and the meanings are very similar, they are treated as a single classifier in this book.

亡 (ボウ/モウ/な・くなる) has 亠 originating in 人 (person) combined with ∟ (screen or fence to hide behind). It means "disappear; non-existence; die."
　　亡命 (ボウ・メイ exile), 亡者 (モウ・ジャ deceased person), 亡くなる (な・くなる pass away)

区 (ク) had blocks (品) originally in an enclosure (匸), and means "section, division"; in Japan, it also means "ward," a section of a city, and is used as a counter of such wards.
　　区別 (ク・ベツ differentiation)

匹 (ヒツ/ひき) was originally two lines under something like "hanging cloth," and seems to have meant "double roll of cloth," that is, a length of cloth with each end rolled toward the other. It is used in the sense of "pair" and as a counter for smaller fauna, including insects and fish, but not birds.
　　匹敵 (ヒッ・テキ rival), 一匹 (イッ・びき one [animal/insect/fish])

匠 (ショウ) combines a hooked measuring rule (匸) and a hatchet (斤) for "craftsman, expert."
　　師匠 (シ・ショウ master)

医 (イ), a box (匸) with an arrow (矢) in it, for "quiver," substitutes for a more complex character, 醫, that includes it as an element and that means "medicine; doctor."
　　医者 (イ・シャ doctor)

冂 (けいがまえ)　　　　　　　　　　　　　　　　　　　　　　　　　(border)

周 (シュウ/まわ・り) has 甩, thought to stand for a field full of rice plants, combined with 口, a square piece of land. It means "universal; all around; be thorough; go around; circumference" and is used as a counter for circuits, revolutions, or orbits.
　　周知 (シュウ・チ common knowledge), 周り (まわ・り circumference)

凵 (かんがまえ)　　　　　　　　　　　　　　　　　　　　　　　　(hollow)

凶 (キョウ) has a mark in a pit (凵) for "calamity, adverse"; the character has close associations with bad harvests. Another sense is "evil," probably through using the character for a different Chinese word.
　　凶作 (キョウ・サク lean crop)

凹 (オウ) simply depicts a depression and means "concave."
　　凹凸 (オウ・トツ unevenness)

凸 (トツ) depicts a bump and means "convex."
　　凸版 (トッ・パン relief printing)

画 (ガ/カク) is an abbreviation of 畫, which combines a hand holding a brush (聿) with a field (田) and a line (一); it means "draw a line, delineate," extended to "plan; picture." Read カク, it is used as a counter for strokes in writing characters.

画廊 (ガ・ロウ picture gallery), 画一 (カク・イツ uniformity)

3-Stroke Classifiers

彳 (ぎょうにんべん) (go; act)

律 (リツ/リチ) combines 彳 and 聿 (holding a brush) for "regulate, rule."
法律 (ホウ・リツ law), 律義 (リチ・ギ upright)

幺 (thin)

幻 (ゲン/まぼろし) combines 幺 (thin thread) with a mark that might be meant to suggest a faint motion. It means " illusory, illusion; phantom."
幻想 (ゲン・ソウ fantasy), 幻 (まぼろし phantom)

玄 (ゲン) has a line drawn across 幺, for "dim." 玄 is a traditional classifier.
幽玄 (ユウ・ゲン profound)

阝 (こざとへん [at left]; おおざと [at right]) (mound; town)

Two classifiers take the form 阝, one appearing on the left side of a kanji, the other on the right, with the respective meanings "mound" or "town."

郭 (カク) combines a castle (享) with a town (阝) to mean "walled town," meaning more often "circumvallate; outline contour."
輪郭 (リン・カク outline)

彡 (さんづくり) (design)

参 (サン/まい・る) is a simplification of 參, supposedly combining a depiction of a woman with a hairpin of three shining jewels (參) with 彡 for original meanings of "three" or "mix." It is currently used for "three" and "attend, participate; present oneself to a superior." The latter has been extended to a humble "go, come," particularly to a shrine or temple, in Japan, where it also is used for "give up, be defeated."
参加 (サン・カ join), 参る (まい・る go, come)

尢 (cripple; elbow)

The classifier 尢 is actually representative of two forms; 尢 itself (meaning "cripple") and the very similar 尤 (meaning "elbow").

就 (シュウ/ジュ/つ・く) combines 京 (town) and 尤 (elbow). Explained as beckoning people to town to work, it means "start work, get employed; accomplish."
就職 (シュウ・ショク find employment), 成就 (ジョウ・ジュ accomplish), 就く (つ・く engage [in])

宀 (うかんむり) (roof)

穴 (ケツ/あな) combines 宀 and ハ (*divide*) . The whole is a traditional classifier

(あなかんむり) meaning "cave, hole" and the target spots for acupuncture and moxacautery. あな is used in the sense of "long shot" at the race track in Japan and can mean "flaw."

穴居 (ケッ・キョ cave dwelling), 穴 (あな hole)

安 (アン/やす・い) has 宀 over a woman (女) to suggest peace and quiet. It means "peaceful, safe, restful; at ease" and, in Japan, "inexpensive."

安心 (アン・シン peace of mind), 安い (やす・い cheap)

守 (シュ/ス/まも・る/もり), with 宀 and 寸 (*hand*), means "protect, safeguard," or "talisman."

看守 (カン・シュ prison guard), 留守 (ル・ス absence from home), 守る (まも・る protect), 子守 (こ・もり baby-sitting)

官 (カン) combines 宀 and ß (pile up); it means "government official, office."

官僚 (カン・リョウ bureaucrat)

宜 (ギ), a roof with meat piled (且) under it, means "proper" or "suitable."

適宜 (テキ・ギ suitable)

実 (ジツ/み/みの・る) simplifies 實, a roof over a fortune (貫), meaning "plenitude; substance; real; fruit" and also, in Japan, "sincerity."

実父 (ジッ・プ real father), 実 (み fruit), 実る (みの・る bear fruit)

宗 (シュウ/ソウ) shows a roof over an altar (示) to suggest perhaps a family mausoleum. It is now used for "family head, originator; religion; Buddhist sect."

宗教 (シュウ・キョウ religion), 宗匠 (ソウ・ショウ master)

宝 (ホウ/たから) is simplified from 寶, a roof with jewels (玉), jars (缶), and money (貝) under it; it means "treasure."

宝石 (ホウ・セキ precious stone), 宝 (たから treasure)

家 (カ/ケ/いえ/や) has a roof with a pig (豕) under it to mean "house," as well as "home, family, and "specialist in."

画家 (ガ・カ painter), 本家 (ホン・ケ head family), 家 (いえ house), 家主 (や・ぬし house owner)

害 (ガイ) can no longer be neatly divided into its original components of a basket inverted over a head (古). It means "obstruct, harm, damage."

公害 (コウ・ガイ environmental pollution)

宮 (キュウ/グウ/ク/みや) combines a roof with two rooms or buildings (呂) to mean "palace." It was applied to members of the Chinese Imperial family; in Japan it may mean "Shinto shrine," or "member of the Imperial family."

宮城 (キュウ・ジョウ Imperial Palace), 東宮 (トウ・グウ Crown Prince), 宮内庁 (ク・ナイ・チョウ Imperial Household Agency), 宮 (みや Shinto shrine; Imperial prince or princess)

宰 (サイ) combines 宀 (*house*) and 辛 (*needle*) and may have originally meant prison but its current senses are "administer" and "chief vassal."

宰相 (サイ・ショウ chief of state)

⊞ (くさかんむり) (grass)

若 (ジャク/ニャク/わか・い/も・しくは) began as a depiction of a woman combing her hair, for something like "supple." It is used for "young" and for "or."
若干 (ジャッ・カン a few), 老若 (ロウ・ニャク young and old), 若い (わか・い young), 若しくは (も・しくは or)

苗 (ビョウ/なえ/なわ) combines grass (⊞) and cultivated field (田) for "seedling, sapling."
種苗 (シュ・ビョウ seeds and saplings), 苗 (なえ seedling), 苗代 (なわ・しろ rice nursery)

薦 (セン/すす・める) combines grass (⊞) and a unicorn-like animal and probably was used to write the name of the grass that the imaginary sacred animal supposedly chose to eat. It now means "recommend."
推薦 (スイ・セン recommendation), 薦める (すす・める recommend)

⊞ (cloth)

希 (キ), a couple of crosses marking 巾, is thought to have meant "fine textured cloth." Its current meaning, "hope," may have derived from that sense, while its sense of "rare; rarefy" is borrowed from another word.
希望 (キ・ボウ hope)

帥 (スイ), combining 𠂤 (corps) and 巾 (banner), means "leader."
元帥 (ゲン・スイ field marshal; admiral)

帝 (テイ), coming from an earlier form variously seen as three strings tied together or a special altar, stands for a major Chinese deity regarded as the creator of the universe, but is most often used for "emperor."
帝王 (テイ・オウ sovereign)

師 (シ) combines 𠂤 (corps) with 帀, a symbol suggesting extensiveness, for a word that seems originally to have meant "big group" but now means "master, teacher,"
教師 (キョウ・シ teacher)

帯 (タイ/おび) is a simplification of 帶, where ⺈⺈ is things strung together and 帀 a long sash. It means "wear, have on oneself; be invested with, assume; sash, belt; zone."
包帯 (ホウ・タイ bandage), 帯びる (お・びる bear), 帯 (おび sash)

夂 (すいにょう [as enclosure]; ふゆがしら [at top]; なつあし [at bottom])
(dragging feet)

処 (ショ) combines 夂 and 几 (table) to suggest "stay at one place; place; settle, decide."
処置 (ショ・チ disposal)

冬 (冫, p.89)

各 (カク/おのおの) has 夂 meeting an obstacle (口) and originally meant "stumble," but took on the more abstract sense of "each, every."

各地（カク・チ every place）, 各（おのおの each）

麦（バク/むぎ）is a simplified form of 麥, combining what originally signified barley（來）and feet（夂）. Mysteriously, the meanings of 麦, now "barley, wheat, rye, oats," and 来（來）, now "come," have switched.

麦芽（バク・ガ malt）, 小麦（こ・むぎ wheat）

夏（カ/ゲ/なつ）began as a picture of a man with a big mask dancing. It is the name of the prehistoric Hsia dynasty, and it means "summer."

初夏（ショ・カ early summer）, 夏至（ゲ・シ summer solstice）, 夏（なつ summer）

廾 （にじゅうあし） (two hands)

弁（ベン）shows two hands 廾 holding a crown ム and properly means "crown," but it has long served as a substitute for three homophonous non-Jōyō Kanji and takes their meaning: 辨（discriminate; apply）, 瓣（petal; valve）, and 辯（argue, eloquence）. In Japan it also means "dialect; take-out lunch."

弁当（ベン・トウ box lunch）

戒 （戈, p.99）

广 （まだれ） (roof; house)

床（ショウ/とこ/ゆか）combining 广 and 木（wood）, means "floor; sleeping place, bed."

温床（オン・ショウ hotbed）, 床屋（とこ・や barbershop）, 床（ゆか floor）

庫（コ/ク）combines 广 and 車（wheel） and means "building, room, or box, for storage."

金庫（キン・コ a safe）, 庫裏（ク・リ living quarters at a temple）

麻（マ/あさ）is a slightly simplified form of 蔴, with 广 and two hemp stalks, for "hemp, flax." It has a borrowed sense of "numbness, palsy" as well. It is a traditional classifier, to which only 麻 of the Jōyō Kanji belongs.

麻薬（マ・ヤク narcotic）, 麻（あさ flax）

尸 （しかばね） (corpse; body; buttocks)

尼（ニ/あま）combines 尸（body）and ヒ（person）for, originally,"intimacy," but its only current meaning is "nun," through its use in the transliteration of the Sanskrit word for "nun," *bhiksuni*, as 比丘尼.

尼僧（ニ・ソウ nun）, 尼寺（あま・でら nunnery）

尿（ニョウ）combines 尸（buttocks）and 水（water）for "urine."
糖尿病（トウ・ニョウ・ビョウ diabetes）

尾（ビ/お）, combining 尸（buttocks）and 毛（hair）, means "tail," figuratively extended to "end, conclusion" and used also as a counter for fish.

尾行（ビ・コウ tailing）, 尾（お tail）

屈（クツ）is a combination of 尸（buttocks）and 出（out）and means "bend over;

submit; bend." It has also picked up, from homophones, the meanings "cave" and "chunky of build."

屈する （クッ・する succumb）

屋 （オク/や）combines 尸, here a variant of 广 (roof), and 至 (terminus), meaning "roof; house," particularly "shop, shop-keeper; one who does. . ." in Japan.

屋内 （オク・ナイ indoors）, 魚屋 （さかな・や fish shop, fish merchant）

□ （くにがまえ）   (enclosure)

囚 （シュウ） combines 口 and 人 (person) for "confine; prisoner."

囚人 （シュウ・ジン prisoner）

因 （イン/よ・る） shows someone spread out （大） on a bed （口） to suggest "rest on, be based on; cause."

原因 （ゲン・イン cause）, 因る （よ・る be based on）

回 （カイ/エ/まわ・る） is two concentric circles, perhaps intended as enclosures, meaning "turn, revolve" and used also as a counter for times, repetitions. It also means "go around"; in this case 回 is a substitute for 廻, a non-Jōyō Kanji.

二回 （ニ・カイ twice）, 回向 （エ・コウ Buddhist memorial service）, 回る （まわ・る revolve; go around）

困 （コン/こま・る）, a tree （木） in an enclosure （口）, means "troubled."

困難 （コン・ナン hardship）, 困る （こま・る have trouble）

図 （ズ/ト/はか・る） is simplified from 圖, a picture of a map; it means "diagram; devise, plan."

地図 （チ・ズ map）, 図書 （ト・ショ books）, 図る （はか・る devise）

辶 （しんにゅう）   (walk)

込 （こ・む） is a Japan-made character, combining 辶 and 入 (enter); it means "enter, crowd in; elaborate, intricate." The word forms compound verbs, adding a sense of "into."

飛び込む （と・び・こ・む jump in）

巡 （ジュン/めぐ・る） combines 辶 and 巛 (river); it means "patrol, tour" and serves as a counter for patrol rounds.

巡回 （ジュン・カイ patrol）, 巡る （めぐ・る go around）

送 （ソウ/おく・る） is a combination of 辶 and 关 (hands holding something up), suggesting conveying something. It means "send," extended to "see someone off."

送料 （ソウ・リョウ postage）, 送る （おく・る send）

退 （タイ/しりぞ・く） is a combination of 辶 and 艮, a unique development here of elements interpreted as something like "not inclined to go on"; it means "retreat."

退屈 （タイ・クツ boredom）, 退く （しりぞ・く retreat）

逐 (チク) is a combination of ⻌ and 豕 (boar), and was apparently meant to evoke a boar hunt. It means "follow; chase; drive away."
　　逐一 (チク・イチ one by one)

連 (レン/つな・なる/つ・れる), combining ⻌ and 車 (wheel), means "go in a row; link, string together; go with, accompany; in succession." It also abbreviates certain words meaning "league, federation, union" in a geopolitical sense. In Japan, it may mean "group."
　　連日 (レン・ジツ day after day), 連なる (つら・なる range), 連れる (つ・れる be accompanied by)

逸 (イツ) is a slightly simplified form of 逸, the combination of ⻌ and 免 (rabbit); it means "get away; lost; idle" and "exceptional, superb."
　　逸品 (イッ・ピン superb article)

進 (シン/すす・む) is a combination of ⻌ and 隹 (bird) and means "go forward, advance; offer, give."
　　進歩 (シン・ポ progress), 進む (すす・む advance)

遅 (チ/おく・れる/おそ・い) is the simplified form of 遲, a combination of 込 and 犀 (rhinocerous) that means "slow."
　　遅刻 (チ・コク tardiness), 遅れる (おく・れる be late), 遅い (おそ・い late)

| 廴 | (えんにょう) | (extand) |

建 (ケン/コン/た・てる) is a combination of 廴 and 聿 (holding a brush); its meaning, apparently derivative, is "erect, build; found, establish."
　　建設 (ケン・セツ constraction), 建立 (コン・リュウ erection of a temple), 建てる (た・てる build)

4-Stroke Classifiers

| 歹 | (しにがまえ [as enclosure]; がつへん [at left]) | (bones) |

死 (シ/し・ぬ), combining 歹 and 匕 (person), means "death."
　　死亡 (シ・ボウ death), 死ぬ (し・ぬ die)

| 方 | (かたへん) | (banner) |

The character 方, originally meaning "spade" and now "direction," is a classifier, but all Jōyō Kanji classified under it include the larger form 𣃧, which signifies "banner" and imparts this meaning to the kanji.

旅 (リョ/たび) combines 𣃧 and two slightly distorted person (人) components to suggest a caravan. It means "journey, travel."
　　旅行 (リョ・コウ travel), 旅 (たび journey)

旋 (セン) consists of 𣃧 and 疋 (foot) and means "go around; revolve; return."
　　旋回 (セン・カイ circling)

族 (ゾク) is a combination of 𣃧 and 矢 (arrow) and means a set of people who have something in common, a "clan" or "tribe."

家族 （カ・ゾク family）

攵 （ぼくづくり）   (beating; action)

更 （コウ/さら/ふ・ける） goes back to a combination of 丙 (desk) and 攵. It means "replace, redo"; in Japan it is used to write adverbs meaning "moreover" or having other "intensifying" functions. It also means "grow late" in Japan.

更新 （コウ・シン renewal）, 更に （さら・に moreover; [not] at all）, 更ける （ふ・ける grow late）

敏 （ビン） is a combination of 毎, interpreted in this case as a depiction of grass growing, and 攵; it means "keen, acute."

敏感 （ビン・カン sensitive）

散 （サン/ち・る） is a combination of a component meant to represent breaking up bamboo leaves or hemp seeds and 攵, and means "scatter, disperse," with derivative meanings of "desultory; medicinal powder."

散歩 （サン・ポ stroll）, 散る （ち・る fall; scatter）

戈 （ほこづくり）   (halberd)

我 （ガ/われ/わ） started as a picture of a halberd with a notched blade, but is used for "me, I, my." (Note: In the second example word below, the symbol 々 indicates a repetition of the previous character.)

自我 （ジ・ガ ego）, 我々 （われ・われ we）, 我が国 （わ・が・くに our country）

戒 （カイ/いまし・める）, two hands 廾 on a halberd 戈, means "be on guard; warn, admonish; Buddhist precept."

戒律 （カイ・リツ Buddhist precepts）, 戒める （いまし・める admonish）

5-Stroke Classifiers

禾 （のぎへん）   (rice plant; crops)

秀 （シュウ/ひい・でる） combines 禾 with 乃 (supple) to suggest rice plants in tassel, and it means "excel, excellent."

秀才 （シュウ・サイ brilliant person）, 秀でる （ひい・でる be superior）

利 （リ/き・く）, a combination of 禾 and 刂 (edged tool), means "sharp, keen; effective; profit"; perhaps the ancient Chinese associated such ideas with plowing.

利害 （リ・ガイ advantages and disadvantages）, 利く （き・く be effective）

委 （イ） combines a rice plant with its drooping tassels 禾 and a woman （女）, perhaps to suggest "drooping," but its current meanings are "entrust (a matter to someone); fine, minute."

委員 （イ・イン committee member）

季 （キ）, a combination of 禾 and 子 (child), suggests the growth period from the time of sowing to harvesting. It means "season, term."

季節 （キ・セツ season）

科 （カ） combines 禾 and 斗 (ladle) to suggest measuring and grading. It means "categorization, division; crime; penalty."

科目 （カ・モク school subject）

香 （コウ/キョウ/か/かお・り）, is a combination of 禾 and 甘 (sweet) and means "aroma, smell, fragrance; incense."   In Japan it refers to a *shōgi* (Japanese chess) piece also known as a やり, or "spear."   香 is a traditional classifier, to which no other Jōyō Kanji belong.

香水 （コウ・スイ perfume）, 香車 （キョウ・シャ "spear"）, 香 （か fragrance; コウ incense）, 香り （かお・り fragrance）

秋 （シュウ/あき） is a combination of 禾 and 火 (fire) and means "harvesting time, autumn."

晩秋 （バン・シュウ late autumn）, 秋 （あき autumn）

秒 （ビョウ）, combining 禾 with 少 (few), meant "very small thing."   It is commonly used only for "second (of time)" and as a counter for seconds of time or arc.

十秒 （ジュウ・ビョウ ten seconds）

稚 （チ）, originally the combination of 禾 and 遲 (slow), means "very young."

幼稚園 （ヨウ・チ・エン kindergarten）

罒 （あみがしら）   (net)

罪 （ザイ/つみ）, a combination of 罒 and 非 (wrong), means "crime; sin."

無罪 （ム・ザイ not guilty）, 罪 （つみ sin; crime）

疒 （やまいだれ）   (disease)

疾 （シツ）, a combination of 疒 and 矢 (arrow), means "illness," especially "acute illness." It also means "fast, rapid."

疾走 （シッ・ソウ dash）

癶 （はつがしら）   (feet turned out)

登 （トウ/ト/のぼ・る） originally had, besides 癶 and 豆 (*dish with tall base*), an element for hands raising the dish up.   It means "go up, climb; rise; attend (as a civic duty); register."

登録 （トウ・ロク register）, 登山 （ト・ザン mountaineering）, 登る （のぼ・る ascend）

6-Stroke Classifiers

聿 （ふでづくり）   (hand holding a brush)

建 （廴, p.98）

律 （彳, p.93）

虍 （とらかんむり）   (tiger)

虐 （ギャク/しいた・げる）, is a combination of 虍 and scratch marks, and means "cruel; torture."

虐待 （ギャク・タイ cruel treatment）, 虐げる （しいた・げる persecute）

| 艮; 𡭴 | (remain) |

即（卩, p.90）

退（辶, p.97）

7-Stroke Classifiers

| 酉 | (とりへん) | (wine jar) |

配（ハイ/くば・る）combines 酉 and 己 (kneeling person), to suggest staying close. It is used for the meaning of "mate, match; allot, distribute."
配偶者（ハイ・グウ・シャ spouse）, 配る（くば・る distribute）

| 辰 | (clam) |

辱（ジョク/はずかし・める）has been intrepreted as a hand（寸）engaged in the action of making something soft, like clam meat（辰）; it means "humiliate, dishonor."
屈辱（クツ・ジョク humiliation）, 辱める（はずかし・める disgrace）

農（ノウ）is a combination of 曲 (for 田, field, by one interpretation or 林, woods, by another）and 辰（shell）, perhaps to suggest spading, and means "farming, agriculture."
農業（ノウ・ギョウ agriculture）

| 豕 | (boar) |

豚（トン/ぶた）, a combination of 月 (meat) and 豕, means "pig; pork."
養豚（ヨウ・トン hog raising）, 豚（ぶた pig; pork）

家（宀, p.94）

逐（辶, p.98）

8-Stroke Classifiers

| 隹 | (ふるとり) | (bird) |

隻（セキ）, a combination of 隹 and 又 (*hand*), means "one" in the sense of the remaining one of a pair; it is used as a counter for ships.
三隻（サン・セキ three ships）

進（辶, p.98）

稚（禾, p.100）

9-Stroke Classifiers

| 頁 | (おおがい) | (head) |

順（ジュン）, a combination of 川 (river)and 頁, means "follow; correct sequence, order; obey; unimpeded."

順番 (ジュン・バン order)

頻 (ヒン) is a combination of 歩 (walk) and 頁; it means approach. It is now used only in the sense of "frequent, persistent."

頻発 (ヒン・パツ frequent occurrence)

11-Stroke Classifiers

 (deer)

麗 (レイ/うるわ・しい), originally a picture of a deer with large antlers, means "beautiful, elegant."

奇麗 (キ・レイ pretty; clean), 麗しい (うるわ・しい beautiful)

As the component inventory increases we also see an increasing number of them that represent the same or a similar sense or thing:

person: 亻(人), 大, 匕, 卩 (㔾), 己, 儿, 〃, 巴, 欠
hand: 扌(手), 又, 寸, ヨ (彐), 尤, 爫
two hands:八, 廾, 关
foot/leg: 足, 疋, 止, 夂
joint/bone:冎, 歹, 号 (另)
walk:歩, 辶
cover/lid:冖, 襾, 入
roof/house:宀, 广

In spite of the fact that the compound kanji introduced in this section are quite complicated in their forms, there are some strikingly similar ones.   The following is a list of them, including kanji introduced in earlier sections:

帥 (leader)	師 (master)
官 (official)	宮 (palace)
因 (cause)	困 (troubled)
凶 (adverse)	区 (division)
今 (now)	令 (command)
名 (name)	各 (each)
思 (think)	恵 (mercy)
善 (good)	喜 (joy)
史 (history)	吏 (official)
司 (control)	同 (same)
失 (lose)	朱 (red)
乗 (ride)	垂 (hang)
歩 (walk)	走 (run)
折 (fold)	析 (analyze)

Combinations of Greater Complexity

The kanji in this section are combinations of more than two components, each component contributing to the meaning of the kanji.   When two of the components together form an element that has already been introduced as a compound kanji in preceding sections, they are not reanalyzed here. In some cases the original elements have so merged as to make them unanalyzable, so many kanji in this section will be in effect analyzed into only two components. Because of the number of components involved, kanji introduced in this section are not cross-listed by every component, but only by traditional classifiers. When more than one such classifier is involved, the kanji is listed under the most common classifier and cross-listed under the others. Remember to look for classifiers first at the top, bottom, left side, right side, or wrapped around two or more sides of a kanji.

1-Stroke Classifiers

| 亅 | (はねぼう) | (no meaning) |

争 (ソウ/あらそ・う) is a simplified form of 爭, a combination of ⺍ (fingers), 亅, and a hand ⺕; think "two hands scrambling for the same thing." It means "struggle, compete, argue, fight."

戦争 (セン・ソウ war), 争う (あらそ・う argue; compete)

| 乙; 乚 | (おつにょう) | (pin down) |

乳 (ニュウ/ちち/ち) may be a combination of ⺍ (fingers), 子 (child), and 乚, a mark descended from a representation of a swallow, a bird associated with babies; or else ⺍ and 孔 (hole, duct). It means "milk, milky; breast."

牛乳 (ギュウ・ニュウ cow's milk), 乳 (ちち milk; breast), 乳飲み子 (ち・のみ・ご baby)

乾 (カン/かわ・く) originated as a combination of 日 (sun) in the middle of the left side of 㐱 (banner) and 乙, perhaps meaning something stretched out under the sun to "dry."

乾杯 (カン・パイ a toast), 乾く (かわ・く get dry)

2-Stroke Classifiers

| 亻 | (にんべん); | 𠆢 | (ひとがしら) | (person) |

命 (ロ, p.107)

便 (ベン/ビン/たよ・り) is a combination of 亻 and 更 (*stretch, stiff*) that is supposed to suggest softening, and thus improving passage. It means "convenience; conveyance; letter" and "void feces/urine."

便利 (ベン・リ convenient), 船便 (ふな・ビン sea mail), 便り (たよ・り letter)

修 (シュウ/シュ/おさ・める) combines 攸 (long and narrow) and 彡 (design) to suggest getting something into good form. It means "learn, master; amend; enhance, decorate; edit."

修理 (シュウ・リ repair), 修行 (シュ・ギョウ training), 修める (おさ・める master)

倉 (ソウ/くら), a combination of 食 (eat; food) and 口 (place), means "barn; warehouse."

倉庫 (ソウ・コ warehouse), 倉 (くら storehouse)

阝; 巳 (kneeling person)

危 (キ/あぶ・ない/あや・ぶむ) is a combination of 人 (person), 厂 (cliff) and 巳; it means "danger."

危機 (キ・キ crisis), 危ない (あぶ・ない dangerous), 危ぶむ (あや・ぶむ be anxious about)

命 (口, p.107)

匕 (person; spoon)

能 (月, p.110)

力 (りきづくり) (strength)

勝 (ショウ/か・つ/まさ・る) combines 朕 (*lift boat; buoyancy*) and 力, to symbolize the power to rise to the top, for "win, excel."

勝利 (ショウ・リ victory), 勝つ (か・つ win), 勝る (まさ・る surpass)

勢 (セイ/いきお・い) consists of 木 (tree) and 土 (earth) now unified on the upper left, 丸 (*someone stretching arms*) and 力; it may suggest the energy to farm. The meaning is "force, vigor; circumstances; force of numbers."

大勢 (おお・ゼイ throngs), 勢い (いきお・い force)

又 (*hand*)

最 (日, p.110)

報 (土, p.105)

刂 (りっとう) (sword)

刷 (サツ/す・る) combines 尸 (buttocks), 巾 (cloth), and 刂. It basically means "rub off," but what is rubbed off gets rubbed onto the cloth, providing another sense, "print."

印刷 (イン・サツ printing), 刷る (す・る print)

匸 (かくしがまえ; はこがまえ) (hide)

匿 (トク) is a combination of 匸 and 若 (young mulberry leaves). It means "conceal."

匿名 (トク・メイ anonymity)

厶 (private),

能 (月, p.110)

十 (ten; full)

率 (玄, p.114)

3-Stroke Classifiers

彳 （ぎょうにんべん）   (go; act)

役 （ヤク/エキ）, a combination of 彳 and 殳 (hand holding a halberd), was meant to suggest working away from home. It means "role, useful role, service, duty; compel" and sometimes "war, campaign."

配役 （ハイ・ヤク cast）, 現役 （ゲン・エキ active service）

後 （ゴ/コウ/のち/うし・ろ/あと/おく・れる） consists of 彳, 幺 (thin), and 夂 (dragging feet); it means "delayed, late; after, later; latter; rear, behind."

午後 （ゴ・ゴ afternoon）, 後半 （コウ・ハン latter half）, 後 （のち/あと later）, 後ろ （うし・ろ behind）, 後れる （おく・れる be delayed）

微 （ビ） combines 彳, what remains of some graphs representing thread and a line (interpreted as adding a sense of "slight") in the middle, and 夂 (action). It means "sneak; covert" and also "minute, tiny."

微妙 （ビ・ミョウ subtle）

徴 （チョウ） is an abbreviated combination of 微 (tiny) and 王 (king) to indicate, it is said, the ruler's ability to spot hidden signs of talent among his subjects. It means "summon; sign, feature."

特徴 （トク・チョウ feature）

山 （やまへん）   (mountain)

峠 （とうげ）, a Japan-made kanji, combines 山 with 上 (ascend) and 下 (descend) for "mountain pass" and, figuratively, "turning point, crisis."

炭 （火, p.111）

土   (earth)

報 （ホウ/むく・いる）, a combination of 幸 (*handcuffs*), 卩 (person kneeling), and 又 (*hand*), suggests a penalty or paying for a crime. It means "repay, requite; report."

報告 （ホウ・コク report）, 報いる （むく・いる reward; revenge）

艹 （くさかんむり）   (grass)

葬 （ソウ/ほうむ・る） has death, or a dead person （死）, between two 艹 (grass) components and means "bury, entomb."

葬式 （ソウ・シキ funeral service）, 葬る （ほうむ・る bury）

夢 （夕, p.105）

繭 （糸, p.115）

夕   (evening)

夢 （ム/ゆめ） includes an eye and something else on top, a cover 冖 in the middle, and a sinking moon 夕 on the bottom. Scholars disagree about the element above the eye, but agree that it was to evoke an inability to see, with the character as a whole meaning what you see with your eyes closed at night: a "dream."

夢中 (ム・チュウ preoccupied), 夢 (ゆめ dream)

| 寸 | ((hand); measure) |

尉 (イ) is a combination of 尸 (buttocks), two parallel lines (to suggest lining up or leveling out) with what remains of 火 (fire) under them, and 寸; it meant "press" (as with an iron). In Japan it has been·used to designate the lowest military rank or set of military ranks among, in modern times, commissioned officers.

大尉 (タイ・イ captain)

尋 (ジン/たず・ねる) consists of 寸 (measure), and 左 (left hand) and 右 (right hand) combined, with ⺕ (hand) doing duty for both the upper parts. It referred to a unit of length, or depth, similar to a fathom.   As a Jōyō Kanji it retains only its other meanings, "inquire, visit; ordinary."

尋常 (ジン・ジョウ ordinary), 尋ねる (たず・ねる ask; visit)

奪 (大, p.106)

| 大 | ((spread-eagle person); large) |

奉 (ホウ/ブ/たてまつ・る) adds another hand (手) to 奉 (holding up an offering) and means "offer; revere; serve."

奉仕 (ホウ・シ service), 奉行 (ブ・ギョウ magistrate), 奉る (たてまつ・る offer)

奔 (ホン) shows a person (大) with three extra legs to represent rapid motion and means "run, dash."

奔走 (ホン・ソウ bustle about)

奏 (ソウ/かな・でる) is a combination of 夫 (two hands holding something) and 夭, here perhaps a sprig of a sacred tree or an animal sacrifice; it meant "offer something to a god."   It is now used for the meaning of "tell" as a humble form and "play music."

演奏 (エン・ソウ musical performance), 奏でる (かな・でる play)

奥 (オウ/おく) combines 宀 (cover), 釆 (scatter), and 大 (two hands) to suggest groping for something in a dark place. It means "deep inside."

奥義 (おく・ギ/オウ・ギ inner mysteries)

奪 (ダツ/うば・う) consists of 大 (person), 隹 (bird), and 寸 (hand) and means "snatch, rob."

略奪 (リャク・ダツ looting), 奪う (うば・う snatch)

器 (ロ, p.107)

奮 (フン/ふる・う) is a combination of 大 (large) and a bird (隹) fluttering over a field (田), to be the imagery for "excite; be stirred up."

興奮 (コウ・フン excitement), 奮う (ふる・う get spirited)

| 女 | （おんなへん） | | (woman) |

婿 （セイ/むこ）, a combination of 女 and 胥 (pair), means "daughter's spouse."
女婿 （ジョ・セイ son-in-law）, 婿 （むこ groom ; son-in-law）

| 尸 | （しかばねかんむり） | | (corpse; body; buttocks) |

尽 （ジン/つ・くす） is a simplification of 盡, of which the components are 聿 (brush in hand), 灬 (drops), and 皿 (dish), suggesting some sort of "last drops" notion. It means "use up, exhaust."
尽力 （ジン・リョク efforts）, 尽くす （つ・くす exhaust）

局 （キョク） may be a variant of 句 (small frame), with a basic sense of partition. It means "delimit, phase, segment; office, bureau," as well as "board; match" for board games such as *go* and *shōgi*. It is also used as a counter for matches played.
結局 （ケッ・キョク after all）

昼 （日, p.110）

展 （テン） has 尸 (buttocks) over an amalgamated symbol for bricks, meaning weight, and 衣 (garment). The whole means "spread out; open up; exhibit."
発展 （ハッ・テン development）

履 （リ/は・く） consists of 尸 (body) and 復 (walk back); it means "carry out, carry on; footwear; wear on feet or legs."
履歴書 （リ・レキ・ショ curriculum vitae）, 履く （は・く put on; wear）

| 口 | （くちへん） | | (mouth; opening) |

命 （メイ/ミョウ/いのち） combines 亼 (lid; cover), 口, and 卩 (person kneeling) to evoke a pronouncement from above. It means "mandate" and, derivatively, "life."
命名 （メイ・メイ naming）, 寿命 （ジュ・ミョウ life span）, 命 （いのち life）

倉 （人, p.103）

啓 （ケイ） consists of 戸 (door), 攵 (beating hand), and 口 and means "open; enlighten." It also serves as a humble term for "tell."
啓示 （ケイ・ジ revelation）

喪 （ソウ/も）, a jumbled combination of 哭 (wail) and 亡 (die), means "mourn; lose."
喪失 （ソウ・シツ loss）, 喪 （も mourning）

嘆 （タン/なげ・く） combines 口 and 莫 (game cooking over a fire); it means "sigh, gasp."
嘆願 （タン・ガン supplication）, 嘆く （なげ・く sigh）

器 （キ/うつわ） is a simplified form of 器, four objects （口）, perhaps dishes, and 犬 (dog). It means "container, utensil; implement; capacity, capability" and sometimes "organ of the body."
器用 （キ・ヨウ dexterous）, 器 （うつわ container; ability）

| 幺 | （いとがしら） | （thin） |

幾 （キ/いく・つ） combines two 幺 components, 人 （person）, and 戈 （halberd）; it is used for the meaning "what amount."

幾何 （キ・カ geometry）, 幾つ （いく・つ how many）

| 宀 | （うかんむり） | （roof） |

宿 （シュク/やど）, a combination of 宀, 人 （person）, and 百 （someone in bed）, means "lodge, dwell."

宿命 （シュク・メイ fate）, 宿 （やど lodging）

寒 （カン/さむ・い） has 宀 over an amalgamation of symbols for bricks and two hands, and 冫 （ice） ; it means "cold." It is also used for the derived meaning of "desolate."

寒波 （カン・パ cold wave）, 寒い （さむ・い cold）

寡 （カ）, a combination of 宀, 頁 （head）, and 分 （divide）, means "alone; scanty."
寡婦 （カ・フ window）

審 （シン）, a combination of 宀 and 番 （watch） means "inspect, ascertain."
不審 （フ・シン suspicion）

| 广 | （まだれ） | （house） |

庶 （ショ） combines 广 with an old variant of a character for light, suggesting a place where people might be found, and means "people, common folk; various."

庶民 （ショ・ミン the people）

慶 （心, p.111）

| 廾 | （にじゅうあし） | （two hands） |

葬 （艹, p.105）

奔 （大, p.106）

算 （竹, p.115）

| 夂 | （なつあし） | （dragging feet） |

慶 （心, p.111）

憂 （心, p.111）

| 辶 | （しんにゅう） | （walk） |

造 （ゾウ/つく・る） combines 辶 and 告 （stick things together） and means "put together, make, construct" or rarely, "reach, get to."

造花 （ゾウ・カ artificial flower）, 造る （つく・る make）

透 （トウ/す・ける）, a combination of 辶 and 秀 （stand out）, means "transparent, show through." In Japan it is also used to write a word meaning "become thin."

透明 （トウ・メイ transparent）, 透ける （す・ける show through）

廴 （えんにょう） (extend)

延 （エン/の・べる） is a combination of 止 (*foot*), with a mark over it that suggests stretching, and 廴. It means "extend, delay." Used as prefix のべ, it means "total" in Japan.

延期 （エン・キ postponement）, 延べる （の・べる extend）

彡 (design)

修 （人, p.103）

阝 （こざとへん [at left]）; （おおざと [at right]） (mound; town)

郵 （ユウ） combines 垂 (border) and 阝 and referred to a post where an orderly was stationed. It now means "postal."

郵便局 （ユウ・ビン・キョク post office）

隆 （リュウ） is a simplification of 降 (descend) and 生 (grow); it means "prosper."
隆盛 （リュウ・セイ prosperity）

4-Stroke Classifiers

止 (*foot*)

歳 （サイ/セイ）actually has 歩 (walk) overlapping 戉 (sickle), to suggest "(annual) harvest; year, age."

万歳 （バン・ザイ Long live...!）, 歳暮 （セイ・ボ year-end gift）

木 （きへん） (tree; wood)

染 （セン/そ・める/し・み） is a combination of 氵 (water) and a much simplified form for a dye box; it means "dye; stain."

伝染 （デン・セン contagion）, 染める （そ・める dye）, 染み （し・み stain）

棄 （キ） consists of an inverted 子 (child), representing a newborn baby, and symbols no longer analyzable for a dustpan and two hands. It means "abandon, discard."

棄権 （キ・ケン abstention）

水；氵 （さんずい） (water)

染 （木, p.109）

涙 （ルイ/なみだ） consists of 氵 and 戻 (come through) and means "tears."
催涙ガス （サイ・ルイ・ガス tear gas）, 涙 （なみだ tears）

湿 （シツ/しめ・る） is a simplified form of 濕, a combination of 氵, 日 (sun), and 絲 (bundle of raw silk); it means "get moist, humid."

湿度 （シツ・ド humidity）, 湿める （しめ・る become damp）

手；扌 （てへん） (hand)

抑 （ヨク/おさ・える） consists of 扌 and 卬 (press) and means "suppress, control."
抑制 （ヨク・セイ control）, 抑える （おさ・える restrain）

承 (ショウ/うけたまわ・る) goes back to a symbol for a person on top of 手, with two more symbols for hands to the left and right. It means "receive; accept," extended to "hear, learn" in a humble sense.

承知 (ショウ・チ acceptance), 承る (うけたまわ・る hear)

拾 (シュウ/ジュウ/ひろ・う), a combination of 扌 and 合 (join together), means "pick up." Read ジュウ, it may substitute for 十 (ten)in writing amounts of money.

収拾 (シュウ・シュウ cope with), 拾万円 (ジュウ・マン・エン hundred thousand yen), 拾う (ひろ・う pick up)

| 犬；犭 | (けものへん) | (dog) |

獄 (ゴク) is two dogs (犭 and 犬) with 言 (say) in the middle. It means "trial" or "prison."

脱獄 (ダツ・ゴク prison break)

獣 (ジュウ/けもの), a combination of a slightly modified 単 (beater), 口 (enclosure) and 犬, means "animal."

怪獣 (カイ・ジュウ monster), 獣 (けもの beast)

| 日 | (ひへん; ひらび) | (sun; say) |

昼 (チュウ/ひる) is a combination of 尺, a replacement for 聿 (holding a brush), 日 (sun), and a line interpreted as representing a time span. It means "daytime; midday, noon; lunch."

昼夜 (チュウ・ヤ day and night), 昼 (ひる noon; lunch)

最 (サイ/もっと・も) is a combination of 日, slightly modified from the original form that represented a cover, and 取 (take). It means "most," derived from some idea of how much one takes under a cover.

最高 (サイ・コウ highest), 最も (もっと・も most)

替 (タイ/か・える) is a combination of two 夫 (man) components and 曰 (say), but regarded as suggesting human activity in this case; it means "take turns."

交替 (コウ・タイ shift), 替える (か・える exchange)

暴 (ボウ/バク/あば・く), 日 (sun) with a composite element that shows a dead animal or hide held in two hands under it, must have meant "expose to the elements," but now means "divulge"; it also has the sense of "violent."

暴力 (ボウ・リョク violence), 暴く (あば・く divulge)

曇 (ドン/くも・る) has 日 (sun) above 雲 (cloud) and means "cloudy."
曇天 (ドン・テン cloudy weather), 曇る (くも・る get cloudy)

| 月 | (つきへん; つくづき) | (moon; meat, flesh) |

能 (ノウ), with a highly simplified form of a character meaning "work hard" on the upper left, 月 (meat), and marks seen as a tortoise's feet on the right, is thought to have suggested tenacity. It means "ability, efficacy." In Japan, it also means "Noh play."

勝 (カ, p.104)

膚（フ）, a combination of a kind of container （盧） abbreviated and 月 (flesh), means "skin."

皮膚（ヒ・フ skin）

| 王; 玉 | （たまへん） | (gem) |

班（ハン）is a combination of two 玉 components and 刂 (sword), representing the cutting of a gem in two. It means "smaller unit," that is "squad; section; team."

班長（ハン・チョウ head of a squad）

| 火 | （ひへん）; | 灬 | （れっか） | (fire) |

炭（タン/すみ）, a combination of 山 (mountain), 厂 (cliff), and 火, means "coal; charcoal."

石炭（セキ・タン coal), 炭（すみ charcoal）

焼（ショウ/や・く）, a combination of 火, 尭 (high), means "burn," in the sense of "change under the influence of heat or light," including cooking without liquid, "fry, bake."

全焼（ゼン・ショウ burn down), 焼く（や・く burn; grill; broil; bake）

然（ゼン/ネン）combines 月 (meat) and 犬 (dog) to mean fatty dog meat; this over 灬 (fire) meant "burn, be aflame." It came to be used, however, for a Chinese homonym meaning "so; state," and is often used after another kanji to form a descriptive word.

平然（ヘイ・ゼン calmly), 天然（テン・ネン natural）

| 心 | （したごころ） | (heart) |

慶（ケイ）combines 鹿 (deer), 心, and 夂 (feet), suggesting "happiness, joy," as for instance one's feeling on bringing venison or a deer skin for a celebration.

同慶（ドウ・ケイ joy at another's good fortune）

憂（ユウ/うれ・える/う・い）is the combination of 頁 (head), 心, and 夂 (dragging feet), and means "pensive; worry."

憂慮（ユウ・リョ anxiety), 憂える（うれ・える worry), 憂き目（う・き・め bitter experience）

| 爫 | （つめかんむり） | (fingers) |

爵（シャク）has on the top and left the descendant of a picture of a decorated flagon and herbs to spice up liquor, and 寸 (*hand*) on the lower right. The combination stood for a liquor container in the shape of a sparrow, presented to honor nobles in ancient China. It is used in the sense of "titled."

爵（シャク・イ peerage）

| 戸 | （とだれ） | (door) |

啓（口, p.107）

| 戈 | （ほこづくり） | (halberd) |

幾（幺, p.108）

賊 (貝, p.117)

斤 (おのづくり)   (hatchet)

断 (ダン/た・つ/ことわ・る) is simplified from 斷, a combination of four 幺 (thin) components, some lines signifying cutting, and 斤 to mean "cut off," now usually in a figurative sense. It also means "decide, decisive," and in Japan "make excuses; decline."

断固 (ダン・コ decisively), 断つ (た・つ sever), 断る (ことわ・る reject; decline)

質 (貝, p.117)

攵 (ぼくづくり)   (beating; action)

修 (人, p.103)

敬 (ケイ/うやま・う) is a slightly simplified 敬, which combines a character meaning "vigilant" with 攵 (action); it means "respect."

敬語 (ケイ・ゴ honorifics), 敬う (うやま・う revere)

数 (スウ/ス/かず/かぞ・える) is simplified from 數, the combination of 母 (mother), 中 (middle), and 女 (woman) linked together, with 攵 (action); it means "count; number; several."

数学 (スウ・ガク mathematics), 人数 (ニン・ズ/ニン・ズウ the number of people), 数 (かず number), 数える (かぞ・える count)

微 (彳, p.105)

徴 (彳 徴, p.105)

欠 (あくび)   (*stooping person with mouth open*)

款 (カン) consists of 柰 (wild apple tree) and 欠; it means "engrave, write; articles, formal document." It sometimes substitutes for 歓 (カン) (p.105), meaning "joy."

落款 (ラッ・カン artist's signature or seal)

殳   (hand holding a halberd; action)

役 (彳, p.105)

殺 (サツ/サイ/セツ/ころ・す) is a modified form of 殺, which is a combination of 乂 (reap), 求 (millet), and 殳 (action). It means "chip away; decrease; do away with; kill, deadly."

自殺 (ジ・サツ suicide), 相殺 (ソウ・サイ/ソウ・サツ offsetting), 殺生 (セッ・ショウ slaughter), 殺す (ころ・す kill)

般 (舟, p.115)

設 (言, p.116)

5-Stroke Classifiers

| 示 ; ネ | (しめすへん) | ((*altar*); indicate) |

祝 (シュク/シュウ/いわ・う) combines ネ (*altar*) and 兄 (someone on knees) and means "priest" ("Shinto priest" in Japan) and "pray; celebrate."

祝日 (シュク・ジツ holiday) , 祝儀 (シュウ・ギ celebration; gift; tip), 祝う (いわ・う celebrate)

祭 (サイ/まつ・る) is a combination of 月 (meat), 又 (*hand*), and 示 (*altar*), reflecting a religious ceremony. It means "worship, enshrine; festival."

祭日 (サイ・ジツ holiday), 祭り (まつ・り festival)

| 禾 | (のぎへん) | (rice plant) |

穂 (スイ/ほ) is a combination of 禾 and 恵, which replaces an element meaning "thin, fine"; it means "tassels" on a plant or "ear of grain."

出穂期 (シュッ・スイ・キ the earing season), 穂 (ほ ear)

| 穴 | (あなかんむり) | (cave) |

突 (トツ/つ・く) originally had a dog (犬) in the mouth of a cave (穴) and means "abruptly; thrust out, protrude."

突然 (トツ・ゼン suddenly), 突つ (つ・く poke; thrust; stab)

| 罒 | (あみがしら) | (net) |

罰 (バツ/バチ), a combination of 詈 (abuse), and 刂 (sword), means "punishment."

罰金 (バッ・キン fine), 罰 (バツ retribution)

罷 (ヒ) combines 罒 and 能 (tenacity) and means "cease; dismiss."
罷免 (ヒ・メン dismissal)

羅 (ラ) consists of 罒 and 維 (string; tie) and means "net, netting." It also names a thin silk fabric, means "enumerate, list"; and is used to transliterate foreign syllables like *la*, especially from Sanskrit.

網羅 (モウ・ラ include all)

| 田 | | (field) |

畝(せ/うね) combines 十 (ten), 田, and 久 (person stooped over, walking), probably to suggest the measuring of farm land. It stands for a unit of land area, approximately 100 square meters in Japan, and also refers to the ridge between two furrows in a plowed field.

一畝 (ひと・せ 100 square meters), 畝 (うね ridge)

畜 (チク) combines 玄 (dark) and 田 to evoke fertile farm soil. It means "breed, raise; farm stock."

家畜 (カ・チク livestock; domestic animal)

留 (リュウ/ル/と・める) combines an element representing a blocked door or window with 田 and means "detain; stay."

留学 （リュウ・ガク studying abroad), 留守番 （ル・ス・バン house-sitting), 留め
る （と・める detain)

異 （イ/こと) is a simplified form of 異, which may consist of elements
representing a large mask and someone holding it with both hands, pretending to
be someone else. It means "different; unusual, strange."

異常 （イ・ジョウ abnormality), 異なる （こと・なる differ)

畳 （ジョウ/たた・む/たたみ) is simplified from 疊, the combination of three
miscellaneous objects （田) and 宜 （big pile); it means "stack up; fold up." It is
also used in Japan to write the word *tatami* and as a counter of *tatami* to measure
room size.

六畳 （ロク・ジョウ six-mat room), 畳む （たた・む fold up), 畳 （たたみ *tatami*)

奮 （大, p.106)

皿 (dish)

盗 （トウ/ぬす・む) is simplified from 盜, which is a combination of 皿 and 次
(covet); which is in turn 冫 （water) and 欠 （someone with mouth open); 盗 means
"steal."

盗難 （トウ・ナン theft), 盗む （ぬす・む steal)

監 （カン) is a combination of 臣 （*big eye*), 人 （person), and 皿 with a line over
it to suggest something in it; it has been suggested that the kanji represents
looking at a reflection in water in a dish. It means "observe from above; oversee,
supervise."

監視 （カン・シ watch)

生 ((*growing grass*); live)

産 （サン/う・む/うぶ) is a modification of 產, combining 文 （letter), 厂 （sharply
defined), and 生 for "give birth." It also has the derived meanings "produce;
product; property."

産業 （サン・ギョウ industry), 産む（う・む give birth to), 産湯（うぶ・ゆ a baby's
first bath)

甘 (sweet)

甚 （ジン/はなは・だ) is a combination of 甘 and 匹 （pair; sex) that obliquely
suggests overindulgence. It means "very much, exceedingly."

甚大 （ジン・ダイ immense), 甚だ （はなは・だ very much)

玄 (dim)

畜 （田, p.113)

率 （ソツ/リツ/ひき・いる) may consist of 玄 straddled by two 八 （brush off)
components, and 十 （join together). It means "bring along, lead; impetuous;
unadorned, unadulterated" and, with the reading リツ, "ratio, rate."

率直 （ソッ・チョク frank), 率 （リツ rate), 率いる （ひき・いる lead)

| 立 | （たつへん） | (standing) |

競 （キョウ/ケイ/きそ・う/せ・る） comprises two modified 言 (say) components and two 儿 (person) components. It means "dispute; vie."

競争 （キョウ・ソウ competition）, 競馬 （ケイ・バ horse racing）, 競う （きそ・う vie）, 競り （せ・り auction）

6-Stroke Classifiers

| 糸 | （いとへん） | (thread) |

給 （キュウ） combines 糸 and 合 (join together) and means "add, supplement; provide; wages; serve."

給料 （キュウ・リョウ wages）

絶 （ゼツ/た・える）, a modification of 絶, consisting of 糸, 刀 (sword), and 巴 (stooping woman), means "cut short, terminate, cease; standing alone, the utmost."

絶対 （ゼッ・タイ absolute）, 絶える （た・える discontinue）

継 （ケイ/つ・ぐ） is simplified from 繼, which combines 糸 and four more pieces of thread （糸） and means "tie, link together." Derivative uses are for "succeed to" and "adoptive" in words meaning "stepmother," "stepfather," and "stepchild."

継続 （ケイ・ゾク continuation）, 継ぐ （つ・ぐ inherit）

綿 （メン/わた） is a combination of 糸, 白 (white), and 巾 (cloth). It means "cotton thread; endless, unbroken; cotton, wadding; fine, minute."

綿密 （メン・ミツ minuteness）, 綿 （メン cotton; わた wadding）

繭 （ケン/まゆ） combines a symbol for thread hanging, 糸, and 虫 (insect; worm) and means "cocoon."

繭糸 （ケン・シ silk thread）, 繭 （まゆ cocoon）

| 舟 | （ふねへん） | (boat) |

般 （ハン）, a combination of an irregular variant of 凡 (board) and 殳 (action), meant "spread out flat." It now means "sort, kind."

全般 （ゼン・パン all its aspects）

| 竹 | （たけかんむり） | (bamboo) |

筋 （キン/すじ） is a combination of 竹 and 肋 (rib), which is in turn 月 (meat) and 力 (strength) combined; the whole means "sinew; line." In Japan it is also used for the extended meanings "story line, plot, (thread of) reasoning; source of information; lineage, stock, natural aptitude" and as an occasional counter for long, thin things.

筋肉 （キン・ニク muscle）, 筋書 （すじ・がき synopsis）

答 （トウ/こた・える） combines 竹 and 合 (fit) to evoke the notion of a bamboo container and lid that correspond to each other. It means "respond, response."

応答 （オウ・トウ response）, 答える （こた・える answer）

算（サン）, a combination of 竹 and 具 (arrange), means "count, calculate."
計算（ケイ・サン calculation）

| 西 | (cover) |

覇（ハ）is a modified form of 覇, a combination of 雨 (rain), 革 (bleached hide), and 月 (moon). The original meaning was the dark part of the disk of the non-full moon. It now means "rule; dominance."
覇権（ハ・ケン hegemony）

| 虍 (とらかんむり) | (tiger) |

膚（月, p.111）

| 血 | (blood) |

衆（シュウ/シュ）was originally a combination of either 日 (sun) or 目 (eye) and three 人 (person) components; it depicted many people working under the sun, or simply many people. It means "crowd, multitude of," and it represents a sporadic noun formant, basically a pluralizer, in Japanese.
大衆（タイ・シュウ the masses）, 衆生（シュ・ジョウ living things）

| 臼 | (mortar) |

興（コウ/キョウ/おこ・る）combined four symbols for hands around 同 (same) and means "raise, arise; emerge as a geo-political reality." Read キョウ it means "fun, merriment."
興行（コウ・ギョウ performance）, 興味（キョウ・ミ interest）, 興る（おこ・る emerge）

| 聿 | (hand holding brush) |

粛（シュク）is a simplified form of 肅, which combines 聿 with an abbreviation of 淵 (deep pool); it means "quiet; restrain."
自粛（ジ・シュク self-control）

| 色 | (color) |

絶（糸, p.115）

| 虫 | (insect) |

繭（糸, p.115）

| 米 | (rice) |

奥（大, p.106）

7-Stroke Classifiers

| 言 (ごんべん) | (say) |

設（セツ/もう・ける）had in earlier forms a symbol for a chisel or a wedge instead of speech, with 殳 (action) on the right. It means "install, set up, establish."

設立 (セツ・リツ establishment), 設ける (もう・ける set up)

| 貝 | (かいへん) | (shell; wealth) |

賊 (ゾク) is a combination of 貝, 戈 (halberd), and between them a cross mark where earlier forms had a symbol for a helmet or sword.   It means "injure with a weapon; rob; robber; rebel."

盗賊 (トウ・ゾク thieves)

賛 (サン) is a simplified form of 贊, which consists of two 先 (*tip of foot*) components and 貝 (ceremonial article) and has been interpreted as suggesting assisting at a ceremony. It means "assist, approve," and, substituting for 讃 (praise), "praise; poetry or prose written on a painting."

賛成 (サン・セイ approval)

質 (シツ/シチ/チ) is a combination of two 斤 (hatchet) components for their use as weights, and 貝, to suggest assaying, evaluation; it means "quality; evaluate; nature; question; plain" and, read シチ, "pawn, something held as security."

質 (シツ quality; シチ pawn), 言質 (ゲン・チ pledge)

| 見 | | (look) |

規 (キ) was originally perhaps 矢 (arrow; straight stick) and 見, suggesting a pair of compasses used to measure off lengths; it means "measure, regulate criterion."

規則 (キ・ソク regulation)

| 角 | (つのへん) | (horn) |

解 (カイ/ゲ/と・く) consists of a horn (角) separated from an ox (牛) with an edged tool (刀) and means "take apart." It also means "dissolve, take off; comprehend."

理解 (リ・カイ comprehension), 解せない (ゲ・せない beyond understanding), 解く (と・く dissolve; solve)

| 臣 | | (*big eye*; vassal) |

臨 (リン/のぞ・む) is a combination of 臣 (*big eye*), 人 (person), and 品 (various unspecified objects) and means "look over, look down on from above," with derivative meanings of "face, have a view of; in the face of, on the verge of; attend, confront; deal with subordinates," and in Japan is used as an abbreviation of the first example below.

臨時 (リン・ジ temporary), 臨む (のぞ・む attend; confront)

8-Stroke Classifiers

| 隹 | (ふるとり) | (bird) |

難 (ナン/かた・い/むずかし・い) is a slight simplification of 難, a combination of 𦰩 (broiling game) and 隹 (bird), presumed to have once meant "broil." Perhaps that represents a kind of disaster, or perhaps this character was substituted for another; scholarly opinions differ. It means "disaster; difficult; censure."

非難（ヒ・ナン censure），有難い（あり・がた・い precious），難しい（むずかし・い difficult）

| 隷 | | (catch) |

隷（レイ）combines 奈（wild apple tree）and 隶, suggesting to one scholar stringing apples together to account for its use to mean "chained people; slave."

隷属（レイ・ゾク slave）

9-Stroke Classifier

| 頁 |（おおがい） | (head) |

類（ルイ）is a slight simplification of 類, a combination of 米（rice），representing one kind of plant, 犬（dog），one kind of animal, and 頁; the whole means "classify, categorize; genus, sort; similar."

類する（ルイ・する similar）

Chapter 4

Phonetic Compound Kanji

Unlike the semantic compound kanji listed in the previous chapter, the majority of kanji were created by combining two components each having a different function: one component that hinted at the meaning of the new kanji and one that suggested the pronunciation of the word the new kanji represented. Often the latter, phonetic, component imparted its meaning to the new kanji as well. Such phonetic compound kanji, the subject of this chapter, amount to about two-thirds of the Jōyō Kanji list.

There were three ways in which this combining process could happen. Sometimes a word, written with a certain character, would develop different senses, which might or might not be accompanied by minor changes in pronunciation. To distinguish the meanings of these cognates in the written language, they could be written with the original character plus a new semantic component (also called simply a "semantic"); such a component might be one of the classifiers seen in the previous chapter. The original character, the phonetic component (or "phonetic"), continued to show the pronunciation; it also helped show the meaning in this case. For example, compare the basic-form kanji 交 (コウ cross; mix) and several of the kanji that include it; 効, 郊, 校, 絞, 較. Theoretically, there might have been one word at one time meaning something like "cross; mix" from which developed new words. For clarity, these words came to be written in different ways;

交 (コウ cross; mix)	＋力 (strength)	→効 (コウ effect)
交	＋阝 (town)	→郊 (コウ suburb)
交	＋木 (tree; wood)	→校 (コウ school)
交	＋糸 (thread)	→絞 (コウ wring)
交	＋車 (wheel)	→較 (カク compare)

The new words (effect, suburb, etc.) were in some sense related to the original meaning of "crossing, mixing, mingling"; the added semantic components (力, 糸, etc.) helped the new kanji depict the more specific meaning of the new word. The component 交 shows the reading コウ for all but the last character. The nature of this apparent exception will be traced below.

The second possibility was that a kanji might be "borrowed" to write an

119

unrelated homophone. We have already seen that 然 (ゼン/ネン) originally meant "burn," but was borrowed to write an abstract word, pronounced the same as the word for "burn," that means "so; like that." To avoid confusion, a semantic component (another "fire") was added to the character to represent the "burn" meaning; the result was 燃 (ネン), and 然 came to be used exclusively for "so." As in the example with 交, above, the phonetic 然, in its original sense, adds to the meaning of the new kanji.

Finally, in some cases a phonetic was chosen purely to show the pronunciation of the new kanji, without regard to the meaning of the phonetic component. For example, the character 十 (ジュウ *needle*; ten) is used as the phonetic of 汁(ジュウ broth), but there seems to be no connection in the latter with the meaning of "needle" or "ten."

Sometimes kanji created by these means were used as phonetics of more complex new characters, which might be used again in still more complex ones. The following is an example of one of the few cases of this found among the Jōyō Kanji:

刀 (トウ as phonetic)＋口 ("mouth" as semantic) →召 (ショウ summon) (トウ
　　and ショウ are related phonetically.)
召 (ショウ as phonetic)＋日 ("sun" as semantic) →昭 (ショウ bright)
昭(ショウ as phonetic)＋照 ("fire" as semantic) →照 (ショウ shine)

As we have seen, the *on-yomi* (Sino-Japanese readings) of a set of kanji containing the same phonetic component are not always identical to the reading of the phonetic component when it appears alone; in fact, sometimes there are a number of variations in pronunciation among kanji containing the same component.

Such natural changes in pronunciation may have been the result of any of a variety of causes: differences in dialects (cf. "drag" vs. "draw" in English), differences in speech styles (cf. "madam" vs. "ma'am"), differences in grammatical functions (cf. "address [the noun]" vs. "address [the verb]"), and so forth.

A given sound almost always changes to a similar one (e.g., $\underline{p}$ to $\underline{b}$, $\underline{b}$ to $\underline{m}$, etc). Likely sound changes can be arranged in a hierarchy, as shown below; sounds usually change in the direction of a neighboring sound, though given a long enough history, one sound might end up as any other. A glance at the diagram will reveal that the initial sounds of the *on-yomi* of 刀 (トウ) and 召 (ショウ) are very close. The final sounds of 較 (カク) and 交 (コウ) are not that far apart either: the final $\underline{k}$ changed to $\underline{g}$ which changed to $\underline{w}$ (the difference between the English "drag" and "draw" is similar). Only a few cases are not explainable in terms of the phonetic hierarchies. The sounds $\underline{k}$ and $\underline{l}$ ($\underline{r}$ in Japanese) alternated in Chinese in such related words as 各 (カク) and 落 (ラク). Likewise, Chinese $\underline{h}$ (later $\underline{k}$ in Japanese) and $\underline{m}$ sometimes alternated, giving such pairs as 海(カイ) and 毎(マイ).

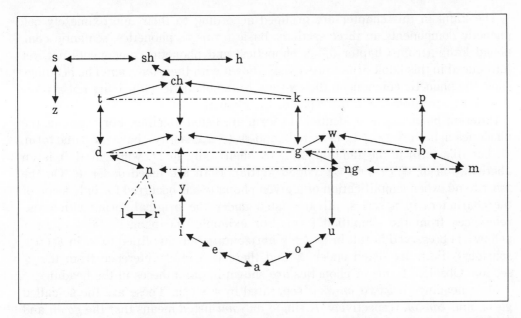

There were a number of differences between early Chinese and Japanese that further separate words that had been similarly pronounced:

Japanese syllables had to end in a vowel. When a word ending in a consonant in Chinese entered Japanese, an u or i had to be added. The kak of 較 became カ ク.

No h sound in Japanese corresponded to the h sound of Chinese. The Chinese h-like sounds became k or g in Japanese, so many of the h-s alternations (similar sounds) in Chinese became k-sh or g-sh alternations (dissimilar sounds).

There was no ng sound in Japanese distinct from a g sound. A final ng was soon lost, leaving only the u or i that had been added in Japanese.

There was no distinction between ch and s in Japanese. The various ch and s sounds of Chinese became s (or sh) sounds in Japanese. The t-ch alternation in Chinese (as with the tau and chieu of 刀 and 召) became even more disparate (タウ and セウ in the early period).

Finally, changes in Japanese itself over the centuries resulted in greater variations in the pronunciation of corresponding kanji:

Vowel sequences ending in u merged into a single long vowel. Thus, 交, originally カウ in Japanese, became the modern コウ, even further from the カク of 較 while 刀 (タウ) and 召 (セウ) became トウ and ショウ.

Pu and mu at the end of words changed. The p of pu sounds at the end of a word vanished; the remaining u then melded with the vowel sound that had preceded the p. For example, 十 (ten), originally pronounced something like zip, in Japanese might have been something like jipu, then ji(w)u and finally ジュウ, as we know it today. A mu at the end of a word became an n. The word 辛 (needle) was sim in early Chinese, something like shimu in early Japanese, and finally シン. (The first and last sounds of zip and sim are relatively close, but the Japanese sounds have grown rather far apart.)

These sorts of changes must be kept in mind when assessing the similarity of pronunciation of a kanji to that of its phonetic.

The kanji in this chapter are grouped according to their approximately 560 phonetic components, in three sections: basic forms as phonetics, semantic compound kanji (from Chapter 3) as phonetics, and phonetic components not yet introduced in this book or not previously shown with their *on-yomi*. The headings show the phonetic component, the *on-yomi* of the phonetic (which are not always Jōyō Kanji readings), and the sense of the phonetic.

Different phonetics now identical in form are listed together. For example, the phonetics in both 敗 (ハイ be defeated) and 貞 (テイ chastity) have the same form, 貝, but this form is the familiar 貝 (ハイ shell) only in 敗, while in 貞 it is an abbreviation of 鼎 (チョウ/テイ tripod kettle). Both are listed under 貝. On the other hand, when simplification of a given phonetic has occurred for only some of the characters in a series, all are listed under the original form, with cross references from the simplified form. For example, the phonetic 黄 (コウ/オウ yellow) is preserved in full in 横 (オウ horizontal) but simplified to ム in 広 (コウ spacious). Both are listed under 黄 and there is a cross-reference from the ム section. Obsolete forms of phonetics are shown in parentheses in the headings.

Most headings list two *on-yomi* separated by a slash. These are the so-called *go-on*, and *kan-on*, respectively. A single *on-yomi* listed means that the *go-on* and *kan-on* are the same. *Go-on* are Japanese approximations of the Chinese pronunciation of words (characters) that entered Japan with Buddhism before the eighth century and survive in vocabulary, much of it Buddhist in origin, popularized then. *Kan-on* are Japanese readings of Chinese words that arrived over the next five centuries; *kan-on* are the most commonly used *on-yomi* today. (Other types of *on-yomi*, the *tō-on*, and *sō-on*, which arrived after the twelfth century along with new products from China, are not included in the headings; neither are the *kan' yō-on*, "improper" *on-yomi* given to kanji in Japan. Except for a few case, as noted, these readings are of little relevance to the *on-yomi* patterns seen in series of similar kanji.)

When there is more than one pair of *on-yomi*, they are separated by the word "or" (in these cases, the Chinese allowed one character to stand for differently pronounced words). Two sets of *on-yomi* on two separate lines of the heading indicate either that the single modern form of the phonetic has derived from two different old forms or that the phonetic is substituting for a more complex form in one of the cases.

The meanings listed for the phonetics are those that the component has as a component, not necessarily as an independent kanji. The distinction between the obsolete and the current meanings of the phonetics is ignored (so there are no italicized glosses). The meaning of the phonetic is repeated in the description of the kanji only when it seems relevant; when it seems to be merely an arbitrary phonetic, such as where it was used merely as an onomatopoeic sign, only the form is mentioned.

Headings are ordered by increasing stroke count. Headings with the same number of strokes are in Japanese syllabary order.

In cases such as that of 召, above, in which newly made kanji act successively as phonetics for further new kanji, all the kanji in the group are shown under the same heading (listed, of course, by stroke order).

Basic Forms as Phonetics

This section contains all the Jōyō Kanji basic forms that are used as phonetics.

1-Stroke Phonetic

| 乙 ; し | (オツ/イツ) | (curve) |

                 (レイ)   (offering in a dish)

礼 (レイ/ライ) has し substituted for the phonetic of the old form 禮, a combination of 示 (altar) with the phonetic 豊 (レイ offering in a dish). It means "courtesy, bow; ceremony; gratitude."

    礼 (レイ bow; thanks), 礼拝 (ライ・ハイ/レイ・ハイ worship)

2-Stroke Phonetics

| 又 | (ウ/ユウ) | (hand) |

    受; 授 (舟, p. 147)

| 九 | (ク/キュウ) | (come to end and curve) |

究 (キュウ/きわ・める) combines 穴 (cave) and the phonetic 九 (come to the end). It means "carry through to the end."

    究明 (キュウ・メイ investigation), 究める (きわ・める go to extremes)

軌 (キ) is a combination of 車 (car) and the phonetic 九 (curve). It means "rut, track."

    軌道 (キ・ドウ tracks)

| 七 | (シチ/シツ) | (cut) |

切 (セツ/サイ/き・る) combines 刀 (knife) and the phonetic 七 (cut). It means "cut; pressing; closeness; earnest" or, read サイ, is used in words meaning "all."

    大切 (タイ・セツ important), 一切 (イッ・サイ all), 切る (き・る cut)

窃 (セツ) is a combination of 穴 (cave) and the phonetic 切 (cut). It means "steal, filch."

    窃盗 (セッ・トウ theft)

| 十 | (ジュウ/シュウ) | (needle; ten; gather) |

汁 (ジュウ/しる) consists of 氵 (water) and the phonetic 十. It means "juice, broth, soup."

    果汁 (カ・ジュウ fruit juice), みそ汁 (みそ・しる *miso* soup)

針 (シン/はり), a combination of 金 (metal) and the phonetic 十 (needle), means "needle."

    方針 (ホウ・シン policy), 針 (はり needle)

人；亻　(ニン/ジン)   (person)

仁 (ジン/ニ) combines 二 (ニ/ジ two) and 亻 (person). With 亻 as phonetic it means "human; humane; consideration, sympathy." In limited use with 二 as phonetic, "two."

　　仁義 (ジンギ humanity and justice), 仁王 (ニ・オウ *niō*, a pair of guardian gods)

丁　(チョウ/テイ or トウ/テイ)   (nail; stay put; strike; T-shape)

打 (ダ/う・つ), a combination of 扌 (hand) and the phonetic 丁 (nail), means "strike, hit." うつ, in the form うち, is used as an emphatic prefix for a verb.
　　打撃 (ダ・ゲキ blow), 打つ (う・つ strike)

庁 (チョウ) is an abbreviation of 廳 with 丁 chosen for its phonetic value nuder 广 (roof). It means "administration building; office, bureau."
　　官庁 (カン・チョウ government agency)

成 (セイ/ジョウ/な・る) combines 戊, a variant of 戈 (halberd), with the phonetic 丁 (strike); an earlier from was 成. It means "achieve; form, become."
　　成功 (セイ・コウ success), 成仏 (ジョウ・ブツ die; entering Nirvana), 成る (な・る become)

灯 (トウ/ひ), a combination of 火 (fire) and the phonetic 丁 (stay put), means "lamp, light."
　　灯台 (トウ・ダイ lighthouse), 灯 (ひ light)

町 (チョウ/まち) consists of 田 (field) and the phonetic 丁 (nail; T-shape), from an original sense of "foot-path between fields," it has come to mean "town." A チョウ is a unit of land area, of about 9,930 square meters, and a unit of length of approximately 109 meters.
　　町長 (チョウ・チョウ town headman), 町 (まち town)

亭 (テイ) has the phonetic 丁 (stay put) added to, and replacing the bottom ロ of, 高 (tall building). It means "inn" and is used in the names of inns and restaurants and even garden pavilions, as well as those of writers or comic storytellers.
　　料亭 (リョウ・テイ Japanese-style restaurant)

訂 (テイ) consists of 言 (say) and the phonetic 丁. It means "correct, revise text" or "conclude, settle," with reference to treaties and the like.
　　訂正 (テイ・セイ correction)

頂 (チョウ/いただ・く/いただき) combines 頁 (head) and the phonetic 丁 (nail). "Nail" and "head" together suggest "top, summit," or as a verb "hold over the head." The Japanese use it for ceremonious acceptance, and as a humble form for "receive."
　　絶頂 (ゼッ・チョウ peak), 頂く (いただ・く receive), 頂 (いただ・き top)

城 (ジョウ/しろ), a combination of 土 (soil) and the phonetic 成 (form up), means "castle."

城下町 (ジョウ・カ・マチ castle town), 城 (しろ castle)

盛 (セイ/ジョウ/も・る/さか・ん) combines 皿 (dish) and the phonetic 成 (form up). It means "dish up, fill; heap up; thrive; prime." In Japan it is also used for "full bloom" and "in heat."

盛大 (セイ・ダイ splendid), 繁盛 (ハン・ジョウ prosperity), 盛る (も・る dish up), 盛ん (さか・ん thriving)

停 (テイ) combines 亻 (person) and the phonetic 亭 (building to stay at) and means "stop, stay."

バス停 (バス・テイ bus stop)

貯 (チョ) consists of 貝 (wealth) and 宁 (spool of thread), not really related to 丁; it means "reserve, save."

貯金 (チョ・キン saving money)

誠 (セイ/まこと) is a combination of 言 (say) and the phonetic 成 (form) meaning "true, sincere."

誠意 (セイ・イ sincerity), 誠に (まこと・に truly)

刀 ; 刂 (トウ)   (edged tool; curved line)

召 (ショウ/め・す) is a combination of 口 (mouth) and the phonetic 刀. It means "summon." Japanese めす is also an honorific word meaning "eat, drink; take; wear."

召集 (ショウ・シュウ convoke), 召す (め・す summon; take; wear)

辺 (ヘン/あた・り/べ) uses 刀, with no phonetic justification, to replace the 臱 (メン/ヘン edge of nose) of the older form 邊. It means "edge, side, boundary, vicinity."

身辺 (シン・ペン around one), 辺り (あた・り vicinity), 海辺 (うみ・べ seaside)

到 (トウ) consists of 至 (reach) and the phonetic 刀 (curved line). It means "reach; approach."

到着 (トウ・チャク arrival)

招 (ショウ/まね・く), a combination of 扌 (hand) and the phonetic 召 (summon), means "invite".

招待 (ショウ・タイ invitation), 招く (まね・く invite)

沼 (ショウ/ぬま), a combination of 氵 (water) and the phonetic 召, means "swamp." One expert claims a connection between the "curved line" in the phonetic and the shape of a marsh's edge.

沼沢 (ショウ・タク marsh), 沼 (ぬま swamp)

昭 (ショウ) is a combination of 日 (sun) and the phonetic 召; it means "bright, clear."

昭和 (ショウ・ワ Showa era, 1926-1988)

倒 (トウ/たお・れる) combines 亻 (person) and the phonetic 到 (reach) and means "fall over, knock over; upside down."

倒産 (トウ・サン bankruptcy), 倒れる (たお・れる fall down)

紹 (ショウ) consists of 糸 (thread) and the phonetic 召 (summon) and means "introduce; succeed."

紹介 (ショウ・カイ introduction)

詔 (ショウ/みことのり) adds 言 (say) to the phonetic 召 (summon) and means "Imperial edict, rescript."

詔勅 (ショウ・チョク Imperial rescript), 詔 (みことのり Imperial edict)

超 (チョウ/こ・える) combines 走 (run) with the phonetic 召. It means "jump over; exceed; super-."

超過 (チョウ・カ excess), 超える (こ・える cross over; exceed)

照 (ショウ/て・る) adds 灬 (fire) to the phonetic 昭 (bright) to mean "shine; illuminate; compare."

照明 (ショウ・メイ lighting), 照る (て・る shine)

二 (ニ)   (two)

仁 (亻, p. 124)

弐 (ニ) combines 弋 (stake) with an extra dot and the phonetic 二 (two). It means "two," used mostly in writing monetary sums, or "double."

弐万円 (ニ・マン・エン 20,000 yen)

3-Stroke Phonetics

干 (カン)   (fork; stick)

刊 (カン) is a combination of 刂 (edged tool) and the phonetic 干 (stick). It means "cut, carve; print, publish."

週刊 (シュウ・カン weekly publication)

汗 (カン/あせ) consists of 氵 (water) and the phonetic 干. It means "sweat." It is used also to transliterate "Khan," the title of a Turkish or Mongolian chieftan.

ジンギス汗 (ジンギス・カン Genghis Khan), 汗 (あせ sweat)

肝 (カン/きも) consists of 月 (flesh) and the phonetic 干 (stick). It means "liver" or "essential." In Japan its meanings extend to "gall bladder; mind, consciousness; guts, nerve, spirit."

肝心 (カン・ジン essential), 肝 (きも liver; spirit)

軒 (ケン/のき) is a combination of 車 (wheel) and the phonetic 干 (stick). It originally referred to a fancy carriage with a high railing and also to curved eaves. It is used now for "eaves," often part of the name of a restaurant; and in Japan it is a counter for houses.

軒数 (ケン・スウ number of houses), 軒 (のき eaves)

幹 (カン/みき) combines 㫃 (banner), 日 (sun), and the phonetic 干 (stick). It means "stem, trunk; main, primary; ability."

新幹線 (シン・カン・セン new trunk line; Shinkansen [train]), 幹 (みき trunk)

岸 (ガン/きし) consists of 山 (mountain) and the phonetic 厈 (ガン), made of 厂 (cliff) and the phonetic 干. It means "shore, bank."

海岸 (カイ・ガン seashore), 岸 (きし shore; riverbank)

弓 (キュウ)   (bow; curve)

強 (キョウ/ゴウ/つよ・い/し・いる) is a combination of ム (round), 虫 (insect), and a reduction of the phonetic 彊 (キョウ strong bow). Originally used to write the name of a hard-shelled beetle, it is now used for "strong, tough; strengthen; force," and, suffixed to a number, (as キョウ) "and a little bit more, plus."

強力 (キョウ・リョク powerful), 強引 (ゴウ・イン coercive), 強い (つよ・い strong), 強いる (し・いる compel)

窮 (キュウ/きわ・める) consists of 穴 (cave) and the phonetic 躬 (キュウ bowed), itself a combination of 身 (body) and the phonetic 弓 (bow). It means "reach the limit; utmost; straits, predicament."

窮乏 (キュウ・ボウ destitution), 窮める (きわ・める reach an extreme)

己 (コ/キ)   (winding thread; design; zigzag line)

妃 (ヒ) is a combination of 女 (woman) and a reduction of 配 (ハイ adjoin) as a phonetic. It refers to a royal wife or female consort.

皇太子妃 (コウ・タイ・シ・ヒ Crown Princess consort)

改 (カイ/あらた・める) combines 攵(action)and the phonetic 己(winding thread). It means "mend, renovate; change; check over, verify."

改良 (カイ・リョウ improvement), 改める (あらた・める rectify; examine)

忌 (キ/い・む) is a combination of 心 (heart) and the phonetic 己 (winding thread). It means "abominate, shun; mourn."

忌中 (キ・チュウ in mourning), 忌む (い・む abhor)

紀 (キ) combines 糸 (thread) and the phonetic 己 (winding thread), originally meaning "starting end of thread, beginning," now "reasoning, the line one should hew to; record, account, chronicle; period, era."

世紀 (セイ・キ century)

記 (キ/しる・す) has 言 (say) with the phonetic 己 (zigzag line), and means "write down, memorize; written record."

　記事 (キ・ジ account; article) , 記す (しる・す write down)

起 (キ/おき・る) is a combination of 走 (move feet) and the phonetic 己 (winding thread). It means "initiate; beginning; get up, arise; occur."

　起源 (キ・ゲン origin), 起きる (お・きる arise)

工 (ク/コウ)　　　　　　　　　　　　(ax; manual work; penetrate; process)

功 (コウ/ク) adds 力 (strength) to the phonetic 工 (manual work). It means "work out; result, effect; merits, successes."

　功 (コウ merit), 功徳 (ク・ドク pious act)

江 (コウ/え) consists of 氵 (water) and the phonetic 工 (penetrate) and means "large river; the Yangtze" and, in Japan, "inlet."

　長江 (チョウ・コウ the Yangtze), 入り江 (い・り・え inlet)

攻 (コウ/せめ・る), a combination of 攵 (action) and the phonetic 工 (ax), means "attack."

　専攻 (セン・コウ academic major), 攻める (せめ・る attack)

空 (クウ/そら/あ・く/から) is a combination of 穴 (cave) and the phonetic 工 (penetrate). It means "empty, void, sky; nothingness."

　空気 (クウ・キ air), 空 (そら sky; から empty), 空く (あ・く become vacant)

紅 (コウ/ク/べに/くれない) consists of 糸 (thread) and the phonetic 工 (process). It used to mean "red thread or cloth," and now means "red, crimson; rouge."

　紅白 (コウ・ハク red & white), 真紅 (シン・ク deep red), 紅 (べに rouge; くれない crimson)

貢 (コウ/ク/みつ・ぐ) is a combination of 貝 (wealth) and the phonetic 工 (penetrate). It means "tribute, tax."

　貢献 (コウ・ケン contribution), 年貢 (ネン・グ land tax; rent), 貢ぐ (みつ・ぐ finance)

項 (コウ), a combination of 頁 (head) and 工 (penetrate), once meant "nape of the neck." It now means "neck" or "item, article, clause" as in a document.

　項目 (コウ・モク item)

恐 (キョウ/おそ・れる) consists of 心 (heart) and the phonetic 巩 (キョウ make hole); the latter is a combination of what once represented a person, accenting the hands, and the phonetic 工 (ax). It means "threaten; fear; fearful," and is used in words in Japan that express apology, embarrassment, and surprise.

　恐縮 (キョウ・シュク feel small), 恐れる (おそ・れる fear)

控 (コウ/ひか・える) is a combination of 扌 (hand) and the phonetic 空 (void, empty). It means "withdraw" as well as a probably unrelated sense. "sue"; and in

Japan "stand by; be in reserve; restrain; refrain; jot down."

控除 (コウ・ジョ deduction), 控える (ひか・える hold back; note down; stand by)

| 才 | (ザイ/サイ) (block off; cutting)

在 (ザイ/あ・る) is a combination of 土 (earth) and the phonetic 才 (block off). It means "stay, remain; exist" and, in Japan, "outlying areas, the suburbs, the country."

在日 (ザイ・ニチ staying in Japan), 在る (あ・る be)

材 (ザイ) consists of 木 (tree) and the phonetic 才 (cutting). It means "lumber" and, derivatively, "material; human resources, talent."

材料 (ザイ・リョウ material)

財 (ザイ/サイ) is a combination of 貝 (wealth) and the phonetic 才 (cutting). It means "property, financial resources; finance."

財界 (ザイ・カイ financial world), 財布 (サイ・フ purse)

栽 (サイ) consists of 木 (tree) and the phonetic 弋 (cutting), a combination of 戈 (halberd) and the phonetic 才 (cutting). It means "prune, trim."

盆栽 (ボン・サイ *bonsai*)

裁 (サイ/た・つ/さば・く) combines 衣 (garment) with the phonetic 弋 (cutting). It means "cut, trim, tailor," and also "decide, pass judgment." As a kind of abbreviation, it may also mean "court" in Japan.

裁量 (サイ・リョウ discretion), 裁つ (た・つ cut), 裁く (さば・く judge)

載 (サイ/の・せる) is a combination of 車 (wheel) and the phonetic 弋 (stop). It means "load, let ride; place on; print."

連載 (レン・サイ serialization), 載せる (の・せる load)

| 士 | (ジ/シ) (male; stand by)

仕 (シ/ジ/つか・える) puts イ (person) alongside the phonetic 士 (stand by). It means "serve, wait on." In Japan it has picked up a sense "do, doing" by phonological association with a form of the verb する (do).

仕事 (シ・ごと job), 給仕 (キュウ・ジ waiter), 仕える (つか・える serve)

| 子 | (シ) (child)

字 (ジ/あざ) has the phonetic 子 (child) under 宀 (roof, house). It originally meant "have children," but came to be used for characters produced by the combination of other characters and was subsequently generalized to "letter, written character." In Japan, as あざ, it refers to named subsections of a town or village.

字 (ジ letter; あざ village section)

勺 (ジャク/シャク) (ladle)

的 (テキ/まと) combines 白 (white) and the phonetic 勺 (ladle). It means something "distinct" or "target; hit the mark." It is used to form adjectives from nouns in Japanese, perhaps partly under the influence of English "-tic."
的確 (テキ・カク exact), 的 (まと target)

酌 (シャク/く・む) adds 酉 (wine jar) to 勺 (ladle), the phonetic. It means "serving of liquor; have a drink" or "arrange, make allowances."
晩酌 (バン・シャク evening drink) , 酌む (く・む decant; drink)

釣 (チョウ/つ・る) is a combination of 金 (metal) and the phonetic 勺 (ladle). It means "to fish, angle" and in Japan also means "change received when paying with too large a denomination."
釣果 (チョウ・カ catch of fish), 釣り合う (つ・り・あ・う be in balance)

小 (ショウ) (small)

肖 (ショウ) is a combination of 月 (flesh) and the phonetic 小 (small) originally meaning something like "a miniature." It now means "model; semblance; resemble."
肖像 (ショウ・ゾウ portrait)

削 (サク/けず・る) consists of 刂 (edged tool) and the phonetic 肖 (diminish). It means "shave, plane, whittle; delete."
削減 (サク・ゲン curtailment), 削る (けず・る scrape off; curtail)

宵 (ショウ/よい) combines 宀 (roof, house) and the phonetic 肖 (diminish). It means "evening, night." One scholar connects it with diminishing light.
徹宵 (テッ・ショウ all-night vigil), 宵 (よい early evening)

消 (ショウ/き・える/け・す) is a combination of 氵 (water) and the phonetic 肖 (diminish). It means "diminish," like evaporating water, or "erase; extinguish."
消費 (ショウ・ヒ consumption), 消える (き・える go out; vanish), 消す (け・す erase; put out)

硝 (ショウ) is a combination of 石 (stone) and the phonetic 肖 (diminish) and means "saltpeter."
硝酸 (ショウ・サン nitric acid)

寸 (スン/ソン) (hand)

村 (ソン/ムラ) is a combination of 木 (tree) and the phonetic 寸 (hand). It means "village."
農村 (ノウ・ソン farm village), 村 (むら village)

討 (トウ/う・つ) combines 言 (say) and a reduction of 肘 (チュウ elbow), a combination of 月 (flesh) and 寸 (hand). It means "inquire into; attack with weapons."

討論 (トウ・ロン debate), 討つ (う・つ attack)

夕 (ジャク/セキ)   (evening)
(ガツ/ゲツ)   (moon, wane)

外 (ガイ/ゲ/そと/ほか/はず・す) is a combination of 卜 (divination) and the phonetic 夕 (moon, wane). It means "outside; other, besides; foreign" and in Japan "not coincide; remove, come off; miss; be away from."

外交 (ガイ・コウ diplomacy), 外科 (ゲ・カ surgery), 外 (そと outside; ほか other),
外す (はず・す remove)

山 (セン/サン)   (mountain)

仙 (セン) combines 亻 (person) and the phonetic 山 (mountain). It means "hermit, ascetic," one associated with such magical powers as levitation.

仙人 (セン・ニン hermit wizard)

川 (セン)   (river; pass through)

訓 (クン) is a combination of 言 (say) and the phonetic 川 (river; pass through). It means "teach, indoctrinate; interpret the written word." From the latter comes its Japanese use as "translation reading of kanji."

教訓 (キョウ・クン teachings)

大 (ダイ/タイ)   (spread-eagle person; large; plenty)

泰 (タイ) consists of 水 (water) and a representation of two hands blended with the phonetic 大 (large; plenty). It means "at peace, composed; extreme."

泰然 (タイ・ゼン calm)

達 (タツ) is a combination of 辶 (walk), 羊 (sheep; easy delivery), and the phonetic, a modified 大 (large; plenty), on top. It means "get there without a hitch, reach, arrive; inform; superior, advanced."

配達 (ハイ・タツ delivery)

土 (ツ/ト)   (earth; ground; soil)

吐 (ト/は・く) is a combination of 口 (mouth) and the phonetic 土 (soil). It means "vomit, spew."

吐息 (ト・いき sigh), 吐く (は・く vomit)

社 (シャ/やしろ) combines 礻 (altar) and the phonetic 土 (earth). It originally meant "earth god, local diety," or a shrine to one, and now means "shrine" or, presumably via a sense like "parish," "group of people with a common interest; company; society, the world."

社会 (シャ・カイ society), 社 (やしろ shrine)

徒 (ト) is a combination of 彳 (go), 止 (foot), and the phonetic 土 (ground). It means "walk, stroll; without purpose; follower, fellow."

徒労 (ト・ロウ fruitless labor)

達 (大, p. 131)

女 (ニョ/ジョ)   (woman)

奴 (ド) is a combination of 又 (hand) and the phonetic 女 (woman). It means "slave, servant," typified originally by female servants.

奴隷 (ド・レイ slave)

如 (ジョ/ニョ) is a combination of 口 (mouth) and the phonetic 女 (woman). The kanji may have been designed to bring out the sense "compliant" of the word used for "woman"; it now means "be like" and has been used as a suffix to make certain descriptive words.

欠如 (ケツ・ジョ deficiency), 如実 (ニョ・ジツ realistic)

努 (ド/つと・める) combines 力 (strength) with the phonetic 奴 (slave). It means "endeavor."

努力 (ド・リョク effort), 努める (つと・める try hard)

怒 (ド/いか・る/おこ・る) is a combination of 心 (heart) and the phonetic 奴 (slave). It means "violent; fury, anger."

喜怒 (キ・ド joy and anger), 怒る (いか・る be furious; おこ・る get mad)

4-Stroke Phonetics

王 (オウ)   (big ax; king)

狂 (キョウ/くる・う) is a combination of 犭 (dog) and the phonetic 王 (big ax). It means "madness; crazy, comic; wild, erratic."

狂気 (キョウ・キ insanity), 狂う (くる・う go crazy; wrong)

往 (オウ) is a combination of 彳 (go), a dot as the remnant of a symbol for a foot, and the phonetic 王 (big ax). It means "go, go away; past."

往復 (オウ・フク going and returning)

皇 (コウ/オウ) consists of 自 (nose; first) reduced by a stroke and the phonetic 王 (king). It referred to a legendary first king of mankind, perhaps, and came to be used for "emperor."

皇居 (コウ・キョ Imperial Palace), 天皇 (テン・ノウ Emperor of Japan)

戸 (コ)   (door)

所 (ショ/ところ) combines 斤 (hatchet) and the phonetic 戸. It means "place, site" and also forms a nominalized passive-like expression, "that which is . . . ," in Chinese and Sino-Japanese and is used for or in counters of places in Japanese.

所得 (ショ・トク income), 所 (ところ place; address)

雇 (コ/やと・う) is a combination of 隹 (bird) and the phonetic 戸. It looks like "keeping a bird," and it means "hire, employ."
　解雇 (カイ・コ dismissal), 雇う (やと・う hire)

顧 (コ/かえり・みる) consists of 頁 (head) and the phonetic 雇 (employ) and means "look back; care for, treasure."
　顧問 (コ・モン advisor), 顧みる (かえり・みる look back)

五 (ゴ)　　　　　　　　　　　　　　　　　　　　　　(spool)

悟 (ゴ/さと・る) is a combination of 忄, a regular variant of 心 (heart) and the phonetic 吾 (ゴ talk), which consists of 口 (mouth) and the phonetic 五 (spool). It means "realize, discern."
　覚悟 (カク・ゴ resolve; readiness), 悟る (さと・る realize; be spiritually awakened)

語 (ゴ/かた・る) adds 言 (say) to the phonetic 吾 (ゴ talk) and means "talk, tell; word; language."
　外来語 (ガイ・ライ・ゴ borrowed word), 語る (かた・る talk)

午 (ゴ)　　　　　　　　　　　　　　　　　　　　　　(pounder)

卸 (おろ・す/おろし) combines 卩 (kneeling person), 止 (foot), and the phonetic 午 (pounder), but the *on-yomi* シャ of this character is not included in the Jōyō Kanji. It means "unload" and in Japan "wholesale."
　卸す (おろ・す sell wholesale), たな卸 (たな・おろし stocktaking; faultfinding)

許 (キョ/ゆる・す) is a combination of 言 (say) and the phonetic 午 (pounder), and means "permit."
　許可 (キョ・カ permission), 許す (ゆる・す allow)

御 (ギョ/ゴ/おん) is a combination of 彳 (go), 止 (foot), 卩 (kneeling person), and the phonetic 午 (pounder). It meant "control a horse, rein" and now means "control, manage." Originally also used as an adjective, or honorific prefix, meaning "His Imperial Majesty's," it has been "debased" in Japan to a prefix for general politeness, and it is also used in place of 禦, a non-Jōyō Kanji meaning "defend."
　御する (ギョ・する control), 御主人 (ゴ・シュ・ジン your/her husband; master),
　御中 (おん・チュウ Messrs.)

月 (ゲツ)　　　　　　　　　　　　　　　　　　　　　(moon)

朝; 潮 (舟, p. 147)

斤 (コン/キン) (hatchet)

近 (キン/ちか・い) combines ⻌ (walk) and the phonetic 斤 (hatchet). It means "approach; near" in the spatial and temporal senses.

近所 (キン・ジョ neighborhood), 近い (ちか・い near)

祈 (キ/いの・る), a combination of ネ (altar) and the phonetic 斤 (hatchet), means "pray."

祈願 (キ・ガン prayer), 祈る (いの・る pray)

止 (シ) (foot; stop)

市 (シ/いち) is a blend of 平 (even) and the phonetic 止 (stop). It means "market; city."

市民 (シ・ミン citizen), 市場 (いち・ば marketplace; シ・ジョウ commodities market)

姉 (シ/あね) is a combination of 女 (woman) and 市. It means "elder sister" and is used in words referring to women honorifically.

姉妹 (シ・マイ older and younger sisters), 姉 (あね elder sister)

祉 (シ) combines ネ (altar) and the phonetic 止 (stop) and means "blessing."

福祉 (フク・シ welfare)

歯 (シ/は) is originally a picture of a mouth showing two rows of teeth, a little easier to see in the older form 齒, marked with the phonetic 止 (stop). It means "tooth; cog; age."

歯科医 (シ・カ・イ dentist), 歯 (は tooth)

氏 (シ) (spoon; flat)

紙 (シ/かみ) combines 糸 (thread, fiber) with the phonetic 氏 (flat) to mean "paper," including "newspaper."

和紙 (ワ・シ Japanese paper), 紙 (かみ paper)

婚 (民, p. 145)

尺 (シャク) (*shaku* [0.3 maters])
(ヤク/エキ) (single out; chained)

(All instances of 尺 among the Jōyō Kanji are actually simplified replacements of 睪, which is a combination of 目 (eye) and 幸 (handcuff).)

択 (タク) combines 扌 (hand) and the phonetic 尺 (single out) and means "select."

選択 (セン・タク selection)

沢 (タク/さわ) is a conbination of ⺡ (water) and the phonetic 尺 (chained). It means "swamp; water; benefit; luster."

光沢 (コウ・タク luster), 沢 (さわ swamp)

釈 (シャク) is a combination of 釆 (scatter) and the phonetic 尺 (single out). It means "undo, disentangle; interpret," and it was also selected for the transliteration and abbreviation of Sakyamuni, the name of the current Buddha.

釈放 (シャク・ホウ release)

訳 (ヤク/わけ) is a combination of 言 (say) and the phonetic 尺 (single out). It means "interpret, translate; meaning; reason."

訳 (ヤク translation; わけ meaning; reason)

駅 (エキ) consists of 馬 (horse) and the phonetic 尺 (chained) and means "post station" or nowadays "train station."

東京駅 (トウ・キョウ・エキ Tokyo Station)

井 (セイ/ショウ)   (well)

　(ケイ)   (square frame)

刑 (ケイ) combines 刂 (edged tool) and a variation of the phonetic 井 (square frame). It means "punishment."

刑事 (ケイ・ジ criminal affairs; police detective)

形 (ケイ/ギョウ/かた/かたち) is a combination of 彡 (design) and a variation of the phonetic 井 (square) meaning "shape, form."

形成 (ケイ・セイ formation), 人形 (ニン・ギョウ doll; puppet), 女形 (おんな・がた male actor in female role), 形 (かた/かたち shape)

耕 (コウ/たがや・す) consists of 耒 (plow) and the phonetic 井 (square). It means "till, cultivate."

耕作 (コウ・サク cultivation), 耕す (たがや・す till)

型 (ケイ/かた) is a combination of 土 (earth) and the phonetic 刑 (carve a square). It means "mold" or in Japan, "model, type."

模型 (モ・ケイ model), 型 (かた mold; model, type)

升 (ショウ)   (ladle up; raise)

昇 (ショウ/のぼ・る) combines 日 (sun) and the phonetic 升 (raise, rise), and means "rise."

昇給 (ショウ・キュウ increase in salary)

中 (チュウ)   (middle, center; inside)

仲 (チュウ/なか) is a combination of 亻 (person) and the phonetic 中 (middle). It means "mediation" or, in Japan, "interpersonal relationship."

仲裁 (チュウ・サイ arbitration), 仲 (なか relation)

沖 (チュウ/おき) consists of 氵 (water) and the phonetic 中 (middle) and means "deep" and, in Japan, "the offing."

沖積層 (チュウ・セキ・ソウ alluvial bed), 沖 (おき offing)

忠 (チュウ), a combination of 心 (heart) and the phonetic 中 (center), means "wholehearted; loyal."

忠告 (チュウ・コク advice)

衷 (チュウ) has the phonetic 中 (inside) inside 衣 (garment); it means "inner, dead center."

衷心 (チュウ・シン innermost heart)

屯 (チュウ or ドン/トン)   (sprout)

純 (ジュン) is a combination of 糸 (thread), and the phonetic 屯 (sprout). It meant "undyed thread" and now means "pure, unsullied."

純情 (ジュン・ジョウ naivety)

鈍 (ドン/にぶ・い) is a combination of 金 (metal) and the phonetic 屯 (sprout). It means "dull, not sharp," and, in Japan, this is extended to the realm of color or sound.

鈍感 (ドン・カン insensitive), 鈍い (にぶ・い dull)

日 (ニチ/ジツ)   (sun)
 (ボウ)   (cover, hide)

冒 (ボウ/おか・す) was earlier written 冐, combining 目 (eye) and the phonetic 冂 (cover, hide); it meant "cover, cap," but came to be used for "venture, dare."

冒険 (ボウ・ケン adventure), 冒す (おか・す dare)

帽 (ボウ) has 巾 (cloth) added to the phonetic 冒 (cover, cap) to keep the original meaning of "hat, cap" of 冒 distinct from "venture, dare."

帽子 (ボウ・シ hat, cap)

比 (ヒ)   (lined up; compare)

批 (ヒ) is a combination of 扌 (hand) and the phonetic 比 (compare). It means "criticize."

批評 (ヒ・ヒョウ critique)

陛 (ヘイ) combines 阝 (mound) and the phonetic 坒 (ヒ/ヘイ stairs), which is in turn a combination of 土 (earth) and the phonetic 比 (lined up). It means the high-rising stone steps to a palace and is used for indirect reference to the emperor in Japan.

陛下 (ヘイ・カ His Majesty the Emperor)

父 (フ)   (father)

布 (フ/ぬの) is a combination of 巾 (cloth) and a modification of 父 as phonetic. It means "cloth; spread, expand."

配布 (ハイ・フ wide distribution), 布 (ぬの cloth)

怖 (フ/こわ・い) is a combination of 忄 (heart) and the phonetic 布 meaning "dread."

恐怖 (キョウ・フ terror), 怖い (こわ・い scary)

不 (フ/フウ)   (calyx; bud)

否 (ヒ/いな) combines 口 (mouth) and the phonetic 不. It means "say no, negate, deny; no."

否定 (ヒ・テイ denial), 否 (いな/ヒ nay)

杯 (ハイ/さかずき) is a combination of 木 (wood) and the phonetic 不 (calyx) to mean "cup, chalice, goblet; bowl" and is used as a counter for cupsful, bowlsful, spoonsful, etc.

祝杯 (シュク・ハイ celebratory drink), 杯 (さかずき *sake* cup)

倍 (バイ) combines 亻 (person) with the phonetic 咅, a variant form of 否 (ブ/フウ) meaning "separate." From a possible original meaning like "divide in two," 倍 developed the sense of "double, -tuple."

二倍 (ニ・バイ double)

剖 (ボウ) combines 刂 (edged tool) and the phonetic 咅 (separate), and means "cut off."

解剖 (カイ・ボウ dissection; autopsy)

培 (バイ/つちか・う) consists of 土 (earth) and the phonetic 咅. It means "foster."

栽培 (サイ・バイ culture), 培う (つちか・う cultivate)

陪 (バイ), a combination of 阝 (mound) and the phonetic 咅, means "stay close to, accompany."

陪審 (バイ・シン jury)

部 (ブ) is a combination of 阝 (village) and the phonetic 咅 (separate). It means "divide; part, section"; it is also used as a counter for parts or sections, and for copies of books, newspapers, etc.

部品 (ブ・ヒン parts)

賠 (バイ) is a combination of 貝 (wealth) and the phonetic 咅. It means "compensate."

賠償 (バイ・ショウ compensation)

方 (ホウ)   (spade; direction; stretch)

芳 (ホウ/かんば・しい) consists of 艹 (plant) and the phonetic 方 (spade). It means "fragrant," like freshly spaded grass, for example, from which comes a use as an honorific modifier. In Japan it also means "flowery; favorable, splendid."

芳香 (ホウ・コウ fragrance), 芳しい (かんば・しい fragrant; favorable)

坊 (ボウ/ボッ) combines 土 (earth) and the phonetic 方 (spade); it means "section of town; living quarters of priests and Imperial princes." In Japan it can mean "priest; little boy."

> 坊さん (ボウ・さん bonze) , 坊ちゃん (ボッ・ちゃん young son; little boy [honorific])

妨 (ボウ/さまた・げる) is a combination of 女 (woman) with the phonetic 方 (direction) meaning "obstruct, interrupt."

> 妨害 (ボウ・ガイ obstruction), 妨げる (さまた・げる disturb)

防 (ボウ/ふせ・ぐ) combines 阝 (mound) and the phonetic 方 (direction) and means "defend; prevent."

> 防犯 (ボウ・ハン crime prevention), 防ぐ (ふせ・ぐ defend)

放 (ホウ/はな・す), a combination of 攵 (action) and the phonetic 方 (stretch), means "turn loose, let go; leave be, let alone."

> 放送 (ホウ・ソウ broadcast), 放す (はな・す let free)

房 (ボウ/ふさ) is a combination of 戸 (door) and the phonetic 方 (direction). It referred to rooms that projected from both sides of a house. It means "chamber, bedroom; house" and it may refer indirectly to the occupant of one of those. In Japan it is further used for "tassle, fringe; tuft; cluster (of flowers), bunch (of grapes), section (of an orange)."

> 暖房 (ダン・ボウ heating), 房 (ふさ fringe; cluster)

肪 (ボウ), a combination of 月 (flesh) and the phonetic 方 (stretch), means "fat, grease."

> 脂肪 (シ・ボウ fat)

紡 (ボウ/つむ・ぐ) is a combination of 糸 (thread) and the phonetic 方 (stretch). It means "spin thread."

> 紡績 (ボウ・セキ spinning), 紡ぐ (つむ・ぐ make yarn)

訪 (ホウ/おとず・れる/たず・ねる) consists of 言 (say) and the phonetic 方; it means "seek out; visit."

> 訪米 (ボウ・ベイ visit to U. S.), 訪れる (おとず・れる visit; arrive), 訪ねる (たず・ねる call upon)

倣 (ホウ/なら・う) combines 亻 (person) and the phonetic 放. It means "emulate."

> 模倣 (モ・ホウ imitation), 倣う (なら・う emulate)

傍 (ボウ/かたわ・ら) combines 亻 (person) with the phonetic 旁 (ボウ both sides) and means "near; alongside."

> 傍観 (ボウ・カン look on), 傍ら (かたわ・ら alongside)

毛 (モウ/ボウ)　　　　　　　　　　　　　　　　　　　　(hair; thin)

耗 (モウ/コウ) is a combination of 耒 (plow) and the phonetic 毛 (thin). It means "lessen, diminish."

消耗 (ショウ・モウ consumption), 耗弱 (コウ・ジャク weaken)

木 (モク/ボク)   (tree; wood)

新; 親; 薪 (辛, p. 150)

文 (モン/ブン)   (design)

蚊 (か) is a combination of 虫 (insect) and the phonetic 文; the Chinese word for "mosquito" probably mimicked a mosquito's hum. The *on-yomi*, モン and ブン, are not included in the Jōyō Kanji.

紋 (モン) combines 糸 (thread) and the phonetic 文 (design). It means "woven design; design, pattern," and, in Japan, "family crest."

指紋 (シ・モン fingerprint), 紋 (モン crest)

予 (ヨ)   (weaving shuttle; stretch)

序 (ジョ) consists of 广 (roof) and the phonetic 予 (stretch). It meant something like "front porch" originally, and is now used in the senses of "starting point; preface; order, sequence."

序幕 (ジョ・マク prologue)

野 (ヤ/の) is a combination of 里 (field) and the phonetic 予 (stretch) and means "moor, field, wilds; wild, untamed" or in Japan "baseball field."

野菜 (ヤ・サイ vegetable), 野原 (の・はら grasslands)

預 (ヨ/あず・ける) is a combination of 頁 (head) and the phonetic 予 (stretch). It meant "in advance, beforehand," and "entrust"; Japanese extends the latter sense just slightly to "check, deposit; be entrusted with, keep for someone."

預金 (ヨ・キン bank deposit), 預ける (あず・ける entrust; deposit)

5-Stroke Phonetics

甘 (カン)   (sweet)

勘 (カン) consists of 力 (strength) and the phonetic 甚 (ジン/カン deep), a combination of 匹 (pair) and 甘 (sweet). It meant "consider; count" and, in Japan, "intuition."

勘定 (カン・ジョウ account; bill)

紺 (コン) combines 糸 (thread) and the phonetic 甘 and means "deep blue."

敢 (カン) consists of 攵 (action) and perhaps a merger of an element for "hand" with the phonetic 甘. It meant "venture, dare."

敢行 (カン・コウ carry out resolutely)

堪 (カン/た・える) is a combination of 土 (earth) and the phonetic 甚 (deep). It means "bear, withstand."

堪忍 (カン・ニン patience), 堪える (た・える endure)

厳 （ゲン／ゴン／おごそ・か／きび・しい） in its old form, 嚴, consists of two mouths carping and the phonetic 厰 （ガン stern）, itself a combination of 厂 （cliff） and the phonetic 敢 （dare）. It means "austere, solemn; stern, strict" and is an element of some honorific words for "father."

　厳格 （ゲン・カク strict）, 荘厳 （ソウ・ゴン solemnity）, 厳か （おごそ・か solemn）, 厳しい （きび・しい severe; stern）

☐甲 （キョウ／コウ）   (shell)

押 （オウ／お・す） is a combination of 扌 （hand） and the phonetic 甲 （shell）. It means "press, stamp; hold down" and, in Japan, "push."

　押収 （オウ・シュウ impoundment）, 押す （お・す push; stamp）

岬 （みさき） combines 山 （mountain） and the phonetic 甲, although the *on-yomi* コウ is not included in the Jōyō Kanji. It means "cape, point."

☐古 （ク／コ）   (hard; stay; old)

居 （キョ／い・る） combines 尸 （buttocks） and the phonetic 古 （stay）. It means "stay; reside."

　別居 （ベッ・キョ separation）, 居る （い・る stay）

苦 （ク／くる・しい／にが・い） consists of 艹 （grass） and the phonetic 古 （hard）. It means "bitter; hard to bear; distress."

　苦労 （ク・ロウ hardship）, 苦しい （くる・しい tormenting）, 苦い （にが・い bitter）

固 （コ／かた・める） is a combination of 囗 （enclosure） and the phonetic 古 （hard）. It means "hard, solid; congeal; unbending."

　頑固 （ガン・コ stubborn）, 固める （かた・める harden; solidify）

故 （コ／ゆえ） consists of 攵 （action） and the phonetic 古 （old）. Its meaning is quite abstract, encompassing "old, the old; the late, dead; obstacle; deliberate, premeditated; cause; foregoing state of affairs."

　事故 （ジ・コ accident）, 故に （ゆえ・に consequently）

枯 （コ／か・れる）, a combination of 木 （tree） and the phonetic 古 （old）, means "wither, die."

　枯渇 （コ・カツ drying up）, 枯れる （か・れる wither）

個 （コ） consists of 亻 （person） and the phonetic 固 （solid）. It means "individual" and is used as a counter for things in general.

　個人 （コ・ジン individual）

据 （す・える） combines 扌 （hand） and the phonetic 居 （stay） for "place, lay, set," although its *on-yomi* キョ is not included in the Jōyō Kanji.

湖 （コ／みずうみ） is a combination of 氵 （water） and the phonetic 胡 （コ large cover）, made up of 月 （flesh） and the phonetic 古. It means "lake."

　人造湖 （ジン・ゾウ・コ man-made lake）, 湖 （みずうみ lake）

箇 (カ) is a combination of 竹 (bamboo) and the phonetic 固 (solid). It means "item" and was used as a counter for things with another reading, コ, a use generally taken over by the related 個 (コ); it is now used as an element of counters for places, articles or clauses of contracts and the like, and months.

一箇所 (イッ・カ・ショ one place)

| 去 | (コ/キョ) | (container; concave) |

却 (キャク) combines 卩 (person kneeling) with the phonetic 去 (concave), and means "leave, depart; remove, get rid of; reject."

退却 (タイ・キャク retreat)

脚 (キャク/キャ/あし) consists of 月 (flesh) and the phonetic 却 (leave) and means "leg; footing." It is also a counter for chairs, desks, and the like.

失脚 (シッ・キャク loss of position), 脚立 (キャ・たつ stepladder), 脚 (あし leg)

| 示 ; ネ | (ジ/シ) | (altar) |

視 (シ) is a combination of 見 (see) and the phonetic ネ. It means "sight; look carefully; regard; consider."

近視 (キン・シ nearsightedness)

| 且 | (シャ or ソ/ショ) | (pile on; heap) |

助 (ジョ/たす・ける/すけ) combines 力 (strength) and the phonetic 且 (pile on) and means "assist, help."

救助 (キュウ・ジョ rescue), 助ける (たす・ける help), 助太刀 (すけ・だ・ち assistance)

阻 (ソ/はば・む) consists of 阝 (mound) and the phonetic 且 (heap) and means "hinder; steep."

阻止 (ソ・シ block), 阻む (はば・む obstruct)

査 (サ) is a combination of 木 (wood) and the phonetic 且 (heap). Its meaning has shifted from "wooden fence" to "inspect."

検査 (ケン・サ inspection)

祖 (ソ) a combination of ネ (altar) and the phonetic 且 (heap), means "ancestor; founder."

祖父 (ソ・フ grandfather)

租 (ソ) consists of 禾 (crops) and the phonetic 且 (heap). It means "tribute."

租税 (ソ・ゼイ levies)

粗 (ソ/あら・い) combines 米 (rice) and the phonetic 且. It means "coarse, crude."

粗末 (ソ・マツ crude; plain), 粗い (あら・い coarse)

組 (ソ/く・む/くみ) is a combination of 糸 (thread) and the phonetic 且 (pile on). It means "plait, unite, assemble." In Japan it is also used as the abbreviation of a word for "labor union" and as a counter for things in sets or pairs.

組閣 (ソ・カク formation of a cabinet), 組む (く・む plait; unite), 組合 (くみ・あい union)

石 (ジャク/セキ)   (stone)

拓 (タク) is a combination of 扌 (hand) and the phonetic 石 (stone). It means "take an ink rubbing" or "develop; open new territory."
　　開拓 (カイ・タク land development)

生 (ショウ/セイ)   (birth, life, live)

姓 (セイ/ショウ) combines 女 (woman) and the phonetic 生 (birth). It once meant "maternal lineage," but now means "surname."
　　姓名 (セイ・メイ full name), 百姓 (ヒャク・ショウ peasant)

性 (セイ/ショウ) is a combination of 忄 (heart) and the phonetic 生 (life). It means "inborn nature; sex, gender; character, quality" and is suffixed to certain Sino-Japanese compounds to form abstract nouns.
　　性能 (セイ・ノウ capacity), 性分 (ショウ・ブン one's nature)

星 (セイ/ショウ/ほし), a reduction of 晶 (star) combined with the phonetic 生, means "star."
　　惑星 (ワク・セイ planet), 明星 (ミョウ・ジョウ the morning star; the evening star), 星 (ほし star)

牲 (セイ) is a combination of 牛 (ox) and the phonetic 生 (live). It originally referred to a live sacrifice to a diety, but now has much the general sense of English "sacrifice."
　　犠牲 (ギ・セイ sacrifice; victim)

申 (シン)   (stretch; lightning)

伸 (シン/の・びる) consists of 亻 (person) and the phonetic 申 (stretch) and means "extend, lengthen; state, say."
　　追伸 (ツイ・シン postscript), 伸びる (の・びる extend; grow)

神 (シン/ジン/かみ/かん/こう) is a combination of 礻 (altar) and the phonetic 申 (lightning). It means "god, divine; spirit, soul."
　　神経 (シン・ケイ nerves), 神社 (ジン・ジャ Shinto shrine), 神 (かみ god), 神主 (かん・ぬし Shinto priest), 神々しい (こう・ごう・しい holy)

陣 (ジン) consists of 阝 (mound) and, originally, the phonetic 申 (stretch; lightning). It means "military encampment, battle array; sudden"; in Japan it is used also for "battle; corps, staff."
　　報道陣 (ホウ・ドウ・ジン press corps)

紳 (シン) combines 糸 (thread) and the phonetic 申 (stretch). Originally referring to a sash worn by high officials, it now means "gentleman."
　　紳士 (シン・シ gentleman)

陳 (チン) is a combination of 阝 (mound) and, originally, the phonetic 申 (stretch). It appears that 陣 and 陳 derive from the same character, with an overlap of meaning like "array." This one means "display; state, expound; outdated."

陳列 (チン・レツ display)

電 (デン) consists of 雨 (rain) and the phonetic 申 (lightning) and means "lightning; electricity"; it can also be short for "telegraph, telegram" and, in Japan, "electric train."

電話 (デン・ワ telephone)

主 (ス/シュ) (lamp; stay in one place)

住 (ジュウ/す・む) is a combination of イ (person) and the phonetic 主 (stay in one place). It means "stay, dwell, inhabit"; in Japan it may be used as an abbreviation of a word for "chief priest."

住民 (ジュウ・ミン residents), 住む (す・む reside)

往 (王, p. 132)

注 (チュウ/そそ・ぐ) combines 氵 (water) and the phonetic 主 (stay in one place), and means "pour; focus." It is also used for "comment, annotation" and in Japan can mean "order (merchandise)."

注文 (チュウ・モン order), 注ぐ (そそ・ぐ pour)

柱 (チュウ/はしら) consists of 木 (wood) and the phonetic 主 (stay in one place). It means "pole, pillar; support" and, in Japan, is used as a counter for gods.

電柱 (デン・チュウ utility pole), 柱 (はしら pillar; support)

駐 (チュウ) is a combination of 馬 (horse) and the phonetic 主 (stay in one place), and it means "station, park; stay, be stationed."

駐車場 (チュウ・シャ・ジョウ parking lot)

出 (スイ or シュツ) (go out; foot in a hole)

拙 (セツ) combines 扌 (hand) and the phonetic 出 (foot in a hole). It means "unskillful, clumsy" and is used in certain compounds with a humble first-person possessive effect.

稚拙 (チ・セツ inexperienced and inept)

田 (デン) (cultivated field)

(シン or セイ) (baby's head)

細 (サイ/ほそ・い/こま・かい) combines 糸 (thread) and the phonetic 田 (baby's head) and 細 means "fine, thin, slender, minute; humble."

細心 (サイ・シン scrupulous), 細い (ほそ・い slender), 細かい (こま・かい detailed; minute)

白 (ビャク/ヒャク)   (acorn; white)

伯 (ハク) is 亻 (person) combined with the phonetic 白. It meant "eldest brother; master." In Japan it stands for the third of the five Japanese ranks of nobility, translated "count."

画伯 (ガ・ハク great artist)

拍 (ハク/ヒョウ) consists of 扌 (hand) and the phonetic 白. It means "clap hands; cadence, beat" and is used as the counter for beats in music.

拍手 (ハク・シュ applause), 拍子 (ヒョウ・シ beat)

泊 (ハク/と・まる) is a combination of 氵 (water) and the phonetic 白. It means "mooring; stay, lodge" and is used as a counter for nights spent in an inn.

宿泊 (シュク・ハク lodging), 泊まる (とま・る stay overnight)

迫 (ハク/せま・る) consists of 辶 (walk) and the phonetic 白 and means "draw near; be pressing; press, urge; oppress."

迫力 (ハク・リョク force), 迫る (せま・る insist on; approach)

舶 (ハク) is a combination of 舟 (boat) and the phonetic 白. It means "ship, vessel."

舶来 (ハク・ライ imported)

丙 (ヒョウ/ヘイ)   (desk; stiff)

柄 (ヘイ/がら/え) consists of 木 (wood) and the phonetic 丙 (stiff). It means "handle, shaft, power, dominance" and, in Japan, "pattern; character."

横柄 (オウ・ヘイ arrogance), 柄 (がら pattern; character; え handle)

病 (ビョウ/ヘイ/や・む/やまい) combines 疒 (disease) and the phonetic 丙 (stiff) and means "disease; sick; suffer."

病院 (ビョウ・イン hospital), 疾病 (シッ・ペイ malady), 病む (や・む fall ill), 病 (やまい illness)

平 (ヒョウ/ヘイ)   (flat, even)

坪 (つぼ) is a combination of 土 (ground) and the phonetic 平 (flat), but the on-yomi ヘイ is not included in the Jōyō Kanji. Originally meaning "flat ground," it is used in Japan as a counter, most importantly for land area units of 3.3 square meters.

建坪 (たて・つぼ floor space)

評 (ヒョウ) is 言 (say) combined with the phonetic 平 (flat). It means "criticism."

評判 (ヒョウ・バン reputation)

北 (ホク)   (two persons back to back)

背 (ハイ/せ/せい/そむ・く) consists of 月 (flesh) and the phonetic 北 (back to back). It means "back, rear; turn one's back on, be against."

背景 (ハイ・ケイ background), 背中 (せ・なか the back), 背 (せい/せ height), 背く (そむ・く disobey)

民 (ミン/ビン)   (gimlet; cannot see)

眠 (ミン/ねむ・る), a combination of 目 (eye) and the phonetic 民 (cannot see), means "sleep."

冬眠 (トウ・ミン hibernation), 眠る (ねむ・る sleep)

婚 (コン) consists of 女 (woman) and the phonetic 昏 (コン dark of night), itself originally a combination of 日 (sun) and the phonetic 民 (cannot see). 婚 means "marry."

結婚 (ケッ・コン marriage)

矛 (ム/ボウ)   (halberd)

務 (ム/つと・める) consists of 力 (strength) and 攵 (action) with the phonetic 矛 (halberd). 務 means "duty, service."

義務 (ギ・ム duty), 務める (つと・める work in the service of)

霧 (ム/きり), a combination of 雨 (weather) and the phonetic 務 means "fog."

濃霧 (ノウ・ム dense fog), 霧 (きり fog)

由 (ユ/ユウ)   (basket; filter; go through)

(カイ)   (lump of dirt)

抽 (チュウ) is a combination of 扌 (hand) and the phonetic 由 (filter). It means "extract."

抽選 (チュウ・セン lottery)

宙 (チュウ) combines 宀 (roof) and the phonetic 由, and means "sky; up in the air."

宇宙 (ウ・チュウ cosmos, outer space)

届 (とど・ける), earlier 屆, combines 尸 (body) and the phonetic 由 (lump of dirt), though its *on-yomi* カイ is not included in the Jōyō Kanji. It may have originally meant "obesity," but is now used to mean "reach" and, in Japan, "deliver; notify, report; written notification."

届ける (とど・ける submit)

油 (ユ/あぶら) consists of 氵 (water) and the phonetic 由; it means "oil."

油田 (ユ・デン oil field), 油 (あぶら oil)

笛 (テキ/ふえ), a combination of 竹 (bamboo) and the phonetic 由 (filter), means "bamboo flute; flute, pipe, whistle."

警笛 (ケイ・テキ warning horn), 笛 (ふえ flute)

軸 (ジク) combines 車 (wheel) and the phonetic 由 (go through). It means "axle; axis; scroll."

掛け軸 (か・け・ジク hanging scroll)

用 (ユウ/ヨウ)   (use)

庸 (ヨウ) is a combination of 庚 (holding a stick) and the phonetic 用 (use). It means "employ, hire; common, mediocre."

中庸 (チュウ・ヨウ moderation)

勇 (ユウ/いさ・む), earlier 勇, is a combination of 力 (strength) and the phonetic 甬 (ヨウ pierce, penetrate), itself a combination of a form of an element for "person" and the phonetic 用. 勇 means "brave."

勇気 (ユウ・キ courage), 勇む (いさ・む get in high spirits)

通 (ツウ/ツ/とお・る/かよ・う) consists of 辶 (walk) and the phonetic 甬 (pierce, penetrate) and means "go through, pass; frequent; inform; informed; general, common." In Japan it is further used for "commute" and "street" and as a counter for letters, pieces of mail.

通じる (ツウ・じる lead to; get well versed), 通夜 (ツ・ヤ wake), 通る (とお・る pass through), 通う (かよ・う commute)

痛 (ツウ/いた・い) consists of 疒 (disease) and the phonetic 甬 (pierce) and means "pain; keen, acute" and, in Japan, "pitiful."

痛感する (ツウ・カン・する feel sharply), 痛い (いた・い painful)

踊 (ヨウ/おど・る) combines 足 (foot, leg) and the phonetic 甬 (pierce) and means "jump, dance."

舞踊 (ブ・ヨウ dance), 踊る (おど・る dance)

立 (リュウ)   (stand)

粒 (リュウ/つぶ), a combination of 米 (rice) and the phonetic 立 (stand), means "grain; very small." It is also used as a counter for grains or pills.

粒子 (リュウ・シ particle), 粒 (つぶ grain)

6-Stroke Phonetics

衣 (エ/イ)   (garment; conceal)

依 (イ/エ) is a combination of 亻 (person) and the phonetic 衣 (garment). It means "depend; unchanged."

依存 (イ・ゾン dependence), 帰依 (キ・エ religious conversion)

哀 (アイ/あわ・れ) combines 口 (mouth) and the phonetic 衣 (conceal), and means "sorrow, pity; pitiful."

哀願 (アイ・ガン supplication), 哀れ (あわ・れ pathos; pity)

交 (キョウ/コウ)   (cross; mix)

効 (コウ/き・く) consists of 力 (strength) and the phonetic 交 (cross, mix). It means "result of effort, effect."

効果（コウ・カ effect）, 効く（き・く be effective）

郊（コウ）, a combination of 阝 (town) and the phonetic 交 (mix), means "suburb."

郊外（コウ・ガイ suburbs）

校（コウ）consists of 木 (wood) and the phonetic 交 (cross). Originally meaning "pillory," it is used in the derived senses "investigate; check for accuracy; school; military officer."

学校（ガッ・コウ school）

絞（コウ/しぼ・る/し・める）combines 糸 (thread) with the phonetic 交 (cross) and means "wring, tighten, squeeze."

絞殺（コウ・サツ strangulation）, 絞る（しぼ・る squeeze）, 絞める（し・める tie; strangle）

較（カク）, a combination of 車 (car) and the phonetic 交 (cross), once referred to part of the structure of a carriage. It was also used to write a different but possibly related word meaning "compare" which would be コウ in Japanese. As a Jōyō Kanji, it is used with the former reading and the latter meaning.

比較（ヒ・カク comparison）

行 （ギョウ/コウ）   (go; straight)

衡（コウ）is a combination of 角 (horn) and 大 (large) with the phonetic 行 (straight). Initially it seems to have meant a block of wood to cover and thus disarm both horns of an ox. It came to be used of the beam of a balance, and also the weights, and now means "weight; balance."

均衡（キン・コウ balance）

舟 （シュ/シュウ）   (boat)

受（ジュ/う・ける）is a combination of 爫 (fingers) and 又 (hand) with a much distorted phonetic 舟 squeezed in between, showing something going from one hand to another. It means "receive, accept."

受験（ジュ・ケン take an examination）, 受ける（う・ける receive）

授（ジュ/さず・ける）consists of 扌 (hand) and the phonetic 受 (receive), and means "bestow; be granted."

教授（キョウ・ジュ professor; instruction）, 授ける（さず・ける grant）

朝（チョウ/あさ）is a much simplified combination of 倝 (rising sun) and the phonetic 舟. It means "morning" and "imperial court." The latter is extended to mean imperial domain in both the temporal sense, thus "dynasty," and the spatial sense, thus, in Japan, "Japan."

朝食（チョウ・ショク breakfast）, 朝（あさ morning）

潮（チョウ/しお）consists of 氵 (water) and the phonetic 朝 (morning). It means "morning tide," but is now generalized to mean "tide."

潮流（チョウ・リュウ tidal current）, 潮（しお tide）

☐虫 (ジュウ/チュウ)　　　　　　　　　　　　　　　　　(insect)

　融 (ユウ) combines 鬲 (tripod kettle, steamer) and the phonetic 虫. It means "melt, fuse," or in Japan "accommodate."
　　融通 (ユウ・ヅウ accommodation; elasticity)

☐兆 (ジョウ/チョウ)　　　　　　　　　　　　　　　　　(cracked, split)

　挑 (チョウ/いど・む), is a combination of 扌 (hand) and the phonetic 兆 (split), and means "challenge."
　　挑戦 (チョウ・セン challenge), 挑む (いど・む challenge)

　逃 (トウ/に・げる/のが・す) consists of 辶 (walk) and the phonetic 兆 (split) and means "flee, run away."
　　逃避 (トウ・ヒ escape), 逃げる (に・げる run away), 逃す (のが・す disregard; lose)

　桃 (トウ/もも), a combination of 木 (tree) and the phonetic 兆 (split), means "peach."
　　白桃 (ハク・トウ white peach); 桃 (もも peach)

　眺 (チョウ/なが・める), a combination of 目 (eye) and the phonetic 兆, means "view, gaze out."
　　眺望 (チョウ・ボウ view), 眺める (なが・める view)

　跳 (チョウ/は・ねる/と・ぶ) combines 足 (foot, leg) and the phonetic 兆 (split) and means "spring, jump."
　　跳躍 (チョウ・ヤク leap), 跳ねる (は・ねる jump), 跳ぶ (と・ぶ leap)

☐竹 (チク)　　　　　　　　　　　　　　　　　　　　　(bamboo)

　築 (チク/きず・く) is a combination of 𥐐 (leveling with a stick), 木 (wood), and the phonetic 竹 (bamboo). It means "build, construct."
　　建築 (ケン・チク architecture), 築く (きず・く build; establish)

　篤 (トク) is a combination of 馬 (horse) and the phonetic 竹. It means "hearty, sincere; grave, serious."
　　危篤 (キ・トク critically ill)

☐耳 (ニ/ジ)　　　　　　　　　　　　　　　　　　　　　(ear)

　恥 (チ/はじ・る/はじ), a combination of 心 (heart) and the phonetic 耳 (ear, soft), means "shame" and, in Japan, "shy."
　　恥辱 (チ・ジョク disgrace), 恥じる (は・じる be ashamed), 恥 (はじ shame)

　敢; 厳 (甘, p. 139, 140)

☐米 (マイ/ベイ)　　　　　　　　　　　　　　　　　　　(rice)

　迷 (メイ/まよ・う) combines 辶 (walk) and the phonetic 米 (rice; too small to see) and means "go astray; vacillate, be in doubt" and, in Japan, "odd."

迷惑 (メイ・ワク annoyance), 迷う (まよ・う wander; vacillate)

羊 (ヨウ)   (sheep)

洋 (ヨウ) consists of 氵 (water) and the phonetic 羊 (sheep). It means "ocean; vast" and, in modern times "Western."

洋服 (ヨウ・フク Western clothes)

祥 (ショウ), a combination of 礻 (altar) and the phonetic 羊 (sheep), means "luck; omen."

吉祥 (キッ・ショウ good omen)

達 (大, p. 131)

詳 (ショウ/くわ・しい) is a combination of 言 (say) and the phonetic 羊 (sheep). It means "detailed; setforth in detail."

詳細 (ショウ・サイ details), 詳しい (くわ・しい detailed)

様 (ヨウ/さま) is the Jōyō Kanji form of 樣, which combines 木 (tree) and the phonetic 羕 (ヨウ drift), a combination of 永 (continuously flowing water) and the phonetic 羊. Thought to originally have been the name of a kind of oak, it came to be used instead for a word meaning "appearance, looks; style." In Japan this was extended to include "way"; after a name or other term of personal reference it is an honorific suffix.

様子 (ヨウ・ス appearance; state of affairs), 神様 (かみ・さま Dear Lord)

養 (ヨウ/やしな・う), a combination of 食 (eating) and the phonetic 羊 (sheep), means "feed, nourish; fosterage."

養成 (ヨウ・セイ training), 養う (やしな・う nourish)

窯 (ヨウ/かま) combines 穴 (cave) and 灬 (fire) combined with the phonetic 羊. It means "kiln."

窯業 (ヨウ・ギョウ pottery industry), 窯 (かま kiln)

7-Stroke Phonetics

亜 (ア)   (basement; secondary)

悪 (アク/オ/わる・い), a combination of 心 (heart) and the phonetic 亜 (secondary), means "hate; detestable, bad, wrong; inferior."

悪質 (アク・シツ bad quality; wicked), 悪寒 (オ・カン chill), 悪い (わる・い bad; at fault)

求 (グ/キュウ)   (pelt; shrink taut)

救 (キュウ/すく・う), a combination of 攵 (action) and the phonetic 求 (shrink taut), means "rescue, save."

救急車 (キュウ・キュウ・シャ ambulance), 救う (すく・う rescue; redeem)

球 (キュウ/たま) consists of 玉 (gem) and the phonetic 求 (shrink taut). It means "ball, globe, bulb" and, in certain compounds in Japan, "lightbulb; baseball."

野球 (ヤ・キュウ baseball), 球 (たま/キュウ ball; sphere)

車 (シャ)   (wheel; car)

陣 (申, p. 142)

辛 (シン)   (needle, awl)

新 (シン/あたら・しい/あら・た/にい) consists of 斤 (hatchet) and the phonetic 亲 (シン cut up a tree), which combines 木 (tree) and the phonetic 辛 (needle). The whole character originally meant "fresh-cut wood" and later just "fresh, new."

新年 (シン・ネン New Year), 新しい (あたら・しい new; fresh), 新た (あら・た new), 新妻 (にい・づま new bride)

薪 (シン/たきぎ) adds 艹 (grass) to the phonetic 新 (fresh-cut wood), and it means "firewood."

薪炭 (シン・タン fuel), 薪 (たきぎ firewood)

親 (シン/おや/した・しい)is a combination of 見 (see) and the phonetic 亲. It means "close, intimate; parent, kin" or, especially of an emperor, "in person."

親類 (シン・ルイ relative), 親 (おや parent), 親しい (した・しい intimate)

臣 (ジン/シン)   (vassal)
  (イ/キ)   (a Chou Dynasty family name)

姫 (ひめ) was formerly written 姫, combining 女 (woman) with the phonetic 匝 (a Chou Dynasty family name). In any event the *on-yomi* キ is not included in the Jōyō Kanji. In Japan it means "princess" or, used as a prefix, "small."

豆 (ズ/トウ)   (dish with tall base; bean)

痘 (トウ) consists of 疒 (disease) and the phonetic 豆 (bean) and means "pox, smallpox, cowpox."

種痘 (シュ・トウ vaccination)

頭 (トウ/ズ/ト/あたま/かしら) consists of 頁 (head) and the phonetic 豆 (tall); it means "head; leader; beginning; vicinity" and is used as a counter for large animals.

年頭 (ネン・トウ beginning of year), 頭脳 (ズ・ノウ brain), 音頭 (オン・ド chorus leading), 頭 (あたま head; brains; かしら head; leader)

樹 (ジュ) combines 木 (tree) and the phonetic 尌 (ジュ stand straight), which consists of 寸 (hand) and 壴 (either "drum" or "dish with a stand"). It means "tree; set up, establish."

樹立 (ジュ・リツ establishment)

闘 (トウ/たたか・う), earlier 鬭, is a combination of 鬥 (fight) and the phonetic 尌 (stand straight). It means "fight, combat."

闘争 (トウ・ソウ struggle), 闘う (たたか・う fight)

足 (ソク/ショク)   (lower leg and foot)

促 (ソク/うなが・す) combines 亻 (person) with the phonetic 足 (foot) and means "urge."

促進 (ソク・シン acceleration), 促す (うなが・す urge)

貝 (ハイ/バイ)   (shell)

(テイ)   (tripod-kettle)

貞 (テイ) combines 卜 (divination) with a vastly simplified 鼎 (テイ tripod kettle) as a phonetic. Originally meaning something like "be in communication with the gods," it now means "faithful, chaste."

貞節 (テイ・セツ faithful)

偵 (テイ), a combination of 亻 (person) and the phonetic 貞 (hear a divine message) means "spy upon, scout."

探偵 (タン・テイ detective)

敗 (ハイ/やぶれ・る) consists of 攵 (action) and the phonetic 貝 (shell). Originally it might have meant "divide into two," but now means "go bad, spoil; fail, be defeated"; it is also used as a counter for losses in sports.

失敗 (シッ・パイ failure), 敗れる (やぶ・れる be defeated)

良 ; 㝵 (ロウ/リョウ)   (clean grain)

郎 (ロウ), a combination of 阝 (town) and the phonetic 㝵 (clean grain), has a meaning involving the concept of a well-groomed man. Its current uses include "young man; servant" and it is a common ending in men's names.

新郎 (シン・ロウ bridegroom)

娘 (むすめ) combines 女 (woman) with the phonetic 良 (clean), but its *on-yomi* ジョウ has been excluded from the Jōyō Kanji. It means "young woman"; in Japan, though, it means "daughter; young miss."

朗 (ロウ/ほが・らか) consists of 月 (moon) and the phonetic 㝵 (clean) and means "clear, bright," and with respect to manifestations of personality or attitude, "bright, cheerful."

朗読 (ロウ・ドク reading aloud), 朗らか (ほが・らか cheery)

浪 (ロウ) is a combination of 氵 (water) and the phonetic 良 (clear) meaning once, "clear running water" and now "big waves; wander; profligate, wasteful."

浪人 (ロウ・ニン masterless *samurai*; student without a school)

廊 (ロウ) consists of 广 (house) and the phonetic 郎 and means "eaves; corridor."

廊下 (ロウ・カ hallway)

8-Stroke Phonetics

易 (イ or ヤク/エキ)   (lizard)

賜 (シ/たまわ・る) is a combination of 貝 (wealth) and the phonetic 易. It means "bestow; have bestowed upon one."
恩賜 (オン・シ Imperial gift), 賜る (たまわ・る be granted)

育 (イク)   (growing up)

充 (ジュウ/あ・てる) is a combination of 儿 (human body) and the phonetic 育 (grow up), abbreviated, and means "full; fill."
充分 (ジュウ・ブン enough), 充てる (あ・てる apply)

統 (トウ/す・べる) combines 糸 (thread) and the phonetic 充 (fill). It means "continuity, lineage; unite; govern."
伝統 (デン・トウ tradition), 統べる (す・べる govern)

銃 (ジュウ) combines 金 (metal) and the phonetic 充 (fill) and means "gun."
銃殺 (ジュウ・サツ execution by firing squad)

京 (キョウ/ケイ)   (house on hill; capital; large)

景 (ケイ), combining 日 (sun) and the phonetic 京 (house on hill), means "sunlight, shade; scene, panorama; large; look up to" and, in Japan, "premium."
景気 (ケイ・キ business conditions)

影 (エイ/かげ), a combination of 彡 (design) and the phonetic 景 (sunlight) means "beam of light, shadow; image, shadow, reflection."
影響 (エイ・キョウ influence), 影 (かげ shadow; image)

鯨 (ゲイ/くじら), a combination of 魚 (fish) and the phonetic 京 (large), means "whale."
捕鯨船 (ホ・ゲイ・セン whaleboat), 鯨 (くじら whale)

斉 (ザイ/セイ)   (uniformity, well-ordered)

剤 (ザイ) is a combination of 刂 (edged tool) and the phonetic 斉 (uniformity). It seems to have meant herbs cut in uniform lengths once; now it means "pill; drug."
薬剤師 (ヤク・ザイ・シ pharmicist)

斎 (サイ) combines 示 (altar) and the phonetic 斉 (well-ordered) and meant "religious purification"; it still means "purification," as well as "a study room." In Japan it may be used in naming such rooms and in pen names.
書斎 (ショ・サイ a study)

済 (サイ/す・む) is a combination of 氵 (water) and the phonetic 斉 (uniform). It means "regulate, control; save, rescue" and, in Japan "finish, settle."

返済 (ヘン・サイ repayment), 済む (す・む be finished)

長 (チョウ) (long; stretch)

張 (チョウ/は・る), combining 弓 (bow) with the phonetic 長 (long), suggests stringing a bow. It means basically "stretch; expand, spread"; in Japan it also means "paste, stick on."

緊張 (キン・チョウ tension), 張る (は・る stretch; plaster)

帳 (チョウ) is a combination of 巾 (cloth) and the phonetic 長 (long) meaning "drape, curtain; notebook, ledger, a type of book in the form of a long folded sheet of paper."

手帳 (て・チョウ pocket notebook)

脹 (チョウ) consists of 月 (flesh) and the phonetic 長 (stretch) and means "swell, bulge."

膨張 (ボウ・チョウ expansion)

東 (ツウ/トウ) (through)
(レン) (select)

凍 (トウ/こお・る/こご・える) is a combination of 冫 (ice) and the phonetic 東 (all the way through); it means "freeze; frozen."

冷凍 (レイ・トウ freezing), 凍る (こお・る freeze), 凍える (こご・える get chilled)

陳 (申, p. 143)

棟 (トウ/むね/むな) consists of 木 (wood) and the phonetic 東 (through) and means "ridge of roof; head, highest point; building"; in Japan it is also used as a counter for houses and other buildings.

病棟 (ビョウ・トウ ward), 棟 (むね ridge), 棟木 (むな・ぎ ridgepole)

練 (レン/ね・る), earlier 練, combines 糸 (thread) and the phonetic 東 (select), which is in turn a combination of 束 (bundle) and 八 (divide). It means "to gloss (as of silk thread); to knead; to temper; to train."

練習 (レン・シュウ practice), 練る (ね・る refine)

錬 (レン), originally a combination of 金 (metal) and the phonetic 東 (select), means "temper metal; knead medicine; train, drill."

錬達 (レン・タツ skill)

欄 (ラン) combines of 木 (wood) and the phonetic 闌 (ラン hinder, bar) which is a combination of 門 (gate) and the phonetic 東 (select). It means "handrail" and, derived from that, "column, section in a newspaper."

非 (ヒ) (wings; left vs. right; split)

俳 (ハイ) combines 亻 (person) and the phonetic 非 (left vs. right) and seems to have originally meant "crosstalk comedians." It means "actor; witty; wander";

it also stands for "*haiku*" in some compounds.

俳句 (ハイ・ク *haiku*)

排 (ハイ) is a combination of 扌 (hand) and the phonetic 非 (left vs. right). Its meaning "expel, get rid of" makes sense if thought of as pushing to one side or the other; it also means "put in line."

排除 (ハイ・ジョ elimination)

悲 (ヒ/かなし・い) consists of 心 (heart) and the phonetic 非 (split), and means "sorrow" or, in Buddhist terminology, "mercy."

悲劇 (ヒ・ゲキ tragedy), 悲しい (かなし・い sad)

扉 (ヒ/とびら) is a combination of 戸 (door) and the phonetic 非 (open wings). It means "door flap, door."

門扉 (モン・ピ gate), 扉 (とびら door)

輩 (ハイ) combines 車 (wheel) and the phonetic 非 (left vs. right) for the original sense of "row of carriages"; it means "in succession; fellow."

先輩 (セン・パイ one's senior)

門 (モン/ブン)   (gate, gateway)

問 (モン/と・う/とん) is a combination of 口 (mouth) and the phonetic 門 (gateway). It means "inquire, question; visit."

問題 (モン・ダイ problem), 問う (と・う inquire), 問屋 (とん・や wholesaler)

聞 (ブン/モン/き・く) consists of 耳 (ear) and the phonetic 門 (gateway). It means "hear; smell; repute." In Japan it also means "listen; ask."

新聞 (シン・ブン newspaper), 前代未聞 (ゼン・ダイ・ミ・モン unprecedented), 聞く (き・く hear; listen)

9-Stroke Phonetics

単 (ゼン/セン or タン)   (duster, beater, oscillate; level)

弾 (ダン/ひ・く/はず・む/たま) is a combination of 弓 (bow) and the phonetic 単 (oscillate). It means "bounce, ricochet; bullet; play, pluck (a stringed musical instrument); rebuke."

弾力 (ダン・リョク elasticity), 弾く (ひ・く play), 弾む (はず・む bounce), 弾 (たま bullet)

戦 (セン/いくさ/たたか・う) consists of 戈 (halberd) and the phonetic 単 (beater). It means "battle, war; fear, fright" or, in Japan, "game, match."

名人戦 (メイ・ジン・セン championship match), 戦 (いくさ combat), 戦う (たたか・う fight)

禅 (ゼン) is a combination of 礻 (altar) and the phonetic 単 (level). It originally meant "worship" or "abdication of throne," but in Japan it refers almost exclusively to Zen Buddhism.

南 (ナン)   (south)

　(ケン)   (ornamental tripod-kettle)

　献 (ケン/コン) is in reality an abbreviation of 獻, consisting of 犬 (dog) and the phonetic 鬳 (ケン ornamental tripod-kettle), which consists of 虍 (tiger) and 鬲 (tripod kettle) and stood for the sort of vessel with which meat offerings were made to gods. 献 means "offer, contribute; text, bibliographical source," and is used in Japan as a counter for offerings of drinks.

　献金 (ケン・キン contribution), 献立 (コン・だて menu)

10-Stroke Phonetics

高 (コウ)   (tall house; high)

　豪 (ゴウ) combines 豕 (boar) with the phonetic 高 (high). It has meant "porcupine, but is used now in such senses as "brave, stout; out of the ordinary." It is also an abbreviation for Australia, based on its Chinese pronunciation.

　豪雨 (ゴウ・ウ heavy rain)

　稿 (コウ) is a combination of 禾 (rice plant) and the phonetic 高 (high). Its original meaning, "straw," has given way to "draft, manuscript."

　原稿 (ゲン・コウ manuscript)

　橋 (キョウ/はし) combines 木 (wood) and the phonetic 喬 (キョウ tall house with a curved roof). It means "bridge."

　陸橋 (リッ・キョウ overpass), 橋 (はし bridge)

　矯 (キョウ/た・める) consists of 矢 (arrow) and the phonetic 喬 (curved); it means "bend, reshape; rectify."

　矯正 (キョウ・セイ correction), 矯める (た・める straighten; bend)

竜 (リュウ)   (dragon)

　滝 (たき) is a combination of 氵 (water) and the phonetic 竜 (dragon); its *on-yomi* ロウ is not included in the Jōyō Kanji. It means "waterfall."

11-Stroke Phonetics

魚 (ギョ)   (fish)

　漁 (ギョ/リョウ) is a combination of 氵 (water) and the phonetic 魚 (fish); the reading リョウ for it is a Japanese innovation based on the reading of a character for "hunt" (猟). It means "fishing."

　漁業 (ギョ・ギョウ fishing industry), 漁師 (リョウ・シ fisherman)

鳥 (チョウ)   (bird)

　島 (トウ/しま) is a combination of 山 (mountain) and the phonetic 鳥 (bird). It means "island."

半島 (ハン・トウ peninsula), 島 (しま island)

12-Stroke Phonetic

象 (ゾウ/ショウ)   (elephant)

像 (ゾウ) is a combination of 亻 (person) and the phonetic 象 (elephant). It means "image, model."

想像 (ソウ・ゾウ imagination)

Semantic Compound Kanji as Phonetics

This section lists all the Jōyō Kanji that have the semantic compound kanji of Chapter 3 as phonetics.

3-Stroke Phonetics

及 (ゴウ/キュウ)   (chase after; follow in series)

吸 (キュウ/す・う), a combination of 口 (mouth) and the phonetic 及 (chase after), means "suck, inhale."

吸収 (キュウ・シュウ absorb), 吸う (す・う suck)

級 (キュウ), combines 糸 (thread) with the phonetic 及 (follow in series). It means "order, grade," and "class," as in school.

級友 (キュウ・ユウ classmate)

急 (キュウ/いそ・ぐ) is a combination of 心 (heart) and the phonetic 及 (chase after), slightly distorted. It means "rush; abrupt; steep."

急行 (キュウ・コウ express train), 急ぐ (いそ・ぐ hurry)

刃 (ニン/ジン)   (edge; forge)

忍 (ニン/しの・ぶ) consists of 心 (heart) and the phonetic 刃 (forge). It means "tolerate, bear; brutal"; in Japan it has picked up the sense of "lurk."

残忍 (ザン・ニン cruel), 忍ぶ (しの・ぶ endure)

認 (ニン/みと・める) combines 言 (say) with the phonetic 忍 (tolerate) to mean "recognize, admit; approve of."

確認 (カク・ニン confirmation), 認める (みと・める recognize; approve)

凡 (ボン/ハン)   (sail; flap)

帆 (ハン/ほ) adds 巾 (cloth) to the phonetic 凡 (sail) to preserve the original meaning of "sail; sailing."

出帆 (シュッ・パン set sail), 帆 (ほ sail)

風 (フウ/フ/かぜ/かざ) combines 虫 (snake), for reasons not agreed on, with the phonetic 凡 (sail; flap). It means "wind, air; atmosphere, style, manner, appearance, scene; permeate, spread."

洋風 (ヨウ・フウ western style), 風情 (フ・ゼイ taste), 風 (かぜ wind), 風上 (かざ・かみ windward)

亡 (モウ/ボウ)　　　　　　　　　　　　　　　　　　　　　　　(disappear; lost)

忙 (ボウ/いそが・しい), a combination of 忄 (heart) and the phonetic 亡 (disappear), means "busy."
　　多忙 (タ・ボウ very busy), 忙しい (いそが・しい busy)

妄 (モウ/ボウ) combines 女 (woman) and the phonetic 亡 (lost) and means "rash, indiscriminate; wild, deceptive."
　　妄信 (モウ・シン blind belief), 妄言 (ボウ・ゲン/モウ・ゲン irresponsible utterance)

忘 (ボウ/わす・れる), a second combination of 心 (heart) and the phonetic 亡 (disappear), means "forget."
　　忘年会 (ボウ・ネン・カイ year-end party), 忘れる (わす・れる forget)

盲 (モウ) combines 目 (eye) and the phonetic 亡 (lost); it means "blind."
　　盲人 (モウ・ジン blind person)

望 (ボウ/モウ/のぞ・む), previously written 望, combines 月 (moon), 壬 (someone looking), and the phonetic 亡 (disappear). It means "wish, aspire; view."
　　望遠鏡 (ボウ・エン・キョウ telescope), 本望 (ホン・モウ long-cherished desire), 望む (のぞ・む wish; view)

網 (モウ/あみ), a combination of 糸 (thread), and the phonetic 罔 (モウ net), means "net"; the phonetic in turn combines a form of 冂 (net) with the phonetic 亡.
　　交通網 (コウ・ツウ・モウ traffic network), 網 (あみ net)

4-Stroke Phonetics

区 (ク or ウ/オウ)　　　　　　　　　　　　　　　　　　　　(small section)

欧 (オウ) combines 欠 (someone stooping and yawning) and the phonetic 区 (small section). It meant "vomit," but is now used only for "Europe" in Japan, from the Chinese rendering of the word's first syllable, "Eu-."
　　欧州 (オウ・シュウ Europe)

殴 (オウ/なぐ・る), a combination of 殳 (action) and the phonetic 区, perhaps onomatopoeic, meant "strike, beat."
　　殴打 (オウ・ダ assault), 殴る (なぐ・る strike)

枢 (スウ) consists of 木 (wood) and the phonetic 区 (finely wrought) and means "hinge, pivot."
　　枢軸 (スウ・ジク axis)

駆 (ク/か・ける) is a combination of 馬 (horse) and the phonetic 区, perhaps onomatopoeic, as with 殴 (strike) above; it means "drive, make run; run, gallop."
　　駆使 (ク・シ having command of), 駆ける (か・ける run)

凶 (ク/キョウ)　　　　　　　　　　　　　　　　　　　　　　(in a hole)

胸 (キョウ/むね/むな) combines 月 (flesh) and the phonetic 匈 (キョウ ribcage), which is a combination of 勹 (wrap) and the phonetic 凶 (in a hole). It means "chest, ribcage; bosom."

胸中 (キョウ・チュウ one's mind), 胸 (むね breast), 胸騒ぎ (むな・さわぎ uneasiness)

公 (ク/コウ)   (public)

松 (ショウ/まつ), a combination of 木 (tree) and the phonetic 公, means "pine."
松竹梅 (ショウ・チク・バイ pine, bamboo and plum), 松 (まつ pine)

翁 (オウ) consists of 羽 (wings) and the phonetic 公. It originally signified a bird's down, but now is used for "old man" or may be attached, as an honorific title, to the name of a man of accomplishments.

訟 (ショウ), a combination of 言 (say) and the phonetic 公 (public), means "dispute, sue."
訴訟 (ソ・ショウ lawsuit)

化 (ケ/カ)   (change)

花 (カ/はな) combines 艹 (plant) and the phonetic 化 (change) and means "flower, blossom."
花壇 (カ・ダン flower bed), 花火 (はな・び fireworks)

貨 (カ) is a combination of 貝 (wealth) and the phonetic 化 (change). It means "money; goods."
外貨 (ガイ・カ foreign currency)

靴 (カ/くつ) combines 革 (hide) and the phonetic 化 (change) and means "shoe."
製靴業 (セイ・カ・ギョウ shoe industry), 靴 (くつ shoe)

介 (ケ/カイ)   (mediate)

界 (カイ) consists of 田 (field) and the phonetic 介 (mediate), and means "boundary, border; area, world."
境界 (キョウ・カイ boundary)

元 (ゲン/ガン)   (big round head)

完 (カン) is a combination of 宀 (roof) and the phonetic 元 (big round head). It means "complete."
完全 (カン・ゼン completion; perfection)

冠 (カン/かんむり) combines 冖 (cover), 寸 (hand) and the phonetic 元 (big head) and means "crown; wear on the head."
栄冠 (エイ・カン garland), 冠 (かんむり crown)

頑 (ガン) consists of 頁 (head) and the phonetic 元 (big head) and originally meant "head," but it now means, "hard-headed, stubborn."
頑張る (ガン・ば・る persevere)

院 (イン) is a combination of 阝 (mound) and the phonetic 完 (complete). It meant "mud wall" originally, shifting to "a building in a walled courtyard," and thus "hall, house, cloister, institute." In Japan it has been further used for the residences of, and honorifically indirect reference to, retired emperors and imperial mothers, as an abbreviation for "hospital," and as the ending of posthumous

Buddhist names.

寺院 (ジ・イン temple)

今 (コン/キン)   (cover)

含 (ガン/ふく・む) consists of 口 (mouth) and the phonetic 今 (cover). It means "have something in the mouth; contain, include."

含有 (ガン・ユウ content), 含む (ふく・む contain)

吟 (ギン) is also a combination of 口 (mouth) and the phonetic 今 (cover); this one means "moan; croon, chant, recite; compose."

吟味 (ギン・ミ investigation)

金 (キン/コン/かね/かな) combines 土 (earth), a couple of specks, and the phonetic 今 (cover), to suggest specks of alluvial gold covered with dirt. It means "gold; metal; money; golden; worthy; beautiful."

金 (キン gold; かね money, metal), 金堂 (コン・ドウ main hall of a Buddhist temple), 金物 (かな・もの hardware)

念 (ネン) combines 心 (heart) and the phonetic 今 (cover). It means "think; idea, sense ; chant" and has a further sense of "attention, care" in Japan.

念じる (ネン・じる pray)

琴 (キン/こと) has the phonetic 今 (cover) under a simplification of a graph for a stringed instrument. Its meaning ranges slightly from "stringed instrument," as in the first example below.

木琴 (モッ・キン xylophone), 琴 (こと koto)

陰 (イン/かげ) is a combination of 阝 (mound) and the phonetic 侌 (イン hidden), which consists of 云 (vapor) and the phonetic 今 (cover). It means "shade; shadowy; negative."

陰気 (イン・キ gloomy), 陰 (かげ shade)

飲 (イン/の・む) began as a combination of 欠 (someone yawning) and a graph for "covered liquor jar," which consists of 酉 (wine jar) and the phonetic 今 (cover). It means "drink."

飲食店 (イン・ショク・テン shop serving food and drink), 飲む (の・む drink)

支 (ギ/キ or シ)   (branch)

岐 (キ), a combination of 山 (mountain), to suggest topography, and the phonetic 支 (branch), means "forked; diverge."

岐路 (キ・ロ forked road)

技 (ギ/わざ) combines 扌 (hand) and the phonetic 支 (branch). It means "art, skill," represented as the manipulation of fine branches.

技師 (ギ・シ engineer), 技 (わざ skill)

枝 (シ/えだ) combines 木 (tree) and the phonetic 支 (branch) and means "branch, limb."

枝葉 (シ・ヨウ/えだ・は branch and leaf; trivial detail), 枝 (えだ branch)

肢 (シ), consisting of 月 (flesh) and the phonetic 支 (branch), means "limb, arm, leg."

肢体 (シ・タイ the body)

少 (ショウ)   (few)

抄 (ショウ) combines 扌 (hand) and the phonetic 少 (few). It means "extract, excerpt; copy" and, in Japan, "annotation."

抄本 (ショウ・ホン an abstract)

砂 (サ/シャ/すな) adds 石 (stone) to an abridged phonetic 沙 (シャ/サ sand), which consists of 氵 (water) and 少 (few); it still means "sand" or "granulated."

砂糖 (サ・トウ sugar), 土砂 (ド・シャ earth and sand), 砂 (すな sand)

太 (タイ)   (thick)

駄 (ダ) is a combination of 馬 (horse) and the phonetic 太 (thick). It means "draft horse; load"; in Japan it is also used as a pejorative prefix meaning "low quality," and as an element meaning "footwear."

駄目 (ダ・め no good)

天 (テン)   (heaven)

蚕 (サン/かいこ) properly テン, meaning "earthworm," has been substituted for 蠶 (サン), meaning "silkworm." The latter consists of two 虫 (insect; worm) components and the phonetic 朁 (サン hidden).

蚕業 (サン・ギョウ sericulture), 蚕 (かいこ silkworm)

添 (テン/そ・える) used to be written 添, a combination of 氵 (water) and the phonetic 忝 (テン thin and flat), which consists of a variant of "heart" and the phonetic 天. It means "add, append" with the special sense in Japan of "stay with, attend."

添加物 (テン・カ・ブツ additive), 添える (そ・える append)

内 (ナイ/ダイ)   (inside)

納 (ノウ/ナッ/ナ/ナン/トウ/おさ・める), a combination of 糸 (thread) and the phonetic 内 (inside), means "store, put in; remit; receive" and, in Japan, "end; last."

納税 (ノウ・ゼイ tax payment), 納得 (ナッ・トク assent), 納屋 (ナ・ヤ barn), 納戸 (ナン・ど closet), 出納 (スイ・トウ revenue and expenditure), 納める (お さ・める store, supply, pay, finish)

反 (ハン/ホン)   (bend; turn back)

坂 (ハン/さか) combines 土 (earth) with the phonetic 反 (turn back) and means "slope, hill."

登坂 (ト・ハン climbing a slope), 坂 (さか slope)

返 (ヘン/かえ・す) consists of 辶 (walk) and the phonetic 反 (turn back). It means "return"; in Japan it also serves as a counter of times something is done.

返事 (ヘン・ジ reply), 返す (かえ・す send back)

板 (ハン/バン/いた), a combination of 木 (wood) and the phonetic 反 (bend back), means "board, plate," including those used for printing.

鉄板 (テッ・パン iron plate), 看板 (カン・バン signboard), 板 (いた board)

版 (ハン) is a combination of 片 (piece of wood) and the phonetic 反 (bend back), it means "tablet; printing block, printing plate; print, publish."

版画 (ハン・ガ woodblock print)

販 (ハン) combines 貝 (wealth) and the phonetic 反 (revert). It means "trade, merchandise."

販売 (ハン・バイ sale)

飯 (ハン/めし), a combination of 食 (eat) and the phonetic 反, means "cooked rice; a meal."

御飯 (ゴ・ハン cooked rice; a meal), 飯 (めし cooked rice; a meal)

夫 (フ)   (man)

扶 (フ) consists of 扌 (hand) and the phonetic 夫 (man). It means "aid."
扶養 (フ・ヨウ support a family)

分 (ブン/フン)   (divide; scatter)

盆 (ボン), a combination of 皿 (dish) and the phonetic 分, means "large dish" and in Japan "tray." It can also refer to the Buddhist festival for the dead, from its use to transcribe the last syllable of the festival's Sanskrit name.

盆踊り (ボン・おど・り Bon Festival dance)

粉 (フン/こ/こな) consists of 米 (grain) and the phonetic 分 (divide) and means "flour; powder."

粉末 (フン・マツ powder), 小麦粉 (こ・むぎ・こ flour), 粉 (こな powder, flour)

紛 (フン/まぎ・れる) is a combination of 糸 (thread) and the phonetic 分 (scatter). It means "entangled, mixed up, confused."

紛失 (フン・シツ loss), 紛れる (まぎ・れる be confused; diverted)

貧 (ヒン/ビン/まず・しい) consists of 貝 (wealth) and the phonetic 分 (divide) and means "impoverished."

貧血 (ヒン・ケツ anemia), 貧乏 (ビン・ボウ poverty), 貧しい (まず・しい poor)

雰 (フン) combines 雨 (weather) and the phonetic 分 (scatter). It means "mist, air."

雰囲気 (フン・イ・キ atmosphere)

頒 (ハン) consists of 頁 (head) and the phonetic 分 (divide) and means "distribute."

頒布 (ハン・プ distribution)

友 (ユウ)   (friend)
   (バツ/ハツ)   (brush aside)

抜 (バツ/ぬ・く) is a combination of 扌 (hand) and a simplified form of the phonetic 犮 (brush aside). It means "pull out, extract; outdo." In Japan it is also used to write ぬく when it means "through, completely," in compound verbs.

抜群 (バツ・グン preeminence), 抜く (ぬ・く pick out; outrun)

髪 (ハツ/かみ) consists of 髟 (hair) and the phonetic 友 (brush aside) and means "head hair."

散髪 (サン・パツ haircut), 髪 (かみ hair)

5-Stroke Phonetics

永 (エイ)   (stretched out)

泳 (エイ/およ・ぐ) consists of 氵 (water) and the phonetic 永 (stretched out) and means "swim."

水泳 (スイ・エイ swimming), 泳ぐ (およ・ぐ swim)

詠 (エイ/よ・む), a combination of 言 (say) and the phonetic 永 (stretched out), means "chant, recite; compose (of poetry)."

朗詠 (ロウ・エイ recitation), 詠む (よ・む compose)

央 (オウ/ヨウ)   (center)

英 (エイ) is a combination of 艹 (plant) and the phonetic 央 (center). It meant "corolla" and "beautiful" and is used today for "superb." The Chinese chose it to write the "Eng-" of "England," and now it also means "England."

英語 (エイ・ゴ English language)

映 (エイ/うつ・る/は・える) consists of 日 (sun) and the phonetic 央 (center). It means "glow; constrast; reflect."

映画 (エイ・ガ movie), 映る (うつ・る be reflected), 映える (は・える show to contrast; glow)

可 (カ)   (husky voice; winding)

何 (カ/なに/なん) is a combination of 亻 (person) and the phonetic 可 (husky voice), unless it originates instead in a picture of someone carrying baggage. It meant "load," but came to be used to write a Chinese homonym meaning the interrogative "what".

幾何 (キ・カ geometry), 何 (なに/なん what, which)

河 (カ/かわ) is composed of 氵 (water) and the phonetic 可 (winding). It was originally the name of the Yellow River, and is used now for "large river."

河川 (カ・セン river), 河 (かわ river)

奇 (キ) is a combination of 大 (man) and the phonetic 可 (winding). With a basic sense apparently in the area of "wayward, eccentric, inclined to one side," it means "singular, strange, unexpected."

奇数 (キ・スウ odd number)

荷 (カ/に), a combination of 艹 (plant) and the phonetic 何, means "load" (the original meaning of 何) and "lotus."

入荷 (ニュウ・カ arrival of goods), 荷 (に load)

崎 (さき) combines 山 (mountain) with the phonetic 奇 (inclined) , but the *on-yomi* キ is not included in the Jōyō Kanji. It means "steep," but in Japan is used only with the sense of "promontory" and only in proper names.

長崎 (なが・さき Nagasaki)

寄 (キ/よる) consists of 宀 (house) and the phonetic 奇 (inclined) and means "draw to; donate; gather."

寄付 (キ・フ donation), 寄る (よ・る draw near; drop in)

歌 (カ/うた) is a combination of 欠 (someone yawning) and the phonetic 哥 (カ shout in a husky voice), a reduplication of 可. It means "sing, song," and in Japan *waka,* the thirty-one-syllable poem.

歌手 (カ・シュ singer), 歌 (うた song; *waka*)

騎 (キ) consists of 馬 (horse) and the phonetic 奇 (inclined) and means "horse-riding; rider" and is used as a counter for mounted horses.

騎手 (キ・シュ jockey)

兄 (キョウ/ケイ)   (big child; brother)

況 (キョウ) is a combination of 氵 (water) and the phonetic 兄 (big child). It means "comparison; state of affairs."

近況 (キン・キョウ the way things have been)

句 (ク)   (framed object)

拘 (コウ) consists of 扌 (hand) and the phonetic 句 (framed object) and means "seize and detain; be held."

拘束 (コウ・ソク restraint)

加 (ケ/カ)   (add)

架 (カ/か・ける) is a combination of 木 (wood) and the phonetic 加 (add). It means "crosspiece, beam; lay across, bridge."

架空 (カ・クウ aerial; fictitious), 架ける (か・ける span with)

賀 (ガ) is made of 貝 (wealth) and the phonetic 加 (add). It means "congratulate," from an earlier sense "bestow congratulatory gifts."

年賀状 (ネン・ガ・ジョウ New Year's card)

玄 (ゲン/ケン)   (fine thread)

弦 (ゲン/つる) is a combination of 弓 (bow) and the phonetic 玄 (fine thread), meaning "bowstring; string of a musical instrument; crescent."

弦楽器 (ゲン・ガッ・キ stringed instrument), 弦 (つる bowstring)

巨 (ゴ/キョ)   (distance)

拒 (キョ/こば・む) consists of 扌 (hand) and the phonetic 巨 (distance) and means "reject."

拒否 (キョ・ヒ denial), 拒む (こば・む refuse)

距 (キョ) adds 足 (foot and leg) to the phonetic 巨 (distance) and preserves the meaning "distance."
距離 (キョ・リ distance)

| 左 | (サ) | (left hand; support) |

佐 (サ) , a combination of 亻 (person) and the phonetic 左 (left hand), means "assist, support"; in Japan it is used for high military ranks roughly equivalent to "colonel".
補佐 (ホ・サ aid)

差 (サ/さ・す) is descended from a combination of a picture of an ear of grain and the phonetic 左 (support). It means "difference, inequality; dispatch a messenger" and, in Japan, "hold up, put forward."
差別 (サ・ベツ discrimination), 差し出す (さ・し・だ・す put forward; proffer)

| 司 | (シ) | (peep through hole) |

伺 (シ/うかが・う) is a combination of 亻 (person) and the phonetic 司 (peeping). With an original sense like "keep an eye on," it has come to be used in Japan for words meaning "humbly ask; visit."
伺候 (シ・コウ courtesy call), 伺う (うかが・う ask; visit)

詞 (シ) combines 言 (say) and the phonetic 司. It means "word; part of speech; sentence, poem."
助詞 (ジョ・シ grammatical particle)

飼 (シ/か・う) combines 食 (eat) and the phonetic 司 and means "raise, breed."
飼育 (シ・イク breeding), 飼う (か・う keep; raise)

嗣 (シ) consists of 口 (mouth), 冊 (bamboo tablet), and the phonetic 司. It means "heir."
嗣子 (シ・シ heir)

| 失 | (シチ/シツ) | (lose) |

迭 (テツ) is a combination of 辶 (walk) and the phonetic 失 (lose). It means "alternate."
更迭 (コウ・テツ shake-up)

秩 (チツ) consists of 禾 (rice plant) and the phonetic 失. From an original sense of "rick of rice plants" perhaps, it has come to mean "order, arrangement."
秩序 (チツ・ジョ order)

鉄 (テツ) long ago lost its original sense through being used as a simpler substitute for 鐵 (テツ iron), which is a combination of 金 (metal), 𢦏 (cut), and 呈 (flat). As such, 鉄 means "iron; hard, strong" and in Japan "railroad."
鉄道 (テツ・ドウ railroad)

| 正 | (ショウ/セイ) | (straight; correct) |

征 (セイ) , a combination of 彳 (go) and the phonetic 正 (straight), means "head straight for," or, now, "conquer."

征服 (セイ・フク conquest)

定 (テイ/ジョウ/さだ・める) consists of 宀 (roof) and a variant of 正 (straight) as phonetic. It means "fix; settle; certain"; in Buddhist writings it may refer to the attainment of a state of tranquillity.

定価 (テイ・カ fixed price), 定規 (ジョウ・ギ ruler; norm), 定める (さだ・める ordain)

政 (セイ/ショウ/まつりごと) is made of 攵 (action) and the phonetic 正 (straight). It means "govern; administration, politics."

政権 (セイ・ケン political power), 摂政 (セッ・ショウ regency), 政 (まつりごと affairs of state)

症 (ショウ) is a combination of 疒 (disease) and the phonetic 正 (straight). It means "disease."

症状 (ショウ・ジョウ symptom)

証 (ショウ) combines 言 (say) and the phonetic 正 (straight) and means "proof, evidence; certificate."

証明 (ショウ・メイ proof)

整 (セイ/ととの・える) is made up of 敕, a variant of 敕 (tighten), and the phonetic 正 (straight). It means "arrange neatly."

整理 (セイ・リ arrangement), 整える (ととの・える arrange)

錠 (ジョウ) is a combination of 金 (metal) and the phonetic 定 (fix; settle). Originally "tin, metal work," it now means, in Japan, "lock" and "pill"; it is also used as a counter for pills.

錠剤 (ジョウ・ザイ pill)

占 (セン)   (occupy; hold)

店 (テン/みせ) combines 广 (house) and the phonetic 占 (occupy) to mean "store, shop."

店員 (テン・イン store clerk), 店 (みせ shop)

点 (テン) is an abbreviation of 點, which combines 黒 (black) and the phonetic 占 (occupy) for the meaning "spot, dot; point, mark." It also means "light, turn on; check into; snack item" and is used as a counter for keeping score, or for art works and furniture.

粘 (ネン/ねば・る) consists of 米 (rice) and the phonetic 占 (hold). It means "sticky, viscid."

粘土 (ネン・ド clay), 粘る (ねば・る stick)

冬 (トウ)   (winter)

終 (シュウ/お・わる), a combination of 糸 (thread) and the phonetic 冬 (winter; end of year), means "end, final; done."

終了 (シュウ・リョウ completion), 終わる (お・わる end)

尼 (ニ/ジ or ネイ/デイ)   (stick to)

泥 (デイ/どろ) combines 氵 (water) and the phonetic 尼 (stick to); it means "mud, mire; bog down," and refers to certain kinds of paint, such as gold paint. In Japan it is associated in some words with the meaning "thief."

泥酔 (デイ・スイ intoxication), 泥 (どろ mud)

半 (ハン)   (half, halve)

伴 (ハン/バン/ともな・う) is a combination of イ (person) and the phonetic 半 (half). It means "companion; accompany."

同伴 (ドウ・ハン accompany), 伴奏 (バン・ソウ accompaniment), 伴う (ともな・う be accompanied by)

判 (ハン/バン) consists of 刂 (edged tool) and the phonetic 半 (halve). It means "divide; judge, distinguish; trial." Special senses in Japan are "hand-stamp, seal" and, with reference to book-pages and certain old gold coins, "size."

判断 (ハン・ダン judgment), 裁判 (サイ・バン trial)

畔 (ハン) combines 田 (field) and the phonetic 半 (halve) and means "path between cultivated fields" and it also has a derived meaning "shore."

湖畔 (コ・ハン lakeshore)

皮 (ビ/ヒ)   (skin; cover)

波 (ハ/なみ) consists of 氵 (water) and the phonetic 皮 (cover) and means "wave."

波紋 (ハ・モン ripples), 波 (なみ wave)

披 (ヒ) is a combination of 扌 (hand) and the phonetic 皮 (cover). It means "push open; uncover."

披露 (ヒ・ロウ announcement)

彼 (ヒ/かれ/かの) combines 彳 (go) and the phonetic 皮 (cover) to suggest pushing aside. It has the sense of "aside, over there, yonder" and is used as a third-person pronoun.

彼岸 (ヒ・ガン the far shore; Nirvana; equinoctial week), 彼 (かれ he), 彼女 (かの・ジョ she)

破 (ハ/やぶ・る) consists of 石 (stone) and the phonetic 皮 (cover) and means "break, tear; penetrate."

破産 (ハ・サン bankruptcy), 破る (やぶ・る tear, break)

疲 (ヒ/つか・れる) combines 疒 (ailment) with the phonetic 皮 (skin), supposedly to suggest limpness. It means "fatigued, tired."

疲労 (ヒ・ロウ fatigue), 疲れる (つか・れる get tired)

被 (ヒ/こうむ・る), a combination of 衤 (garment) and the phonetic 皮 (cover), means "cover; put on" with the abstract derived sense of "take on oneself, bear, suffer" from which it derives use as a passive-voice marker.

被害 (ヒ・ガイ damage), 被る (こうむ・る be subjected to)

婆 (バ) combines 女 (women) and the phonetic 波 (wave). It means "old woman."

老婆 (ロウ・バ old woman)

必 (ヒチ/ヒツ)   (wrap tight; squeeze; closed)

泌 (ヒツ/ヒ) combines 氵 (water) and the phonetic 必 (squeeze). It means "ooze out."

分泌 (ブン・ピツ/ブン・ピ secretion), 泌尿器科 (ヒ・ニョウ・キ・カ urology)

秘 (ヒ/ひ・める) used to be written 祕, combining 示 (altar) and the phonetic 必 (closed). It means "closed off; secret."

秘書 (ヒ・ショ secretary), 秘める (ひ・める keep secret)

密 (ミツ) consists of 山 (mountain) and the phonetic 宓 (closed-up house), the phonetic being a combination of 宀 (house) and the phonetic 必 (closed). It means "secret; close, dense" and refers to Esoteric Buddhism.

密度 (ミツ・ド density)

包 (ヒョウ/ホウ)   (enclose, wrap)

抱 (ホウ/だ・く/いだ・く/かか・える) has 扌 (hand) combined with the phonetic 包 (enclose) and means "embrace."

抱負 (ホウ・フ aspiration), 抱く (だ・く/いだ・く embrace), 抱える (かか・える hold in one's arms)

泡 (ホウ/あわ) is a combination of 氵 (water) and the phonetic 包 (enclose). It means "bubble, foam."

水泡 (スイ・ホウ bubble), 泡 (あわ bubble)

胞 (ホウ) combines 月 (flesh) and the phonetic 包 (enclose) and means "placenta; surrounding membrane."

細胞 (サイ・ボウ cell)

砲 (ホウ) consists of 石 (stone) and the phonetic 包 (wrap) and once referred to a military catapult, from which derives today's sense of "gun, firearm."

鉄砲 (テツ・ポウ gun)

飽 (ホウ/あ・きる) is a combination of 食 (eat) and the phonetic 包 (enclose); it means "full, satiated; cloy."

飽和 (ホウ・ワ saturation), 飽きる (あ・きる tire of)

付 (フ)   (attach)

府 (フ), a combination of 广 (house) and the phonetic 付 (attach), originally referred to a government vault for storing documents and valuables; now it means "administrative office; seat of government, capital." In Japan, it is translated "prefecture" with reference to Osaka or Kyoto only.

政府 (セイ・フ government)

附 (フ) is 阝 (mound) and the phonetic 付 (attach). It once referred to a kind of mound, but now means "attach, annex."

附属 （フ・ゾク attached to）

符 （フ） consists of 竹 (bamboo) and the phonetic 付 (attach) and means "tally, ticket," originating in halves of a split piece of wood or bamboo which would match when be placed together.

切符 （キッ・プ ticket）

腐 （フ/くさ・る） combines 肉 (meat) and the phonetic 府 (storage) and means "rot, putrefy."

腐敗 （フ・ハイ decomposition）, 腐る （くさ・る rot）

末 （マツ/バツ）   (branch tips)

抹 （マツ）, a combination of 扌 (hand) and the phonetic 末 (branch tips), means "rub out; powder."

抹殺 （マッ・サツ erasure）

未 （ミ/ビ）   (delicate young branch)

妹 （マイ/いもうと） consists of 女 (woman) and the phonetic 未 (young branch) and means "younger sister."

姉妹 （シ・マイ sisters）, 妹 （いもうと younger sister）

味 （ミ/あじ） combines 口 (mouth) and the phonetic 未 (delicate). It means "taste, flavor" and is used sometimes as a counter for ingredients or seasonings in a food or condiment.

意味 （イ・ミ meaning）, 味 （あじ taste）

魅 （ミ） combines 鬼 (spirit) and the phonetic 未. It refers to a certain magical spirit and also means "charm, enchant."

魅力 （ミ・リョク charm）

令 （リョウ/レイ）   (clear and cold)

冷 （レイ/つめ・たい/ひ・える/さ・める） is a combination of 冫 (ice) and the phonetic 令 (clear and cold). It means "cold."

冷静 （レイ・セイ composure）, 冷たい （つめ・たい cold）, 冷える （ひ・える get chilly）, 冷める （さ・める get cold）

鈴 （レイ/リン/すず） consisting of 金 (metal) and the phonetic 令 (clear and cold), is pronounced something like *ling* in Chinese and means "bell, chime."

電鈴 （デン・レイ electric bell）, 風鈴 （フウ・リン wind bells）, 鈴 （すず small bell）

零 （レイ） combines 雨 (weather) and the phonetic 令 (clear), and means "rain drop; drop, fall; very small; zero."

領 （リョウ）, a combination of 頁 (head) and the phonetic 令, means "neck; nod; gist; dominion; control; the person in power."

大統領 （ダイ・トウ・リョウ president of a nation）

齢 （レイ） consists of 歯 (tooth) and the phonetic 令; it means "age."

年齢 （ネン・レイ age）

6-Stroke Phonetics

安 (アン)   (ease; rest)

案 (アン) is a combination of 木 (wood) and the phonetic 安 (rest). It means "desk," from which derive "think; idea" and, in Japan, "plan, proposal, draft."

宴 (エン) consists of 宀 (house) and the phonetic 晏 (エン/アン sunset), a combination of 日 (sun) and the phonetic 安 (rest), without the 宀. It means "take it easy, find pleasure; party, feast."
　宴会 (エン・カイ banquet)

因 (イン)   (bed; press)

姻 (イン), a combination of 女 (woman) and the phonetic 因 (bed), means "matrimony."
　婚姻 (コン・イン marriage)

恩 (オン) has 心 (heart) combined with the phonetic 因 (press). It means "owe; debt."

有 (ユウ)   (possess)

賄 (ワイ/まかな・う) consists of 貝 (wealth) and the phonetic 有 (possess). Originally "possessions," it now means "bribe," or in Japan "board, provide meals for; manage, make do; provide, accommodate."
　賄賂 (ワイ・ロ bribery), 賄う (まかな・う manage)

会 (エ/カイ)   (gather; united)

絵 (カイ/エ) is a combination of 糸 (thread) and the phonetic 会 (united). Probably associated with colorful weaving or embroidery originally, it means "picture."
　絵画 (カイ・ガ painting), 絵 (エ picture)

各 (カク or ラク)   (foot; stop; stiffen)

客 (キャク/カク) is a combination of 宀 (house) and the phonetic 各 (stop). It means "guest, visitor; customer; outsider."
　客 (キャク guest; customer), 刺客 (シ・カク/シ・キャク assassin)

格 (カク/コウ) consists of 木 (wood) and the phonetic 各 (stop). It meant a piece of wood to block a wheel originally, and its derived senses range through "lattice, frame; rank, status; norm; grammatical case."
　合格 (ゴウ・カク qualifying), 格子 (コウ・シ lattice)

略 (リャク) has 田 (field) together with 各 (foot) and once meant "shortcut." Its current meanings are "scheme, plot; transgress, assault; abbreviation, curtailment."

絡 (ラク/から・む) is a combination of 糸 (thread) and the phonetic 各. It means "tie, link; connection; tangle, snare, enmesh."
　連絡 (レン・ラク contact), 絡む (から・む tangle)

酪 (ラク) is 酉 (wine jar) and the phonetic 各 (stiffen) and means "dairy product, dairy."

酪農 (ラク・ノウ dairy farming)

路 (ロ/じ) is a combination of ⻊ (foot and leg) and the phonetic 各 (foot). It means "road, route."

道路 (ドウ・ロ road), 旅路 (たび・じ journey)

閣 (カク) combines 門 (gate) with the phonetic 各 (stop). From an original sense of "doorstop," it has evolved to mean "grand building" and "cabinet of the goverment."

内閣 (ナイ・カク Cabinet)

落 (ラク/お・ちる) consists of ⺿ (plant) and the phonetic 洛 (ラク), a combination of 氵 (water) and the phonetic 各. It means "fall, drop; finish, end; hamlet."

落第 (ラク・ダイ flunk), 落ちる (お・ちる fall)

額 (ガク/ひたい), a combination of 頁 (head) and the phonetic 客, means "forehead." It has the derived senses of "picture frame; amount, sum."

額 (ガク frame; amount; ひたい forehead)

露 (ロ/ロウ/つゆ) consists of 雨 (weather) and the phonetic 路. It means "dew; expose, reveal" and "Russia," through its use to render the "Ru-" of that name.

露出 (ロ・シュツ exposure), 抜露 (ヒ・ロウ announcement), 露 (つゆ dew)

吉 (キチ/キツ)   (full; tightly closed, tighten)

壱 (イチ) is an abbreviation of 壹, which can be traced back to a combination of 壺 (covered jar) and the phonetic 吉 (full). It is often used as a substitute for 一 (one) in writing amounts of money, because it is more difficult to alter.

壱万円 (イチ・マン・エン 10,000 yen)

結 (ケツ/むす・ぶ/ゆ・う) consists of 糸 (thread) and the phonetic 吉 (tighten). It means "tie, bond; conclude." "Last" and "rice ball" are senses added in Japan.

結果 (ケッ・カ result), 結ぶ (むす・ぶ bind), 結納 (ゆい・ノウ betrothal present)

詰 (キツ/つ・める) is a combination of 言 (say) and the phonetic 吉 (tighten). It means "rebuke, pick on over a fault"; the Japanese sense of "pack, cram in" is probably derived from that. It also means "end" in Japan.

詰問 (キツ・モン harsh interrogation), 詰める (つ・める pack)

共 (ク/キョウ)   (offer; together)

供 (キョウ/ク/そな・える/とも) consists of 亻 (person) and the phonetic 共 (offer) and means "offer, supply." In Japan it also means "attendant, companion."

供給 (キョウ・キュウ supply), 供物 (ク・モツ votive offering), 供える (そな・える make an offering of), 子供 (こ・ども child)

洪 (コウ) combines 氵 (water) and the phonetic 共 (together) and means "flood."

洪水 (コウ・ズイ flood)

恭 (キョウ/うやうや・しい), a combination of a variant of 心 (heart) and the phonetic 共 (offer), means "revere."

恭順 (キョウ・ジュン allegiance), 恭しい (うやうや・しい reverant)

港 (コウ/みなと) is a slight revision of 港, a compound of 氵 (water) and the phonetic 巷 (コウ passage), which combines 巳, originally 邑 (village), and the phonetic 共. 港 means "port, harbor."

空港 (クウ・コウ airport), 港 (みなと harbor)

旨 (シ)   (tasty)

指 (シ/ゆび/さ・す), a combination of 扌 (hand) and the phonetic 旨, means "finger; point out, aim."

指導 (シ・ドウ guidance), 指 (ゆび finger; toe), 指す (さ・す point at)

脂 (シ/あぶら) consists of 月 (flesh) and the phonetic 旨 (tasty). It means "fat, grease," extended to "resin" and "rouge."

脂粉 (シ・フン rouge and powder), 脂 (あぶら fat)

至 (シ)   (reach, come to the end)

室 (シツ/むろ) is a combinatiom of 宀 (house) and the phonetic 至 (come to an end). It means "room," with extensions in "Imperial family; wife of ruler."

室内 (シツ・ナイ indoors), 室 (むろ cellar)

致 (チ/いた・す) was originally a combination of 夂 (feet) and the phonetic 至 (reach). It means "reach, attain; cause, invite; style"; it is used further in Japan for a humble word meaning "do."

致命的 (チ・メイ・テキ fatal), 致す (いた・す do)

窒 (チツ) consists of 穴 (cave) and the phonetic 至 (come to the end) and means "suffocate."

窒息 (チッ・ソク suffocation)

次 (シ)   (arrange)

姿 (シ/すがた) combines 女 (woman) and the phonetic 次 (arrange) and means "figure, appearance, the way one looks."

姿勢 (シ・セイ posture), 姿 (すがた figure)

資 (シ) consists of 貝 (wealth) and the phonetic 次 (arrange). It means "fund, capital; innate qualities, gifts, endowments."

資金 (シ・キン fund)

諮 (シ/はか・る) is a combination of 言 (say) and the phonetic 咨 (シ discuss), which is 口 (mouth) combined with the phonetic 次 (arrange). 諮 means "counsel."

諮問 (シ・モン inquiry), 諮る (はか・る consult over)

守 (シュ/シュウ)   (chase into pen)

狩 (シュ/か・る), a combination of 犭 (animal) and the phonetic 守 (chase), means "chase, hunt."

狩猟 (シュ・リョウ hunting), 狩る (か・る hunt)

朱 (ス/シュ)　　　　　　　　　　　　　　　　　　　　　　(stump; red)

株 (かぶ) consists of 木 (tree) and the phonetic 朱 (stump), but the *on-yomi* シュ is not included in the Jōyō Kanji. It means "stump, stub; stock, shares" and can also be used to count them, as well as to count plants. It also has some of the figurative senses of English "stock," such as "public esteem; assets; one's stock-in-trade, forte."
　　株式会社 (かぶ・シキ・ガイ・シャ joint-stock company)

殊 (シュ/こと) consists of 歹 (dead) and the phonetic 朱 (stump) and originally means "fell, chop down," but has come to mean "special, distinctive."
　　特殊 (トク・シュ distinctive), 殊に (こと・に especially)

珠 (シュ), a combination of 王 (gem) and the phonetic 朱 (red) means "jewel, bead."
　　真珠 (シン・ジュ pearl)

州 (ス/シュウ)　　　　　　　　　　　　　　　　　　　　　(go around)

酬 (シュウ), combination of 酉 (wine jar) and the phonetic 州 (go around), means "repay a drink; repay."
　　報酬 (ホウ・シュウ remuneration)

庄 (ショウ/ソウ)　　　　　　　　　　　　　　　　　　　　(house)

粧 (ショウ), a combination of 米 (rice) and the phonetic 庄, means "adorn."
　　化粧 (ケ・ショウ makeup)

争 (ショウ/ソウ)　　　　　　　　　　　　　　　　　　　　(fight)

浄 (ジョウ) consists of 氵 (water) and the phonetic 争 and means "clean; purity."
　　浄化 (ジョウ・カ purge)

舌 (ゼツ)　　　　　　　　　　　　　　　　　　　　　　　(tongue)
　 (カツ)　　　　　　　　　(whittling knife; smooth, vigorous motion)

活 (カツ) is a combination of 氵 (water) and the phonetic 舌 which is not 舌 (tongue), but 舌 (whittling knife; smooth vigorous motion). It means "liveliness, vigor."
　　生活 (セイ・カツ living)

括 (カツ) consists of 扌 (hand) and the phonetic 舌 (knife) and means "bundle, bunch."
　　一括 (イッ・カツ lumping together)

話 (ワ/はな・す/はなし) is a combination of 言 (say) and the phonetic 舌 (knife; vigorous) it means "talk, tell; tale."
　　民話 (ミン・ワ folktale), 話す (はな・す talk), 話 (はなし a talk)

憩 (ケイ/いこ・い) combines 息 (breathing) and the phonetic 舌 (smooth motion) and means "a breather; relax, rest."
　　休憩 (キュウ・ケイ rest), 憩い (いこ・い relaxation)

先 (セン)   (tiptoe, foot)

洗 (セン/あら・う) combines 氵 (water) and the phonetic 先 (foot) to symbolize "wash."

洗剤 (セン・ザイ detergent), 洗う (あら・う wash)

銑 (セン) consists of 金 (metal) and an abbreviation of the phonetic 洗 (wash). It means "pig iron."

銑鉄 (セン・テツ pig iron)

全 (ゼン/セン)   (round and whole)

栓 (セン), a combination of 木 (wood) and the phonetic 全 (round and whole), means "stopper, cork."

早 (ソウ)   (early)

草 (ソウ/くさ) consists of 艹 (grass) and the phonetic 早. It means "grass, plant" and also has the senses of "rough, unpolished; a draft; cursive (style of writing kanji)."

草案 (ソウ・アン rough idea), 草 (くさ grass)

多 (タ)   (plenty)

移 (イ/うつ・る) consists of 禾 (rice plant) and the phonetic 多. It means "move, shift, transfer."

移住 (イ・ジュウ migration), 移る (うつ・る move)

同 (ズウ/ドウ)   (hollow)

洞 (ドウ/ほら), a combination of 氵 (water) and the phonetic 同 (hollow), means "cave; see through."

洞察 (ドウ・サツ insight), 洞穴 (ほら・あな/ドウ・ケツ cave)

胴 (ドウ), a combination of 月 (flesh) and the phonetic 同 (hollow), means "torso, trunk, body."

筒 (トウ/つつ), a combination of 竹 (bamboo) and the phonetic 同 (hollow), means "tube, cylinder."

封筒 (フウ・トウ envelope), 筒 (つつ cylinder)

銅 (ドウ) consists of 金 (metal) and the phonetic 同 (hollow) for the malleable metal "copper."

伐 (ボチ/バツ)   (chop; show off)

閥 (バツ) is a combination of 門 (gate) and the phonetic 伐 (show off). It means "clique, sect."

派閥 (ハ・バツ faction)

毎 (マイ/バイ)   (mother; dark)

侮 (ブ/あなど・る) consists of 亻 (person) and the phonetic 毎; it means "despise."

侮辱 (ブ・ジョク insult), 侮る (あなど・る despise)

海 (カイ/うみ) is a combination of 氵 (water) and the phonetic 毎 (dark). It means "sea."

海外 (カイ・ガイ abroad), 海 (うみ sea)

悔 (カイ/く・いる/くや・しい), a combination of 忄 (heart) and the phonetic 毎 (dark), means "repent, regret; remorse" and in Japan, "condolence."

後悔 (コウ・カイ regret), 悔いる (く・いる repent), 悔しい (くや・しい vexatious)

梅 (バイ/うめ) is a combination of 木 (tree) and the phonetic 毎 (mother) and means "plum," a tree that seems to have symbolized fertility.

梅雨 (バイ・ウ rainy season), 梅 (うめ plum)

名 (ミョウ/メイ)   (name)

銘 (メイ) consists of 金 (metal) and the phonetic 名 (name). It means "inscribe, inscription" and is used to indicate a special name on a high-grade product.

銘柄 (メイ・がら brand)

列 (レチ/レツ)   (break up; dissect)

例 (レイ/たと・え) is a combination of 亻 (person) and the phonetic 列 (dissect). It means "example; typical case; normal, usual."

例年 (レイ・ネン ordinary year; annually), 例えば (たと・えば for example)

烈 (レツ) is a combination of 灬 (fire) and the phonetic 列 (break up). It means "severe, violent, intense."

熱烈 (ネツ・レツ ardent)

裂 (レツ/さ・く), 衣 (garment) combines with the phonetic 列 (break up), means "tear, rend."

分裂 (ブン・レツ dissolution), 裂く (さ・く rip)

7-Stroke Phonetics

我 (ガ)   (halberd; jagged)

義 (ギ) is a combination of 羊 (sheep) and the phonetic 我 (halberd). It means "right, justice; significance, meaning; in-law."   In Japan it also means "duty."

義理 (ギ・リ social obligations)

餓 (ガ) combines 食 (eat) and the phonetic 我 (jagged). It means "hunger."

餓死 (ガ・シ death by starvation)

儀 (ギ) is a combination of 亻 (person) and the phonetic 義 (right). It means "ritual, ceremony; model, replica" and in Japan, "case, matter to be handled."

儀式 (ギ・シキ rite)

犠 (ギ) combines 牜 (ox) and the phonetic 義 (right), and means "sacrifice."

犠牲 (ギ・セイ sacrifice)

議 (ギ) is a combination of 言 (say) and the phonetic 義 (right), means "debate, discussion."

議会 （ギ・カイ Congress; Parliament)

孝 （キョウ/コウ)   (mix; exchange)

教 （キョウ/おし・える/おそ・わる), previously 敎, is a combination of 攵(action), 子 (child), and the phonetic 爻 （コウ cross; exchange). It means "teach, educate; religion."

教育 （キョウ・いく education), 教える （おし・える teach), 教わる （おそ・わる learn)

酵 （コウ) combines 酉 (wine jar) with the phonetic 孝 (mix) for the meaning "ferment."

発酵 （ハッ・コウ fermentation)

呉 （グ/ゴ)   (delight; dismay)

娯 （ゴ) combines 女 (woman) and the phonetic 呉 (delight). It means "enjoy."
娯楽 （ゴ・ラク amusement)

虞 （おそれ), a combination of 虍 (tiger) and the phonetic 呉 (dismay), meaning "fear, worry."   Its *on-yomi* グ is not included in the Jōyō Kanji.

誤 （ゴ/あやま・る) consists of 言 (say) and the phonetic 呉 (dismay); it means "error."
誤解 （ゴ・カイ misunderstanding), 誤る （あやま・る mistake)

戒 （ケ/カイ)   (holding halberd)

械 （カイ) is a combination of 木 (wood) and the phonetic 戒 (holding halberd). It originally meant a wooden manacle and now means "device, machine."
機械 （キ・カイ machinery)

系 （ゲ/ケイ)   (tie)

係 （ケイ/かか・る/かかり) consists of 亻 (person) and the phonetic 系 (tie); it means "connect" and in Japan, "in charge."
関係 （カン・ケイ connection), 係る （かか・る connect), 係の人 （かかり・の・ひと person in charge)

見 （ゲン/ケン)   (see)

現 （ゲン/あらわ・れる) is 王 (gem) and the phonetic 見 (see). It means "visible; appearance; presence; present, actual."
現在 （ゲン・ザイ the present), 現れる （あらわ・れる appear)

更 （コウ)   (stiff)

硬 （コウ/かた・い) consists of 石 (stone) and the phonetic 更 (stiff) and means "hard, rigid."
硬貨 （コウ・カ coin), 硬い （かた・い hard)

谷 （コク)   (valley; go inside; hollow; spacious)

俗 （ゾク) combines 亻 (person) and the phonetic 谷 (go inside); it means "the world, society; common, ordinary; vulgar; lay, not clerical; custom."

俗説 （ゾク・セツ popular belief）

容 （ヨウ） consists of 宀 (house) and the phonetic 谷 (valley); it means "put in, let in; contain; looks, appearance."
内容 （ナイ・ヨウ content）

浴 （ヨク/あ・びる）, a combination of 氵 (water) and the phonetic 谷 (go in), means "bathe, shower."
浴室 （ヨク・シツ bath room）, 浴びる （あ・びる bathe in）

欲 （ヨク/ほっ・する/ほ・しい） combines 欠 (someone stooping down) and the phonetic 谷 (hollow) for "desire, want."
欲 （ヨク desire）, 欲する （ほっ・する want）, 欲しい （ほ・しい want）

裕 （ユウ） is a combination of 衤 (garment) and the phonetic 谷 (spacious). It means "abundance; generosity."
裕福 （ユウ・フク affluent）

溶 （ヨウ/と・ける） is a combination of 氵 (water) and the phonetic 容 (put in). It means "dissolve, melt."
溶液 （ヨウ・エキ solution）, 溶ける （と・ける melt）

告 （コク）   (tighten)

酷 （コク） is a combination of 酉 (wine jar) and the phonetic 告 (tighten). It originally meant "strong liquor" and now means "harsh."
残酷 （ザン・コク cruel）

赤 （シャク/セキ）   (red)

赦 （シャ） consists of 攵 (action) and the phonetic 赤. It means "pardon."
容赦 （ヨウ・シャ pardon）

秀 （シュ/シュウ）   (leading)

誘 （ユウ/さそ・う）, 言 (say) and the phonetic 秀 (leading), means "lead, guide; invite; entice."
誘導 （ユウ・ドウ induction）, 誘う （さそ・う tempt）

折 （セチ/セツ）   (break off, snap)

逝 （セイ/ゆ・く） consists of 辶 (walk) and the phonetic 折 (break off) and means "depart, pass away."
急逝 （キュウ・セイ untimely death）, 逝く （ゆ・く pass away）

哲 （テツ）, combining 口 (mouth) and the phonetic 折 (snap), probably to suggest articulateness, means "wise; wise man." In Japan it is also used to abbreviate the word for "philosophy."
哲学 （テツ・ガク philosophy）

誓 （セイ/ちか・う） is a combination of 言 (say) and the phonetic 折 (break off), perhaps to symbolize making contract-proving tallies; it means "oath; swear."

宣誓 (セン・セイ oath), 誓う (ちか・う swear)

即 (ソク)　　　　　　　　　　　　　　　　　　　　　　　　(kneeling person)

節 (セツ/セチ/ふし), combining 竹 (bamboo) and the phonetic 即 (kneeling person), means basically "joint"; as of bamboo or knees, or "section"; figurative uses have expanded its range of meaning to include "knot, node, lump; identifying tally; measure in music; paragraph; air, tune; moderate; segmentations of the year into seasons."　It also has limited use as a counter for joints, knots, and pieces of music, and in Japan it can mean "juncture, occasion."

節度 (セツ・ド moderation), お節料理 (お・セチ・リョウ・リ dishes served at New Years), 節 (ふし joint; tune; セツ occasion)

束 (ソク/ショク)　　　　　　　　　　　　　　　　　(shove together, bundle)

速 (ソク/はや・い/すみ・やか) consists of 辶 (walk) and the phonetic 束 (shove together) and means "fast, speedy."

時速 (ジ・ソク speed per hour), 速い (はや・い swift), 速やか (すみ・やか prompt)

頼 (ライ/たの・む/たよ・る) , until recently also written in its earlier form 賴, combined 貝 (wealth) and the phonetic 剌 (ラツ) which consists of 刂 (edged tool) and 束 (bundle). It means "rely" and in Japan "request."

依頼 (イ・ライ request), 頼む (たの・む rely; request), 頼る (たよ・る rely)

瀬 (せ) consists of 氵 (water) and, the phonetic 頼; the *on-yomi* ライ is not included in the Jōyō Kanji. 瀬 means "shoal; rapids"; via an implicit sense of "place to cross a river" it acquired the sense of "chance, opportunity" in Japan.

弟 (ダイ/テイ)　　　　　　　　　　　　　　　　　　　　　　　(step)

第 (ダイ), a combination of 竹 (bamboo) and a reduction of 弟 (step), means "order, rank" and is used as a prefix to form ordinal numbers; it also may mean "qualifying examination."

第三者 (ダイ・サン・シャ a third party)

役 (ヤク/エキ)　　　　　　　　　　　　　　　　　　　　　　(hard duty)

疫 (エキ/ヤク), a combination of 疒 (disease) and a reduction of the phonetic 役 (hard duty) means "plague."

免疫 (メン・エキ immunity), 疫病神 (ヤク・ビョウ・がみ pest)

余 (ヨ)　　　　　　　　　　　　　　　　　　　(shovel; stretch out; relax)

舎 (シャ) used to be written 舍, and earlier still combined 口 (space) and the phonetic 余 (stretch out). It means a place to stretch out and relax; "bunkhouse, barracks, dormitory, temporary residence." It also occurs in forms referring humbly to one's brothers.

寄宿舎 (キ・シュク・シャ dormitory)

叙 (ジョ), combination of 又 (hand) and the phonetic 余 (stretch out), means "relate in rational order; rank, order."

叙述 (ジョ・ジュツ description)

茶 (チャ/サ) combines 艹 (plant) with the phonetic 余 (relax), one stroke reduced. It means "tea," the plant and the beverage.

茶 (チャ tea; green tea), 喫茶店 (キッ・サ・テン coffee house)

除 (ジョ/ジ/のぞ・く) consists of 阝 (mound) and the phonetic 余 (shovel) and means "remove, exclude; arithmetic division."

除夜 (ジョ・ヤ New Year's Eve), 掃除 (ソウ・ジ cleaning), 除く (のぞ・く exclude)

徐 (ジョ) is 彳 (go) combined with the phonetic 余 (shovel) and means "slowly."

徐行 (ジョ・コウ going slowly)

途 (ト) consists of 辶 (walk) and the phonetic 余 (stretch out) and means "road, route, course."

途中 (ト・チュウ on the way)

斜 (シャ/なな・め) is a combination of 斗 (dipper) and the phonetic 余 (shovel); its current meaning, "oblique; slant," may or may not have been the original sense.

斜面 (シャ・メン slope), 斜め (なな・め oblique)

塗 (ト/ぬ・る) is a combination of 氵 (water), 土 (earth), and the phonetic 余 (shovel). It means "paint, plaster."

塗料 (ト・リョウ paint), 塗る (ぬ・る paint)

捨 (シャ/すて・る) consists of 扌 (hand) and the phonetic 舎. It means "discard, throw away."

取捨 (シュ・シャ selection), 捨てる (す・てる discard)

里 (リ)   (divide, section off)

厘 (リン) consists of 厂 (cliff) and the phonetic 里 (divide). It means "very small unit; one one-hundredth; one one-thousandth," as used variously in weights and measures.

九分九厘 (ク・ブ・ク・リン nearly all)

埋 (マイ/う・める) is a combination of 土 (earth) and the phonetic 里. It means "bury."

埋葬 (マイ・ソウ burial), 埋める (う・める bury)

理 (リ) combines 王 (gem) and the phonetic 里 (section off). It had a meaning like "the inherent sectioning, or grain, of a gem-stone" and more broadly means "lines, grain; principle, reason, logic; put right, manage, control."

理由 (リ・ユウ reason)

童; 鐘 (重, p.187, 188)

裏 (リ/うら) has 衣 (garment) with the phonetic 里 (section off) inside. It referred to a striped material that was used for linings of clothing and means "lining; the other side, the reverse."

表裏 (ヒョウ・リ front and back), 裏 (うら undersurface; back)

利 (リ)   (go through easily)

痢 (リ) consists of 疒 (sick) and the phonetic 利 (go through easily) and means "diarrhea."

　下痢 (ゲ・リ diarrhea)

8-Stroke Phonetics

延 (エン)   (extend)

誕 (タン) is a combination of 言 (say) and the phonetic 延 (extend). It originally meant "lie, whopper," but is used today for the borrowed meaning of "be born."

　誕生日 (タン・ジョウ・ビ birthday)

炎 (エン)   (flame)

淡 (タン/あわ・い) consists of 氵 (water) and the phonetic 炎. It means "light, faint, thin," typically in reference to such things as flavor, color, and feelings.

　淡水 (タン・スイ fresh water), 淡い (あわ・い faint)

談 (ダン) combines 言 (say) and the phonetic 炎 (flame); its meaning has weakened from "spirited discourse" to "talk."

　談話 (ダン・ワ talk)

果 (カ or ラ)   (fruit)

菓 (カ), with 艹 (plant) added to the phonetic 果 (fruit), is used for an extension of the meaning "fruit" to something like "pleasure food," namely "candy, cracker, cooky; confection, sweets."

　菓子 (カ・シ candy)

裸 (ラ/はだか) is a combination of 衤 (garment) and the phonetic 果 (fruit); it means "naked."

　裸体 (ラ・タイ naked body), 裸 (はだか naked)

課 (カ) combines 言 (say) and the phonetic 果 (fruit) and means "impose, assign; lesson; section; department."

　課長 (カ・チョウ section chief)

官 (カン)   (building in walled yard; surround)

棺 (カン) combines 木 (wood) and the phonetic 官 (surround); it means "coffin."

管 (カン/くだ) combines 竹 (bamboo) and the phonetic 官 (surround) and means "pile, tube; writing brush; wind instrument; control, administer."

　管理 (カン・リ administration), 管 (くだ pipe)

館 (カン) consists of 飠 (eat) and the phonetic 官 (building). The meaning has generalized from "inn" to "large building," especially a public building.

　旅館 (リョ・カン inn)

屈 (クツ)   (dent)

掘 (クツ/ほ・る), a combination of 扌 (hand) and the phonetic 屈 (dent), means "dig, excavate."

発掘 (ハッ・クツ excavation), 掘る (ほ・る dig)

堀 (ほり) consists of 土 (earth) and the phonetic 屈 (dent), but its *on-yomi* クツ is not included in the Jōyō Kanji. It means "pit," and, in Japan, "moat, canal."

昆 (コン)   (abundant)

混 (コン/まじ・る) consists of 氵 (water) and the phonetic 昆 (abundant); it means "mix."

混雑 (コン・ザツ crowdedness), 混じる (ま・じる get mixed)

参 (サン)   (three)

惨 (サン/ザン/みじ・め) consists of 忄 (heart) and the phonetic 参. It means "misery; atrocity."

惨事 (サン・ジ disaster), 惨殺 (ザン・サツ slaughter), 惨め (みじ・め miserable)

直 (ジキ/チョク)   (set straight)

値 (チ/ね/あたい) is a combination of 亻 (person) and the phonetic 直 (straight). The basic meaning was something like "match up with, correspond to" and the prevailing sense is "value" and, in Japan, "price, cost."

価値 (カ・チ worth), 値段 (ね・ダン price), 値 (あたい value; ね price)

植 (ショク/う・える) consists of 木 (tree) and the phonetic 直 (set straight), and means "plant; settle"; in Japan it also means "set type."

植物 (ショク・ブツ plants), 植える (う・える plant)

殖 (ショク/ふ・える), a combination of 歹 (die) and the phonetic 直 (straight), means "procreate, propagate, accrue." There is no consensus on why the word is written this way, but the meaning may be related to that of the preceding character, 植.

繁殖 (ハン・ショク propagation), 殖える (ふ・える accrue)

置 (チ/お・く) consists of 罒 (net) and the phonetic 直 (straighten); it means "put, place."

位置 (イ・チ position), 置く (お・く set)

徳 (トク) is made up of 彳 (go), 心 (heart), and a slightly modified form of the phonetic 直 (straight); it means "virtue, grace" and, in Japan, "profit."

者 (シャ)   (fireplace; gather)

書 (ショ/か・く) is a combination of 聿 (brush) and a reduction of the phonetic 者. It means "write; calligraphy; document, book."

書道 (ショ・ドウ calligraphy), 書く (か・く write)

著 (チョ/あらわ・す/いちじる・しい), combining 艹 (plant) and the phonetic 者 (gather). It originally meant "chopsticks," but is now used for "distinct, evident, striking; authorship."

著者 (チョ・シャ author), 著す (あらわ・す write [a book]), 著しい (いちじる・
しい distinct)

都 (ト/ツ/みやこ), consisting of 阝 (town) and the phonetic 者 (gather), means
"metropolis; capital; all together; govern" and, in Japan, may refer to Tokyo.

都心 (ト・シン heart of big city), 都合 (ツ・ゴウ circumstances), 都 (みやこ capital)

煮 (シャ/に・る), adding 灬 (fire) to the phonetic 者 (fire), means "boil, cook."

煮沸 (シャ・フツ boiling), 煮る (に・る cook)

暑 (ショ/あつ・い) combines 日 (sun) with the phonetic 者 (fire) and means
"hot; heat."

暑中 (ショ・チュウ midsummer), 暑い (あつ・い hot)

着 (チャク/ジャク/き・る/つ・く) originated as a variant form of 著 (distinct),
listed above, which also used to have readings and meanings now assigned
exclusively to this Jōyō Kanji. The meanings are "stick to, attach; arrive; settle;
wear." In Japan it is also used as a counter for sets of clothing and for finishing
positions in a race.

着陸 (チャク・リク landing), 愛着 (アイ・チャク/アイ・ジャク attachment), 着る
(き・る don), 着く (つ・く arrive)

署 (ショ) combines 罒 (net) and the phonetic 者. It means "division of labor;
government office; to sign."

署名 (ショ・メイ signature)

緒 (ショ/チョ/お) is a combination of 糸 (thread) and the phonetic 者 (gather).
Originally "spool" and then "end of a thread," it means "beginning, starting point;
string, cord."

一緒 (イッ・ショ together), 情緒 (ジョウ・チョ emotion), 緒 (お cord)

諸 (ショ), a combination of 言 (say) and the phonetic 者 (gather), means
"various."

諸国 (ショ・コク various countries)

昔 (シャク/セキ)   (many days; pile up)

借 (シャク/か・りる) is a combination of 亻 (person) and the phonetic 昔 (pile
up); it means "borrow, rent."

借金 (シャッ・キン debt), 借りる (か・りる borrow)

惜 (セキ/お・しい), consisting of 忄 (heart) and the phonetic 昔 (many days),
means "regret; begrudge, spare."

惜別 (セキ・ベツ sad farewell), 惜しい (お・しい regretable, precious)

措 (ソ) combines 扌 (hand) and the phonetic 昔 (pile up) and means "posit."

措置 (ソ・チ measures)

錯 (サク), a combination of 金 (metal) and the phonetic 昔 (pile up), means
"mix up; confusion, disorder."

錯覚 (サッ・カク misjudge)

籍 (セキ) consists of 竹 (bamboo) and the phonetic 耤 (セキ pile of earth), which is a combination of 耒 (plow) and the phonetic 昔 (pile up). 籍 means "document, book; register."

取 (シュ)   (catch)

趣 (シュ/おもむき) combines 走 (run) and the phonetic 取 (catch) and means basically "head for" with the derived sense "inclination, predilection."
趣味 (シュ・ミ taste; hobby), 趣 (おもむき taste; purport)

青 (ショウ/セイ)   (clear; clean)

清 (セイ/ショウ/きよ・い), 氵 (water) and the phonetic 青 (clear), means "clear, pure."
清潔 (セイ・ケツ cleanliness), 清浄 (セイ・ジョウ/ショウ・ジョウ immaculacy), 清い (きよ・い pure)

情 (ジョウ/セイ/なさ・け) is a combination of 忄 (heart) and the phonetic 青. It means "emotion, feeling; affection, love; state of affairs."
情報 (ジョウ・ホウ information), 風情 (フ・ゼイ taste; air), 情け (なさ・け sympathy; mercy)

晴 (セイ/は・れる) combines 日 (sun) and the phonetic 青 (clear). It means "unclouded, fair; clear up" and, in Japan, "festive."
晴天 (セイ・テン clear sky), 晴れる (は・れる clear up)

静 (セイ/ジョウ/しず・か) consists of 争 (fight) and the phonetic 青 (clear) and means "silent, still." Another view takes 争 (ソウ) to be the phonetic and 青 the semantic of this kanji.
静止 (セイ・シ standstill), 静脈 (ジョウ・ミャク vein), 静か (しず・か quiet)

精 (セイ/ショウ) is 米 (rice) and the phonetic 青 (clean) to mean "polished rice"; the modern meanings are "refined; exact; spirit; vigor."
精 (セイ spirit; vigor), 不精 or 無精 (ブ・ショウ indolence)

請 (セイ/シン/う・ける/こ・う) is 言 (say) and the phonetic 青. It means "request" and, in Japan, "redeem."
請求 (セイ・キュウ demand), 普請 (フ・シン construction), 請う (こ・う request), 請け負う (う・け・お・う contract for)

尚 (ジョウ/ショウ)   (rise; spread)

当 (トウ/あ・たる) is a replacement for 當, which consists of 田 (field) and the phonetic 尚 and means "allot; assigned; confront; hit, not miss; proper; the one concerned, in question." In certain Japanese expressions its use is equivalent to "per."
当分 (トウ・ブン for the time being), 当たる (あ・たる hit)

党 (トウ) consists of 儿 (person) and the phonetic 尚 and was used to write a Tibetan clan name, but cane to be used for a homophone 黨 (トウ), a combination of 黒 (dark) and the phonetic 尚 that meant "village community." 党 now means "gang, group; political party."

野党 (ヤ・トウ party out of power)

常 (ジョウ/つね/とこ) is a combination of 巾 (cloth) and the phonetic 尚 (spread). It originally meant "long skirt," but is now used in the senses of "long time; always, usual; ordinary."

日常 (ニチ・ジョウ everyday), 常 (つね normalcy), 常夏 (とこ・なつ everlasting summer)

堂 (ドウ), a combination of 土 (earth) and the phonetic 尚 (rise), once meant "large foundation"; it now means "stately house, building, hall; stately, majestic." It is used to name halls and stores, in pen names, and in honorific reference to someone else's mother.

国会議事堂 (コッ・カイ・ギ・ジ・ドウ Diet Building)

掌 (ショウ) consists of 手 (hand) and the phonetic 尚 (spread) and means "palm of the hand; control."

合掌 (ガッ・ショウ hands together in prayer)

賞 (ショウ) is a combination of 貝 (wealth) and the phonetic 尚. It means "prize, reward; praise, appreciate."

賞金 (ショウ・キン prize money)

償 (ショウ/つぐな・う) combines 亻 (person) and the phonetic 賞 (prize); it means "compensate."

償却 (ショウ・キャク repayment), 償う (つぐな・う compensate)

周 (ス/シュウ)   (around, all over)

週 (シュウ) a combination of 辶 (walk) and the phonetic 周 (around), means "go around" and "week."

週末 (シュウ・マツ weekend)

彫 (チョウ/ほ・る), a combination of 彡 (design) and the phonetic 周 (all over), means "engrave."

彫刻 (チョウ・コク sculpture), 彫る (ほ・る engrave)

調 (チョウ/しら・べる/ととの・える) combines 言 (say) with the phonetic 周 (all over) for "arrange, regulate, harmonize; check, investigate; tone, harmony; rhythm."

調和 (チョウ・ワ harmony), 調べる (しら・べる investigate), 調う (ととの・う get well-arranged)

垂 (ズイ/スイ)   (hang)

睡 (スイ) consists of 目 (eye) and the phonetic 垂 (hang) and means "slumber."
睡眠 (スイ・ミン sleep)

錘 (スイ/つむ) a combination of 金 (metal) and the phonetic 垂 (hang), means "weight used on a balance" and "spindle."

紡錘 (ボウ・スイ spindle), 錘 (つむ spindle)

叔 (スク/シュク)　(pick beans)

　寂 (ジャク/セキ/さび・しい) is a combination of 宀 (house) and the phonetic 叔; it means "quiet; solitary, lonely"
　　静寂 (セイ・ジャク still), 寂 (セキ silent), 寂しい (さび・しい lonesome)

　淑 (シュク) consists of 氵 (water) and the phonetic 叔; it means "gentle, genteel," likely as a "borrowed" meaning.
　　淑女 (シュク・ジョ lady)

　督 (トク) combines 目 (eye) and the phonetic 叔 (pick beans) and means "supervise; urge."
　　監督 (カン・トク supervision; director)

制 (セイ)　(cut)

　製 (セイ) a combination of 衣 (garment) and the phonetic 制 (cut) means "manufacture; production."
　　製作 (セイ・サク production)

宗 (ソ/ソウ)　(family altar)

　崇 (スウ), combining 山 (mountain) and the phonetic 宗 (altar), means "lofty; adore."
　　崇拝 (スウ・ハイ worship)

卒; 卆 (ソチ/ソツ or シュチ/シュツ)　(small; uniform; finish)

　砕 (サイ/くだ・く) is a combination of 石 (stone) and the phonetic 卆 (small), a simplified form of 卒. It means "shatter."
　　粉砕 (フン・サイ pulverization), 砕く (くだ・く shatter)

　粋 (スイ), a combination of 米 (rice) with the phonetic 卆 (uniform), means "pure, unadulterated; fine" and, in Japan, "essence; smart, chic; delicacy, tact."
　　純粋 (ジュン・スイ pure)

　酔 (スイ/よ・う), a combination of 酉 (wine jar) and the phonetic 卆 (finish), means "drunk; motion sickness."
　　陶酔 (トウ・スイ intoxication), 酔う (よ・う get drunk)

卓 (タク)　(prominent)

　悼 (トウ/いた・む), a combination of 忄 (heart) and the phonetic 卓 means "grief; lament."
　　哀悼 (アイ・トウ condolence), 悼む (いた・む lament)

知 (チ)　(intelligence)

　痴 (チ) uses the phonetic 知 to simplify 癡, a combination of 疒 (disease) and 疑 (perplexed), that means "foolish, misguided," particularly as "befuddled with carnal desire."
　　痴漢 (チ・カン molester)

若 (ニャク/ジャク)   (young)

諾 (ダク), a combination of 言 (say) and the phonetic 若, means "assent."
承諾 (ショウ・ダク consent)

表 (ヒョウ)   (front)

俵 (ヒョウ/たわら) is made of 亻 (person) and the phonetic 表 (front). It properly
means "spread," but it refers in Japan to straw bags used to transport rice,
charcoal, and other goods, and it is used as a counter for such bags.
土俵 (ド・ヒョウ sumo ring), 俵 (たわら straw bag)

奉 (ブ/ホウ)   (hold in two hands)

俸 (ホウ) combines 亻 (person) and the phonetic 奉 (hold in two hands) and
means "salary."
俸給 (ホウ・キュウ salary)

棒 (ボウ) consists of 木 (wood) and the phonetic 奉 (hold in two hands). It
means "stick, rod; beat with a stick"; in Japan it also refers to written dashes and
straight lines.

奔 (ホン)   (dash out)

噴 (フン/ふ・く) is a combination of 口 (mouth) and the phonetic 賁 (フン puff
up), which consists of 貝 (shell) and a reduced form of the phonetic 奔 (dash out).
噴 means "spurt, spew, emit."
噴火 (フン・カ eruption), 噴く (ふ・く gush)

墳 (フン) combines 土 (earth) and the phonetic 賁 (puff up). It means "burial
mound, tomb."
古墳 (コ・フン ancient burial mound)

憤 (フン/いきどお・る) consists of 忄 (heart) and the phonetic 賁 (puff up). It
means "resent; get stirred up."
憤慨 (フン・ガイ indignation), 憤る (いきどお・る resent)

苗 (ミョウ/ビョウ)   (seedling; small)

描 (ビョウ/えが・く) consists of 扌 (hand) and the phonetic 苗 (small); it means
"describe, draw."
描写 (ビョウ・シャ depiction; sketch), 描く (えが・く depict)

猫 (ビョウ/ねこ) is a combination of 犭 (animal) and the phonetic 苗, which
sounds something like *mao* in Chinese dialects, thus used onomatopoeically; it
means "cat."
愛猫家 (アイ・ビョウ・カ lover of cats), 猫 (ねこ cat)

明 (ミョウ/メイ)   (clear, clarify)

盟 (メイ) combines 皿 (dish) and the phonetic 明 (clarify) and means "pledge,
oath; ally."
連盟 (レン・メイ league)

武 (ム/ブ)   (martial)

賦 (フ) is a combination of 貝 (wealth) and the phonetic 武 (martial). It means "levy, allot"; and its sense of "compose a poem" and its use as a name for a style of Chinese verse are probably borrowed.

月賦 (ゲッ・ブ monthly installment)

免 (メン/ベン)   (try hard)

勉 (ベン) adds 力 (strength) to the phonetic 免 (bear down) to mean "make an effort, endeavor."

勉強 (ベン・キョウ study; discount)

晩 (バン) combines 日 (sun) and the phonetic 免. It means "evening, night; late."

9-Stroke Phonetics

為 (イ)   (train an animal)

偽 (ギ/いつわ・る/にせ) consists of 亻 (person) and the phonetic 為 (train animal) and means "false, sham."

偽造 (ギ・ゾウ forgery), 偽る (いつわ・る dissemble), 偽 (にせ spurious)

屋 (オク)   (cover)

握 (アク/にぎ・る) is a combination of 扌 (hand) and the phonetic 屋 (cover). It means "grip, grasp."

握手 (アク・シュ handshake), 握る (にぎ・る grip)

音 (オン/イン)   (something in mouth; hide)

暗 (アン/くら・い) combines 日 (sun) and the phonetic 音 (hide); it means "dark; clandestine" and also, by substitution for another kanji, "memorize."

暗殺 (アン・サツ assassination), 暗い (くら・い dark)

軍 (クン)   (encircle, around)

運 (ウン/はこ・ぶ), a combination of 辶 (walk) and the phonetic 軍 (around), means "go around; move, transpot; fate, destiny."

運転 (ウン・テン operation), 運ぶ (はこ・ぶ carry)

揮 (キ) consists of 扌 (hand) and the phonetic 軍 (around) and means "wield, brandish; disperse."

指揮者 (シ・キ・シャ conductor; leader)

輝 (キ/かがや・く) consists of 光 (light) and the phonetic 軍 (around) and means "bright; shine."

輝石 (キ・セキ pyroxene), 輝く (かがや・く shine)

皆 (ケ/カイ)   (even)

階 (カイ), a combination of 阝 (mound) and the phonetic 皆 (even) means "stairs, steps; story, floor" and is also used as a counter for floors.

二階 (ニ・カイ second floor)

☐建☐ (コン/ケン) (build)

健 (ケン/すこ・やか) consists of 亻 (person) and the phonetic 建 (build) and means "healthy, sound."

健全 (ケン・ゼン sound), 健やか (すこ・やか healthy)

☐食; 飠☐ (ジキ/ショク) (eat)

飲 (今, p.159)

飾 (ショク/かざ・る) is a combination of 人 (person), 巾 (cloth), and the phonetic 飠. It means "decorate."

修飾 (ショウ・ショク decoration; modification), 飾る (かざ・る decorate)

☐首☐ (シュ/シュウ) (head; heading)

道 (ドウ/トウ/みち) combines 辶 (walk) and the phonetic 首 (heading). It means "way, road"; with derived senses of "tell; moral; Taoism" and, in Japan, "Hok-kaido."

道具 (ドウ・グ tool), 神道 (シン・トウ Shintoism), 道 (みち road; way)

導 (ドウ/みちび・く), a combination of 寸 (hand) and the phonetic 道 (way), means "lead, guide."

導入 (ドウ・ニュウ introduction), 導く (みちび・く guide)

☐秋☐ (シュ/シュウ) (autumn)

愁 (シュウ/うれ・い) consists of 心 (heart) and the phonetic 秋 (autumn). It means "sorrow; anxiety."

郷愁 (キョウ・シュウ nostalgia), 愁い (うれ・い melancholy)

☐重☐ (ジュウ/チョウ) (weight)

動 (ドウ/うご・く) combines 力 (strength) with the phonetic 重 (weight), perhaps to symbolize exertion of a force. It means "move."

動員 (ドウ・イン mobilization), 動く (うご・く move)

童 (ドウ/わらべ) originated in a combination of 辛 (needle) with the phonetic 重 and meant "blinded slave," but is now used only in the sense of "child."

童話 (ドウ・ワ nursery tale), 童 (わらべ child)

働 (ドウ/はたら・く), a Japanese-made combination of 亻 (person) and the phonetic 動 (move), means "work, labor."

労働 (ロウ・ドウ labor), 働く (はたら・く work)

種 (シュ/たね) consists of 禾 (rice plant) and the phonetic 重 (press down) and means "sow; seed; species, sort"; it is also used as a counter of varieties. In Japan it has the meanings "breed, stock; cause, source."

種類 (シュ・ルイ kind), 種 (たね seed; stock; source)

衝 (ショウ) combines 行 (go) with the phonetic 重 (weight) and means "collide, crash; pivotal point."

衝突 （ショウ・トツ collision）

鐘 （ショウ/かね） is a combination of 金 (metal) and the phonetic 童 used in the sense of 撞 (strike). It means "bell, chime."

警鐘 （ケイ・ショウ alarm bell）, 鐘 （かね bell）

盾 （ジュン/シュン）   (shield)

循 （ジュン） combines 彳 (go) and the phonetic 盾 (shield); it means "go along, go around," perhaps a substitute meaning.

循環 （ジュン・カン circulation）

乗 （ジョウ/ショウ）   (multiply)

剰 （ジョウ） is a combination of 刂 (edged tool) and the phonetic 乗 (multiply). It means "excess, surplus."

剰余 （ジョウ・ヨ surplus）

是 （ゼ/シ）   (straight)

堤 （テイ/つつみ） combines 土 (earth) with the phonetic 是 (straight) and means "bank, levee."

堤防 （テイ・ボウ bank）, 堤 （つつみ levee）

提 （テイ/さ・げる）, a combination of 扌 (hand) and the phonetic 是 (straight), means "carry in one's hand; hold forth, present; lead."

提案 （テイ・アン proposition）, 提げる （さ・げる carry in hand）

題 （ダイ） consists of 頁 (head) and the phonetic 是 (straight). Its meanings "heading, title, theme" derive from an earlier sense, "forehead." In Japan it is also used as a counter for questions or problems.

泉 （ゼン/セン）   (fountainhead)

線 （セン）, a combination of 糸 (thread) and the phonetic 泉, seems to have been another way to write 綫 （セン thin thread）, where the phonetic is 戔 （セン thin）. It has much the sense of English "line," extending from the mathematical meaning to those of "electric wire; vehicular route."

相 　　　　　　　（ソウ/ショウ）　　　　　　　　(face-to-face; mate)

想 （ソウ/ソ） consists of 心 (heart) and the phonetic 相 (face-to-face); it means "image; imagine; idea; think."

理想 （リ・ソウ ideal）, 愛想 （アイ・ソ/アイ・ソウ amiability）

箱 （はこ） is a combination of 竹 (bamboo) and the phonetic 相 (mate); its *on-yomi*, ソウ, is not included in the Jōyō Kanji. It means "box,"(originally "box and lid," where the lid was a matching box inverted over the container box). Its use is extended in Japan to other somewhat box-like objects such as train cars, and to samisen.

霜 (ソウ/しも) combines 雨 (weather) and the phonetic 相 (face-to-face); it means "frost."

霜髪 (ソウ・ハツ white hair), 霜 (しも frost)

則 (ソク)   (stay close; standard)

側 (ソク/かわ) is a combination of 亻 (person) and the phonetic 則 (stay close). It means "near; side."

側面 (ソク・メン side; aspect), 右側 (みぎ・がわ right side)

測 (ソク/はか・る), made up of 氵 (water) and the phonetic 則 (standard), means "sound, measure; guess."

推測 (スイ・ソク conjecture), 測る (はか・る measure)

帝 (タイ/テイ)   (put together; one line)

締 (テイ/し・める) consists of 糸 (thread) and the phonetic 帝 (put together); it means "tie tightly, fasten; conclude, decide."

締結 (テイ・ケツ conclusion), 締める (し・める tie, tighten)

嫡 (チャク) combines 女 (woman) and the phonetic 商 (テキ one line), a simplification of another character that consists of 口 (mouth) under the phonetic 帝 (put together). It means "legal wife" and, derivatively, "legitimate heir."

嫡子 (チャク・シ heir)

摘 (テキ/つ・む) is a combination of 扌 (hand) and the phonetic 商 (one line). It means "pluck, pick."

指摘 (シ・テキ point out), 摘む (つ・む pluck)

滴 (テキ/しずく/したた・る) combines 氵 (water) and the phonetic 商 (one line); it means "drip; drop" and is used as a counter for drops.

点滴 (テン・テキ intravenous drip), 滴 (しずく drop), 滴る (したた・る drip)

適 (テキ) combines 辶 (walk) and the phonetic 商 (one line) and means "head straight for," with the derived sense of "proper, suitable."

適する (テキ・する be suited)

敵 (テキ/かたき) combines 攵 (beating) and the phonetic 商. It means "foe, enemy, adversary."

敵対 (テキ・タイ hostility), 敵 (テキ/かたき enemy)

某 (ム/ボウ)   (unidentified; unforeseeable)

媒 (バイ), a combination of 女 (woman) and the phonetic 某 (unidentified), means "go-between, medium."

媒酌 (バイ・シャク matchmaking)

謀 (ボウ/ム/はか・る) consists of 言 (say) and the phonetic 某 (unforeseeable). It means "scheme, plot, conspire."

無謀 (ム・ボウ reckless), 謀反 (ム・ホン rebellion), 謀る (はか・る plot)

卑 (ヒ)　　　　　　　　　　　　　　　　　　　　　(thin and flat)

碑 (ヒ) combines 石 (stone) and the phonetic 卑 (thin and flat); it means "stone slab memorial; monument; inscription."

記念碑 (キ・ネン・ヒ monument)

要 (ヨウ)　　　　　　　　　　　　　　　　　　　　(waist)

腰 (ヨウ/こし) adds 月 (flesh) to the phonetic 要 (waist) to preserve the original meaning "waist, hips" of the latter which has come to be used for a different meaning ("necessary").

腰痛 (ヨウ・ツウ lumbago), 腰 (こし waist, hip)

10-Stoke Phonetics

員 (ウン/イン or エン)　　　　　　　　　　　　　　(round)

円 (エン/まる・い) is a simplified form of 圓, which is 囗 (enclosure) added to the phonetic 員 (round) to preserve the latter's original meaning. 円 means "circle; round; full" and in Japan "yen."

百円 (ヒャク・エン 100 yen), 円い (まる・い round)

韻 (イン) combines 音 (sound) and the phonetic 員 (round) and means "harmony, resonance; rhyme."

余韻 (ヨ・イン reverberation)

害 (ガイ/カイ)　　　　　　　　　　　　　　　　　(hold down)

割 (カツ/わ・る/わり/さ・く) combines 刂 (edged tool) and the phonetic 害. It means "divide, cut"; in Japan it also means "tenths."

割愛 (カツ・アイ relinquish), 割る (わ・る cut; break), 割 (わり proportion), 割く (さ・く split)

轄 (カツ) consists of 車 (wheel) and the phonetic 害 (hold down); from "linchpin" it derived the meaning "control."

管轄 (カン・カツ jurisdiction)

鬼 (キ)　　　　　　　　　　　　　　　　　　　　(round head)

塊 (カイ/かたまり) is a combination of 土 (earth) and the phonetic 鬼 (round) meaning "lump, clod."

金塊 (キン・カイ nugget), 塊 (かたまり lump)

家 (ケ/カ)　　　　　　　　　　　　　　　　　　　(house)

嫁 (カ/よめ/とつ・ぐ) consists of 女 (woman) and the phonetic 家 (house); it means "marry, become a bride; bride, wife; ascribe to another."

転嫁 (テン・カ imputation), 嫁 (よめ bride), 嫁ぐ (とつ・ぐ marry)

稼 (カ/かせ・ぐ), a combination of 禾 (crop) and the phonetic 家 (house), meant "plant, farm; crops," but in Japan is used only to mean "work for pay; earn."

稼業 (カ・ギョウ business), 稼ぐ (かせ・ぐ earn)

兼 (ケン)　　　　　　　　　　　　　　　　　　　　(bring two things together)

嫌 (ケン/ゲン/きら・う/いや) is a combination of 女 (woman) and the phonetic 兼, meaning "dislike, hate; doubt, suspicion."

嫌悪 (ケン・オ disgust), 機嫌 (キ・ゲン mood), 嫌う (きら・う dislike), 嫌 (いや disgusting)

廉 (レン), a combination of 广 (house) and the phonetic 兼 (bring two things together), means "corner, cornered," and, said to be derived from that, "decent, incorruptible; inexpensive."

廉価 (レン・カ bargain price)

謙 (ケン), a combination of 言 (say) and the phonetic 兼, means "humble."

謙虚 (ケン・キョ modest)

骨 (コチ/コツ)　　　　　　　　　　　　　　　　　　　　　　　(joint)

滑 (カツ/すべ・る/なめ・らか), consisting of 氵 (water) and the phonetic 骨 (joint), means "smooth; slide, slip; slick, cunning, smooth-tongued."

滑走路 (カッ・ソウ・ロ runway), 滑る (すべ・る slide). 滑らか (なめ・らか smooth)

原 (ゴン/ゲン)　　　　　　　　　　　　　　　　　　　　　　　(spring)

源 (ゲン/みなもと) is a combination of 氵 (water) and the phonetic 原 (spring). It means "river source; source, origin."

源泉 (ゲン・セン wellspring), 源 (みなもと source)

願 (ガン/ねが・う) is a combination of 頁 (head) and the phonetic 原 (spring). It means "wish, desire; supplicate, beg."

願望 (ガン・ボウ desire), 願う (ねが・う wish; beg)

射 (シャ)　　　　　　　　　　　　　　　　　　　　　　　　(release)

謝 (シャ/あやま・る) combines 言 (say) and the phonetic 射 (release); it means "apologize; thank, reward; decline, refuse."

感謝 (カン・シャ gratitude), 謝る (あやま・る apologize)

真 (シン)　　　　　　　　　　　　　　　　　　　　　　(thorough, full)

慎 (シン/つつし・む), a combination of 忄 (heart) and the phonetic 真 (thorough), means "prudent, discreet."

慎重 (シン・チョウ caution), 慎む (つつし・む be discreet)

鎮 (チン/しずめ・る), a combination of 金 (metal) and the phonetic 真 (full), means "weight; press, quell."

鎮痛剤 (チン・ツウ・ザイ anodyne), 鎮める (しず・める calm; quell)

朕 (ジン/チン)　　　　　　　　　　　　　　　　　　　　　(rise, raise)

謄 (トウ) consists of 言 (say) and the phonetic 朕 (put upon) and means "copy."

謄本 (トウ・ホン certified copy)

騰 (トウ) is a combination of 馬 (horse) and the phonetic 朕 (rise), and it means "go up, rise."

　高騰 (コウ・トウ sudden price rise)

倉 (ソウ) (barn)

創 (ソウ) combines 刂 (edged tool) with the phonetic 倉. It means "wound, hurt" and also "originate."

　創立 (ソウ・リツ establishment)

帯 (タイ) (sash)

滞 (タイ/とどこお・る) consists of 氵 (water) and the phonetic 帯 (sash) and means "stagnate."

　滞在 (タイ・ザイ sojourn), 滞る (とどこお・る get overdue)

畜 (チク) (raise stock)

蓄 (チク/たくわ・える), consisting of 艹 (plant) and the phonetic 畜 (raise stock), means "store, stock up," originally with particular reference to a winter's store of vegetables.

　貯蓄 (チョ・チク savings), 蓄える (たくわ・える stock)

唐 (ドウ/トウ) (Tang, China)

糖 (トウ), a combination of 米 (rice) and the phonetic 唐, means "sugar."

　糖分 (トウ・ブン sugar content)

能 (ノウ/ドウ or ナイ/ダイ) (ability)

態 (タイ), a combination of 心 (heart) and the phonetic 能 (ability), means "attitude; figure, appearance."

　態度 (タイ・ド attitude)

般 (バン/ハン) (board)

搬 (ハン), consisting of 扌 (hand) and the phonetic 般 (board), means "convey, transport."

　運搬 (ウン・パン transfer)

盤 (バン) adds 皿 (dish) to the phonetic 般 (board) to mean "plate, platter, dish" and other plate or disk-shaped things. It can also mean "large flat stone; base, foundation" and in Japan "game board; development of play."

　円盤 (エン・バン disk)

11-Stroke Phonetics

尉 (イ) (press, iron out)

慰 (イ/なぐさ・める), a combination of 心 (heart) and the phonetic 尉 (iron out), means "console, soothe," with the added senses in Japan of "fun, diversion."

　慰安 (イ・アン recreation), 慰める (なぐさ・める comfort)

[異] (イ) (differ)

翼 (ヨク/つばさ), 羽 (feather) and the phonetic 異 (diverge), means "wings; wing; protect."

左翼 (サ・ヨク left wing), 翼 (つばさ wing)

翌 (ヨク) is 立 (start up) combined with an abbreviation of the phonetic 翼; it means "the next, the following (day, morning, year)."

翌日 (ヨク・ジツ the next day)

[黄; ム] (オウ/コウ) (yellow light; spread)

広 (コウ/ひろ・い) consists of 广 (roof) and ム (spread), a substitute for the phonetic 黄, and it means "spacious; wide, broad,"

広報 (コウ・ホウ publicity), 広い (ひろ・い spacious)

横 (オウ/よこ) is a combination of 木 (wood) and the phonetic 黄 (spread). It seems to be based on some concept of horizontal wood; it means "horizontal; alongside; perverse."

横断 (オウ・ダン crosscut), 横 (よこ the side)

拡 (カク) combines 扌 (hand) and the phonetic 広 (broad) and means "extend."

拡大 (カク・ダイ enlargement)

鉱 (コウ) is a combination of 金 (metal) and the phonetic 広; it means "ore" or "mine."

鉱山 (コウ・ザン mine)

[貫] (カン) (run through)

慣 (カン/な・れる) combines 忄 (heart) and the phonetic 貫 (run through). It means "accustom; accustomed."

慣例 (カン・レイ custom), 慣れる (な・れる get used to)

[黒] (コク) (black; silent)

墨 (ボク/すみ) consists of 土 (earth) and the phonetic 黒 (black) and means "ink."

白墨 (ハク・ボク chalk), 墨 (すみ *sumi,* India ink)

黙 (モク/だま・る), is a combination of 犬 (dog) and the phonetic 黒 (silent), meaning "silence; tacit."

黙認 (モク・ニン tacit approval), 黙る (だま・る fall silent)

[祭] (サイ/セイ) (rub clean; purify)

際 (サイ/きわ) combines 阝 (mud wall) and the phonetic 祭 (rub). It means "hem, edge, border; meet, contact; juncture, occasion."

際 (サイ occasion; きわ edge)

察 (サツ), a combination of 宀 (house) and the phonetic 祭 (rub clean) means "discern."

警察 (ケイ・サツ police)

擦 (サツ/す・る) combines 扌 (hand) and the phonetic 察, used for the sense of 祭 (rub clean); it means "rub, chafe."
　摩擦 (マ・サツ rub; friction), 擦る (す・る rub)

庶 (ショ)   (gather)

度 (ド/ト/タク/たび) is a combination of 又 (hand) and an abbreviation of the phonetic 庶. It means "measure; degree; frequency; time, occasion" and is used as counter of degrees and times.
　今度 (コン・ド this/next time), 法度 (ハッ・ト prohibition), 仕度 (シ・タク preparation), 度 (たび time)

席 (セキ) is 巾 (cloth) and an abbreviation of the phonetic 庶; it means "seat."

遮 (シャ/さえぎ・る) combines 辶 (walk) and the phonetic 庶 (gather) and means "interrupt."
　遮断 (シャ・ダン interception), 遮る (さえぎ・る block)

渡 (ト/わた・る) is 氵 (water) and the phonetic 度 (measure); it means "cross over; ferry" and, in Japan, "hand over."
　渡米 (ト・ベイ visit to the U.S.A.), 渡る (わた・る go over)

章 (ショウ)   (period; pause; mark off)

商 (ショウ/あきな・い) is a combination of 冏 (elevation) and an abbreviation of the phonetic 章. It meant "heights, highlands," with special reference to an early Chinese seat of power whose people were later reduced to peddlers, whence its usual meaning, "merchant; commerce; merchandise."
　商社 (ショウ・シャ trading company), 商い (あきな・い business)

彰 (ショウ) combines 彡 (design) and the phonetic 章 (mark off) and means "distinct; publicize."
　表彰 (ヒョウ・ショウ award)

障 (ショウ/さわ・る), a combination of 阝 (wall) and the phonetic 章 (mark off), means "obstacle."
　障子 (ショウ・ジ shōji, sliding door), 障る (さわ・る hinder)

宿 (スク/シュク)   (inn; pack in)

縮 (シュク/ちぢ・む) is made of 糸 (thread) and the phonetic 宿 (pack in). It means "shrink, reduce in size."
　縮図 (シュク・ズ reduced-scale drawing), 縮む (ちぢ・む shrink)

曹 (ゾウ/ソウ)   (throng)

遭 (ソウ/あ・う), combining 辶 (walk) and the phonetic 曹 (throng), means "encounter."
　遭難 (ソウ・ナン meet disaster), 遭う (あ・う encounter)

槽 (ソウ) is 木 (wood) and the phonetic 曹 (throng). It means "tub, tank," originally a ubiquitous type of wooden tub holding feed or water.

浴槽 （ヨク・ソウ bathtub）

| 票 | （ヒョウ）   (float on air)

漂 （ヒョウ/ただよ・う）, consisting of 氵 （water） and the phonetic 票 （float）, means "drift; bleach."

漂白 （ヒョウ・ハク bleaching）, 漂う （ただよ・う drift）

標 （ヒョウ） is a combination of 木 （tree） and the phonetic 票 （float on）, which is said to have orginally meant a high branch; 標 means "mark, sign."

標準 （ヒョウ・ジュン standard）

| 麻 | （メ/バ）   (hemp)

摩 （マ）, a combination of 手 （hand ） and the phonetic 麻 （hemp）, means "rub, scrape."

摩滅 （マ・メツ defacement）

磨 （マ/みが・く） combines 石 （stone） with the phonetic 麻 （hemp） to write another sense of the word written with the preceding kanji; it means "polish, burnish."

研磨 （ケン・マ polish）, 磨く （みが・く polish）

魔 （マ） is a combination of 鬼 （spirit） and the phonetic 麻; it means "demon; magic," perhaps an abbreviation of a Sanskirt word.

魔法 （マ・ホウ magic）

12-Stroke Phonetics

| 貴 | （キ）   (prominent)

遺 （イ/ユイ）, a combination of 辶 （walk） and the phtnetic 貴 （prominent）, means "leave behind; remains."

遺失物 （イ・シツ・ブツ lost article）, 遺言 （ユイ・ゴン will）

| 敬 | （キョウ/ケイ）   (on guard)

警 （ケイ）, combining 言 （say） and the phonetic 敬 （on guard）, means "warn; guard; pithy" and, in Japan, "police."

警官 （ケイ・カン policeman）

驚 （キョウ/おどろ・く）, a combination of 馬 （horse） and the phonetic 敬 （on guard）, means "surprise, astonish."

驚異 （キョウ・イ wonder）, 驚く （おどろ・く be surprised）

| 幾 | （ケ/キ）   (small, fine)

機 （キ/はた） combines 木 （wood） and the phonetic 幾 （minute）. It means "weaver's loom" or a key part thereof, from which derived the senses of "machinery, mechanism; chance, opportunity." In Japan, it can mean "airplane" and is used as a counter for airplanes.

ジェット機 （ジェット・キ jet plane）, 機 （はた loom; キ chance）

間 (ケン/カン)   (space)

簡 (カン) is a combination of 竹 (bamboo) and the phonetic 間 (space) that originally referred to a section of bamboo for writing on that would be strung together with others into a notebook, with "spaces" in between. It means "tablet; letter; simple; pick out, select."

　　簡単 (カン・タン simple)

最 (サイ)   (pinch)

撮 (サツ/と・る), 扌 (hand) and the phonetic 最 (pinch), means "pick, pinch off," but has been given the special meaning of "take (a photo)."

　　撮影 (サツ・エイ filming), 撮る (と・る take [photos])

集 (シュウ)   (gather)

雑 (ザツ/ゾウ) is simplified from 雜, originally a combination of 衣 (garment) and the phonetic 集 (gather) to suggest an accumulation of old clothes and symbolize "miscellany; motley; crude, unrefined."

　　雑用 (ザツ・ヨウ chores), 雑木林 (ゾウ・き・ばやし coppice)

焦 (ショウ)   (char)

礁 (ショウ), a combination of 石 (rock) and the phonetic 焦 (charred color), means "submerged rock, reef."

　　暗礁 (アン・ショウ submerged rock)

善 (ゼン/セン)   (good)

繕 (ゼン/つくろ・う) consists of 糸 (thread) and the phonetic 善 (good) and means "mend, repair."

　　修繕 (シュウ・ゼン repair), 繕う (つくろ・う mend)

尊 (ソン)   (value)

遵 (ジュン), combining 辶 (walk) and the phonetic 尊 (value), means "observe, abide by."

　　遵守 (ジュン・シュ observance)

替 (タイ)   (replace)
　 (シン)   (ornamental hair pin; insert)

潜 (セン/ひそ・む/もぐ・る) combines 氵 (water) and, as phonetic, what looks like 替 (タイ) but is actually a simplification of 朁 (シン onamental hairpin, insert). 潜 means "submerge; latent."

　　潜水艦 (セン・スイ・カン submarine), 潜む (ひそ・む lurk), 潜る (もぐ・る dive)

登 (トウ)   (go up)

澄 (チョウ/す・ます), a combination of 氵 (water) and the phonetic 登, means "clear, limpid; get clear; clarify" and, in Japan, "act in an affected manner, assume an innocent air."

　　清澄 (セイ・チョウ limpid), 澄ます (す・ます clarify; look innocent)

然 (ネン/ゼン) (burn)

燃 (ネン/も・える) adds 火 (fire) to the phonetic 然 (burn) to preserve its original meaning, "burn."

燃料 (ネン・リョウ fuel), 燃える (も・える burn)

普 (フ/ホ) (flat)

譜 (フ), a combination of 言 (say) and the phonetic 普 (flat), represents an ordering of information, "chart; record; notebook" and also the meaning "successive."

楽譜 (ガク・フ musical score)

番 (ホン/ハン) (spread)

翻 (ホン/ひるがえ・す) consists of 羽 (wing) and the phonetic 番 (spread) and means "flutter, flap," with derivative senses of "turn over; rearrange; translate."

翻訳 (ホン・ヤク translation), 翻す (ひるがえ・す reverse)

藩 (ハン), consists of 艹 (plant) and the phonetic 潘 (ハン spreading of water), a combination of 氵 (water) and the phonetic 番 (spread). It originally meant "hedge" and thus "wall; territory." In Japan it refers to a *han*, an Edo-period feudal domain or clan.

買 (メ/バイ) (trade)
(イク/ショク) (continue)

売 (バイ/う・る) is a simplified form of 賣, combining an abbreviation of 出 (take out) and the phonetic 買 (trade). It means "sell."

特売 (トク・バイ special sale), 売る (う・る sell)

続 (ゾク/つづ・く) is a combination of 糸 (thread) and a simplified form of the phonetic 賣 (continue), which is slightly different from 賣. 続 means "continue."

続行 (ゾッ・コウ proceeding), 続く (つづ・く continue)

読 (ドク/トク/よ・む) combines 言 (say) and a simplified form of 賣 (pause and go on) and means "read."

読者 (ドク・シャ reader), 読本 (トク・ホン reader), 句読点 (ク・トウ・テン punctuation marks), 読む (よ・む read)

量 (ロウ/リョウ) (measure)

糧 (リョウ/ロウ/かて), consisting of 米 (rice) and the phonetic 量 (measure), means "provisions, rations; food."

食糧 (ショク・リョウ food), 兵糧 (ヒョウ・ロウ provisions), 糧 (かて food)

13-Stroke Phonetics

意 (イ) (think)

億 (オク) combines 亻 (person) and the phonetic 意 (think) and means "think, guess"; it is also used for "hundred million."

一億 (イチ・オク one hundred million)

憶 (オク) is 忄 (heart) combined with the phonetic 意 (think) and means "think of; keep in mind; memory."

記憶 (キ・オク memory)

楽 (ガク/ラク)   (kind of oak tree; acorn)

薬 (ヤク/くすり) is a combination of 艹 (plant) and the phonetic 楽 (acorn). It means "medicinal herb, nut, or root; medicine, drug; power."

薬局 (ヤッ・キョク pharmacy), 薬 (くすり medicine)

禁 (コン/キン)   (close up)

襟 (キン/えり) combines 衤 (garment) and the phonetic 禁 (close up) and means "collar; heart, bosom."

開襟 (カイ・キン open-necked), 襟 (えり collar)

農 (ノウ/ドウ)   (glutinous)

濃 (ノウ/こ・い), a combination of 氵 (water) and the phonetic 農 (glutinous), means "thick, dense."

濃淡 (ノウ・タン light and dark, shading), 濃い (こ・い thick)

14-Stroke Phonetics

需 (ス/シュ)   (soft and wet)

儒 (ジュ) is a combination of 亻 (person) and the phonetic 需 (soft and wet). It means "cultured," a Confucian ideal.

儒教 (ジュ・キョウ Confucianism)

徴 (チョウ)   (sign, indication)

懲 (チョウ/こ・りる) consists of 心 (heart) and the phonetic 徴 (sign) and means "chastise, punish."

懲罰 (チョウ・バツ punishment), 懲りる (こ・りる learn one's lesson)

15-Stroke Phonetics

監 (ケン/カン)   (look down on water in dish; oversee)

塩 (エン/しお) is a simplified form of 鹽, which has 鹵 (rock salt) intruding in the phonetic 監. It means "salt; chlorine."

食塩 (ショク・エン table salt), 塩 (しお salt)

覧 (ラン) adds 見 (see) to an abbreviation of the phonetic 監 (look down over) and means "survey, view."

万国博覧会 (バン・コク・ハク・ラン・カイ world's fair)

濫 (ラン) combines 氵 (water) and the phonetic 監 (water in dish); it means "overflow; excessive."

濫造 (ラン・ゾウ overproduction)

艦 (カン) consists of 舟 (boat) and the phonetic 監 (oversee) and means "battleship."

艦隊 (カン・タイ fleet)

鑑 (カン) is a combination of 金 (metal) and the phonetic 監 (reflection); it means "mirror; inspect; specimen; reference book."

鑑賞 (カン・ショウ appreciation)

| 暴 | (ボウ/ホウ or ボク/ホク) | (burst open) |

爆 (バク), consisting of 火 (fire) and the phonetic 暴 (burst), means "explode" and, in Japan, "bomb."

爆弾 (バク・ダン bomb)

| 憂 | (ウ/ユウ) | (supple) |

優 (ユウ/やさ・しい/すぐ・れる) is a combination of 亻 (person) and the phonetic 憂 (supple). It means "actor; gentle, graceful; superior, excellent."

俳優 (ハイ・ユウ actor), 優しい (やさ・しい gentle), 優れる (すぐ・れる excel)

Other Phonetic Components

This section lists phonetic components not previously introduced and completes the presentation of the Jōyō Kanji. The new phonetic components are of the following nature:

1. Independent kanji that are not included in the Jōyō Kanji. Some of them are nonetheless quite commonly used in newspapers and magazines, especially for proper names. Examples include 之 (シ/の tip of foot), 也 (ヤ/なり scorpion), 云 (ウン/い・う vapor), 旦 (タン/あした sunrise), 坐 (ザ/すわ・る sit), 朋 (ホウ two in a row), 頃 (キョウ/ころ incline), 寅 (エン/とら straight).

2. Basic forms that are not included in the Jōyō Kanji, most of which lost their independent usage very early. Some of them were introduced as semantic components in Chapter 3. Examples include the following: 几 (キ stool), 厶 (シ private), 卜 (ボク divination), 乂 (ガイ cross), 彡 (セン/サン design), 弋 (イキ/ヨク stake), 亢 (neck), 禾 (ワ/カ millet plant), 艮 (コン mark), 酉 (ユ/ユウ wine jar), 隹 (スイ bird), 亥 (ガイ skeleton of pig).

3. Compound kanji almost all of which have fallen into disuse as independent characters, such as 劦 (キョウ joining forces), 戔 (セン chopping up), 夋 (シュン lanky), 荅 (トウ small bean), 袁 (エン/オン loose), 曼 (マン cover), 褱 (カイ keep in bosom), 喿 (ソウ fidget).

2-Stroke Phonetics

| 乂 | (ガイ) | (various crossed things, such as shears) |

刈 (か・る) combines 刂 (edged tool) and the phonetic 乂 (shears) and means "mow, clip." Its *on-yomi* ガイ is not included in the Jōyō Kanji.

| 厂 | (カン) | (cliff) |

涯 (ガイ) consists of 氵 (water) and the phonetic 厓 (ガイ cliff), which comprises 圭 (high ground) and the phonetic 厂 (cliff). It means "bank, shore; stopping point, end."

生涯 (ショウ・ガイ lifetime)

顔 (ガン/かお), a combination of 頁 (head) and the phonetic 彦 (ガン handsome man), means "face; color." The phonetic is made of 文 (design), 彡 (design), and the phonetic 厂 (cliff), the notion supposedly being that a steep forehead marked a handsome face.

顔面 (ガン・メン face)

几 (キ)   (stool)

机 (キ/つくえ), a combination of 木 (wood) and the phonetic 几 (stool), means "desk."

机上 (キ・ジョウ desktop), 机 (つくえ desk)

肌 (はだ) is a combination of 月 (flesh) and the phonetic 几, but the *on-yomi* キ is not included in the Jōyō Kanji. It means "human skin," with metaphorical extensions to "exterior surface; temperament, disposition."

拠 (キョ/コ), was formerly 據, 扌 (hand) and the phonetic 豦 (キョ) combined; 処 (place) now replaces the old phonetic. It means "base, foundation."

根拠 (コン・キョ basis), 証拠 (ショウ・コ evidence)

飢 (キ/う・える) combines 食 (eat) and the phonetic 几, an early replacement of the phonetic 幾 (キ a little); it means "hunger; starve."

飢餓 (キ・ガ starvation), 飢える (う・える starve)

丂 (コウ)   (winding)

巧 (コウ/たく・み) combines 工 (ax) and the phonetic 丂 (winding) and means "skillful, deft."

巧妙 (コウ・ミョウ skillful), 巧み (たく・み dexterous)

朽 (キュウ/く・ちる) is a combination of 木 (tree) and the phonetic 丂 (winding). It once meant "dead tree," but now means "rot, decay."

不朽 (フ・キュウ immortal), 朽ちる (く・ち・る decay)

汚; 誇 (于, p. 202, 203)

考 (コウ/かんが・える) merges an abbreviated form of 老 (old man) and the phonetic 丂 (winding). It once had the meaning of "old man," still approximated rarely as "deceased father," but it is usually used for "think, thought ; examine."

考慮 (コウ・リョ consideration), 考える (かんが・える think)

拷 (ゴウ) combines 扌 (hand) and the phonetic 考 (examine) and means "beat, thrash."

拷問 (ゴウ・モン inquisition by torture)

厶 (シ)   (private)
  (イ)   (plow)

仏; 払 (弗 p. 216)

台 (ダイ/タイ) is originally a combination of 口 (mouth) and the phonetic ム (plow) with the meaning "begin; work on," but its current meaning and reading come from its use as a substitute for 臺 (ダイ/タイ observation platform), a merger of 土 (earth), 至 (reach), and an abbreviation of 高 (high), that means "platform; table, board." In Japan 台 is additionally used as "base, stand, support, level (of prices, age) and as a counter for machines and vehicles.

台 (ダイ stand), 台風 (タイ・フウ typhoon)

私 (シ/わたくし), combining 禾 (crop) and the phonetic ム (private), means "private, secret," and, in Japan, "I, me."

私的 (シ・テキ private), 私 (わたくし I)

始 (シ/はじめ・る), a combination of 女 (woman) and the phonetic 台 (イ/タイ begin), means "begin; inauguration."

開始 (カイ・シ commencement), 始める (はじ・める begin)

治 (ジ/チ/おさ・める/なお・る) is a combination of 氵 (water) and the phonetic 台 (イ/タイ work on); it meant "flood," from which it gained the senses of "govern, put in order; remedy."

政治 (セイ・ジ politics), 治療 (チ・リョウ remedy), 治める (おさ・める govern), 治る (なお・る be cured)

怠 (タイ/おこた・る/なま・ける) combines 心 (heart) and the phonetic 台 (タイ); it means "lazy, negligent."

怠慢 (タイ・マン negligence), 怠る (おこた・る neglect), 怠ける (なま・ける slack off)

胎 (タイ) is a combination of 月 (flesh) and the phonetic 台 (タイ begin). It means "embryo, fetus; uterus."

胎児 (タイ・ジ embryo)

| 㔾 | (ハン) | (frame; fence) |

犯 (ハン/おか・す) is a combination of 犭 (animal) and the phonetic 㔾 (fence). It means "violate, commit an illegal or sinful act; crime, offence; criminal" and is a counter for a criminal's convictions.

犯罪 (ハン・ザイ crime), 犯す (お・か・す violate)

範 (ハン) merges 車 (wheel) into an abbreviation of the phonetic 笵 (ハン bamboo hoop), itself a combination of 竹 (bamboo) and the phonetic 氾 (ハン overflow), a combination in turn of 氵 (water) and 㔾 (frame). 範 may have meant "wheel rim"; now it means "norm, model; range."

範囲 (ハン・イ range)

| 匕 | (ヒ) | (spoon) |

蛇 (它 p. 214)

| 勹 | (ヒョウ/ホン) | (enclosure) |

旬; 殉 (勹 p. 206)

ト (ボク)   (divination)

朴 (ボク) combines 木 (tree) and the phonetic ト. It means "artless, simple."
    素朴 (ソ・ボク naive)

赴 (フ/おもむ・く), combining 走 (run) and an abbreviation of the phonetic 仆 (フ tumble), meant "run pell mell" and now means "hasten off to; go, proceed." Substituting for a non-Jōyō kanji of the same *on-yomi*, it means "news of a death."
    赴任 (フ・ニン go to a new post), 赴く (おもむ・く go)

3-Stroke Phonetics

弋 (イキ/ヨク)   (stake)

代 (ダイ/タイ/か・わる/よ/しろ) is a combination of 亻 (person) and the phonetic 弋. It means "take over for; substitute, deputy, generation, period" and, in Japan, "fee."
    代表 (ダイ・ヒョウ representation), 交代 (コウ・タイ alternation), 代わる (か・わる replace), 君が代 (きみ・が・よ name of Japanese national anthem), 代物 (しろ・もの goods)

式 (シキ), combining 工 (ax) and the phonetic 弋 (stake), meant "build with tools," evolving to "style, mode; form, ceremony; formula."

袋 (タイ/ふくろ), a combination of 衣 (garment) and the phonetic 代 means "bag, sack."
    風袋 (フウ・タイ tare), 袋 (ふくろ bag)

貸 (タイ/か・す) is a combination of 貝 (wealth) and the phonetic 代 (take over for) ; it means "lend, rent."
    貸借 (タイ・シャク debit and credit), 貸す (か・す lend)

試 (シ/こころ・みる/ため・す) is a combination of 言 (say) and the phonetic 式 (build); it means "try, test."
    入試 (ニュウ・シ entrance exam), 試みる (こころ・みる try), 試す (ため・す test)

于 ; 亏 (ウ)   (big curve; big concavity)

芋 (いも) combines 艹 (plant) and the phonetic 于 (big curve) for the meaning "potato"; the *on-yomi* ウ is not included in the Jōyō Kanji.

宇 (ウ) combines 宀 (roof) and the phonetic 于 (big curve) to mean originally "big roof; eaves," coming later to refer to the building thereunder and thence something like "realm, sphere."
    宇宙 (ウ・チュウ universe; outer space)

汚 (オ/きたな・い/けが・らわしい/よご・れる) joins 氵 (water) and a variant of the phonetic 亏 (big concavity). Referring earlier to mud puddles, it now means "dirty, impure, defiled."
    汚職 (オ・ショク corruption), 汚い (きたな・い dirty), 汚らわしい (けが・らわし

い filthy), 汚れる (よご・れる　get dirty)

華 (カ/ケ/はな) originates in a combination of ⺿ (plant), 垂 (hang), and the phonetic 于 (big). It means "flower; flowery, gorgeous; China."
　　豪華 (ゴウ・カ splendor), 香華 (コウ・ゲ incense and flowers), 華やか (はな・やか flowery)

誇 (コ/ほこ・る) is a combination of 言 (say) and the phonetic 夸 (カ/コ spread-legged stance), which is made of 大 (spread-eagle person) and another variant of the phonetic 于 (big curve) . It means "brag, boast."
　　誇張 (コ・チョウ exaggeration), 誇る (ほこ・る boast)

4 (ク/キョウ)　　　　　　　　　　　　　　　　　　　　　　　(twist)
　　叫 (キョウ/さけ・ぶ) combines 口 (mouth) and the phonetic 4 (twist). It means "scream, shout."
　　絶叫 (ゼッ・キョウ yell), 叫ぶ (さけ・ぶ shout)

糾 (キュウ) is a combination of 糸 (thread) and the phonetic 4 (twist). Originally "twine, cord," its meaning now ranges through "tangle" and "inquire into, examine."
　　糾明 (キュウ・メイ close examination)

彡 (サン)　　　　　　　　　　　　　　　　　　　　　　　　　(design)
　　杉 (すぎ) combines 木 (tree) and the phonetic 彡 (design), although the *on-yomi* サン is not included in the Jōyō Kanji; it means "cedar; Japanese cedar."

之 (シ)　　　　　　　　　　　　　　　　　　　　(tip of foot; keep going)
　　芝 (しば) is a combination of ⺿ (plant) and the phonetic 之, but the *on-yomi* シ is not included in the Jōyō Kanji. It means "turf, lawn grass" in Japanese only.

寺 (ジ/てら) combines 寸 (hand) and a variant of the phonetic 之 (foot). It once meant "work, serve; government office," but has long been specialized for "Buddhist temple."
　　寺院 (ジ・イン temple), 寺 (てら temple)

志 (シ/こころざ・す/こころざし) combines 心 (heart) and a variant of the phonetic 之 (keep going). It means "intend, aspire to."
　　意志 (イ・シ will), 志す (こころざ・す aspire to), 志 (こころざし aim)

侍 (ジ/さむらい) is a combination of 亻 (person) and the phonetic 寺 (serve) meaning "attend, be in the service of" and, in Japan, *samurai*.
　　侍従 (ジ・ジュウ chamberlain), 侍 (さむらい *samurai*)

持 (ジ/も・つ) is made from 扌 (hand) and the phonetic 寺 (work). It means "hold; keep; own."
　　持続 (ジ・ゾク maintain), 持つ (も・つ hold; own)

待 (タイ/ま・つ) is a combination of 彳 (conduct) and the phonetic 寺 (serve). It means "receive, entertain; await."

接待 (セッ・タイ reception), 待つ (ま・つ wait for)

時 (ジ/とき) combines 日 (sun) and the phonetic 寺 in the sense of its top element 之 (move ahead). It means "time, hour; o'clock."

時差 (ジ・サ time difference), 時 (とき time)

特 (トク) is a combination of 牛 (ox) and the phonetic 寺. It meant "bull ox," but now means "singular, special."

特別 (トク・ベツ special)

等 (トウ/ひと・しい) is made up of 竹 (bamboo) and the phonetic 寺. It may have had to do with joints of bamboo; its meaning is "equal; rank; et cetera, the likes of."

等級 (トウ・キュウ rank), 等しい (ひと・しい equal)

詩 (シ), a combination of 言 (say) and the phonetic 寺 (work), means "poem, poetry." Until modern times it was used in Japan only in regard to Chinese poetry.

誌 (シ) combines 言 (say) and the phonetic 志 (aim) and means "note, write down"; in Japanese it also means "magazine."

雑誌 (ザッ・シ magazine)

卂 (シン)   (fly fast)

迅 (ジン) is ⻌ (walk) combined with the phonetic 卂 (fast) and means "swift."
迅速 (ジン・ソク speedy)

巛 (セン)   (river)

災 (サイ/わざわ・い) was originally a combination of 火 (fire) and the phonetic 巛 (サイ blocked river), simplified to 巛 (river). It means "natural disaster, calamity."

災難 (サイ・ナン disaster), 災い (わざわ・い misfortune)

爿 ; 丬 (ソウ/ショウ)   (long board)

壮 (ソウ), 士 (male) combined with the phonetic 爿 (long board) for an original meaning of "tall man," now means "stalwart, vigorous; prime of manhood; grand, magnificent."

壮観 (ソウ・カン grand sight)

状 (ジョウ) is a combination of 犬 (dog) and the phonetic 爿. It means "appearance, state; document, letter."

状態 (ジョウ・タイ state)

将 (ショウ) is the Jōyō Kanji variant of 將, combining 月 (flesh), 寸 (hand), and the phonetic 爿 (long board) and was used to refer to the middle, or longest, finger. From that derived the meaning "lead, conduct; military patrol leader"; its idiomatic sense of "be on the verge of, about to" came from that.

将軍 (ショウ・グン shogun)

荘 (ソウ) combines 艹 (grass) and the phonetic 壮 (vigorous) for "thick grass;

thatched cottage or barn." It now has senses of "majestic; country house, villa" and is much used in the names of villas and apartment houses in Japan.

別荘 (ベッ・ソウ villa)

装 (ソウ/ショウ/よそお・う) is a combination of 衣 (garment) and the phonetic 壯 meaning "dress, adorn; feign."

装飾 (ソウ・ショク decoration), 衣装 (イ・ショウ clothes), 装う (よそお・う dress up; simulate)

奨 (ショウ) is a combination of 大 (large) and the phonetic 将 (lead); it means "encourage, urge on."

奨学金 (ショウ・ガッ・キン scholarship)

蔵 (ゾウ/くら) is the Jōyō Kanji simplification of 藏, which combines 艹 (plants) and the phonetic 臧 (ゾウ), a combination of 臣 (vassal), 戊 (halberd), and the phonetic 爿 (long board). It means "stock, store; cache away."

冷蔵庫 (レイ・ゾウ・コ refrigerator), 蔵 (くら storehouse)

臓 (ゾウ), a combination of 月 (flesh) and the phonetic 蔵 (store), means "internal organ."

心臓 (シン・ゾウ heart)

| 乇 (タク) | (rooted) |

宅 (タク) combines 宀 (roof) and the phonetic 乇 (rooted) and means "house." As an independent word in Japan it can mean "(our)home; my husband," or, with the honorific prefix お, "you; your home."

住宅 (ジュウ・タク residence)

託 (タク) combines 言 (say) and the phonetic 乇 (rooted) and means "entrust."

託す (タク・す entrust)

| 夂 (チ) | (draggimg feet) |

条 (攸, p. 229)

| 也 (ヤ) | (scorpion) |

他; 地; 池; 施 (它, p. 214)

| 幺 (ヨウ) | (faint) |

幼 (ヨウ/おさな・い), a combination of 力 (strength) and the phonetic 幺 (faint), means "young, infant."

幼児 (ヨウ・ジ infant), 幼い (おさな・い infantile)

幽 (ユウ) is a combination of 山 (mountain) with the phonetic 㐀 (ユウ thin thread) and means "dim, obscure."

幽霊 (ユウ・レイ ghost)

4-Stroke Phonetics

尹 （イン）　　　　　　　　　　　　　　　　　　　　　　　　　　　(control)

君 （クン/きみ） is a combination of 口 (mouth) and the phonetic 尹 (control). It originally meant something like "priest, prophet" and later "lord, gentleman." Via usage like that of "milord," it has come to be in Japan a non-honorific "you" in male language, as well as a semi-formal name-suffix, mostly of male names.

諸君 （ショ・クン gentlemen）, 君 （きみ you）

郡 （グン） combines 阝 (town) with the phonetic 君 (control). It means "county," an administrative unit within a prefecture.

奈良県吉野郡 （ナ・ら・ケン・よし・の・グン Yoshino-gun, Nara Prefecture）

群 （グン/む・れ/むら・がる）, 羊 (sheep) combined with the phonetic 君 (control), means "flock, herd, group, crowd."

群集 （グン・シュウ crowd）, 群れ （む・れ flock）, 群がる （むら・がる throng）

勻 （イン or キン）　　　　　　　　　　　　　　　　　　　　　　　(even)

旬 （ジュン） merges 日 (sun) with the phonetic 勻 (even). It means "go around; a circuit; one of the three ten day periods in the old thirty-day month."

上旬 （ジョウ・ジュン first ten days of a month）

均 （キン） adds 土 (earth) to the phonetic 勻 (even), distinguishing one of the latter's original meanings, "level."

平均 （ヘイ・キン average）

殉 （ジュン） is a combination of 歹 (die) and the phonetic 旬 (go around) and refers to the practice of a lord's retainers surrounding his corpse and following him in death. In modern times it is more likely to be used in the sense of "martyr-dom."

殉じる （ジュン・じる sacrifice oneself）

云 （ウン）　　　　　　　　　　　　　　　　　　　　　　　　　　(vapor)

伝; 転 （軎, p. 222）

芸 （埶, p. 250）

魂 （コン/たましい） combines 鬼 (ghost) and the phonetic 云 (mist) and means "soul, spirit."

商魂 （ショウ・コン commercial spirit）, 魂 （たましい soul）

夬 （ケ/カイ）　　　　　　　　　　　　　　　　　　　　　　　(scoop out)

快 （カイ/こころよ・い） is a combination of 忄 (heart) and the phonetic 夬 (scoop out). It means "pleasant; get well," apparently likened to bailing the bad feelings out.

快適 （カイ・テキ comfortable）, 快い （こころよ・い pleasant）

決 (ケツ/き・める) is 氵 (water) combined with the phonetic 夬 (scoop out)for a sense of a river breaking through its banks. It means "break; vigorous, resolute, decisive; determine, decide."

決裂 (ケツ・レツ break down), 決める (き・める decide)

| 気 | (ケ/キ) | (steam) |

気 (キ/ケ) is the Jōyō Kanji abbreviation of 氣, which adds 米 (rice) to the phonetic 气 (steam), presumably to clarify the original meaning "steam" by showing it rising over rice. It now means "air, atmosphere; spirit, mind" and, in Japan, "temper; feeling; intention."

気持ち (キ・も・ち feeling), 気配 (ケ・ハイ indication)

汽 (キ) adds 氵 (water)to the phonetic 气 (steam), again retaining the latter's meaning, "steam."

汽車 (キ・シャ steam train)

| 开 | (ケン) | (grind, polish) |

研 (ケン/と・ぐ) adds 石 (stone) to the phonetic 开 (grind, polish) and means "grind, polish; study."

研究 (ケン・キュウ research), 研ぐ (と・ぐ grind)

| 亢 | (コウ) | (neck; stand straight) |

坑 (コウ) is 土 (earth) combined with the phonetic 亢 (straight) and means "pit."

坑夫 (コウ・フ miner)

抗 (コウ) combines 扌 (hand) and the phonetic 亢 (stand straight) for "resist, object."

抗議 (コウ・ギ protest)

航 (コウ), a combination of 舟 (boat) and the phonetic 亢 (straight), means "sail to; voyage."

航海 (コウ・カイ voyage)

| 厷 | (コウ) | (spread elbows) |

雄 (ユウ/お/おす) combines 隹 (bird) and the phonetic 厷 (stick elbows out) for "male; brave; grand."

雄大 (ユウ・ダイ grand), 雄牛 (お・うし bull), 雄 (おす male)

| 卬 | (ゴウ) | (kneeling before someone standing) |

仰 (ギョウ/コウ/あお・ぐ/おお・せ) adds 亻 (person) to the phonetic 卬 (kneel before), retaining the latter's meaning, "look up to; command from a superior."

仰天 (ギョウ・テン astonishment), 信仰 (シン・コウ faith), 仰ぐ (あお・ぐ look up), 仰せ (おお・せ order)

迎 (ゲイ/むか・える) combines 辶 (walk) and the phonetic 卬 (kneel to someone); it means "greet, receive."

迎賓館 (ゲイ・ヒン・カン guesthouse), 迎える (むか・える greet)

从 (ジュ or ジュウ/ショウ)   (two people; follow)

従 (ジュウ/ショウ/ジュ/したが・う), is the Jōyō Kanji version of 從 with 彳 (go) and 止 (foot) added to the phonetic 从 (follow); it means "follow; secondary; comply with, obey."

従来 (ジュウ・ライ formerly), 追従 (ツイ・ショウ flattery), 従五位 (ジュ・ゴ・イ secondary fifth rank), 従う (したが・う obey)

縦 (ジュウ/たて) combines 糸 (thread) and the phonetic 従 (follow). It means "vertical; length; free, arbitrary."

縦横 (ジュウ・オウ vertical and horizontal), 縦 (たて length)

殳 (ズ/シュ)   (weapon in hand)
(ボツ)   (dive)

投 (トウ/な・げる), a combination of 扌 (hand) and the phonetic 殳 (weapon in hand), means "throw, cast."

投書 (トウ・ショ letter to editor), 投げる (な・げる throw)

没 (ボツ) is a revised form of 沒, which has 氵 (water) and 殳 (dive) combined. It means "submerge, sink; nullify; die" and shows up as a negative prefix meaning "without."

日没 (ニチ・ボツ sunset)

段; 鍛 (耑, p. 240)

壬 (チョウ/テイ)   (straight shin; extend)
(ニン/ジン)   (pregnant; loaded)

任 (ニン/まか・せる) is a combination of 亻 (person) and the phonetic 壬 (loaded). It means "task, responsibility; entrust."

任期 (ニン・キ term of office), 任せる (まか・せる entrust)

呈 (テイ) combines 口 (mouth) and a variant of the phonetic 壬 (straight shin). It means "state (straightforwardly); offer, present."

贈呈 (ゾウ・テイ presentation)

廷 (テイ) is 廴 (extend) and the phonetic 壬 (straight shin). It designated a place for political assemblies and now means "court of law."

法廷 (ホウ・テイ court of justice)

妊 (ニン) combines 女 (woman) and the phonetic 壬 (pregnant) and means "pregnancy."

避妊 (ヒ・ニン contraception)

庭 (テイ/にわ) is 广 (house) and the phonetic 廷 (courtyard). It means "garden, yard, court."

庭園 (テイ・エン garden), 庭 (にわ garden)

程 (テイ/ほど), a combination of 禾 (crop) and the phonetic 呈 (straight), means "standard, norm; extend, distance."

程度 (テイ・ド degree), 三日程 (みっ・か・ほど some three days)

聖 (セイ) rearranges 耳 (ear) and the phonetic 呈 (straight). It means "sage; saint; holy."
聖書 (セイ・ショ the Bible)

艇 (テイ) combines 舟 (boat) and the phonetic 廷 and means "boat."
競艇 (キョウ・テイ motorboat race)

賃 (チン) is a combination of 貝 (money) and the phonetic 任 (task). It means "hire, employ; wages, fee."
家賃 (や・チン rent)

聴 (チョウ/き・く) is the Jōyō Kanji variant of 聽, a combination of 耳 (ear), 悳 (straight), and the phonetic 壬 (extend). It means "listen."
聴衆 (チョウ・シュウ audience), 聴く (き・く listen)

冘	(チン/ニン)	(sink)

沈 (チン/しず・む) adds 氵(water) to the phonetic 冘 (sink) and means "submerge, sink; quiet, calm."
沈黙 (チン・モク silence), 沈む (しず・む sink)

朮	(ハツ)	(bud opening, sprout)

肺 (ハイ), 月 (flesh) and a slightly modified 朮 (open), means "lungs."

鉢 (ハチ/ハツ), a combination of 金 (metal) and another variant of the phonetic 朮, means "bowl, pot."
鉢 (ハチ bowl), 衣鉢 (イ・ハツ a master's secrets)

𠬝	(フク)	(attach, stick)

服 (フク) goes back to a combination of 舟 (boat) and the phonetic 𠬝 (attach) and had reference to the boards making up the sides of a boat. Now it means "clothes; wear; dose; obey."
制服 (セイ・フク uniform)

巴	(ヘ/ハ)	(lie prostrate, contact)

把 (ハ) joins 扌 (hand) and 巴 (contact) and means "grasp; handle"; it is also a counter for bundles.
把握 (ハ・アク grip)

肥 (ヒ/こ・える/こえ) is 月 (flesh) and a 巴 of contested origin, perhaps an expansion of ヒ (ヒ) or perhaps 己 as an abbreviation of 配 (ハイ). It means "fat; fertile."
肥満 (ヒ・マン obesity), 肥える (こ・える fertile), 肥 (こえ fertilizer)

丯	(ホウ)	(ear of rice ; pyramid ; cone)

邦 (ホウ), combination of 阝 (mound) and the phonetic 丯 (cone), meant something like "territory," of a sort demarcated by earthen pyramids or conical

mounds. It means "a land; the nation" and thus, in Japan, "Japan."
邦楽 (ホウ・ガク Japanese music)

封 (フウ/ホウ) was originally written with 土 (earth) on the right and the phonetic 丰 (triangle) on the left. It referred to a triangular mound or cone of earth of a sort used to demarcate territory. It now means "mound; fence off; close; seal."
封 (フウ seal), 封建時代 (ホウ・ケン・ジ・ダイ feudal period)

峰 (ホウ/みね) combines 山 (mountain) and the phonetic 夆 (ホウ meet), a combination of 夂 (dragging feet) and the phonetic 丰 (cone). It means "peak, ridge."
処女峰 (ショ・ジョ・ホウ virgin peak), 峰 (みね mountain peak)

豊 (ホウ/ゆた・か) is a simplification of 豐, combining 山 (mountain), 豆 (stemmed dish), and two instances of the phonetic 丰 (ear of rice). It means "abundance; plenty."
豊作 (ホウ・サク good crop), 豊か (ゆた・か plentiful)

縫 (ホウ/ぬ・う), combination of 糸 (thread) and the phonetic 逢 (ホウ meet), made of 辶 (walk) and the phonetic 夆 (meet); 逢 means "sew."
裁縫 (サイ・ホウ sewing) , 縫う (ぬ・う sew)

勿 (モチ/ブツ)   (streamers; mixed)

物 (ブツ/モツ/もの) is a combination of 牛 (ox) and the phonetic 勿 (mixed) . It may have originally related to pied oxen, but it developed the very abstract sense of "thing." Apparently oxen epitomized the notion of "things."
物価 (ブッ・カ commodity prices), 荷物 (に・モツ load), 物 (もの thing)

5-Stroke Phonetics

㠯 (イ)   (plow)

以 (イ) combines a variant of the phonetic 㠯 (plow) on the left with 人 (person). It means "with, using; from there."
以前 (イ・ゼン before)

似 (ジ/に・る) is a combination of 亻 (person) and the phonetic 以. It means "resemble."
類似 (ルイ・ジ resemblance), 似る (に・る look like)

𦥑 (エイ/ケイ)   (surrounding fire)
(ガク)   (exchange)

学 (ガク/まな・ぶ) combines 子 (child) and a Japanese simplification of the phonetic 學 (exchange), made up of 冖 (roof) and an element originally showing two hands holding the phonetic 爻 (コウ cross). It means "school; study, learn; learning, -logy."
学期 (ガッ・キ semester), 学ぶ (まな・ぶ learn)

栄 (エイ/さか・える/は・える) is 木 (tree) and a simplified 𤇾 (surrounding), which combines two 火 (fire) and the phonetic 冂 (ケイ surround) . It means "bloom, flourish; glory."

栄養 (エイ・ヨウ nourishment), 栄える (さか・える thrive; は・える glory)

蛍 (ケイ/ほたる), 虫 (insect) and the simplified form of the phonetic 熒 (surrounding fire), means "firefly."

蛍光灯 (ケイ・コウ・トウ flourescent lamp), 蛍 (ほたる firefly)

営 (エイ/いとな・む) combines 宮 (building), abbreviated to 呂, and the simplified form of the phonetic 熒 (surrounding fire) and means "encampment, barrack; build, carry on, operate."

営業 (エイ・ギョウ business), 営む (いとな・む conduct)

覚 (カク/おぼ・える/さ・ます) combines 見 (see) and the simplification of the phonetic 學 (exchange), it means "sense; waken; awake, enlightened; enlightened one."

味覚 (ミ・カク taste), 覚える (おぼ・える memorize), 覚ます (さ・ます awaken)

| 戉 | (エツ) | (broad-ax) |

越 (エツ/こ・す) combines 走 (run) and the phonetic 戉. It means "go over; surpass."

卓越 (タク・エツ excellence), 越す (こ・す go over)

| 㕣 | (エン) | (running water) |

沿 (エン/そ・う) adds 氵 (water) to the phonetic 㕣 (running water), which itself combines 八 (water) and 口 (hole); 沿 means "alongside; flank."

沿線 (エン・セン along the railroad line), 沿う (そ・う go alongside)

船 (セン/ふね/ふな) is a combination of 舟 (boat) and the phonetic 㕣 (running water), meaning "boat, ship."

船員 (セン・イン sailor), 船 (ふね ship), 船出 (ふな・で setting sail)

鉛 (エン/なまり), 金 (metal) and the phonetic 㕣 (running water), means "lead," the metal.

鉛筆 (エン・ピツ pencil), 鉛 (なまり lead)

| 夗 | (オン/エン) | (two persons bending down) |

腕 (ワン/うで) is a combination of 月 (flesh) and the phonetic 宛 (オン/エン bending), which joins 宀 (roof) and the phonetic 夗 (two persons bending). An earlier sense of "wrist" has expanded to "arm" and "dexterity, ability."

腕力 (ワン・リョク physical force), 腕 (うで arm)

| 圣 | (カイ) | (clod) |
| | (ケイ) | (vertical, straight) |

怪 (カイ/あや・しい) is a combination of 忄 (heart) and the phonetic 圣 (clod), made of 又 (hand) and 土 (earth). It means "mysterious; suspicious."

怪談 (カイ・ダン ghost story), 怪しい (あや・しい suspicious)

径 (ケイ) combines 彳 (go) and the Jōyō Kanji abbreviation of the phonetic 巠 (straight), probably to suggest a sense like "direct route"; it means "lane, straight; diameter."

　　直径 (チョッ・ケイ diameter)

茎 (ケイ/くき) is 艹 (plant) and the phonetic 巠 (straight); it means "stalk, stem."

　　地下茎 (チ・カ・ケイ subterranean stem), 茎 (くき stalk)

経 (ケイ/キョウ/へ・る) is 糸 (thread) and the phonetic 巠 (vertical). It basically means "warp threads," but it has important derived senses: "longitude; pass by; elapse; thread of logic; unchangeable; control, administer." It is what is translated as "the Book of" in the names of the Confucian classics and, read キョウ, means "sutra."

　　経済 (ケイ・ザイ economy), 経 (キョウ sutra), 経る (へ・る pass through)

軽(ケイ/かる・い/かろ・やか)has 車 (car) combined with the phonetic 巠 (straight). It seems to have referred to a light carriage or chariot for use in war, but is used in the senses of "light, not heavy; not serious; careless."

　　軽視 (ケイ・シ make light of), 軽い (かる・い light), 軽やか (かろ・やか springy)

| 旡 | (キ/カイ) | (person bending backward) |

既 (キ/すで・に) combines a now modified 皀 (food) and the phonetic 旡 (person bending backward) to suggest someone with a full stomach, that is, someone who has eaten already. The meaning is "already; completely, full."

　　既製 (キ・セイ　ready-made), 既に (すで・に already)

愛 (アイ) is a combination of 夂 (dragging feet), 心 (heart) and, originally, the phonetic 旡 (person bending backward). The result means "affection, love."

慨 (ガイ) is 忄 (heart) and the phonetic 既 (full); it means "heart-felt; lament."
　　感慨 (カン・ガイ deep emotion)

概(ガイ)is 木 (wood) and the phonetic 既 (full). It means "approximate, general," derived from an original sense of "strickle."

　　概略 (ガイ・リャク outline)

| 牙 | (ゲ/ガ) | (fang; gear) |

芽 (ガ/め) is a combination of 艹 (plant) and the phonetic 牙 (fang); it means "bud, sprout."

　　発芽 (ハツ・ガ germination), 芽 (め sprout)

邪 (ジャ) unites 阝 (town) and the phonetic 牙; originally a place name, it now means "evil, wicked."

　　無邪気 (ム・ジャ・キ innocence)

雅 (ガ) combines 隹 (bird) and the phonetic 牙. Originally "crow, raven," perhaps onomatopoeically, it now means "grace, elegance" and is the name of a kind of Chinese music and poetry presentation.

雅楽 （ガ・ガク *gagaku*, Japanese court music）

| 乎 | （コ） | (exhale) |

呼 （コ/よ・ぶ） adds 口 (mouth) to the phonetic 乎 (exhale) to preserve the latter's original meaning, but the kanji also means "call, name, invite."

呼吸 （コ・キュウ breath）, 呼ぶ （よ・ぶ call）

| 此 | （シ） | (unevenly placed feet; odd) |

紫 （シ/むらさき）combines 糸 (thread) and the phonetic 此 (odd); it means "purple, violet," apparently conceived of as an "odd" color, not really blue and not really red. In Japan むらさき also refers to soy sauce.

紫外線 （シ・ガイ・セン ultraviolet rays）, 紫 （むらさき purple）

雌 （シ/め/めす） combines 隹 (bird) and the phonetic 此 and means "female," used of animals, and "puny, frail."

雌伏 （シ・フク bide one's time）, 雌牛 （め・うし cow）, 雌 （めす female）

| 乍 | （ジャ/サ） | (carving; intentional) |

作 （サク/サ/つく・る） combines 亻(person) and 乍 (carving) and means "make, produce; action; a product; one's works." In Japan it also means "farming; grow; crop."

作曲 （サッ・キョク musical composition）, 作業 （サ・ギョウ operation）, 作る （つく・る make）

昨 （サク） is 日 (day) and the phonetic 乍. It means "past, last."

昨年 （サク・ネン last year）

詐 （サ） is made of 言 (say) and the phonetic 乍 (intentional), and means "lying, falsity."

詐称 （サ・ショウ false statenent）

酢 （サク/す）, meaning "vinegar; acetic," is a combination of 酉 (wine jar) and the phonetic 乍.

酢酸 （サク・サン acetic acid）, 酢 （す vinegar）

搾 （サク/しぼ・る） is a Japanese combination of 扌 (hand) and the phonetic 窄 （サク　squeeze in）, which is 穴 (hole) and the phonetic 乍 (intentional). 搾 means "squeeze, press out."

搾取 （サク・シュ exploitation）, 搾る （しぼ・る wring out）

| 朮 | （ジュツ） | (millet ear; hang on, adhere) |

述 （ジュツ/の・べる） is a combination of 辶 (walk) and the phonetic 朮 (adhere). It means "state, make a statement."

述懐 （ジュッ・カイ reminiscence）, 述べる （の・べる state）

術 （ジュツ） puts 行 (route) and the phonetic 朮 (adhere) together, originally for the sense of "path," but it now means "skill, art; tactics."

手術 （シュ・ジュツ surgery）

| 疋 | (ショ/ソ) | (foot) |

従; 縦 (从, p. 208)

疎 (ソ/うと・んじる) originally had 㐬 (flow) on the right of the phonetic 疋 (foot). The meaning has changed as well, from "go through" to "sparse, loose; estranged, distant."

过疎 (カ・ソ depopulation), 疎んじる (うと・んじる neglect)

礎 (ソ/いしずえ), meaning "cornerstone, footstone," is a compound of 石 (stone) and the phonetic 楚 (ソ firewood), which combines two 木 (wood) and the phonetic 疋 (foot) .

礎石 (ソ・セキ cornerstone), 礎 (いしずえ cornerstone)

| 尒 | (ショウ) | (lift and weigh) |

称 (ショウ) is a combination of 禾 (crop) and 尒, a simplified form of 爯 (weigh). It now means "esteem, praise; name; designation."

称する (ショウ・する call)

| 㐱 | (シン/チン) | (thick hair; tight packed) |

珍 (チン/めずら・しい) combines 玉 (gem) and the phonetic 㐱 (tightly packed). Originally meaning "quality gem," it means "rare, unusual; strange."

珍重 (チン・チョウ value highly), 珍しい (めずら・しい rare)

診 (シン/み・る), 言 (say) combined with the phonetic 㐱, originally had to do with interpretation of dreams and now means "diagnose."

診察 (シン・サツ medical examination), 診る (み・る examine a patient)

| 它; 也 | (タ or ヤ) | (snake; stretch) |

他 (タ), 亻 (person) and 也, a variant of the phonetic 它 (snake), once meant "wrong thing," but now means "other."

他人 (タ・ニン others)

池 (チ/いけ) is a combination of 氵 (water) and the phonetic 也 (stretch). Its meaning has generalized from "irrigation pond" to "pond, pool."

貯水池 (チョ・スイ・チ reservoir), 池 (いけ pond)

地 (チ/ジ) combines 土 (earth) the phonetic 也 (stretch). It means "ground, land; place, base; indigenous; in Japan it is further used for "fabric; texture."

地理 (チ・リ geography), 地元 (ジ・もと local)

施 (シ/セ/ほどこ・す) is 㫃 (banner) combined with the phonetic 也 (stretch), and originally meant "extend, stretch," but now means "perform; bestow."

施政方針 (シ・セイ・ホウ・シン administrative policy), 施主 (セ・ぬし donor), 施す (ほどこ・す donate; perform)

蛇 (ジャ/ダ/へび) combines 虫 (snake) with the phonetic 它 (snake) and still means "serpent, snake."

蛇 (ジャ/へび snake), 蛇足 (ダ・ソク superfluity)

氏 (タイ/テイ)   (dirt pile; low)

低 (テイ/ひく・い) originated in a combination of 亻(person) and the phonetic 氏 (low) to mean "lowly, lacking in stature ; short person," but has generalized to include "low, not high."

最低 (サイ・テイ the lowest), 低い (ひく・い low)

底 (テイ/そこ) combines 广 (house) and the phonetic 氏 (low) for the meaning "bottom, basis"; in Japan it further means "a kind, a sort."

徹底 (テッ・テイ thoroughness), 底 (そこ bottom)

抵 (テイ), meaning "hamper, obstruct; equivalence," is a combination of 扌 (hand) and the phonetic 氏.

抵抗 (テイ・コウ resistance)

邸 (テイ), made of 阝 (town) and the phonetic 氏 (low), seems to have referred to a townhouse where provincial lords resided when in town; it then developed the sense of "residence, mansion."

官邸 (カン・テイ official residence)

旦 (タン)   (sunrise)
      (セン)   (weigh heavily)

但 (ただ・し) joins 亻(person) and the phonetic 旦 for the meaning "however, except for the fact that." Its *on-yomi*, タン, is not included in the Jōyō Kanji.

但し書き (ただ・し・が・き proviso)

担 (タン/かつ・ぐ/にな・う) combines 扌 (hand) and the phonetic 旦 substituted for 詹 (weigh heavily). It means "carry on the shoulders, bear; burden."

担保 (タン・ポ collateral), 担ぐ (かつ・ぐ shoulder), 担う (にな・う bear)

胆 (タン) combines 月 (flesh) and 旦 substituted for phonetic 詹; it means "gall bladder; courage, spirit."

大胆 (ダイ・タン daring)

壇 (ダン/タン) is 土 (earth) and the phonetic 亶 (タン foundation), a combination of 㐭 (barn) and the phonetic 旦. It means "platform; circles, those involved."

仏壇 (ブツ・ダン Buddhist altar), 土壇場 (ド・タン・バ last moment)

癶 (ハチ/ハツ)   (ready to move)

発 (ハツ/ホツ) is the Jōyō Kanji form of 發, a combination of 弓 (bow), 殳 (action), and the phonetic 癶 (ready to move). It means "fire, shoot; burst forth, emerge, issue, start; spread; depart, leave." In Japan it is also used as a counter of rounds of ammunition and of shots fired.

発見 (ハッ・ケン discovery), 発足 (ホッ・ソク/ハッ・ソク inauguration)

廃 (ハイ/すた・れる) combines 广 (house) and the phonetic 発 (burst); it means "get dilapidated; ruined, useless; outdated; abolish."

廃品 (ハイ・ヒン waste articles), 廃れる (すた・れる become outdated)

弗；ム （ホチ／フツ）　　　　　　　　　　　　　　　　　　　　　（brush off）

仏 （ブツ／ほとけ） combines 亻(person) and ム substituted for the phonetic 弗; it once meant "vague," but long ago came to be used as a transliteration of the first syllable of "Buddha," of which it is also an abbreviation.
　　仏教 （ブッ・キョウ Buddhism）, 仏 （ほとけ Buddha）

払 （フツ／はら・う） adds 扌(hand) to ム, a replacement for the phonetic 弗 (brush off), and it does in fact mean "brush off, sweep away," with the additional meaning in Japan of "pay."
　　払底 （フッ・テイ shortage）, 払う （はら・う pay）

沸 （フツ／わ・く） is a combination of 氵(water) and the phonetic 弗; it means "seethe, bubble up; boil."
　　沸騰 （フッ・トウ boiling）, 沸く （わ・く boil）

費 （ヒ／つい・やす） combines 貝 (money) and the phonetic 弗 (brush off) and means "spend; expense."
　　生活費 （セイ・カツ・ヒ living expenses）, 費やす （つい・やす spend）

卯 （ミョウ／ボウ）　　　　　　　　　　　　　　　　　　　　　（open a gate）
　（リュウ）　　　　　　　　　　　　　　　　　　　　　　　　　（slippery）

柳 （リュウ／やなぎ）, 木 (tree) and the phonetic 卯 (slippery), means "willow."
　　川柳 （セン・リュウ *senryū*, satirical haiku）, 柳 （やなぎ willow）

貿 （ボウ） combines 貝 (wealth) and the phonetic 卯 (open a gate) and means "trade, commerce."
　　貿易 （ボウ・エキ trade）

戊 （モ／ボウ）　　　　　　　　　　　　　　　　　　　　　　　（broad-ax）

茂 （モ／しげ・る） is a combination of 艹 (plant) and the phonetic 戊. It means thrive."
　　繁茂 （ハン・モ luxuriance）, 茂る （しげ・る grow thick）

厉 （ライ／レイ）　　　　　　　　　　　　　　　　　　　　　　（whetstone）

励 （レイ／はげ・む）is the Jōyō Kanji form of 勵, combining 力 (strength) and the phonetic 厲 (whetstone) for "strive; encourage."
　　激励 （ゲキ・レイ encouragement）, 励む （はげ・む strive）

禾 （ワ／カ）　　　　　　　　　　　　　　　　　　　　　　（drooping millet plant）

和 （ワ／オ／やわ・らげる／なご・やか）is a combination of 口 (mouth) and the phonetic 禾 (drooping millet plant) meaning "calm, peaceful; harmony, getting along together, concord; mix; sum." In Japan it additionally means "Japanese."
　　和解 （ワ・カイ reconciliation）, 和尚 （オ・ショウ Buddhist priest）, 和らげる （やわ・らげる soften）, 和やか （なご・やか peaceful）

6-Stroke Phonetics

亥 (ガイ/カイ)　　　　　　　　　　　　　　　　　(boar skeleton; stiff, hard)

劾 (ガイ) is a combination of 力 (strength) and the phonetic 亥 (stiff). It means "reproach."
　　弾劾 (ダン・ガイ impeachment)

刻 (コク/きざ・む), a combination of 刂 (edged tool) joined with the phonetic 亥 (hard), means "carve, notch," with derived senses "segment of time; cruel." In Japan it also means "chop, mince."
　　即刻 (ソッ・コク instantly), 刻む (きざ・む carve)

核 (カク) combines 木 (tree) and the phonetic 亥 (hard). It means "core, seed, kernel; core, nucleus"; in Japan it also means "nuclear weapon."
　　核家族 (カク・カ・ゾク nuclear family)

該 (ガイ) is a combination of 言 (say) and the phonetic 亥 (stiff). An early meaning seems to have been something like "military standard operations procedure; it now means "applicable; general, prevailing."
　　該当 (ガイ・トウ fall within the purview of)

契 (カツ/カチ or ケイ)　　　　　　　　　　　　　　　　(notch)

契 (ケイ/ちぎ・る) joins together 大 (person) and the phonetic 㓞 (notch), which is 刀 (knife) and the phonetic 丰 (カイ notched stick) combined. 契 used to mean "tally" but now means "sign of agreement; pledge."
　　契約 (ケイ・ヤク contract), 契る (ちぎ・る pledge)

喫 (キツ) is 口 (mouth) and the phonetic 契 (tally; carve) and may have meant "gnaw, nibble"; now it means "eat, drink" and in the case of tobacco smoke, "inhale."
　　喫煙 (キツ・エン smoking)

潔 (ケツ/いさぎ・よい) combines 氵 (water) and the phonetic 絜 (ケツ control), which is 糸 (thread) and the phonetic 㓞. It means "clean, pure."
　　潔白 (ケッ・パク purity), 潔い (いさぎ・よい upstanding)

关 (カン)　　　　　　　　　　　　　　　　　　　　(binding cord)
　(ショウ)　　　　　　　　　　　　　　　　　　　(slender)

咲 (さ・く) combines 口 (mouth) and the phonetic 关 (slender); it properly means "smile, laugh," but in Japan is used only for "bloom." Its *on-yomi*, ショウ, is not included in the Jōyō Kanji.

関 (カン/せき) is the Jōyō Kanji version of 門 (gate) and the phonetic 丱 (binding cord). It means "barrier station; checkpoint; important device; connect with."
　　関連 (カン・レン relationship), 関所 (せき・ショ checkpoint)

屰 (ギャク/ゲキ)　　　　　　　　　　　　　　　(someone upside down)

逆 (ギャク/さか・さ) adds 辶 (walk) to the phonetic 屰 (someone upside down);

it means "backwards, contrary; go against."

逆境（ギャッ・キョウ adversity），逆さ（さか・さ upside-down)

劦（キョウ） (united forces)

協（キョウ）adds 十 (gather) to the phonetic 劦 (united forces) and means "cooperate; agreement; harmonize."

協会（キョウ・カイ association)

脅（キョウ/おびや・かす/おど・す）is a combination of 月 (flesh) and the phonetic 劦 (united forces). It means "side, under the arm," but in Japan is used for "threaten, menace."

脅迫（キョウ・ハク threat），脅かす（おびや・かす menace），脅す（おど・す threaten)

夾（キョウ/コウ） (put between)

峡（キョウ）combines 山 (mountain) and a simplification of the phonetic 夾 (squeeze between) and means "valley, glen."

海峡（カイ・キョウ strait)

挟（キョウ/はさ・む）adds 扌(hand) to the phonetic 夾 (put between) and still means "interpose, insert."

挟撃（キョウ・ゲキ attack on both sides），挟む（はさ・む insert)

狭（キョウ/せま・い/せば・める）is 犭(dog) and the phonetic 夾 (put between), and means "narrow."

狭量（キョウ・リョウ narrow-minded），狭い（せま・い narrow），狭める（せば・める make narrow)

虍（ク/コ） (tiger)

炉（ロ）is an abbreviation of 爐, which combines 火 (fire) and the phonetic 盧 (ロ food container); and the latter in turn has 皿 (dish) and 田 (food container) with the phonetic 虍. It means "furnace, fireplace."

虚（キョ/コ）is the Jōyō Kanji form of 虛, combining an ancient form of 丘 (hill) and the phonetic 虍. It means "empty; vain; false."

虚栄（キョ・エイ vanity），虚空（コ・クウ empty sky)

虜（リョ）is a combination of 力(strength)，田, a simplification of a form meaning "transfix", and the phonetic 虍. It means "captive."

捕虜（ホ・リョ prisoner of war)

戯（ギ/たわむ・れる）is a combination of 戈 (halberd) and the phonetic 虛 (vain); it means "play, jest."

戯曲（ギ・キョク drama），戯れる（たわむ・れる play)

慮（リョ）melds 心 (heart) and the phonetic 盧. It means "consider, deliberate."
遠慮（エン・リョ reserve)

西（ケ/カ） (store)

価（カ/あたい）is 亻(person) and 西, which is reduced from the phonetic 賈

(ケ/カ store), a combination of 襾 (cover) and 貝 (wealth). It probably once meant "merchant," but now means "price, worth."

価 (ヒョウ・カ evaluation), 価 (あたい price)

☐ 瓜 (ケ/カ) (melon; round)

孤 (コ) combines 子 (child) and the phonetic 瓜. From "orphan," it has developed the sense of "solitude; alone."

孤児 (コ・ジ orphan)

弧 (コ), uniting 弓 (bow) and the phonetic 瓜 (round), means "bow, arc."

☐ 圭 (ケ/ケイ) (neat pile; boundary)

佳 (カ) is a combination of 亻 (person) and the phonetic 圭 (pile); it means "beautiful; fine, fair."

佳作 (カ・サク fine piece of work)

封 (ヲ, p. 210)

涯 (厂, p. 199)

掛 (か・ける/かかり) combines 扌 (hand) and the phonetic 卦 (ケイ divine), made of 卜 (divination) and the phonetic 圭 (pile); its *on-yomi* ケイ is not included in the Jōyō Kanji. It means basically "hook on, hang" and has a broad range of meanings in Japan, including "place on, cover, spread; charge, levy; spend; cost; multiply" and, as a verb suffix, "start, begin."

掛ける (か・ける hang; place; spend; multiply), 掛 (かかり expense)

街 (ガイ/カイ/まち) has 行 (go) split by the phonetic 圭 (boundary); it means "street; town."

商店街 (ショウ・テン・ガイ shopping district), 街道 (カイ・ドウ highway), 街 (まち town)

☐ 关 (ケン) (fist)

券 (ケン) has 刀 (knife) under the phonetic 关 (fist). It stood for one kind of tally and currently means "ticket; certificate card."

乗車券 (ジョウ・シャ・ケン passenger ticket)

巻 (カン/ま・く/まき) is the Jōyō Kanji form of 已 (kneeling person) and the phonetic 关 (fist). It means "roll up, book, volume" and serves as a counter for volumes.

巻頭 (カン・トウ beginning of book/magazine), 巻く (ま・く roll up), 巻 (カン/まき volume)

圏 (ケン) wraps 囗 (enclosure) around the phonetic 巻 (roll up) and means "zone, sphere."

勢力圏 (セイ・リョク・ケン sphere of influence)

| 㐬 | (コウ) | (missing ; empty) |

荒 (コウ/あら・い/あ・れる) combines 艹 (grass) and the phonetic 㐬 (missing) for "barren, wild"; in Japan it also means "rough, crude."

荒廃 (コウ・ハイ devastation), 荒い (あら・い rough), 荒れる (あ・れる get stormy)

慌 (コウ/あわ・てる) combines 忄 (heart) and the phonetic 荒 (barren); it means "lose one's head, get flustered; get in a rush."

恐慌 (キョウ・コウ panic), 慌てる (あわ・てる flurry)

| 亙 | (コウ) | (bowstring) |
| | (セン or カン) | (encircle) |

恒 (コウ) is a combination of 忄 (heart) and a simplification of the phonetic 亙 (bowstring). It may originally have meant "taut, tense," but its meaning has usually been close to "constant."

恒例 (コウ・レイ usual practice)

垣 (かき), combining 土 (dirt) and the phonetic 亙 (encircle), means "fence"; its *on-yomi* エン is not included in the Jōyō Kanji.

垣根 (かき・ね fence)

宣 (セン), with 宀 (house) over the phonetic 亙 (encircle), is thought to have once meant "fenced-off residence," but it means "announce, declare."

宣伝 (セン・デン advertisement)

| 艮 | (コン) | (sign, mark; remain) |

限 (ゲン/かぎ・る) puts 阝 (mound) alongside 艮 (mark); it meant "landmark," a meaning since abstracted to "limit; restriction."

限界 (ゲン・カイ boundary), 限る (かぎ・る limit)

恨 (コン/うら・む), a combination of 忄 (heart) and the phonetic 艮 (mark; remain), means "grudge."

悔恨 (カイ・コン remorse), 恨む (うら・む bear a grudge)

根 (コン/ね) combines 木 (tree) and the phonetic 艮 (remain) for the concrete and figurative meanings of "root."

根本 (コン・ポン roots), 根 (ね/コン root)

眼 (ガン/ゲン/まなこ), 目 (eye) combined with the phonetic 艮 (remain), means "eye; judgment, perspicacity."

眼前 (ガン・ゼン before one's eyes), 開眼 (カイ・ゲン enlightenment; カイ・ガ ン gaining eyesight), 眼 (まなこ eye)

銀 (ギン) is 金 (metal) and the phonetic 艮 (remain). It was used for "silver," supposedly because silver does not rust away; it also means "money" and, in Japan as a word element, "bank."

墾 (コン) combines 土 (earth) and the phonetic 豤 (コン labor), which is a variant of 豕 (pig) and the phonetic 艮. 墾 means "till, cultivate."

開墾 (カイ・コン cultivation)

懇 (コン/ねんご・ろ) combines 心 (heart) and the phonetic 貇 (labor) combined. It means "whole-hearted"; in Japan it also means "intimate, congenial."

懇意 (コン・イ intimate), 懇ろ (ねんご・ろ cordial)

束 (シ) (thorn; harass)

刺 (シ/さ・す) combines 刂 (edged tool) and the phonetic 朿 (thorn). It means "thorn; stab; sting."

名刺 (メイ・シ name card), 刺す (さ・す stab)

責 (セキ/せ・める) is a combination of 貝 (wealth) and a much-modified 朿 (harass). The basic idea must have once been that of indebtedness, or dunning for debts; it means "blame; burden." In some of the following kanji, some find a sense of "pile up" in it.

責任 (セキ・ニン responsibility), 責める (せ・める blame)

策 (サク) combines 竹 (bamboo) and the phonetic 朿 (thorn). It referred to bamboo riding crops and to canes on the one hand, and to bamboo writing tablets on the other, perhaps applied to homophonous words. The derived meanings are "written order; appointment; plan, plot, stratagem."

策略 (サク・リャク strategy)

債 (サイ) puts 亻 (person) beside the phonetic 責 (dun); it means "debt; press for payment"; in Japan it may, as a word element, signify "bond" in the sense of "stocks and bonds."

債券 (サイ・ケン bond)

漬 (つ・ける) is a combination of 氵 (water) and the phonetic 責 (pile up) and means "pickle; soak." The *on-yomi* シ is not included in the Jōyō Kanji.

積 (セキ/つ・む), combining 禾 (crop) and the phonetic 責 (pile up), means "pile up, accumulate; measure."

積雪 (セキ・セツ snowfall), 積む (つ・む pile up)

績 (セキ) puts 糸 (thread) together with the phonetic 責 (pile up) and means "spin thread; merit, achievement."

成績 (セイ・セキ achievement)

丞 (ジョウ) (raise)

蒸 (ジョウ/む・す) adds 艹 (plant) to the phonetic 烝 (ジョウ steam), which is in turn a combination of 灬 (fire) and the phonetic 丞 (raise). It meant "hemp stalk," a fuel, but now is used only in the sense of "steam."

蒸発 (ジョウ・ハツ evaporation), 蒸す (む・す steam)

聿 (イツ) (holding a brush)
(シン) (dripping brush)

津 (シン/つ) has 氵 (water) and a phonetic 聿 (dripping brush), which used to have an additional three strokes representing dripping; the three strokes have since been eliminated. It means "drip, spill over" and "inlet, harbor."

興味津々 (キョウ・ミ・シン・シン growing interest), 津波 (つ・なみ *tsunami*)

戋 (セン or サン/ザン)   (cut into pieces; little)

浅 (セン/あさ・い) is a combination of 氵 (water) and the Jōyō Kanji simplification of the phonetic 戔 (little), a reduplication of 戈 (halberd). It means "shallow" and "light in color."
浅薄 (セン・パク shallow), 浅い (あさ・い shallow)

桟 (サン) unites 木 (wood) and the phonetic 戋 (little) and refers to various stiffening crosspieces or the framework of flooring, bridges, shelves, and *shōji*.

残 (ザン/のこ・る), a combination of 歹 (bone) and the phonetic 戋 (cut into pieces), means "remainder, leave behind" and also "merciless."
残念 (ザン・ネン regret), 残る (のこ・る remain)

践 (セン) is 足 (foot) and the phonetic 戋. It means "tread on; carry out, put in practice."
実践 (ジッ・セン practice)

銭 (セン/ぜに) joins 金 (metal) and the phonetic 戋 (little) for "copper coin; money, cash" and the old Japanese *sen*, ¥0.01.
銭湯 (セン・トウ public bath), 銭 (ぜに money)

甫 (セン or タン)   (spindle)

専 (セン/もっ・ぱら) joins 寸 (hand) and 甫, which stands for the phonetic 甫 (spindle), for a possible original meaning of "spinning." It means "concentrate; exclusive" and in certain words in Japan is understood as an abbreviation of the first example below, "professional school."
専門学校 (セン・モン・ガッ・コウ professional school), 専ら (もっぱ・ら exclusively)

団 (ダン/トン) is the Jōyō Kanji simplification of 團, combining 囗 (circle) and the phonetic 専. It means "round; group, team."
団体 (ダン・タイ group), 布団 (フ・トン *futon*)

伝 (デン/つた・える) is the form of 傳 chosen for the Jōyō Kanji, 亻 (person) combined with the phonetic 専 (spinning). Its meanings are "transmit, pass on; legend; annotation; annotated text."
伝説 (デン・セツ legend), 伝える (つた・える transmit)

転 (テン/ころ・がる) is 車 (wheel) and 云 again serving for the phonetic 専 (spinning); it means "roll, revolve; turn, change course."
運転 (ウン・テン driving), 転がる (ころ・がる roll about)

𠂤 (タイ or カイ)   (pile)

追 (ツイ/お・う) is 辶 (walk) and the phonetic 𠂤. It means "follow, chase, pursue."
追加 (ツイ・カ addition), 追う (お・う follow)

帰 (キ/かえ・る) is an abbreviation of the non-Jōyō Kanji form 歸, combining 帚 (broom, possibly as an abbreviation of 婦, woman), 止 (foot), and the phonetic 𠂤. 帰 means "return."

帰宅（キ・タク returning home），帰る（かえ・る go/come back）

而 （ニ/ジ）   (beard)

耐（タイ/た・える），a combination of 寸（hand）and the phonetic 而（beard），means "tenacious; endure."

耐久力（タイ・キュウ・リョク durability），耐える（た・える endure）

厎 （ハ）   (branch off)

派（ハ）adds 氵（water）to the phonetic 厎（branch off）; it means "branch; derivation; sect."

流派（リュウ・ハ school）

脈（ミャク），月（flesh）and the phonetic 厎（branch off），means "blood vessel; pulse; vein, lode, row."

并 （ヒョウ/ヘイ）   (stand together)

併（ヘイ/あわ・せる）adds 亻（person）to a simplified form of 幷（stand together）. It means "conjoin; stand together."

併用（ヘイ・ヨウ joint usage），併せる（あわ・せる put together）

瓶（ビン）combines 瓦（earthenware）with the phonetic 并（stand together）; the *on-yomi* ビン is a *tō-on*, a later development. The kanji meant "well bucket," the kind used in pairs, one at each end of the rope. Now it means "pot, vase, bottle."

塀（ヘイ）is a Japanese-made combination of 土（soil）and the phonetic 屛（ビョウ/ヘイ screen），made of 尸（cover）and the phonetic 并（stand together）. It means "earthen wall" or more generally, "wall, fence."

亦 （ヤク/エキ）   (armpits; intervals)
（ラン/レン）   (tangle)

夜（ヤ/よ/よる）merges 夕（moon）with the phonetic 亦（intervals）and means "night."

昨夜（サク・ヤ last night），夜中（よ・なか late night），夜（よる night）

変（ヘン/かわ・る）is a combination of 夂 for 攵（beat）and the phonetic 亦（tangled）as a simplified form of 䜌. It means "change; tumult, disorder; strange."

変人（ヘン・ジン eccentric person），変わる（か・わる change）

恋（レン/こ・う/こい）combines 心（heart）and the phonetic 亦（tangled）. It means "love, tender passion."

恋愛（レン・アイ love），恋う（こ・う long for），恋（こい love）

液（エキ）is a combination of 氵（water）and the phonetic 夜（night）used, they say, only for its element 亦（armpits）; if so, it could suggest sweat, and through that its meaning of "juice, broth; fluid, liquid."

液体（エキ・タイ liquid）

蛮（バン）combines 虫（snake）with the phonetic 亦（tangled）. The ancient Chinese used it to refer to some of their southern neighbors whom they regarded as less civilized. It now means "barbaric."

野蛮 (ヤ・バン barbarous)

湾 (ワン) is the Jōyō Kanji form of 灣, 氵 (water) and the phonetic 彎 (ワン bowed), which combines 弓 (bow) and the phonetic 䜌 (tangled). It means "bay, gulf; bowed."

東京湾 (トウ・キョウ・ワン Tokyo Bay)

興 (ヨ)   (four hands working together)

挙 (キョ/あ・げる) combines 手 (hand) and 興 as a simplified form of the phonetic 與 (four hands working together; see 与, p. 47). It means "raise, lift up; hold; perform; behavior, action."

挙式 (キョ・シキ hold a ceremony), 挙げる (あ・げる raise; perform; mention; arrest)

誉 (ヨ/ほま・れ), 言 (say) combined with the phonetic 興 (four hands working together), means "praise; honor, fame."

名誉 (メイ・ヨ honor), 誉 (ほま・れ fame)

嬰 (ヨウ/エイ)   (necklace)

桜 (オウ/さくら) unites 木 (tree) and a simplified form of the phonetic 嬰 (necklace), which is 女 (woman) and two 貝 (shell) components. In China it names the cherry tree *Prunus tomentosa* and in Japan the flowering cherry tree, or, in particular, its blossoms. It also means "pink," and an extended sense in Japan is "horse meat."

桜桃 (オウ・トウ cherry), 桜 (さくら cherry blossom)

7-Stroke Phonetics

疑 (イ)   (turn around; wonder)

疑 (ギ/うたが・う) started out with 子 (child), now reduced to マ, in combination with 疋 (foot), and the phonetic 疑 (wonder); it means "doubt."

疑惑 (ギ・ワク suspicion), 疑う (うたが・う doubt)

凝 (ギョウ/こ・る) combines 冫 (ice) and the phonetic 疑 (doubt). It means "coagulate, curdle" and, in Japan, "get stiff; get deeply engrossed in, devoted to; elaborate, exquisite, painstaking."

凝結 (ギョウ・ケツ coagulation), 凝る (こ・る become absorbed in)

擬 (ギ) combines 扌 (hand) and the phonetic 疑 (doubt); it means "imitation; mimic."

模擬 (モ・ギ sham)

串 (カン)   (skewer)

患 (カン/わずら・う) mates 心 (heart) and the phonetic 串 (skewer) for the meaning of "affliction; sickness."

急患 (キュウ・カン emergency case), 患う (わずら・う suffer)

箚 (カン) (falling)

陥 (カン/おちい・る/おとしい・れる) is a combination of 阝 (mound) and the phonetic 臽 (falling), which is in turn 人 (person) and 臼 (pit), with the last replaced by its regular Jōyō Kanji version 旧. It means "fall into" and figuratively "get involved in; lapse into; be reduced to; entrap, capture."

欠陥 (ケッ・カン defect), 陥る (おちい・る fall in), 陥れる (おとしい・れる entrap)

肙 (ケン) (worm)

絹 (ケン/きぬ) is 糸 (thread) and the phonetic 肙 (worm), which combines ロ (originally a little circle to suggest roundness) and 月 (flesh). It means "silk," the thread made by silk-worms.

正絹 (ショウ・ケン pure silk), 絹 (きぬ silk)

夅 (コウ) (descend)

降 (コウ/お・りる/ふ・る) is a combination of 阝 (hill) and the phonetic 夅 (descend). It means "descend; come down from the sky, surrender."

降参 (コウ・サン surrender), 降りる (お・りる descend), 降る (ふ・る fall from the sky)

矦 (コウ) (target)

侯 (コウ) is a combination of 亻 (person) and the phonetic 矦 (target), of which the top was originally a figure representing hanging cloth and the bottom is 矢 (arrow). The combination has been used in the sense of the phonetic, "target, mark," but usually means "feudal lord; marquis," with perhaps a similar history to that of "marquis."

諸侯 (ショ・コウ feudal lords)

候 (コウ/そうろう) combines 亻 (person) with 侯 (lord), minus its first stroke, as phonetic. It means "wait upon, attend; spy on; sign, mark of, indication, feature; season." In Japan one of the verbs expressing its meaning "be in attendance" came to be used as a very polite "be" and is used at the end of the sentence in the old epistolary style.

気候 (キ・コウ climate), 候文 (そうろう・ブン old epistolary style)

売 (コク) (strung shells)

殻 (カク/から) combines 殳 (action) and the phonetic 売 (strung shells) and means "shell; husk."

地殻 (チ・カク lithosphere), 殻 (から shell)

穀 (コク) is a combination of 禾 (crop) and the phonetic 殻 (husk), reduced; it means "grain, cereals."

穀物 (コク・モツ grain)

坐 (ザ)   (sit)

座 (ザ/すわ・る) adds 广 (house) to the phonetic 坐 (sit), which is a combination of 土 (earth) and two 人 (person) components. It means "seat; sit; stellar constellation"; in Japan it is used for a gathering, a kind of trade union (called a *za*), and a theatrical troupe and as a suffix for theater names.

座 (ザ seat; gathering), 座る (すわ・る sit)

夋 (シュン)   (tall and thin)

俊 (シュン) combines 亻(person) and the phonetic 夋 (tall) and means "stand out, excel."

俊英 (シュン・エイ man of talent)

唆 (サ/そそのか・す) is a combination of 口 (mouth) and the phonetic 夋, meaning "incite."

教唆 (キョウ・サ instigation), 唆す (そそのか・す incite)

酸 (サン/す・い) combines 酉 (wine jar) and the phonetic 夋; it means "acid; sour" and is used in words meaning "oxide, oxygen."

酸素 (サン・ソ oxygen), 酸い (す・い sour)

㑴 (シン)   (go into every corner)

侵 (シン/おか・す) is a combination of 亻(person) and the phonetic 㑴 (go into every corner), itself a combination of 又 (hand) and most of 帚 (broom). It means "invade, attack, trespass."

侵入 (シン・ニュウ trespass; invasion), 侵す (おか・す invade)

浸 (シン/ひた・す), 氵(water) and the phonetic 㑴 (go into every corner), means "soak."

浸水 (シン・スイ submergence), 浸す (ひた・す soak)

寝 (シン/ね・る) is the Jōyō Kanji form of 寢, combining 宀 (house), 爿 (bed), and the phonetic 㑴, possibly as an abbreviation of 侵 (invade). It means "go to bed, lie down; sleep."

寝室 (シン・シツ bedroom), 寝る (ね・る sleep)

辰 (ジン/シン)   (clam; vibrate, shake)

唇 (シン/くちびる) combines 口 (mouth) with the phonetic 辰 (clam); it means "lip."

口唇 (コウ・シン lips), 唇 (くちびる lip)

娠 (シン), a combination of 女 (woman) and the phonetic 辰 (shake), to suggest fetal quickening, means "pregnant."

妊娠 (ニン・シン pregnancy)

振 (シン/ふ・る) combines 扌(hand) and the phonetic 辰 (shake). It means "shake, swing." In Japan it is particularly associated with "batting" in baseball. It can mean "bearing, carriage, gestures, action" as in dance and theater. As a suffix on words expressing duration it means "after a lapse of. . ., for the first time in. . .";

it is also used as a counter for swords.

振興 (シン・コウ promotion), 振る (ふ・る swing)

震 (シン/ふる・う), 雨 (weather) combined with 辰 (shake), means "tremble, quake."

地震 (ジ・シン earthquake), 震う (ふる・う quiver)

叟 (ソウ)　　　　　　　　　　　　　　　　　　　　　　　　(search)

捜 (ソウ/さが・す) adds 扌 (hand) to the phonetic 叟 (search), which was originally a combination of 宀 (house), 火 (fire), and 又 (hand). It still means "search."

捜索 (ソウ・サク searching), 捜す (さが・す search)

甬 (ソウ)　　　　　　　　　　　　　　　　　　　　　　　　(put in)

挿 (ソウ/さ・す) is the Jōyō Kanji simplification of the combination of 扌(hand) and the phonetic 臿 (put in), which shows a 千 (pounder) in a 臼 (mortar). It means "put in, insert, interpose."

挿入 (ソウ・ニュウ insert), 挿す (さ・す stick in)

兌 (ダイ/タイ or エイ or エツ)　　　　　　　　　(strip off, remove)

悦 (エツ) combines 忄(heart) and a version of 兌 (strip off), which is ハ (separate) combined with 兄 (big-headed child), to suggest something akin to "a load off one's mind." But the meaning is closer to "joy, delight."

御満悦 (ゴ・マン・エツ his/her delight)

脱 (ダツ/ぬ・ぐ) is 月 (flesh) and the phonetic 兌 (strip off). It means "undress; slip out of, escape; peel off, remove."

脱する (ダッ・する escape from), 脱ぐ (ぬ・ぐ take off)

税 (ゼイ), combining 禾 (crop) and the phonetic 兌 (strip off), means 'tax.'

説 (セツ/ゼイ/と・く) combines 言 (say) and the phonetic 兌 (strip off) to suggest a "verbal disencumbrance." It means "explain, elucidate; persuade; view; story; theory."

説明 (セツ・メイ explanation), 遊説 (ユウ・ゼイ campaigning), 説く (と・く persuade)

鋭 (エイ/するど・い) combines 金 (metal) with the phonetic 兌 (strip off); it means "pointed, sharp."

鋭気 (エイ・キ vigor), 鋭い (するど・い sharp)

閲 (エツ) has 門 (gate) and the phonetic 兌 (strip off), apparently indicating some kind of formal inspection; it means "inspect, examine."

検閲 (ケン・エツ inspection, censorship)

彔 (テイ)　　　　　　　　　　　(sideways-walking tiger-like animal)

逓 (テイ) is simplified from a combination of 辶 (walk) and 彔 (side-stepping tiger), which is made of 虍 (tiger) and 厂 (horizontal extension). It means "relay; one after another."

逓信事務（テイ・シン・ジ・ム postal and telegraphic services）

図 （ノウ）   (head)

悩 （ノウ/なや・む） is a combination of 忄 (heart) and the phonetic 図 (head), simplified from 𱶛, namely 巛 (hair) combined with 図 (head). It means "affliction, agony."

悩殺 （ノウ・サツ captivate）, 悩む （なや・む be in torment）

脳 （ノウ）, 月 (flesh) added to the phonetic 図 (head), means "brain; head."

孚 （フ）   (lightweight)

浮 （フ/う・く） combines 氵 (water) and the phonetic 孚 (light), which is made of 爪 (fingers) and 子 (child); it means "float; come to the surface; rootless; at loose ends" and, in Japan, "end up costing less (time or money), get left over."

浮力 （フ・リョク buoyancy）, 浮く （う・く float; get left over）

甫 （フ/ホ）   (rice-seedling nursery; spread)

捕 （ホ/と・らえる/つか・まえる） combines 扌 (hand) and the phonetic 甫 and means "catch, capture."

捕鯨 （ホ・ゲイ whaling）, 捕らえる （と・らえる capture）, 捕まえる （つか・まえる catch）

浦 （ホ/うら）, 氵 (water) and the phonetic 甫, properly means "beach," but is also used for "bay, inlet" in Japan.

曲浦 （キョク・ホ winding creek）, 浦 （うら inlet）

補 （ホ/おぎな・う）, a combination of 衤 (garment) and the phonetic 甫 (spread), means "patch up, mend"; it is used especially in the sense of "supplement."

補助 （ホ・ジョ assistance）, 補う （おぎな・う compensate for）

舗 （ホ） has 舎 (house), originating as an error for 金 (metal), combined with the phonetic 甫 (spread), to refer to a metal plate, part of a knocker on a gate. Now it means "shop, store; pave."

舗道 （ホ・ドウ pavement）

博 （ハク/バク） combines 十 (put together) and the phonetic 尃, the Jōyō Kanji form of 尃 （フ/ハク spread flat）, which is 寸 (hand) and the phonetic 甫 (spread). It means "extend; extensive, gamble" and in certain cases abbreviates Japanese words meaning "doctorate; exposition."

万国博 （バン・コク・ハク world's fair）, 博徒 （バク・ト gambler）

敷 （フ/し・く） adds 攵 (action) to the phonetic 尃 (spread flat), a combination of 方 (stretch) and the phonetic 甫 (spread), and 敷 means "spread, lay."

敷設 （フ・セツ laying [roadway]）, 敷く （し・く spread）

縛 （バク/しば・る）, a combination of 糸 (thread) and the phonetic 尃 (spread flat), means "tie up, bind."

束縛 （ソク・バク restraint）, 縛る （しば・る bind）

薄 (ハク/うす・い) is 艹 (grass) and the phonetic 溥 (フ/ホ　spread), now slightly modified, which is a combination of 氵 (water) and the phonetic 博 (extensive), of which people quit writing the 十. It means "thin; light; approach."
薄情 (ハク・ジョウ heartlessness), 薄い (うす・い thin; light)

簿 (ボ), 竹 (bamboo) and a slightly modified phonetic 溥 (spread), was first created when notebooks were thin sheets of bamboo. It means "notebook, ledger."
名簿 (メイ・ボ roster)

呆 (ホウ)　(diapered infant)

保 (ホ/たも・つ) adds 亻(person) to the phonetic 呆 (diapered infant) and means "protect, sustain, keep, maintain."
保険 (ホ・ケン insurance), 保つ (たも・つ maintain)

褒 (ホウ/ほ・める) interposes the phonetic 保 (wrap protectively) in 衣 (clothing). Originally referring to a kind of coat, it now means "reward; praise."
褒美 (ホウ・ビ reward), 褒める (ほ・める praise)

㒼 (マン)　(cover)

満 (マン/み・たす) is the Jōyō Kanji form of 滿, which combines 氵(water), 从 (line up), and the phonetic 㒼 (cover), itself a combination of 廿 (pelt) and 巾 (cloth). The whole thing simply means "fill; full." Having been used to write the first syllable of the name of Manchuria, it has also picked up the meaning "Manchuria."
満員 (マン・イン full house), 満たす (み・たす fill)

酉；酋 (ユウ or シュウ)　(wine jar)

猶 (ユウ), 犭 (animal) and the phonetic 酋, referred to a gibbon originally, but is used in the sense of "waver, dawdle."
猶予 (ユウ・ヨ extension of time)

醜 (シュウ/みにく・い) combines 鬼 (ghost) and the phonetic 酉 (wine jar) for the meaning "ugly."
醜聞 (シュウ・ブン scandal), 醜い (みにく・い ugly)

攸 (ユウ)　(long and narrow)

条 (ジョウ) is the Jōyō Kanji-sanctioned abbreviation of 條, which drapes the phonetic 攸 (long and narrow), consisting of 亻 (person) and a vertical line once written as dots for a dribble of water and 攵 (do), over 木 (tree). It means "thin branch," but is most often used in senses of "stripe, strip; line, item, clause, act."
条約 (ジョウ・ヤク treaty)

悠 (ユウ) is a combination of 心 (heart) and the phonetic 攸 (long) for "calm, composed; long, everlasting."
悠然 (ユウ・ゼン composed)

[充] (リュウ)   (flow)

流 (リュウ/ル/なが・れる) adds 氵(water) to the phonetic 充 (flow), represented according to one scholar by a suggestion of amniotic fluid under a symbol of "upside-down newborn." The result still means "flow, stream; current," with derived senses including "float, wander; exile; smooth-running; style, school; class." Japanese usage adds "lineage; foreclosure."

一流 (イチ・リュウ first-rank), 流布 (ル・フ circulation), 流れる (なが・れる flow)

硫 (リュウ), a combination of 石 (stone) and the phonetic 充 (flow), means "sulphur."

硫酸 (リュウ・サン sulfuric acid)

8-Stroke Phonetics

[曷] (ガチ/ガツ)   (shout; hoarse; coarse)

喝 (カツ) is a combination of 口 (mouth) and the Jōyō Kanji simplification of the phonetic 曷 (shout), consisting of 日 (say) and the phonetic 匂 (カイ restrain someone). It means "shout, yell at."

恐喝 (キョウ・カツ threat)

渇 (カツ/かわ・く) combines 氵(water) and the phonetic 曷 (hoarse) for "thirst."
渇望 (カツ・ボウ longing), 渇く (かわ・く get thirsty)

掲 (ケイ/かか・げる) is 扌(hand) and the phonetic 曷, and means "put up, display."
掲示 (ケイ・ジ notice), 掲げる (かか・げる display)

褐 (カツ), a combination of 衤(garment) and the phonetic 曷 (coarse), refers to a coarse fabric and a brown color.
褐色 (カッ・ショク brown)

謁 (エツ) is 言 (say) and the phonetic 曷 (shout). It means "meet, call on (a superior)."
拝謁 (ハイ・エツ audience)

[其] (ギ/キ)   (winnow; square; regular)

基 (キ/もと/もとい) combines 土 (ground) and the phonetic 其 (square); it means "base, foundation"; it is also used as a counter of certain things that stand on a foundation, such as machines, gravestones, and pagodas.
基金 (キ・キン fund), 基づく (もと・づく be based on), 基 (もとい basis)

棋 (キ) consists of 木 (wood) and the phonetic 其 (square) and refers to either of two games, *go* and *shōgi*, played on square boards.
棋士 (キ・シ player of *go/shōgi*)

期 (キ/ゴ) is 月 (moon) and the phonetic 其 (regular); it means "term, period; expect."
期待 (キ・タイ expectation), 最期 (サイ・ゴ one's death)

欺 (ギ/あざむ・く), a combination of 欠 (stooping person) and the phonetic 其, means "deceive."

詐欺 (サ・ギ fraud), 欺く (あざむ・く deceive)

碁 (ゴ), 石 (stone) and the phonetic 其 (square), writes the name of the game *go*.

旗 (キ/はた) combines 㫃 (banner) and the phonetic 其 (square) and means "flag, pennant."

国旗 (コッ・キ   national flag), 旗 (はた flag)

菊 (キク)   (wrapped rice)

菊 (キク) is a combination of 艹 (plant) and the phonetic 匊 (wrapped rice), which consists of 勹 (wrap) and 米 (rice). キク alone means "chrysanthemum," and in compound words it includes some other members of the daisy family.

庚 (キョウ/コウ)   (hard)

康 (コウ) is an old blending of what would be 米 (rice) and the phonetic 庚 (hard). It may have meant "rice bran"; now it means "peace, calm; healthy."

健康 (ケン・コウ health)

尭 (ギョウ)   (tall person)

暁 (ギョウ/あかつき) combines 日 (sun) and the Jōyō Kanji simplification of the phonetic 堯, comprising 儿 (man) and 垚 (high pile of dirt). It means "dawn," but also "well versed."

通暁 (ツウ・ギョウ well-informed), 暁 (あかつき dawn)

奚 (ゲ/ケイ)   (string)

渓 (ケイ) is the Jōyō Kanji sanctioned simplification of 溪, which consists of 氵 (water) and the phonetic 奚 (string), which in turn consists of 爪 (fingers) and a slightly miswritten 糸 (thread). It means "mountain stream; ravine, gorge."

渓流 (ケイ・リュウ mountain torrent)

鶏 (ケイ/にわとり) combines 鳥 (bird) and the phonetic 奚 and means "chicken," probably onomatopoeic in origin.

養鶏場 (ヨウ・ケイ・ジョウ chicken farm), 鶏 (にわとり chicken)

岡 (コウ)   (thick rope; hard and strong)

剛 (ゴウ) is 刂 (edged tool) and the phonetic 岡 (hard and strong). It means "tough, staunch."

剛健 (ゴウ・ケン virile)

綱 (コウ/つな) combines 糸 (thread) and the phonetic 岡 (hard and strong). It means "rope; code, rules, discipline."

綱紀 (コウ・キ official discipline), 綱 (つな rope)

鋼 (コウ/はがね), 金 (metal) and the phonetic 岡 (hard and strong), means "steel."

鋼鉄 (コウ・テツ steel), 鋼 (はがね steel)

囷 (コン/キン)   (round)

菌 (キン) combines ⺾ (plant) and the phonetic 囷 (round), made of 囗 (enclosure) and 禾 (crop). It means "fungus," generalized from "mushroom, toadstool" and now extended to "germ."

釆 (サイ)   (pluck)

採 (サイ/と・る) adds 扌 (hand) to the phonetic 釆 (pluck), a combination of ⺥ (fingers) and 木 (tree), and still means "pluck, nip off" as well as "pick up, adopt."
採用 (サイ・ヨウ adoption; employment), 採る (と・る pick up)

菜 (サイ/な) analyzes into ⺾ (plant) and the phonetic 釆 (pluck). It means "vegetable, greens; dish, prepared food."
菜食 (サイ・ショク vegetarian diet), 菜っ葉 (な・っ・ぱ greens)

彩 (サイ/いろど・る) is a combination of 彡 (design) and the phonetic 釆 (pick). It means "hue, coloring."
水彩画 (スイ・サイ・ガ watercolor), 彩る (いろど・る color)

炗 (シュウ)   (stop)

渋 (ジュウ/しぶ・い), a combination of 氵 (water) and the Jōyō Kanji replacement for the phonetic 歮 (stop), means "not progress smoothly; astringent; sour, glum; sedate, tasteful."
渋滞 (ジュウ・タイ traffic jam; delay), 渋い (しぶ・い astringent)

妾 (ショウ)   (female slave)

接 (セツ/つ・ぐ) combines 扌 (hand) and the phonetic 妾 (female slave), which originated in a combination of 女 (woman) and 辛 (tattooing needle). It means "contact, connect; approach."
接する (セッ・する get close to), 接ぐ (つ・ぐ put together)

昌 (ショウ)   (say clearly)

唱 (ショウ/とな・える) adds 口 (mouth) to the phonetic 昌 (say clearly), a combination of 日 (sun) and 曰 (say); it means "intone, recite; advocate, sing."
唱歌 (ショウ・カ singing), 唱える (とな・える recite)

帚 (ス/シュウ)   (broom)

帰 (⺲, p. 222)

掃 (ソウ/は・く) is 扌 (hand) and the Jōyō Kanji form of the phonetic 帚 (broom); it means "sweep."
清掃車 (セイ・ソウ・シャ garbage truck), 掃く (は・く sweep)

隹 (スイ)   (fat bird; heavy)

推 (スイ/お・す) combines 扌 (hand) and the phonetic 隹 (heavy); it means "push, propel; recommend, propose; infer, surmise."

推理小説 (スイ・リ・ショウ・セツ detective story), 推す (お・す infer; recommend)

唯 (ユイ/イ), a combination of 口 (mouth) and the phonetic 隹, means "yes; only, uniquely."

唯一 (ユイ・イツ one and only), 唯々諾々 (イ・イ・ダク・ダク quite willingly)

催 (サイ/もよお・す) is a combination of 亻 (person) and the phonetic 崔 (サイ), which consists of 山 (mountain) and the phonetic 隹 (fat bird). It means "urge, bring on, provoke" and, in Japanese, "hold, put on, organize (a social event)."

催促 (サイ・ソク urging), 催す (もよお・す hold; provoke)

維 (イ) consists of 糸 (thread) and the phonetic 隹 and means "rope; tie together."

維持 (イ・ジ maintenance)

| 僉 | (セン) | (gather, sharp) |

倹 (ケン) is a combination of 亻 (person) and the Jōyō Kanji form of the phonetic 僉 (gather), which consists of 亼 (gather), two 口 (mouth) components, and two 人 (person) components. It means "collected, disciplined; sparing, modest."

倹約 (ケン・ヤク frugality)

剣 (ケン/つるぎ) combines 刂 (edged tool) with the phonetic 僉 (sharp). It means "double-edged sword"; in Japan it refers to swords in general, and "sting, stinger" (as of a bee).

剣 (ケン/つるぎ sword)

険 (ケン/けわ・しい), 阝 (mound) and the phonetic 僉 (sharp), means "severe; risky; venture" and in Japan "steep."

危険 (キ・ケン danger), 険しい (けわ・しい steep)

検 (ケン) consists of 木 (wood) and the phonetic 僉 (gather) and originally meant "seal wooden tablets." It now means "inspect, investigate"; in Japan, it also refers to a public prosecutor's office.

検事 (ケン・ジ public prosecutor)

験 (ケン/ゲン) is a combination of 馬 (horse) and, originally, the phonetic 検 (inspect), but the 木 is no longer written. It means "try out, examine, proof, results."

経験 (ケイ・ケン personal experience), 霊験 (レイ・ゲン miraculous efficacy)

| 蚤 | (ソウ) | (flea) |

騒 (ソウ/さわ・ぐ) joins 馬 (horse) with a simplified form of the phonetic 蚤 (flea), which goes back to a combination of 虫 (insect) and 爪 (fingernails). It means "restive, agitated; commotion."

騒音 (ソウ・オン noise), 騒ぐ (さわ・ぐ raise a ruckus)

| 悤 | (ソウ) | (put together) |

窓 (ソウ/まど) was originally 穴 (dwelling) put together with the phonetic 囱 (ソウ skylight); the phonetic was expanded with 心 (heart), presumably as a common error, to the phonetic 息 (put together), and subsequently simplified to 悤. 窓 means "window" or, figuratively, "room."

同窓会 (ドウ・ソウ・カイ alumni meeting/society), 窓 (まど window)

総 (ソウ) is a combination of 糸 (thread) and the phonetic 悤 (put together). It means "tuft; combine and tie together; have under control; all together, complete."

総理大臣 (ソウ・リ・ダイ・ジン Prime Minister)

隶 (ダイ/タイ)   (catch up)

康 (庚, p. 231)

逮 (タイ) adds 辶 (walk) to the phonetic 隶 (catch up); it still means "catch up, overtake."

逮捕 (タイ・ホ arrest)

罙 (シン)   (deep)

深 (シン/ふか・い) adds 氵(water) to the phonetic 罙 (deep), which began as 穴 (cave), 火 (fire) and 又 (hand); it means "deep," literally, and figuratively.

深刻 (シン・コク serious), 深い (ふか・い deep)

探 (タン/さぐ・る/さが・す) is a combination of 扌 (hand) and the phonetic 罙 (deep). It means "grope for, seek; search, explore" and, in Japan, "reconnoiter."

探検/探険 (タン・ケン exploration), 探る (さぐ・る grope after; spy on), 探す (さが・す search for)

沓 (ドウ/トウ)   (repetition)

踏 (トウ/ふ・む) is a combination of 足 (foot) and the phonetic 沓 (repetition), which is 水 (fluid) and 曰 (say). It means "mark time; stamp one's feet; tread on."

雑踏 (ザッ・トウ bustle), 踏む (ふ・む tread on)

匋 (ドウ/トウ)   (pottery)

陶 (トウ) adds 阝 (mound of earth) to the phonetic 匋 (pottery), which combines 缶 (earthenware) and 勹 (wrap). It means "pottery, ceramics" and has the derived senses of "mold character, educate, cultivate; rapt, vacant."

陶器 (トウ・キ ceramics)

㝵 (トク)   (obtain)

得 (トク/え・る/う・る) adds 彳 (go) to the phonetic 㝵 (obtain), which long ago was a combination of what should have become 貝 (wealth) and 寸 (hand). It means "obtain, gain; able, capable."

得 (トク profit), 得る (え・る get), あり得る (あり・う・る be possible)

畀 (ヒ)   (give)

鼻 (ビ/はな) consists of 自 (nose) and the phonetic 畀, originally showing a ball of something and two hands. It means "nose; foremost, beginning."

耳鼻科 (ジ・ビ・カ otorhinology), 鼻 (はな nose)

宀 (ヒン)   (arrange closely)

賓 (ヒン) consists of 貝 (wealth) and of the phonetic 宀 (arrange closely), originally a combination of 宀 (roof) and 豕 (pig), just like 家(カ/ケ family). It means "honored guest, entertain; grammatical object."

賓客 (ヒン・キャク honored guest)

浜 (ヒン/はま) abbreviates 濱, which combines 氵 (water) with the phonetic 賓 (close). It means "beach, shore"; in Japan it is used as short for the place name Yokohama.

海浜 (カイ・ヒン seaside), 浜 (はま beach)

舞 (ブ)   (dance)

無 (ム/ブ/な・い) was originally equivalent to the phonetic 舞 and meant "dance," but came to be used for a homophone that means "non-existent; nil; non-, -less, lacking."

無理 (ム・リ unreasonable), 無事 (ブ・ジ safety), 無い (な・い not exist)

舞 (ブ/ま・う/まい) adds 舛 (left and right feet) to the phonetic 舞 (dance), to preserve the meaning, "dance."

舞台 (ブ・タイ stage), 舞う (ま・う dance), 舞 (まい dance)

朋 (ボウ/ホウ)   (double)

崩 (ホウ/くず・れる) combines 山 (mountain) and the phonetic 朋 (make two), slightly modified from 朋, which traces back to a representation of two strings of shells. It means "landslide, crumble" and is used in reference to the death of an emperor.

崩壊 (ホウ・カイ collapse), 崩れる (くず・れる break down)

棚 (たな) is a combination of 木 (wood) and the modified phonetic 朋 (double); the *on-yomi* ホウ is not included in the Jōyō Kanji. It means "shelf."

孟 (ミョウ/モウ)   (vigorous)

猛 (モウ) is 犭 (animal) with the phonetic 孟 (vigorous), consisting of 子 (child) and 皿 (dish, cover); it means "violent, fierce."

猛烈 (モウ・レツ violent)

坴 (リク)   (spacious land)

陸 (リク) adds 阝 (mound) to the phonetic 坴 (spacious land), which is two 土 (earth) components and 八 (separate); it means "land, continent."

大陸 (タイ・リク continent)

陵 (リョウ/みささぎ) is 阝 (mound) and the phonetic 夌 (リョウ long trek), a melding of 夂 (feet) and the phonetic 坴 (spacious land). It means "hill, mound; Imperial mausoleum."

丘陵 (キュウ・リョウ hill), 陵 (みささぎ Imperial mausoleum)

| 侖 | （リン） | (orderly) |

倫（リン）combines 亻(person) with the phonetic 侖 (orderly), which is made up of ㅅ (gather) and 冊 (bamboo tablets). It means "ethics, mores; peers."

不倫（フ・リン immoral)

輪（リン/わ）consists of 車 (wheel) and the phonetic 侖 (orderly). It means "wheel; ring, hoop"; in Japan it is further used as a counter for flowers.

年輪（ネン・リン growth ring)、輪（わ wheel; circle)

論（ロン）、言 (say) and the phonetic 侖 (orderly), means "discuss, debate; theory."

論じる（ロン・じる argue)

| 巤 | （リョウ） | (mane; hirsute) |

猟（リョウ）is made of 犭(dog) and the Jōyō Kanji form of the phonetic 巤, which combines ``` (hair)、囟 (head), and a few strokes surmised to represent animal legs. It means "hunt."

| 录 | （ロク） | (peel off) |

緑（リョク/ロク/みどり）is a combination of 糸 (thread) and the phonetic 录 (peel off). It means "green," or, with reference to hair, "black."

新緑（シン・リョク fresh verdure)、緑青（ロク・ショウ verdigris)、緑（みどり green)

録（ロク）、金 (metal) and the phonetic 录 (peel off) combined, means "record," originally by scratching through bamboo skin or thin metal.

録音（ロク・オン audio recording)

| 或 | （ワク/コク） | (territory; frame) |

国（コク/くに）is the Jōyō Kanji variant of 國, which adds 囗 (boundary) to the phonetic 或 (territory), a combination of 戈 (halberd), a small square to represent land area, and two lines, now one line, surmised to suggest extent of territory. 国 means "country, land, nation"; it is what was used in Japan to refer to the provinces, and in Japan it also means "hometown" and, of course, "Japan, Japanese."

国宝（コク・ホウ national treasure)、国（くに country)

域（イキ）is 土 (earth) and the phonetic 或 (territory); it means "territory, area; sphere, province."

領域（リョウ・イキ domain)

惑（ワク/まど・わす）combines 心 (heart) and the phonetic 或 (frame, limit). It means "be a slave to; misguide" and, in Japan, "not know where to turn."

誘惑（ユウ・ワク temptation)、惑わす（まど・わす mislead)

9-Stroke Phonetics

禹 (ウ)   (lizard)

属；嘱 (蜀, p. 256)

亜 (エン)   (smoke)

煙 (エン/けむり/けむ・たい) adds 火 (fire) to the phonetic 亜 (smoke), which is a pictograph of smoke over an incense burner. It means "smoke; smoking; soot; haze, mist."

禁煙 (キン・エン No Smoking), 煙 (けむり smoke), 煙たい (けむ・たい smoky; feel awkward)

爰 (オン/エン)   (tug; something in between)

援 (エン) consists of 扌 (hand) and the phonetic 爰 (tug), which shows something between two hands, ⺨ and 又. It means "pull; help, aid."

援助 (エン・ジョ assistance)

暖 (爰, p. 241)

緩 (カン/ゆる・める) is 糸 (thread) with the phonetic 爰 (something in between), and means "loose."

緩和 (カン・ワ relief), 緩める (ゆる・める loosen)

昷 (オン)   (warm)

温 (オン/あたた・かい) adds 氵 (water) to the phonetic 昷 (warm), originally a dish (皿) and something under a cover. It means "warm, warmth; calm, gentle."

温度 (オン・ド temperature), 温かい (あたた・かい warm)

咼 (カ)   (round; fit in; fall into)

過 (カ/す・ぎる/あやま・ち) combines 辶 (walk) with the phonetic 咼 (fit in), consisting of 冎 (round bone joint) and 口 (opening). It means "go past; go too far; mistake."

過保護 (カ・ホ・ゴ overprotectiveness), 過ぎる (す・ぎる pass), 過ち (あやま・ち error)

渦 (カ/うず) joins 氵 (water) and the phonetic 咼 (round); it means "whirlpool."
渦中 (カ・チュウ turmoil), 渦 (うず whirlpool)

禍 (カ) is a combination of 礻 (altar) and the phonetic 咼 (fall into), meaning "calamity."

惨禍 (サン・カ disaster)

奐 (カン)   (assist in childbirth; take out)

換 (カン/か・える) joins 扌 (hand) and the phonetic 奐 (take out), which originates in a combination of symbols for a squatting woman and two hands. 換 means "exchange, change."

交換手（コウ・カン・シュ telephone operator）, 換える（か・える exchange）

喚（カン）combines 口（mouth）and the phonetic 奐. It means "call, summon; shout."

召喚（ショウ・カン subpoena）

|禺| （グ/グウ）   (monkey; alike)

偶（グウ）is 亻（person）and the phonetic 禺（alike）, originally a pictograph of a monkey with a big head and long tail. It means "wooden figure, doll; twin, pairing; fortuity, happenstance."

偶然（グウ・ゼン coincidence）

遇（グウ）combines 辶（walk）and the phonetic 禺（monkey）and means "encounter; treat, entertain."

冷遇（レイ・グウ cold treatment）

隅（グウ/すみ）joins 阝（mound）and the phonetic 禺（alike）; it means "corner, nook."

一隅（イチ・グウ a corner）, 隅（すみ nook）

愚（グ/おろ・か）, combining 心（heart）and the phonetic 禺（monkey）, means "stupid, silly." Used for self-reference, it expresses humility.

愚痴（グ・チ grumbling）, 愚か（おろ・か foolish）

|叚| （ケ/カ）   (cover, mask)

仮（カ/ケ/かり）is the Jōyō Kanji form of 假, 亻（person）and the phonetic 叚（mask）, which goes back to a hand or two, one of which, 又, is still recognizable, with some kind of cover. 仮 means "temporary, provisional; borrow; sham, false."

仮説（カ・セツ supposition）, 仮病（ケ・ビョウ feigned illness）, 仮（かり provisional）

暇（カ/ひま）joins 日（day）with the phonetic 叚; it means "leisure, free time."

休暇（キュウ・カ holiday; vacation）, 暇（ひま leisure）

|臤| （ケン）   (stiffened)

堅（ケン/かた・い）adds 土（earth）to the phonetic 臤（stiffened）, which consists of 臣（vassal）and 又（hand）; it means "hard, firm, solid."

堅実（ケン・ジツ steadfast）, 堅い（かた・い firm）

緊（キン）combines 糸（thread）and the phonetic 臤（stiffened）for the sense "tauten; tight, tense."

緊急（キン・キュウ emergency）

賢（ケン/かしこ・い）, 貝（wealth）and the phonetic 臤（stiffened）, means "wise, smart."

賢明（ケン・メイ wise）, 賢い（かしこ・い smart）

|㬎| （ケン）   (exposed)

顕（ケン）is the Jōyō Kanji form of 顯, comprising 頁（head）and the phonetic

顯 (exposed), which is a combination of 日 (sun) and 絲 (thread); 顯 means "manifest."

  顕著 (ケン・チョ notable)

咸 (ゲン/カン) (keep in)

  減 (ゲン/へ・らす) is a combination of 氵 (water) and the phonetic 咸 (keep in), which is made of 口 (mouth) and 戌 (halberd in hand); it means "decrease."

  減退 (ゲン・タイ decrease), 減らす (へ・らす reduce)

  感 (カン), a combination of 心 (heart) and the phonetic 咸 (keep in), means "stir emotion; sense, feel."

  感じる (カン・じる feel)

  憾 (カン) joins another heart 忄 to the phonetic 感 (stir emotion) and means "rue."

  遺憾 (イ・カン regret)

亟 (コク/キョク) (ridgepole)

  極 (キョク/ゴク/きわ・まる) combines 木 (wood) and the phonetic 亟 (ridgepole). It means "acme, polar extremity."

  極端 (キョク・タン extreme), 極上 (ゴク・ジョウ best), 極まる (きわ・まる reach an extreme)

兹 (ジ/シ) (luxuriant)

  滋 (ジ) adds 氵 (water) to the phonetic 兹 (luxuriant), a combination of 艹 (grass) and the phonetic 絲 (シ thread) abbreviated. It means "grow thick; nutritious."

  滋養 (ジ・ヨウ nourishment)

  慈 (ジ/いつく・しむ) is a combination of 心 (heart) and the phonetic 兹 (luxuriant). It means "love, parental care."

  慈善 (ジ・ゼン charity), 慈しむ (いつく・しむ love)

  磁 (ジ) is 石 (stone) and the phonetic 兹 (luxuriant). It means "magnet, lodestone; porcelain."

  磁器 (ジ・キ porcelain)

酋 (シュウ) (chief brewer)

  猶 (酋, p. 229)

育 (ダ or ズイ) (uneven; zigzag)

  随 (ズイ) has 辶 (walk) partially splitting a simplified version of the phonetic 隋 (ダ or ズイ fall), which is a combination of 阝 (mound) and the phonetic 育 (zigzag). 随 means "follow, accompany."

  随意 (ズイ・イ one's own accord)

  堕 (ダ) adds 土 (earth) to the phonetic 隋 (fall), simplified, and means "fall, collapse; wane, deteriorate."

堕落 (ダ・ラク degradation)

惰 (ダ) combines 忄 (heart) with a reduction of the phonetic 隋. It means "lethargy, indolence."

惰性 (ダ・セイ inertia)

髄 (ズイ) is a combination of 骨 (bone) and a reduction of the phonetic 隨. It means "marrow; pith."

彖 (タン)   (hang down)

縁 (エン/ふち) combines 糸 (thread) with the phonetic 彖, a slight variant of 彖 (hang down), originally representing a fat pig with a sagging belly. It means, nonetheless,"fringe, hem, edge, relation, bond, ties." In Japan it further refers to a veranda-like part of a house.

縁 (エン relation; ふち rim)

耑 (タン)   (cloth hanging doubled over)

段 (ダン) is a combination of 殳 (weapon in hand) and a part of the phonetic 耑 (hanging cloth). It means "section; chapter; stair step; stage," being used also to count steps; it is but a short leap to the Japanese use for "rank, grade," that is, competitive level in the martial arts, *go*, and so forth.

階段 (カイ・ダン staircase)

端 (タン/はし/は/はた) combines 立 (stand) with the phonetic 耑 (doubled-over cloth). It means "straight, edge, brink; start" and, in Japan,"odd, left-over."

発端 (ホッ・タン origin), 端 (はし edge), 端数 (は・スウ fraction), 道端 (みち・ばた roadside)

鍛(タン/きた・える), 金(metal)and the phonetic 段(steps), means "forge, anneal."

鍛練 (タン・レン training), 鍛える (きた・える forge)

冢 (チュウ/チョウ)   (mound; grave)

塚 (つか) adds 土 (earth) to the phonetic 冢 (mound; grave), which is 冖 (cover) over 豕 (pig with legs tied) less one stroke. The *on-yomi* チュウ/チョウ have never been used in Japan. 塚 means "mound, grave."

豙 (ツイ)   (heavy pig)

遂 (スイ/と・げる) combines 辶 (walk) and the phonetic 豙 (heavy pig) and means "accomplish."

未遂 (ミ・スイ attempted), 遂げる (と・げる accomplish)

隊 (タイ) combines 阝 (mound) with the phonetic 豙 (heavy pig) and seemingly meant "heavy pile of earth," but is used instead for "band, troop; troops."

墜 (ツイ) consists of 土 (earth) and the phonetic 隊 (heavy clump). It means "plunge to earth."

墜落 (ツイ・ラク plunge to earth)

屍 (デン)   (buttocks)

殿 (デン/テン/との/どの) is a combination of 殳 (action) and the phonetic 屍 (buttocks), which is made of 尸 (body) and what once represented a stool. From humble beginnings as "spank" and "heavy," it has come to mean "rear, last; large building, palace, hall" and provides for honorific reference to Imperial family members. In Japan it has meant "lord; Your/His Lordship" and is used as a generalized personal honorific.

殿下 (デン・カ Your/His/Her Highness), 御殿 (ゴ・テン palace), 殿方 (との・がた gentleman), 山田太郎殿 (やま・だ・タ・ロウ・どの Taro Yamada, Esq.)

荅 (トウ)   (small bean)

塔 (トウ) joins 土 (earth) to the phonetic 荅, a combination of 艹 (plant) and 合 (put together) presumably suggesting a pod of beans or peas. It is believed to have been created expressly to render the -tup- of "stupa," the Sanskrit word for "pagoda, tower," and it indeed means "stupa, pagoda."

五重の塔 (ゴ・ジュウ・の・トウ five-story pagoda)

搭 (トウ) is a combination of 扌 (hand) and the phonetic 荅. It means "board, get on; load."

搭乗 (トウ・ジョウ boarding)

耎 (ネン/ゼン)   (soft)

軟 (ナン/やわ・らかい) originated in the combination of the early forms of 車 (wheel) and the phonetic 耎 (soft), consisting of 而 (beard) and 大 (big). It means "soft, tender."

柔軟 (ジュウ・ナン flexible), 軟らかい (やわ・らかい soft)

暖 (ダン/あたた・かい), formerly meaning "spreading sunlight," became confused with, and replaced, a combination of 日 (sun) and the phonetic 耎 (soft). The Kanji now means "warm."

暖冬 (ダン・トウ mild winter), 暖かい (あたた・かい warm)

畐 (フク)   (bottle of liquor)

副 (フク) is 刂 (knife) and the phonetic 畐, which goes back to a picture of a round-bottomed liquor bottle. The original meaning was "cut in two, halve," but it is now used for meanings like "sub-; vice-; secondary."

副作用 (フク・サ・ヨウ side effect)

富 (フ/フウ/と・む/とみ), 宀 (house) and the phonetic 畐 (bottle of liquor), means "wealth; rich."

貧富 (ヒン・プ wealth and poverty), 富貴 (フウ・キ/フッ・キ wealth and fame), 富む (と・む get wealthy), 富 (とみ wealth)

幅 (フク/はば) combines 巾 (cloth) and the phonetic 畐; it meant "shin guards" earlier, but now means "width, span" and "hanging scroll" and is used to count instances of the latter.

幅 (フク hanging scroll; はば width)

福 (フク) consists of ネ (altar) and the phonetic 畐 (bottle of liquor) and means "blessings, good fortune."

復 (フク) combines 彳 (go) with the phonetic 复 (フク double back), which is a melding of 夂 (feet) and the phonetic 畐. It means "go back; retrieve; again, respond."

　復活 (フッ・カツ revival; rebirth)

腹 (フク/はら) is a combination of 月 (flesh) and the phonetic 复 (double back) meaning "belly, innards" and, the belly considered the seat of thoughts and emotions, "mind, heart." Another figurative use is "hillside, mountainside."

　空腹 (クウ・フク hunger), 腹 (はら belly; mind)

複 (フク), ネ (garment) and the phonetic 复 (double back), means "lie one upon another; double, duplicate."

　複雑 (フク・ザツ complex)

覆 (フク/おお・う/くつがえ・す) combines 襾 (cover) and the phonetic 復 (go back) and means "cover, veil; overturn, upset, repeat, reproduce."

　覆面 (フク・メン mask), 覆う (おお・う cover), 覆す (くつがえ・す upset)

復 (フク)　　　　　　　　　　　　　　　　　　　　　(double back)

復; 腹; 複; 覆 (畐, p. 242)

扁 (ヘン)　　　　　　　　　　　　　　　　　　　(thin and flat; tablets)

偏 (ヘン/かたよ・る) consists of 亻 (person) and the phonetic 扁 (thin and flat), composed of 戸 (door-flap) and 冊 (tablets). It means "incline toward; one-sided, partial" and refers to left-side classifiers of kanji.

　偏見 (ヘン・ケン prejudice), 偏る (かたよ・る be one-sided)

遍 (ヘン) comprises 辶 (walk) and the phonetic 扁 (thin and flat); it means "all over, everywhere" and is used as a counter for repetitions.

　普遍的 (フ・ヘン・テキ universal)

編 (ヘン/あ・む) is a combination of 糸 (thread) and the phonetic 扁 (tablets) and means "book-binding; binding thread, basting thread; knit, braid; assemble, compile; edit; edition,"

　編集 (ヘン・シュウ compilation), 編む (あ・む knit)

俞 (ユ)　　　　　　　　　　　　　　　　　　　　　(scoop out)

愉 (ユ) combines 忄 (heart) and the phonetic 俞 (scoop out), of which the early forms show a boat graph, now 月, and a couple of tools; the combination may have been meant to suggest the removal of worries, relief; it means "pleasant; delight."

　愉快 (ユ・カイ delightful)

諭 (ユ/さと・す), a combination of 言 (say) and the phonetic 俞 (scoop out), means "admonish."

　教諭 (キョウ・ユ instructor), 諭す (さと・す admonish)

輸 (ユ) is a combination of 車 (car) and the phonetic 俞 (scoop out) and it means "transport."
　輸出 (ユ・シュツ export)

癒 (ユ), meaning "cure; heal," consists of 疒 (disease) and the phonetic 愈(ユ relief), which is 心 (heart) and the phonetic 俞 (scoop out).
　癒着 (ユ・チャク pathological adhesion)

游 (ユ/ユウ)　　　　　　　　　　　　　　　　　　　　　　(wander)

遊 (ユウ/ユ/あそ・ぶ) adds 辶 (walk) to the phonetic 斿 (wander), a combination of 㫃 (banner) and 子 (child). It means "wander, meander; have fun, play; enjoyment."
　遊園地 (ユウ・エン・チ amusement park), 遊山 (ユ・サン jaunt), 遊ぶ (あそ・ぶ have fun)

昜 (ヨウ)　　　　　　　　　　　　　　　　　　　　　　　(sunrise)

場 (ジョウ/ば) combines 土 (earth) and the phonetic 昜 (sunrise), which is made of 日 (sun) and a melding of a graph meaning "rise" with 彡 (design). It means "ceremonial arena, site, place"; in Japanese usage it also means "scene, occasion, time and place; scene of a play" and is a counter of scenes of plays.
　会場 (カイ・ジョウ meeting place), 場 (ば scene)

湯 (トウ/ゆ) comprises 氵 (water) and the phonetic 昜 (sunrise) and means "hot water; bath."
　湯治 (トウ・ジ hot-spring cure), 湯 (ゆ hot water)

揚 (ヨウ/あ・げる) joins 扌 (hand) to the phonetic 昜 (sunrise); it means "raise, lift" and in Japanese usage, "profit; fry."
　掲揚 (ケイ・ヨウ hoist), 揚げる (あ・げる raise; fry)

陽 (ヨウ) combines 阝 (mound) and the phonetic 昜 (sunrise) and means "sunshine; sunny; positive, favorable, "
　太陽 (タイ・ヨウ the sun)

傷 (ショウ/きず/いた・める) is a combination of 亻 (person) and the phonetic 昜, which has historically alternated with 昜 in certain characters. It means "injury, wound,"
　重傷 (ジュウ・ショウ serious injury), 傷 (きず injury), 傷める (いた・める injure; damage)

腸 (チョウ), a combination of 月 (flesh) and the phonetic 昜, means "intestines."

枼 (ヨウ)　　　　　　　　　　　　　　　　　　　　　　　(leaves)

葉 (ヨウ/は) adds 艹 (plant) to the phonetic 枼 (leaves) and still means "leaves." The phonetic originally depicted leaves on a tree(木).
　紅葉 (コウ・ヨウ autumn tints), 葉 (は leaf)

舀 (ヨウ) (knead)

稲 (トウ/いね/いな) combines 禾 (rice plant) with the phonetic 舀, which is ⺈ (fingers) and the Jōyō Kanji form of 臼 (mortar). It means "rice plant."
水稲 (スイ・トウ wet-field rice), 稲 (いね rice plant), 稲穂 (いな・ほ ear of rice)

揺 (ヨウ/ゆ・れる) is a combination of 扌 (hand) and a variant of the phonetic 舀. It means "shake, wobble, sway."
動揺 (ドウ・ヨウ rolling; agitation), 揺れる (ゆ・れる quake)

謡 (ヨウ/うた・う/うたい), comprising 言 (say) and a variant of the phonetic 舀, means "chant, sing; song."
民謡 (ミン・ヨウ folk song), 謡う (うた・う perform a Nō song), 謡 (うたい Nō song)

䍃 (ヨウ) (knead)

揺; 謡 (舀, p. 244)

畾 (ライ/ルイ) (pile; continue)

累 (ルイ) is a combination of 糸 (thread) and an abbreviation of 畾 (pile). It means "pile up; cumulate; tie; connected."
累積 (ルイ・セキ accumulation)

塁 (ルイ) is 土 (soil) and another abbreviation of 畾 (pile) and means "fort, fortress" and, in baseball, "base."
一塁 (イチ・ルイ first base)

雷 (ライ/かみなり) consists of 雨 (rain) and the phonetic 畾 (continue) abbreviated. It means "thunder."
雷雨 (ライ・ウ thundershower), 雷 (かみなり thunder)

婁 (ル/ロウ) (linked together)

楼 (ロウ) is 木 (wood) and the Jōyō Kanji abbreviation of 婁 (linked togther), originally composed of 母 (mother), 中 (inside), and 女 (woman). It means "tall building."
摩天楼 (マ・テン・ロウ skyscraper)

10-Stroke Phonetics

韋 (イ) (go around; opposite)

囲 (イ/かこ・む) consists of 囗 (enclosure) and 井 replacing the phonetic 韋 (go around), which depicts two feet at the top and bottom going in opposite directions around 口 (place). It means "enclose, surround."
周囲 (シュウ・イ circumference), 囲む (かこ・む surround)

偉 (イ/えら・い) combines 亻 (person) and the phonetic 韋. It means "great, emminent."

偉大 (イ・ダイ great), 偉い (えら・い great)

違 (イ/ちが・う) adds 辶 (walk) to the phonetic 韋 (opposite). It means "go in a different direction; go in the wrong direction; differ."
　　違反 (イ・ハン violation), 違う (ちが・う differ)

緯 (イ) is a combination of 糸 (thread) and the phonetic 韋 (go around). It means "woof; latitude."
　　緯度 (イ・ド latitude)

衛 (エイ) has 行 (go) surrounding the phonetic 韋 (go around). It means "patrol; guard; defense."
　　防衛 (ボウ・エイ defense)

雋 (エ/ケイ)　　　　　　　　　　　　　　　　　　　　　　　　(swallow)

携 (ケイ/たずさ・わる) is 扌 (hand) and 雟, an unexplained substitute for the phonetic 雟, comprising 山 (mountain), 隹 (bird), and what probably represents a window. The whole means "carry in hand; hold hands."
　　携帯 (ケイ・タイ portable), 携わる (たずさ・わる engage in)

袁 (オン/エン)　　　　　　　　　　　　　　　　　　　　　　(loose; circle)

園 (エン/その) combines 囗 (enclosure) and the phonetic 袁 (circle), without the *hane*; the phonetic shows 衣 (garment) merged with something it is draped loosely over. The kanji means "fenced ground, garden."
　　保育園 (ホ・イク・エン nursery school), 園 (その garden)

猿 (エン/さる), 犭 (animal) and the phonetic 袁, a substitute for 爰 (オン/エン pull); it means "monkey."
　　類人猿 (ルイ・ジン・エン anthropoid), 猿 (さる monkey)

遠 (エン/オン/とお・い) is a combination of 辶 (walk) and the *hane*-less form of the phonetic 袁 (loose); it means "far, remote."
　　遠足 (エン・ソク excursion), 久遠 (ク・オン eternity), 遠い (とお・い distant)

還 (カン) is a combination of 辶 (walk) and the phonetic 睘 (カン circle), which is 罒 (eye) merged with the phonetic 袁 (circle). It means "circle around, return."
　　生還 (セイ・カン come back alive)

環 (カン), adding 王 (gem) to the phonetic 睘 (circle), means "ring, circle."
　　環境 (カン・キョウ environment)

崔 (カク)　　　　　　　　　　　　　　　　　　　　　　　　(white bird)

確 (カク/たし・か) combines 石 (stone) and the phonetic 隺, which is 隹 (bird) with some additional marks. It means "firm; certain."
　　確実 (カク・ジツ certainty), 確か (たし・か certain)

莧 (カン)　　　　　　　　　　　　　　　　　　　　　　　　(goat)

寛 (カン) consists of 宀 (house) and the phonetic 莧; it means "spacious; generous."

寛大（カン・ダイ generosity)

鬲 (キャク/カク) (partition)

隔(カク/へだ・てる)is a combination of 阝(mound)and the phonetic 鬲(partition), originally a depiction of a tripod-steamer. It means "partition, separate; separated by, at intervals of; apart, away, distant,"

隔日（カク・ジツ every other day), 隔てる（へだ・てる set apart)

堇 (キン) (dried-up; exhaust)

勤（キン/ゴン/つと・める）joins 力（strength) and the phonetic 堇（exhausting), which is a merger of 革 (pelt), 火 (fire), and 土 (soil). It means "toil, work hard, persevere, serve; be employed."

勤労（キン・ロウ labor), 勤行（ゴン・ギョウ Buddhist service), 勤める（つと・める work for)

漢（カン）is a combination of 氵(water) and an old variant of the phonetic 堇 (dried up). Its earliest uses were as the name of a river and of the Milky Way, and the Han people or kingdom and then the Han dynasty, whence it became a metonym for China. It also means "guy, chap, bloke."

漢字（カン・ジ Chinese character)

謹（キン/つつし・む）combines 言 (say) and the phonetic 堇 (exhaust). It means "be discreet; humble oneself."

謹賀新年（キン・ガ・シン・ネン Happy New Year), 謹む（つつし・む be discreet)

冓 (ク/コウ) (framework)

溝（コウ/みぞ）is a combination of 氵(water) and the phonetic 冓 (framework). It means "ditch, trench."

排水溝（ハイ・スイ・コウ drainage ditch), 溝（みぞ ditch)

構（コウ/かま・え）adds 木 (wood) to the phonetic 冓 (framework) and means "put together, construct; structure." In Japanese, further senses are "posture, attitude, concern oneself with, mind; meddle."

構造（コウ・ゾウ structure), 構え（かま・え structure; posture)

講（コウ）is a combination of 言 (say) and the phonetic 冓 (framework). It means "lecture"; in Japanese use, certain groups and organizations, particularly religious and mutual financing associations, are referred to by this kanji.

講演（コウ・エン lecture)

購（コウ), 貝 (money) and the phonetic 冓 (framework), means "purchase."

購買力（コウ・バイ・リョク purchasing power)

𠳋 (ケン) (give)

遣（ケン/つかう）combines 辶 (walk) and the phonetic 𠳋 (give), which is 𠂤 (things in a pile) and a sketch of two hands. It means "send, dispatch" and, in Japan,"use; usage."

派遣 （ハ・ケン dispatch）, 小遣い （こ・づか・い pocket money）

| 貟 | （サ） (small)

鎖 （サ/くさり） is a combination of 金 （metal） and the phonetic 貟 （small）, composed of 小 （small） and 貝 （shell）; it means "chain; lock, close."
閉鎖 （ヘイ・サ closure）, 鎖 （くさり chain）

| 朔 | （サク） (first day of month)

塑 （ソ） is 土 （soil） and the phonetic 朔, which combines 月 （moon） and 屰 （upside down）. It means "mold, form of clay."
塑像 （ソ・ゾウ clay figure）

| 隼 | （ジュン） (falcon)

准 （ジュン） was an abbreviation of 準 （level）, described below, that has achieved independence and means "grant, authorize; accept,"
批准 （ヒ・ジュン ratification）

準 （ジュン） consists of 氵 （water） and the phonetic 隼. It means "level; follow, imitate, conform to; prepare; quasi-, semi-, associate."
準備 （ジュン・ビ preparation）

| 歬 | （ゼン） (advance)

前 （ゼン/まえ） is a melding of 刂 （edged tool） and the phonetic 歬 （advance）, a combination of 止 （foot） and 舟 （boat）. It has been associated with a sense of "cut evenly," but more importantly means "advance, front, before, previous, earlier" and in Japan "a share, one person's worth of" and "you."
前半 （ゼン・ハン/ゼン・パン first half）, 前 （まえ before; front）

| 壽 | （トウ/チュウ） (long footpath)

寿 （ジュ/ことぶき） is a greatly simplified alternate for 壽, which itself is a melding of 耂 （old man） and the phonetic 𡕥 （long footpath）, which is believed to be what is left of a depiction of a path between fields combined with 寸 （hand）. It means "longevity; celebration of longevity" and, in Japan, "felicitations, best wishes."
長寿 （チョウ・ジュ longevity）, 寿 （ことぶき felicitations）

鋳 （チュウ/い・る） is a combination of 金 （metal） and the phonetic 寿 meaning "cast, pour, mint."
鋳造 （チュウ・ゾウ casting）, 鋳る （い・る cast）

| 聶 | （ニョウ/ジョウ） (gather)

摂 （セツ） consists of 扌 （hand） and a Jōyō Kanji simplification of the phonetic 聶 （gather）, three 耳 （ear） components. It means "hold, take; rule, control; serve in joint capacity; deputy."
摂取 （セッ・シュ intake）

葡 (ビ)   (equipped)

備 (ビ/そな・える) adds 亻(person) to the phonetic 葡 (equipped), which once depicted a quiver full of arrows. It means "equip, prepare, provide."
　準備 (ジュン・ビ preparation), 備える (そな・える make provision)

莫 (マク/バク or モ/ボ)   (not visible; missing; gone)

募 (ボ/つの・る) combines 力 (strength) and the phonetic 莫 (not visible), which shows 日 (sun) behind 艹 (grass) and 大 (also originally 艹, grass). The kanji means "raise (funds), advertise for, collect."
　募集 (ボ・シュウ recruiting), 募る (つの・る raise)

漠 (バク) is a combination of 氵(water) and the phonetic 莫 (not visible). It means "desert, wasteland; ill-defined, vague."
　砂漠 (サ・バク desert)

墓 (ボ/はか) consists of 土 (ground) and the phonetic 莫 (gone). It means "grave, tomb."
　墓地 (ボ・チ cemetery), 墓 (はか grave)

幕 (マク/バク) adds 巾 (cloth) to the phonetic 莫 (screen off); it means "drape, curtain; tent; camp." It is also a counter for acts of a play.
　幕 (マク curtain), 幕府 (バク・フ shogunate)

慕 (ボ/した・う) combines 心 (heart) and the phonetic 莫 (not visible) and means "long for, love."
　慕情 (ボ・ジョウ longing), 慕う (した・う yearn for)

暮 (ボ/く・らす) adds 日 (sun) to the phonetic 莫 (not visible), preserving an original meaning of the latter, "nightfall" and, derivatively, "end." Idiomatic Japanese has added the meaning of "live; daily life."
　歳暮 (セイ・ボ year's end; year-end gift). 暮らす (く・らす live)

膜 (マク), a combination of 月 (flesh) and the phonetic 莫 (not visible), means "membrane."

模 (モ/ボ) combines 木 (wood) and the phonetic 莫 (not visible); it means "model, form" and, in Japanese only, "grope for."
　模様 (モ・ヨウ pattern), 規模 (キ・ボ scale)

滅 (メツ/ベツ)   (extinguish)

滅 (メツ/ほろ・びる) adds 氵(water) to the phonetic 威 (extinguish), a combination of 火 (fire) and 戌 (cropping). The whole means "perish, come to an end, die out" and is a word for "death" in Buddhist usage.
　不滅 (フ・メツ immortality), 滅びる (ほろ・びる cease to exist)

厤 (レキ)   (line up)

暦 (レキ/こよみ) combines 日 (day) and the Jōyō Kanji simplification of the phonetic 厤 (line up), which is made of two 禾 (cereal plants) under 厂 (roof). It means "calendar."

西暦 (セイ・レキ A.D.), 暦 (こよみ calendar)

歴 (レキ), 止 (foot) and the phonetic 厤 (line up), means "pass by successively; one after another, successive; history; distinct, unmistakable."

歴史 (レキ・シ history)

11-Stroke Phonetics

寅 (イン)   (straight, stretch)

演 (エン), is made of ⺡ (water) and the phonetic 寅 (stretch), a combination of 宀 (house) and what was once a depiction of an arrow held in two hands. It meant something like "flow on and on; inundate," but now it means "state, expound, lecture; do for an audience, perform; practice, exercise."

演説 (エン・ゼツ speech)

㥯 (イン)   (hide away)

隠 (イン/かく・れる) adds 阝 (mound) to the Jōyō Kanji form of the phonetic 㥯 (hide away), which is a combination of ⺍ (fingers), 工 (a hidden object), ⼹ (hand), and 心 (heart). The whole means "conceal, hide."

隠居 (イン・キョ retirement), 隠れる (かく・れる hide)

穏 (オン/おだ・やか) combines 禾 (crop) with the phonetic 㥯 (hide away). It probably once meant "store crops," but now means "placid, mild."

穏健 (オン・ケン moderate), 穏やか (おだ・やか calm)

雚 (カン)   (cry out)

勧 (カン/すす・める) combines 力 (strength) and the Jōyō Kanji simplification of the phonetic 雚 (cry out), consisting of 隹 (bird) plus a few strokes and the phonetic 吅 (カン), made of a plurality of mouth graphs. The whole means "recommend, urge."

勧告 (カン・コク advice), 勧める (すす・める recommend)

歓 (カン) combines 欠 (person with mouth open) with the phonetic 雚 (cry out); it means "joy."

歓待 (カン・タイ warm reception)

権 (ケン/ゴン) is a combination of 木 (wood) and the phonetic 雚; it means "beam balance; power, authority, right; plan, strategm; provisional."

権利 (ケン・リ rights), 権化 (ゴン・ゲ incarnation)

観 (カン) consists of 見 (see) and the phonetic 雚 and means "look, observe, view."

観客 (カン・キャク audience)

轂 (キャク/ケキ)   (strike against)

撃 (ゲキ/う・つ) consists of 手 (hand) and the phonetic 轂 (strike against), which combines 車 (wheel) and 殳 (action). The whole means "strike, hit; shoot; attack."

攻撃 (コウ・ゲキ attack), 撃つ (う・つ shoot)

境 (キョウ/ケイ)   (end)

境 (キョウ/ケイ/さかい) comprises 土 (ground) and the phonetic 竟 (end), which is a meld of 章 (movement) and 儿 (person). It means "border, boundary; place, where/how something ends up; state, circumstances."

心境 (シン・キョウ state of mind), 境内 (ケイ・ダイ precincts), 境 (さかい border)

鏡 (キョウ/かがみ) combines 金 (metal) and the phonetic 竟. It means "mirror" and corresponds to "-scope" in the names of optical instruments.

鏡台 (キョウ・ダイ dresser), 鏡 (かがみ mirror)

頃 (キョウ/ケイ)   (incline)

傾 (ケイ/かたむ・く) adds 亻(person) to the phonetic 頃 (incline), which is a combination of 頁 (head) and 匕 (someone leaning over). The whole preserves the original meaning of the phonetic, "incline, lean; decline."

傾向 (ケイ・コウ tendency), 傾く (かたむ・く incline)

埶 (ゲ/ゲイ)   (planting)

芸 (ゲイ) is an abbreviation of 藝 (ウン cultivate) which, ironically, replaced its synonym 埶 (ゲイ cultivate), a combination of 艹 (plant) and the phonetic 埶 (planting); the latter in early forms comprises what would now be 木 (tree), 土 (earth), and a graph of two hands. The whole can mean "plant, cultivate," but usually means "art, skill."

熱 (ネツ/あつ・い) is a combination of 灬 (fire) and the phonetic 埶; it means "hot; heat; fever; feverish."

熱 (ネツ heat; fever), 熱い (あつ・い hot)

桀 (ケチ/ケツ)   (conspicuous)

傑 (ケツ) joins 化 (person) with the phonetic 桀 (conspicuous), which is 舛 (feet) atop 木 (tree). It means "prominent, outstanding."

傑作 (ケッ・サク masterpiece; blunder)

桼 (シツ)   (dripping of sap)

漆 (シツ/うるし) combines 氵 (water) and the phonetic 桼 (dripping), which shows liquid (氽) coming out of a tree (木). It means "lacquer."

漆器 (シッ・キ lacquerware), 漆 (うるし lacquer)

孰 (ジュク/シュク)   (wall-making)

塾 (ジュク) combines 土 (dirt) and the phonetic 孰 (wall-making), which is formed of 享 (wall) and 丸 (two hands). It means "private school."

熟 (ジュク/う・れる) consists of 灬 (fire) and the phonetic 孰 (cook), which included 羊 (mutton) in its ancient form. It means "boil, cook; ripe, mature."

半熟 (ハン・ジュク half-ripe; soft-boiled), 熟れる (う・れる ripen)

斬 (セン/サン)   (cleave; gash)

漸 (ゼン) consists of 氵(water) and the phonetic 斬 (gash), which is a combination of 車 (car) and 斤 (hatchet). It means "move gradually; gradual."

漸次 (ゼン・ジ gradually)

暫 (ザン) combines 日 (sun) and the phonetic 斬 (cleave); it means "awhile."

暫定 (ザン・テイ tentative)

韱 (セン)   (fine, thin)

繊 (セン) adds 糸 (thread) to the Jōyō kanji simplification of the phonetic 韱
(fine), a combination of 韭 (chives) and the phonetic 㦰 (セン chopping). The
whole means "fiber; fine, thin."

繊維 (セン・イ fiber)

曽 (ソ/ゾウ or ソ/ソウ)   (pile up)

僧 (ソウ) combines 亻(person) with the Jōyō Kanji simplification of the phonetic
曽, a pictograph of a food steamer. It means "monk, priest."

層 (ソウ) puts 尸 (roof) on top of the phonetic 曽 (pile up). It means "multi-storied
building, story, floor; layer, stratum."

増 (ゾウ/ま・す/ふ・える) joins 土 (dirt) and the phonetic 曽 (pile up) and means
"increase."

増減 (ゾウ・ゲン increase and decrease), 増す (ま・す increase), 増える (ふ・
える increase)

憎 (ゾウ/にく・む) combines 忄(heart) and the phonetic 曽 (pile up), perhaps
to suggest the feeling of things "piling up" on one. It means "hate; hatred."

憎悪 (ゾウ・オ hatred), 憎む (にく・む hate)

贈 (ゾウ/ソウ/おく・る) combines 貝 (wealth) and the phonetic 曽 (pile up). It
means "give, gift."

贈賄 (ゾウ・ワイ bribery), 寄贈 (キ・ゾウ/キ・ソウ presentation), 贈る (おく・
る present)

曼 (マン/バン)   (cover; spread)

漫 (マン) joins 氵(water) to the phonetic 曼 (cover), which was originally a
combination of 冃 (cover), 罒 (eye), and 又 (hand). It means "vast, expansive;
rambling, random, desultory."

漫画 (マン・ガ cartoon)

慢 (マン) joins 忄(heart) to the phonetic 曼 (spread) and means "loose, lax;
slow-going; haughty."

自慢 (ジ・マン boast)

离 (リ)   (large snake)

離 (リ/はな・れる) combines 隹 (bird) and the phonetic 离 (large snake). The kanji may have originally referred to the Korean nightingale, its use for the current meaning of "part, separate" being a borrowing.

離婚 (リ・コン divorce), 離れる (はな・れる separate)

扁 (ロウ)   (leak)

漏 (ロウ/も・れる) adds 氵 (water) to the phonetic 扁 (leak), which is 雨 (rain) under 尸 (roof). It means "leak; let be known."

漏電 (ロウ・デン electric leakage), 漏れる (も・れる leak out)

12-Stroke Phonetics

郷 (キョウ/ケイ)   (dine together)

郷 (キョウ/ゴウ) is a variant of 鄉, and that is a melding customization of 阝 (village) and the phonetic 郷 (dine together), which in turn shows two seated persons with 皀 (food) between them. The whole means "village; rural."

郷里 (キョウ・リ hometown), 近郷 (キン・ゴウ neighboring district)

響 (キョウ/ひび・く) combines 音 (sound) and the phonetic 郷 (village). It means "resound, echo"; in Japanese use it can stand for "symphony orchestra."

影響 (エイ・キョウ influence), 響く (ひび・く resound)

𡨄 (ケン)   (restrain)

憲 (ケン) combines 心 (heart) with the phonetic 𡨄 (restrain), apparently an eye (罒) with something covering it. It means "rules, constitution."

憲法 (ケン・ポウ constitution)

戠 (シキ/ショク)   (mark)

織 (ショク/シキ/お・る) is 糸 (thread) and the phonetic 戠 (mark), which originates as 弋 (post) combined with 辛 (awl). It means "weave."

織機 (ショッ・キ loom), 組織 (ソ・シキ organization), 織る (お・る weave)

職 (ショク) combining 耳 (ear) and the phonetic 戠 (mark) means "profession. occupation."

識 (シキ) combines 言 (say) and the phonetic 戠 (mark). It means "sign, mark; recognize; recognition, knowledge."

常識 (ジョウ・シキ common sense)

舄 (シャク/セキ)   (magpie)

写 (シャ/うつ・す) is a simplified form of 寫, combining 宀 (house) and the phonetic 舄 (magpie). It probably once meant "move something," but now it means "copy, reproduce; cast an image of."

写真 (シャ・シン photograph), 写す (うつ・す copy)

潟 (かた) is a combination of 氵 (water) and the phonetic 舄, of which the *on-yomi* セキ is not listed for Jōyō Kanji. It means "lagoon."

干潟 (ひ・がた tideland)

☐ (セン)   (departure of the soul)

遷 (セン) adds 辶 (walk) to the phonetic 䙴 (departure of the soul), which combines 西 (basket), a sign for " two hands", and 己 (someone squatting). It means "move, change."
    変遷 (ヘン・セン transition)

巽 (セン)   (put together)

選 (セン/えら・ぶ) is a combination of 辶 (walk) and the phonetic 巽 (put together), which comprises two 己 (bow) components and 共 (two hands holding some king of stand); it means "select, elect."
    選挙 (セン・キョ election), 選ぶ (えら・ぶ select)

㪘 (テツ)   (pass through)

徹 (テツ) consists of 彳 (go) and the phonetic 㪘 (pass through), which is a combination of 育 (childbearing) and 攵 (action). The whole means "through, throughout."
    徹する (テッ・する pierce)

撤 (テツ), a combination of 扌 (hand) and the phonetic 㪘 (pass through), means "remove, withdraw."
    撤回 (テッ・カイ retraction)

閏 (ニュン/ジュン)   (ooze out)

潤 (ジュン/うるお・う/うる・む) combines 氵 (water) and the phonetic 閏 (ooze out), which also means "intercalary" as an independent, non-Jōyō kanji. It is speculated that the combination of 門 (gate) and 王 (king) indicates the latter meaning, supposing that a king stayed indoors on the extra day or days of a leap year. 潤 means "moist, damp; benefit, enrich."
    利潤 (リ・ジュン profit), 潤う (うるお・う be moistened; benefit), 潤む (うる・む be wet)

寍 (ネイ)   (restful)

寧 (ネイ) combines 丁 (originally 丂, wish to grow) and the phonetic 寍 (restful), which is made up of 宀 (house), 心 (heart), and 皿 (dish). It means "calm."
    丁寧 (テイ・ネイ polite)

敏 (ハン)   (tufted)

繁 (ハン) is a merger of 攵 (do) and a phonetic 敏 (tufted), made of 糸 (thread) and 毎 (grow). It means "luxuriant; thrive; frequent; excessive."
    繁華街 (ハン・カ・ガイ shopping district)

敝 (ヘイ)   (rip, tear)

幣 (ヘイ) adds another 巾 (cloth) to the phonetic 敝 (tear), which is a combination of 攵 (action) and 巾 (cloth) melded with two ハ (divide) components. It refers to strips of silk, or paper offered to a deity; it also means "money."

紙幣 （シ・ヘイ paper currency）

弊 （ヘイ） consists of 廾 (two hands) and the phonetic 敝 (tear). It means "torn, ragged," and functions in some words as a humble possessive.

弊害 （ヘイ・ガイ ill effect）

彭 （ボウ/ホウ）   (drum)

膨 （ボウ/ふく・れる） combines 月 (flesh) and the phonetic 彭 (drum), made of 壴 (drum) and 彡 (decoration). It means "swell, bulge."

膨大 （ボウ・ダイ huge）, 膨れる （ふく・れる swell）

業 （ボク）   (slave)

僕 （ボク） adds 亻 (person) to the phonetic 業 (slave); it means "male servant" and, via "(your) servant," it has come to be used as a first person pronoun by Japanese males.

撲 （ボク） combines 扌 (hand) and the phonetic 業 (slave) for the meaning "beat, flog."

撲滅 （ボク・メツ extermination）

尞 （リョウ）   (bonfire, light)

僚 （リョウ） is a combination of 亻 (person) and the phonetic 尞 (bonfire); it means "peer; government official."

同僚 （ドウ・リョウ colleague）

寮 （リョウ） combines 宀 (house) with the phonetic 尞 (light). It has meant "public office," but now usually means "dormitory" and, in Japanese usage, "villa."

療 （リョウ）, 疒 (disease) and the phonetic 尞, means "cure."

診療所 （シン・リョウ・ジョ clinic）

13-Stroke Phonetics

褱 （カイ）   (put in one's bosom)

懐 （カイ/ふところ/なつ・かしい） adds 忄 (heart) to the Jōyō Kanji simplification of the phonetic 褱 (put in one's bosom), symbolized by 罒 (eye) and some teardrops below it inside 衣 (garment). It means "bosom, pocket; keep in one's bosom; embrace" and, in Japan, "yearning."

懐中 （カイ・チュウ one's pocket）, 懐 （ふところ bosom）, 懐かしい （なつ・かしい brings back memories）

壊 （カイ/こわ・れる）, 土 (soil) and the phonetic 褱, means "break, destroy."
破壊 （ハ・カイ destruction）, 壊れる （こわ・れる break）

蒦 （カク/キャク）   (seize)

獲 （カク/え・る） adds 犭 (animal) to the phonetic 蒦 (seize), which combines 艹 (plant) and 隻 (bird in hand). It means "get, catch, seize."

獲得 （カク・トク acquisition）, 獲物 （え・もの game; catch; prize）

穫 （カク）, 禾 （crop） and the phonetic 蒦 （seize）, means "harvest."
収穫 （シュウ・カク harvest）

護 （ゴ） is a combination of 言 （say） and the phonetic 蒦. It means "guard, protect."
保護 （ホ・ゴ protection）

囲 （カン）   (circle)

還; 環 （袁, p. 245）

豦 （キョ）   (fighting)

劇 （ゲキ） was originally a combination of 力 （strength）, since long ago
alternating with 刂 （edged tool）, and the phonetic 豦 （fighting）, which puts 虍
（tiger） and 豕 （wild boar） together. It means "severe, fierce"; it also means "drama,
play."

熏 （クン）   (smoke)

勲 （クン） is a combination of 力 （strength） and the simplification of the phonetic
薰, which has 灬 （fire） combined with the descendant of a pictograph of a smoking
chimney. The kanji means "exploit, feat; merit."
勲章 （クン・ショウ decoration）

薫 （クン/かお・る） combines 艹 （plant） and the phonetic 熏 （smoke）; it means
"aroma, fragrance; burning incense; influence."
薫陶 （クン・トウ education）, 薫る （かお・る be aromatic）

舜 （シュン）   (quick movement)

瞬 （シュン/まばた・く） combines 目 （eye） and the phonetic 舜 （quick movement）,
which long ago consisted of early forms of 炎 （flame）, 冖 （frame）, and 舛 （feet）.
It means "blink, wink."
一瞬 （イッ・シュン an instant）, 瞬く （まばた・く blink）

襄 （ジョウ）   (stir up; soft)

壌 （ジョウ） consists of 土 （soil） and the phonetic 襄 （stir up）, which is made
of a medley of strokes for "mixture of things" in 衣 （garment）. It meant "arable
soil, fertilized earth."
土壌 （ド・ジョウ soil）

嬢 （ジョウ） combines 女 （woman） and the phonetic 襄 （soft）. It properly means
"woman, mother," but in Japanese use means instead "Miss; young lady."
お嬢さん （お・ジョウ・さん young lady; your daughter）

譲 （ジョウ/ゆず・る） combines 言 （say） and the phonetic 襄. It means "concede,
yield; be humble."
譲渡 （ジョウ・ト transfer）, 譲る （ゆず・る concede）

醸 (ジョウ/かも・す) is 酉 (wine jar) and the phonetic 襄 (stir up). It means "brewing,"

醸造 (ジョウ・ゾウ brewing), 醸す (かも・す brew)

喿 (ソウ)　　　　　　　　　　　　　　　　　　　　　　　　　　　(fidget)

操 (ソウ/みさお/あやつ・る) joins 扌 (hand) with the phonetic 喿 (fidget), a combination of 木 (tree) and three 口 (mouth) conponents. It once meant "make a racket, bustle," but now means "fiddle with, manipulate, handle, operate; fidelity, adherence to one's principles."

操作 (ソウ・サ operation), 操 (みさお chastity), 操る (あやつ・る manipulate)

燥 (ソウ), 火 (fire) with the phonetic 喿, means "dry up."

乾燥 (カン・ソウ dessication)

繰 (く・る), meaning "reel, wind," combines 糸 (thread) and the phonetic 喿 (fidget), but the *on-yomi* ソウ is not included in the Jōyō Kanji. In Japanese, it also means "turn, flip; count."

藻 (ソウ/も) has 艹 (plant) over the phonetic 澡 (ソウ wash), which consists of 氵 (water) and the phonetic 喿 (fidget). It means "seaweed" and, actually derived therefrom, "rhetorical flourish."

海藻 (カイ・ソウ seaweed), 藻 (も seaweed)

蜀 (ゾク/ショク)　　　　　　　　　　　　　　　　　　　　　　　(stick to)

独 (ドク/ひと・り) is reduced from the non-Jōyō kanji 獨, which is a combination of 犭 (dog) and the phonetic 蜀 (stick to), which in turn comprises 虫 (insect) and a picture of a big-eyed worm. The whole means "alone, solitary, single, solo." Used to transcribe the beginning of the word "Deutschland," it has picked up the meaning "Germany."

独立 (ドク・リツ independence), 独り (ひと・り alone)

属 (ゾク) is a simplifying restructuring of 屬, which is a combination of 尾 (tail) and the phonetic 蜀 (stick to). It means "attach; belong; genus."

属する (ゾク・する belong)

触 (ショク/ふ・れる/さわ・る) is reduced from the non-Jōyō kanji 觸, which consists of 角 (horn) and the phonetic 蜀 (stick to). The whole means "butt, rush against; touch; feel."

接触 (セッ・ショク contact), 触れる (ふ・れる touch; touch on), 触る (さわ・る touch)

濁 (ダク/にご・る) combines 氵 (water) and the phonetic 蜀; it means "muddy, turbid" and is also used to describe such consonant sounds in Japanese as *b, d, g*.

濁流 (ダク・リュウ muddy stream), 濁る (にご・る get turbid)

嘱 (ショク) is a combination of 口 (mouth) and the phonetic 属 (attach). It means "request, charge."

嘱託 (ショク・タク part-time service)

辟 (ヒャク/ヘキ or ヒ/ビ)　　　　　　　　　　　　　　　　(split; off-center; flat)

避 (ヘキ/さ・ける) consists of ⻌ (walk) and the phonetic 辟 (split), which is 尸 (body), 辛 (pointed tool), and 口 (opening) combined to suggest "punishment, putting to death." The whole means "avoid, evade."

避暑 (ヒ・ショ summering), 避ける (さ・ける avoid)

壁 (ヘキ/かべ), meaning "wall," is a combination of 土 (soil) and the phonetic 辟 (flat).

壁画 (ヘキ・ガ mural), 壁 (かべ wall)

癖 (ヘキ/くせ) conjoins 疒 (disease) and the phonetic 辟 (off-center). It means "habit; eccentricity."

悪癖 (アク・ヘキ bad habit), 癖 (くせ habit)

敫 (ヤク)　　　　　　　　　　　　　　　　　　　　　　　　(spray)

激 (ゲキ/はげ・しい) combines 氵 (water) and the phonetic 敫 (spray), which is 白 (white) and 放 (emit). The whole means "violent, vehement."

激流 (ゲキ・リュウ torrent), 激しい (はげ・しい violent)

雍 (ユ/ヨウ)　　　　　　　　　　　　　　　　　　　　　(bird in cage)

擁 (ヨウ) combines 扌 (hand) with the phonetic 雍, which originates in 隹 (bird) and a phonetic character for "water-surrounded dwelling"; it means "embrace; support, protect."

擁護 (ヨウ・ゴ protection)

雁 (ヨウ)　　　　　　　　　　　　　　　　　　　　　　　(catch)

応 (オウ) is a reduction of 應, which is 心 (heart) and the phonetic 雁 (catch), in turn a combination of 广 (cover), 亻 (person), and 隹 (bird). The whole means "respond, react."

応じる (オウ・じる respond)

粦 (リン)　　　　　　　　　　　　　　　　　(will-o'-the wisp, in a row)

隣 (リン/とな・る/となり) is a variant of original non-Jōyō kanji 鄰, which is 阝 (village) and the phonetic 粦 (in a row). The latter originally had the old equivalent of 炎 (flame) on top instead of 米; with 舛 (staggering), it is thought to have represented a string of ghostly lights. The whole means "neighbor, next door."

隣接 (リン・セツ contiguity), 隣り合う (とな・り・あう be next door to each other), 隣 (となり neighbor)

14-Stroke Phonetics

赫 (キャク/カク)　　　　　　　　　　　　　　　　　　　　(deep red)

嚇 (カク) conjoins 口 (mouth) and the phonetic 赫 (deep red), a reduplication of 赤 (red); it means "rage."

威嚇 (イ・カク threat)

爾 (ジ)   (seal)

璽 (ジ)is a combination of 玉(gem)and the phonetic 爾(seal). It means "Imperial seal."

国璽 (コク・ジ the Seal of State)

翟 (ジャク/タク or ジャク/テキ)   (gleam; jut up)

濯 (タク) combines 氵(water) and the phonetic 翟, which began as 羽 (feather) above 隹 (bird), to suggest a peacock's tail feathers. It means "rinse."

洗濯 (セン・タク laundry)

曜 (ヨウ), 日 (sun) and the phonetic 翟 (gleam), referred to certain celestial luminaries, in particular, the sun, moon, and five naked-eye planets, and when Japan adopted the Western week it used this kanji in the calques of the weekday names.

火曜日 (カ・ヨウ・ビ Tuesday)

躍 (ヤク/おど・る) consists of 足 (foot) and the phonetic 翟 (jut up). It means "leap, jump."

躍進 (ヤク・シン rapid advance), 躍る (おど・る leap)

16-Stroke Phonetics

縣 (ケン)   (hang)

懸 (ケン/ケ/か・ける) adds 心 (heart) to the phonetic 縣 (hang), which is a combination of 県 (gibbeted head) and 系 (extended thread). It means "hanging, pendant."

懸賞 (ケン・ショウ prize), 懸念 (ケ・ネン anxiety), 懸かる (か・かる hang)

龍 (トウ)   (one upon another)

襲 (シュウ/おそ・う) consists of 衣 (garment) and 龍 (dragon), the latter standing for its reduplication, the old phonetic meaning "one upon another". It means "put one garment on over another; succeed, inherit; attack, raid."

世襲 (セ・シュウ inheritance by descent), 襲う (おそ・う attack)

17-Stroke Phonetic

霝 (レイ)   (drip)

霊 (レイ/リョウ/たま) is the Jōyō Kanji simplification of 靈, which combines 巫 (medium) and the phonetic 霝 (drip), which is 雨 (rain) with three big drops under it. The Kanji means "spirit; mystic, mysterious; soul, departed spirit."

霊 (レイ departed soul), 悪霊 (アク・リョウ evil spirit), 霊屋 (たま・や mausoleum)

Chapter 5

Special Japanese Uses of Kanji

In this chapter we analyze in more detail the *kun-yomi*, or native Japanese readings, of kanji; list irregular readings of kanji *ateji*; and describe the use of kanji in proper names.

Usage and Readings of *Kun-yomi*

Kanji have been used in Japan for about fifteen hundred years. During that period a large number of native Japanese words have been "assigned" to kanji of appropriate meaning, with the result that the kanji *kun-yomi* inventory has greatly proliferated. It was only in the 1950s that the Japanese government began regulating kanji readings, to make learning to read and write easier.

As an example of the large number of readings, the officially accepted *kun-yomi* for 生 are listed as follows (生, along with 下, has the largest number of officially accepted *kun-yomi*):

い   for 生きる (live), 生かす (keep alive), 生ける (alive)
う   for 生む (give birth), 生まれる (be born)
お   for 生う (grow)
は   for 生える (grow), 生やす (grow)
き   for 生 (raw) as in 生糸 (きいと raw silk)
なま for 生 (raw) as in 生魚 (なまざかな raw fish)

Excluded from the Jōyō Kanji listing are the following *kun-yomi*:

な   for 生る (bear), 生す (bear)
うぶ for 生な (naive)

How much of a *kun-yomi* word should be "assigned" to the kanji and how much should be written with trailing *kana*, called *okurigana*, is also prescribed in the Jōyō Kanji listing. The basic *okurigana* rules prescribed by the government are as follows:

1. No *okurigana* for uninflected words, such as nouns, e.g., 光 (ひかり light), 氷 (こおり ice), 話 (はなし story).

Exception: To avoid misreading when a character has more than one reading as nouns, the last syllable is written in *okurigana*, e.g., 一つ (ひとつ one), as opposed to 一(イチ); 半ば (なかば middle) as opposed to 半 (ハン half).

2. For inflected words (verbs and adjectives), the root is written in kanji, the

259

inflectional ending in *okurigana*, e.g., 書く (かく write), 赤い (あかい red).

Exception 1: The last syllable of the root is written with *okurigana* to help distinguish different words written with the same kanji, e.g., 大きい (おおきい large), as opposed to 大いに (おおいに greatly); 静か (しずか quiet), as opposed to 静まる (しずまる become quiet).

Exception 2: The last syllable of the root is written with *okurigana* to indicate (a) adjectives ending in -しい, e.g., 美しい (うつくしい beautiful), and (b) *-eru/-iru* verbs, e.g., 考える (かんがえる think).

3. For compounds words, the above *okurigana* rules apply, e.g., 流れ込む (ながれこむ flow into), 長引く (ながびく prolonged), 旅立つ (たびだつ go on a journey).

Exception 1: Compound words not liable to misreading can be written (a) without the "internal" *okurigana*, if there is one, e.g., 申し込む/申込む (もうしこむ propose), 待ち遠しい/待遠しい (まちどおしい be impatient for) or (b), without the single *okurigana* at the end if this is the only *okurigana*, e.g., 田植え/田植 (たうえ rice planting).

Exception 2: Some words are written without any *okurigana* simply because of established practice (frequent use on signs, printed forms, etc.), e.g., 切手 (きって stamp), 待合室 (まちあいシツ waiting room), 受取 (うけとり receipt).

Irregular Readings of Kanji: *Ateji*

Sometimes kanji, usually two or more in combination, are "assigned" to a word without regard to their *on-* and *kun-yomi*. For example, the word おとな (adult) was "given" the two kanji 大人, which are appropriate in terms of meaning but have no readings anything like おとな. When used in such a way, the kanji are called *ateji*.

The list below contains the government-approved irregular readings in Japanese syllabary order. The irregular portions of words (where the kanji and reading do not match) are underlined. The following are points to bear in mind while studying the list:

1. Some of the readings are regular *on-yomi* that have been excluded from the Jōyō Kanji or are slight variations on regular *on-yomi*, e.g., 一言居士 (イチゲンコジ), 友達 (ともダチ), 砂利 (ジャリ), 数珠 (ジュズ), and 読経 (ドキョウ).

2. Some of the irregularities result from *okurigana* irregularities or from the combination of two words, e.g. 浮気 (うわき), 行方 (ゆくえ), 息吹 (いぶき), 海原 (うなばら), 河原/川原 (かわら), and 若人 (わこうど).

3. Many are *ateji* pure and simple, a kanji compound being used to write a simple Japanese word, or a Japanese compound without a one-to-one relationship of its parts to the kanji, e.g., 田舎 (いなか), 竹刀 (しない), 山車 (だし), 七夕 (たなばた), 雪崩 (なだれ), 土産 (みやげ), and 浴衣 (ゆかた).

4. Some of the kanji compounds listed here with "special readings" also have regular *on-yomi*, with the same or related meanings, e.g., 今日 (コンニチ/きょう), 白髪 (ハクハツ/しらが), 梅雨 (バイウ/つゆ), 仲人 (チュウニン/なこうど), and 紅葉 (コウヨウ/もみじ).

あす	明日	(tomorrow)	しぐれ	時雨	(drizzling rain in
あずき	小豆	(red bean)			early winter)
あま	海女	(woman diver)	しない	竹刀	(bamboo sword)
イオウ	硫黄	(sulfur)	しばふ	芝生	(lawn)
イクジ	意気地	(spirit)	しみず	清水	(clear water)
イチゲンコジ	一言居士	(ready critic)	シャミセン	三味線	(samisen)
いなか	田舎	(the country)	ジャリ	砂利	(gravel)
いぶき	息吹	(breath)	ジュズ	数珠	(rosary)
うなばら	海原	(the main)	ジョウズ	上手	(skillfulness)
うば	乳母	(wet nurse)	しらが	白髪	(white hair)
うわキ	浮気	(inconstancy)	しろうと	素人	(amateur)
うわつく	浮つく	(be flippant)	シわす/シはす	師走	(December)
おかあさん	お母さん	(mother)	すもう	相撲	(sumo wrest-
おじ	叔父/伯父	(uncle)			ling)
おとうさん	お父さん	(father)	ゾウリ	草履	(sandals)
おとな	大人	(adult)	だし	山車	(float)
おとめ	乙女	(maiden)	タち	太刀	(sword)
おば	叔母/伯母	(aunt)	たちのく	立ち退く	(move out)
おまわりさん	お巡りさん	(policeman)	たなばた	七夕	(Festival of
おみき	お神酒	(sacred sake)			the Weaver)
おもや	母屋/母家	(main house)	たび	足袋	(tabi, Japanese
かぐら	神楽	(kagura;Shinto			socks)
		music and dance)	チご	稚児	(child in fes-
かし	河岸	(riverside)			tival procession)
かぜ	風邪	(a cold)	ついたち	一日	(the first day
かや	蚊帳	(mosquito net)			of a month)
かわせ	為替	(exchange)	つきやま	築山	(miniature hill
かわら	河原/川原	(dry river bed)			in a garden)
きのう	昨日	(yesterday)	つゆ	梅雨	(rainy season)
きょう	今日	(today)	でこぼこ	凹凸	(unevenness)
くだもの	果物	(fruit)	手伝う	手伝う	(help with)
くろうと	玄人	(expert)	テンまセン	伝馬船	(barge)
けさ	今朝	(this morning)	トあみ	投網	(cast net)
ケシキ	景色	(scene)	とえはたえ	十重二十重	(ten -and
ここチ	心地	(feeling)			twentyfold)
ことし	今年	(this year)	ドキョウ	読経	(sutra chanting)
さおとめ	早乙女	(rice-planting			
		girl)	とケイ	時計	(clock)
ざこ	雑魚	(small fish)	ともダチ	友達	(friend)
サじき	桟敷	(gallery)	なこうど	仲人	(go-between)
さしつかえる	差し支える	(have trouble)	なごり	名残	(parting)
さつきばれ	五月晴れ	(fine weather	なだれ	雪崩	(snowslide)
		during the rainy season)	にいさん	兄さん	(older brother)
さなえ	早苗	(rice sprouts)	ねえさん	姉さん	(older sister)
さみだれ	五月雨	(early summer	のら	野良	(farm)
		rain)	のりと	祝詞	(Shinto prayer)

ハカセ	博士	(doctor)	みやげ	土産	(souvenir)
はたち	二十/二十歳	(twenty years old)	むすこ	息子	(son)
			めがね	眼鏡	(glasses)
はつか	二十日	(twenty days; the twentienth day of a month)	モサ	猛暑	(stalwart man)
			もみじ	紅葉	(maple; autumnal tints)
ひとり	一人	(one person)			
ひより	日和	(weather)	モメン	木綿	(cotton)
ふたり	二人	(two persons)	もより	最寄り	(the nearest)
ふつか	二日	(two days; the second day of a month)	やおチョウ	八百長	(fixed fight)
			やおや	八百屋	(greengrocer)
ふぶき	吹雪	(snowstorm)	やまと	大和	(Japan)
へた	下手	(unskillful-ness)	ゆかた	浴衣	(summer kimono)
へや	部屋	(room)	ゆくえ	行方	(whereabouts)
まいご	迷子	(lost child)	よせ	寄席	(variety house)
まっか	真っ赤	(deep red)	わこうど	若人	(youth)
まっさお	真っ青	(deep blue)			

Special Kanji for Personal Names

Governmental regulation of kanji usage meets with a major problem when it comes to proper names, especially place names and personal names. If all the kanji used traditionally for place and personal names were included in the Jōyō Kanji, the number of kanji in the list would be far beyond the present 1945, defeating the purpose of the Jōyō Kanji. On the other hand, replacing an excluded kanji in place names or family names with another kanji of a similar reading or meaning or with *kana* would be unacceptable to the vast majority of people. Replacement with a simplified form of the same kanji, however, has been fairly well accepted.

The solution has been to ignore the Jōyō Kanji list for place names, family names, and given names already in use, but to limit the use of kanji for given names for new babies. Two hundred eighty-four addititional kanji were selected by the Ministry of Justice as Jinmei-yō Kanji (kanji for names only), so that together with the 1945 Jōyō Kanji, a total of 2,229 kanji are available for given names.

The Jinmei-yō Kanji list does not provide the reading of the kanji, so people are free to use various readings of them. Jōyō Kanji too may have unlisted readings when used in names. For instance, when 洋 (ヨウ ocean) is used for a given name, in addition to the Jōyō Kanji reading, ヨウ, the traditional readings of うみ, きよ, なみ, ひろ, ひろし, and み become possible.

The readings for given names include some irregular *on-yomi* that have no relationship to the Chinese reading of the kanji; for example, 嵩 (コウ) and 絢(ジュン). (The regular *on-yomi* 嵩 and 絢 are スウ/シュウ and ケン respectively.) Such readings treat parts of the characters as if they were phonetics (they usually are in some other characters). *Kun-yomi* for names are vestiges of the unrestricted *kun-yomi* of the past. Some readings are apparently based on vague associations with the meaning of the kanji, while some are regular readings of the kanji. For instance, かめ (turtle) is the regular reading of the kanji 亀 (turtle), and its name-only readings すすむ (go forward) and ひさ/ひさし (long) can be attributed to the characteristics of turtles, which include "slow walking" and "longevity" respectively, but its other name-only readings, あま and あや have no obvious relationship with the meaning of " turtle."   Note that *kun-yomi* for names include many premodern Japanese grammatical forms; for example, きよし (圭, 汐, 浩, 靖) for modern Japanese きよい (pure) and たすく (匡, 丞, 佑, 祐, 亮, 輔) for modern Japanese たすける (assist).

The following is the list of Jinmei-yō Kanji with some of their possible readings. The kanji are arranged by order of increasing stroke count; kanji with the same stroke count are given in Japanese-syllabary order, based on the first *on-yomi* listed.   The general meanings of the kanji are shown in parentheses.

2 strokes 乃 (or; your) ダイ　ナイ　おさむ　の

3 strokes 之 (go; this) シ　いたる　くに　これ　の　のぶ　ひさ　ゆき　よし
　　　　　巳 (the sixth of the twelve horary signs; snake) シ　み
　　　　　也 (be; particle for emphasis) ヤ　あり　これ　なり

4 strokes 允 (harmonious) イン　じょう　すけ　ただし　まこと　まさ　まさし　みつる
　　　　　丑 (the second of the twelve horary signs; ox) チュウ　うし　ひろ
　　　　　巴 (lie on stomach) ハ　ヘ　とも　ともえ

5 strokes 叶 (fulfillment) キョウ　かな　かのう　かない　やす
　　　　　弘 (extensive) グ　コウ　お　ひろ　ひろし　ひろむ　みつ
　　　　　只 (only) シ　これ　ただ
　　　　　旦 (dawn) タン　あき　あきら　あけ　あさけ
　　　　　汀 (water's edge) テイ　みぎわ　なぎさ
　　　　　卯 (the fourth of the twelve horary signs; hare) ボウ　う　しげ　しげる

6 strokes 伊 (this; he) イ　おさむ　これ　ただ　ただし　はじめ　よし
　　　　　亦 (also) エキ　ヤク　また
　　　　　亥 (the twelfth of the twelve horary signs; boar) ガイ　い
　　　　　伎 (technique) キ　ギ
　　　　　匡 (correct) キョウ　たすく　ただ　ただし　まさ　まさし
　　　　　旭 (morning sun) キョク　コク　あき　あきら　あさひ　てる
　　　　　圭 (fief) ケ　ケイ　か　かど　きよ　きよし　たま　よし
　　　　　伍 (five; group) ゴ　いつつ　くみ　とも
　　　　　亘 (extend) コウ　とおる　のぶ　わたる
　　　　　汐 (evening tide) ジャク　セキ　うしお　きよ　きよし　しお
　　　　　庄 (farm house; village) ショウ　ソウ　ホウ　たいら　まさ
　　　　　丞 (assist) ジョウ　すけ　すすむ　たすく
　　　　　凪 (calm) なぎ

7 strokes 杏 (apricot) アン　キョウ　ギョウ　コン
　　　　　佑 (assist) ウ　ユウ　すけ　たすく
　　　　　伽 (keep company with) カ　とぎ
　　　　　玖 (black gemstone) キュウ　ク　たま　き　ひさ

亨 (go through) キョウ　コウ　あき　あきら　すすむ　たか　とおる　とし
　　みち　ゆき

芹 (parsley) キン　せり

冴 (freeze) コ　ゴ　さえ

吾 (I) ゴ　あ　みち　わが　われ

宏 (large) コウ　あつ　ひろ　ひろし

沙 (sand) サ　シ　シャ　すな　まさご

辰 (the fifth of the twelve horary signs; dragon; time) シン　ジン　たつ
　　とき　のぶ　よし

那 (what) ダ　ナ　とも　やす

汰 (cleanse) タ　よなぐ

杜 (wood) ト　ヅ　もり

甫 (rice-plant nursery) フ　ホ　すけ　とし　はじめ　まさ　もと

芙 (lotus) フ　ブ　はす

酉 (the tenth of the twelve horary signs; hen) ユ　ユウ　とり　なが　みのる

李 (plum) リ

呂 (linked) リョ　ロ　おと　とも　なが

伶 (musician) リョウ　レイ　さと　さとし　わざおぎ

冶 (melt) ヤ

邑 (town) ユウ　オウ　むら　さと　さとし　くに　すみ

8 strokes 阿 (right angle) ア　オ　お　くま

侑 (assist; offer) ウ　ユウ　すけ　すすむ　たすく　ゆき

苑 (garden) エン　オン　その

於 (oh) オ　ウ　うえ　おおい

旺 (extensive) オウ　あきら　さかん

茄 (eggplant) カ　なす

侃 (incorruptible) カン　ただし　ただ　なお　やす　あきら　つよし

欣 (rejoice) キン　コン　ゴン　やす　やすし　よし

尭 (tall) ギョウ　たか　たかし

虎 (tiger) ク　コ　たけ　とら

昂 (look up) コウ　ゴウ　あき　あきら　たか　たかし

采 (pluck) サイ

迪 (walk) ジャク　テキ　すすむ　ただ　ただす　ひら　ふみ　みち

昌 (bright; flourish) ショウ　あき　あきら　さかえ　すけ　まさ　よし

奈 (how) ダイ　ナ　いかん　なに

茉 (jasmine) バツ　マ　マツ　ま

弥 (extend) ビ　ミ　ひさ　ひさし　ひろ　ます　みつ　や　やす

朋 (friend) ホウ　とも

茅 (kind of reed) ボウ　かや　ち

孟 (first child; beginning) ボウ　マン　ミョウ　モウ　おさ　たけ　たけし
　　つとむ　はじめ

怜 (clever) リョウ　レイ　さと　さとし

9 strokes 郁 (flowery) イク　あや　か　かおり　かおる　たかし　ふみ

胤 (breed) イン　かず　たね　つぎ　つぐ　み

衿 (collar) キン　コン　えり

虹 (rainbow) グ　グウ　コウ　にじ

勁 (vigorous) ケイ　キョウ　つよし

奎 (stride) ケイ　ふみ

彦 (handsome man) ゲン　さと　ひこ　ひろ　やす　よし

胡 (foreign) コ　ゴ　ひさ

洸 (extensive) コウ　たけ　たけし　ひろし

哉 (how; what; if) サイ　か　かな　すけ　ちか　とし　はじめ　や

柊 (holly) シュウ　シュ　ひいらぎ　ひらぎ　くき

洲 (islet) シュウ　ス　しま　くに

洵 (whirlpool; truly) シュン　ジュン　まこと

茜 (madder) セイ　あかね

眉 (eyebrow) ビ　まゆ

昴 (the Pleiades) ボウ　すばる

柾 (straight grain) まさ　まさき

耶 (or; or not) ヤ　か　しゃ

宥 (forgiving) ユウ　ウ　すけ　ひろ

柚 (citron) ユウ　ユ　ゆず

祐 (help) ユウ　さち　すけ　たすく　まさ　ます　むら　よし

亮 (bright) リョウ　あき　あきら　すけ　たすく　とおる　ふさ　まこと

玲 (clear sound) リョウ　レイ　あき　あきら　たま

10 strokes 晏 (peaceful) アン　やす　はる　さだ

紘 (rope; extensive) オウ　コウ　つな　ひろ　ひろし

莞 (kind of reed) カン　い

栞 (guide) カン　しおり

赳 (strong) キュウ　たけ　たけし　つよし

矩 (square) ク　かど　つね　のり

桂 (fragrant olive) ケ　ケイ　かつ　かつら　よし

拳 (fist) ケン　ゲン　つとむ　たかし

倖 (lucky) コウ

晃 (shine) コウ　あき　あきら　てる　ひかる

浩 (extensive) コウ　ゴウ　いさむ　きよし　はる　ひろ　ひろし　ゆたか

紗 (silk gauze) サ　シャ

朔 (the first day of a month) サク　はじめ　きた　もと

峻 (high mountain) シュン　たか　たかし　ちか　みち

隼 (peregrine falcon) シュン　ジュン　たか　とし　はや　はやぶさ

恕 (sympathy) ジョ　ショ　ひろし　みち　よし　のり　ただし　しのぶ

晋 (go forward) シン　くに　すすむ　ゆき

秦 (name of country) シン　はた　まさ

晟 (bright) セイ　あきら　まさ　てる

悌 (obedient) ダイ　テイ　とも　やす　やすし　よし

桐 (paulownia) トウ　ドウ　きり　ひさ　ひら

唄 (song) バイ　うた

莉 (jasmine) ライ　リ　レイ

栗 (chestnut) リチ　リツ　くり

凌 (endure) リョウ　しのぐ

倭 (small man; Japanese) ワ　イ　しず　やまと　やす　まさ　かず

11 strokes 惟 (think) イ　エイ　ユイ　あり　これ　ただ　のぶ
　　　　　寅 (the third of the twelve horary signs; tiger; discreet) イン　つら　とも
　　　　　　とら　のぶ　ふさ
　　　　　亀 (turtle) キ　キン　ク　コン　あま　あや　かめ　すすむ　ひさし　ひさ
　　　　　毬 (ball) キュウ　まり
　　　　　菫 (violet) キン　すみれ
　　　　　袈 (priest's robe) ケ
　　　　　絃 (string) ゲン　ケン　いと　お　つる
　　　　　梧 (Chinese parasol tree) ゴ　きり
　　　　　笹 (bamboo grass) ささ
　　　　　梓 (catalpa) シ　あずさ
　　　　　偲 (recollect) シ　サイ　しのぶ
　　　　　脩 (dried meat; long) シュ　シュウ　ス　おさむ　すけ　なが　のぶ
　　　　　淳 (sincere) シュン　ジュン　あき　あつ　あつし　ただし　とし
　　　　　惇 (sincere) シュン　ジュン　トン　あつ　あつし　まこと
　　　　　渚 (beach) ショ　なぎさ　みぎわ
　　　　　梢 (treetop) ショウ　そう　こずえ　すえ
　　　　　捷 (surpass) ショウ　かつ　はや　とし　さとし　まさる
　　　　　笙 (a musical pipe instrument) ショウ
　　　　　菖 (iris) ショウ　あやめ
　　　　　晨 (morning) シン　ジン　とき　あき　とよ
　　　　　彗 (broom) スイ
　　　　　爽 (quick) ソウ　あきら　さわ　さ
　　　　　啄 (peck) タク
　　　　　琢 (polish) タク　あや　たか　みがく
　　　　　紬 (pongee) チュウ　つむぎ
　　　　　猪 (wild boar) チョ　い　いのこ　しし
　　　　　捺 (press) ナツ　ナ
　　　　　彬 (be endowed) ヒン　あき　あきら　よし
　　　　　彪 (design) ヒョウ　あや　たけし　たけ　とら　つよし　あきら
　　　　　萌 (sprout) ホウ　ボウ　ミョウ　モウ　めばえ　もえ
　　　　　眸 (pupil) ボウ　ム　ひとみ
　　　　　梨 (pear) リ　なし
　　　　　崚 (towering) リョウ
　　　　　鹿 (deer) ロク　か　しか　しし

12 strokes 渥 (moist) アク　あつ　あつし　やすし
　　　　　瑛 (gem) エイ　ヨウ　あき　あきら　てる
　　　　　媛 (belle) エン　オン　ひめ
　　　　　凱 (triumph) ガイ　よし　とき　たのし
　　　　　稀 (rarity) キ　ケ　まれ
　　　　　葵 (hollyhock) キ　ギ　あおい　まもる
　　　　　喬 (tall) キョウ　ギョウ　すけ　たか　たかし　ただ　ただし　もと
　　　　　欽 (stand on ceremony) キン　コン　こく　ただ　ひとし　まこと　よし
　　　　　絢 (pattern) ケン　ジュン　あや
　　　　　皐 (eminent) コウ　すすむ　たかし
　　　　　皓 (white) コウ　ゴウ　あき　あきら　てる

萩 (mugwort; bush clover) シュ　シュウ　はぎ
須 (wait; need) シュ　ス　まつ　もち　もとむ
竣 (complete) シュン
翔 (flying) ショウ　ゾウ
惣 (all) ス　ソウ　おさむ　のぶ　ふさ　みち　みな
巽 (southeast) ソン　たつみ　ゆき　よし
智 (wise) チ　あきら　さと　さとし　さとる　とし　とも　のり　まさる
椎 (sweet acorn tree) ツイ　しい　つち
敦 (thick and heavy) トン　あつ　あつし　おさむ　つとむ　つる　のぶ
斐 (pattern) ハイ　ヒ　あきら　あや　よし
遥 (far) ヨウ　のぶ　はる　はるか
湧 (bubble up) ヨウ　ユウ　わき　わく　わか
嵐 (storm) ラン　あらし
椋 (tree of elm family) リョウ　むく　くら
琳 (gem) リン
禄 (blessing; stipend) ロク　さち　とし　とみ　よし

13 strokes 暉 (shine) キ　あき　あきら　てる
鳩 (pigeon) キュウ　ク　あつむ　はと　やす
瑚 (sacrificial vessel) コ　ゴ
嵩 (high) コウ　シュウ　ショウ　スウ　かさ　たか　たかし　たけ　たけし
滉 (wide) コウ　ひろ　ひろし
裟 (surplice) サ
嵯 (rugged) サ
蒔 (sow) ジ　まき
頌 (recite) ジュ　ショウ　ス　うた　おと　つぐ　のぶ
舜 (rose of Sharon) シュン　きよ　とし　みつ
詢 (consult) ジュン　まこと
靖 (peaceful) ジョウ　セイ　おさむ　きよし　しず　のぶ　やす　やすし
稔 (harvest) ジン　ニン　ネン　とし　なり　なる　みのる　ゆたか
瑞 (felicity) ズイ　たま　みず
蒼 (pale blue) ソウ　しげ　しげる
禎 (happy) チョウ　テイ　さだ　さち　ただ　ただし　つぐ　とも　よし
椿 (camellia) チン　つばき　つば
楠 (camphor tree) ナン　くす　くすのき
楓 (maple) フウ　ホウ　かえで
睦 (friendly) ボク　モク　あつし　ちか　ちかし　のぶ　まこと　むつ　むつみ
椰 (palm tree) ヤ　やし
蓉 (lotus) ユウ　ヨウ　ひろ　ひろし　よし
瑶 (gem) ヨウ　たま
楊 (willow) ヨウ　やなぎ　やな　や　やな
稜 (dignity) リョウ　ロウ　いず　たか
蓮 (lotus) レン　はす

14 strokes 熊 (bear) ウ　ユウ　くま
樺 (birch) カ　かば　から
嘉 (good; felicity) カ　ひろ　よし　よしみ　よみし

魁 (leader) カイ　ケ　いさお　いさむ　つとむ
綺 (twill) キ　あや
熙 (shine) キ　ひかる　てる　ひろ　のり
瑳 (polish) サ
颯 (gust) サツ　サ　ソウ
爾 (that; you) ジ　ニ　あきら　しか　ちか　ちかし　み　みつる
肇 (begin) ジョウ　チョウ　ただ　ただし　とし　はじむ　はじめ
槙 (black pine) シン　テン　こずえ　まき
榛 (hazel alder) シン　ジン　はり　はる
聡 (sagacity) ス　ソウ　あき　あきら　さと　さとし　さとる　ただし　とし
翠 (green) スイ　あきら　みどり
碩 (full) セキ　みつる　ゆたか　ひろ　みち
漱 (rinse out) ソウ
綜 (control) ソウ　おさ
蔦 (ivy) チョウ　つた
暢 (carefully) チョウ　いたる　かど　とおる　なが　のぶ　まさ　みつる
緋 (scarlet) ヒ　あか　あけ
碧 (bluegreen) ヒャク　ヘキ　あお　たま　みどり
輔 (help) フ　ブ　ホ　すけ　たすく
鳳 (phoenix) ホウ　たか
瑠 (emerald) リュウ　ル　るり
綾 (figured satin) リョウ　リン　あや
綸 (thread) リン　いと

15 strokes 慧 (clever) エ　ケイ　あき　あきら　さと　さとし　さとる
毅 (strong) キ　ギ　ゲ　かた　こわし　しのぶ　たけ　たけし　つよし　とし　よし
嬉 (joy) キ　よし
槻 (zelkova tree) キ　つき
誼 (proper) ギ　よし
駒 (colt) ク　こま
醇 (pure) ジュン　あつ　あつし
諄 (steadfast) ジュン　あつ　さね　しげ　まこと
蕉 (banana) ショウ
蝶 (butterfly) ジョウ　チョウ
憧 (longing) ドウ
璃 (emerald) リ　たま　るり
遼 (far) リョウ　とお　とおる　はるか
諒 (clear) リョウ　ロウ　まこと
凛 (cold) リン
黎 (dark) レイ　たみ

16 strokes 叡 (wise) エイ　さと　さとし　あきら　とおる　とし　まさ　よし
橘 (wild orange) キチ　キツ　たちばな
錦 (brocade) キン　コン　かね　にしき
黛 (artifical eyebrows) タイ　まゆずみ
鮎 (catfish; sweetfish) デン　ネン　あい　あゆ
燎 (bonfire) リョウ

蕗 (butterbur) ル ロ ふき
澪 (channel) レイ リョウ みお

17 strokes 霞 (mist) カ ゲ かすみ
磯 (seashore) キ ケ いそ
鞠 (ball) キク まり
鴻 (large) コウ ひろ ひろし
燦 (resplendent) サン あき
駿 (steed) シュン たか たかし とし
瞳 (pupil) ズウ ドウ トウ あきら ひとみ
檀 (spindle tree) ダン タン まゆみ
瞭 (clarity) リョウ あき あきら
嶺 (summit) リョウ レイ たけ ね みね

18 strokes 鎌 (sickle) ケン レン かた かね かま
曙 (dawn) ショ あけ あきら
穣 (rich) ジョウ ニョウ おさむ しげ みのる ゆたか
雛 (chick) ス スウ ひな
藤 (wisteria) トウ ドウ ひさ ふじ
麿 (Ⅰ) まろ
燿 (shine) ヨウ てる
藍 (indigo) ラン あい
鯉 (carp) リ こい

19 strokes 艶 (glossy) エン おう つや もろ よし
鯛 (sea bream) チョウ たい
鵬 (phoenix) ホウ とも ゆき
蘭 (orchid) ラン か

20 strokes 巌 (precipitous) ガン ゲン いわ いわお お みち みね よし
馨 (fragrance) キョウ ケイ か かおり かおる きよ よし
耀 (sparkle) ヨウ あきら

21 strokes 鶴 (crane) カク ガク ず たず つ つる

24 strokes 鷹 (hawk) オウ ヨウ たか
麟 (imaginary animal) リン

Old Forms of Kanji Approved for Given Names

Old forms of 195 Jōyō Kanji and 10 Jinmei-yō Kanji may be used for given names.
The following lists new and old forms (the latter in parentheses) of these kanji, by
stroke count of the new forms.

3	与(與)	収(收)	6	気(氣)	壮(壯)
4	仏(佛)	庁(廳)		亘(亙)	争(爭)
5	広(廣)	払(拂)		尽(盡)	団(團)

伝(傳)	祐(祐)	圏(圈)	暦(曆)
灯(燈)	郎(郞)	検(檢)	歴(歷)
毎(每)	10 桜(櫻)	湿(濕)	練(練)
7 亜(亞)	陥(陷)	煮(煮)	15 謁(謁)
応(應)	恵(惠)	暑(暑)	縁(緣)
芸(藝)	倹(儉)	焼(燒)	横(橫)
児(兒)	剣(劍)	畳(疊)	器(器)
社(社)	従(從)	装(裝)	戯(戲)
寿(壽)	将(將)	弾(彈)	勲(勳)
条(條)	祥(祥)	晩(晚)	撃(擊)
状(狀)	真(眞)	揺(搖)	諸(諸)
即(卽)	粋(粹)	塁(壘)	穂(穗)
売(賣)	捜(搜)	禄(祿)	蔵(藏)
抜(拔)	帯(帶)	13 禍(禍)	鋳(鑄)
来(來)	梅(梅)	楽(樂)	賓(賓)
8 価(價)	秘(祕)	寛(寬)	黙(默)
祈(祈)	敏(敏)	漢(漢)	16 衛(衞)
国(國)	勉(勉)	署(署)	壊(壞)
祉(祉)	竜(龍)	奨(獎)	懐(懷)
者(者)	涙(淚)	寝(寢)	薫(薰)
斉(齊)	朗(朗)	慎(愼)	獣(獸)
突(突)	11 悪(惡)	摂(攝)	縦(縱)
拝(拜)	逸(逸)	節(節)	嬢(孃)
侮(侮)	渇(渴)	戦(戰)	繁(繁)
歩(步)	偽(僞)	禅(禪)	薬(藥)
弥(彌)	虚(虛)	僧(僧)	謡(謠)
9 為(爲)	掲(揭)	滞(滯)	頼(賴)
悔(悔)	険(險)	嘆(嘆)	錬(鍊)
海(海)	黄(黃)	禎(禎)	録(錄)
巻(卷)	黒(黑)	福(福)	17 謹(謹)
峡(峽)	視(視)	虜(虜)	厳(嚴)
狭(狹)	渋(澁)	廊(廊)	繊(纖)
県(縣)	渚(渚)	14 穀(穀)	聴(聽)
恒(恆)	渉(涉)	雑(雜)	覧(覽)
砕(碎)	剰(剩)	緒(緒)	18 顕(顯)
臭(臭)	酔(醉)	静(靜)	験(驗)
祝(祝)	巣(巢)	層(層)	騒(騷)
叙(敍)	琢(琢)	増(增)	贈(贈)
乗(乘)	猪(猪)	憎(憎)	懲(懲)
浄(淨)	著(著)	徴(徵)	穣(穰)
神(神)	転(轉)	稲(稻)	鎮(鎭)
専(專)	都(都)	徳(德)	難(難)
祖(祖)	盗(盜)	髪(髮)	翻(飜)
荘(莊)	12 奥(奧)	碑(碑)	類(類)
単(單)	温(溫)	墨(墨)	19 鶏(鷄)
昼(晝)	暁(曉)	様(樣)	瀬(瀨)
卑(卑)	勤(勤)	緑(綠)	臓(臟)

20 巌(巖)
　　響(響)
　　譲(讓)
　　醸(釀)
　　欄(欄)

Chapter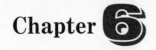

Rules for Kanji Compounds

As seen in the vocabulary examples in the preceding chapters, kanji are used not only individually but also in compound words, or *jukugo*. Indeed, among the 1,945 Jōyō Kanji, there are approximately 370 that are no longer used independently but only to form compounds; another 170 or so are rarely used singly. Although there are compounds of three or more kanji, the majority are compounds of two kanji; these latter form the bulk of this chapter.

Kanji are not put together randomly to form compounds. A number of rules can be discerned, and these are discussed in this chapter's two main sections: compounds whose two elements are in a syntactic relationship (e.g., verb—object and subject—predicate) and compounds whose two elements are juxtaposed in a sort of "and" or "or" relationship.

Most of the compounds listed involve the *on-yomi* of the kanji. A large number of *on-yomi* combinations used in modern Japanese originated in Chinese classical wrtitings. Over the long history of Japanese usage, some of these have undergone a change in meaning, such as 遠慮(エンリョ reserve [originally "forethought"]) and 迷惑(メイワク trouble [originally "be at a loss"]). A few native-Japanese words, originally pronounced with their *kun-yomi*, are now read with their *on-yomi*. Examples include 大根(ダイコン radish [formerly read おおね])and 返事(ヘンジ [formerly read かえりごと]). Aside from these, quite a number of kanji compounds were created in Japan on contact with Western cultures just a century or so ago, using the *on-yomi* of the kanji. Examples are 会社(カイシャ company) and 銀行(ギンコウ bank). Compounds such as these are still being created today.

Kun-yomi compounds also exist. Many compound words are made up of purely Japanese elements; for example, 草木(くさき vegetation) and 山川(やまかわ mountains and rivers). Additionally, a few compounds used to be read with *on-yomi*, but are now pronounced with their *kun-yomi* instead. Examples include 日暮/日暮れ(ひぐれ nightfall) and 耳鳴/耳鳴り(みみなり ringing in the ears).

Two Kanji in a Syntactic Relationship

Subject-Predicate

A good example of a compound word whose elements have a subject-predicate relationship—in both English and Japanese—is "earthquake," or 地震(ジシン): the "earth" (subject) "quakes" (predicate). The number of kanji compounds of this type is, however, small. While for many such compounds the meaning is direct, some compounds have indirect and figurative meanings, for example 蛇行 (ダコウ meander, lit., "snake-go"). The subject kanji often have something to do with nature (日 [sun; day], 鳥 [bird], 地 [earth]); with the human body (目 [eye], 歯 [tooth]); or with abstract concepts (年 [year; age]; 国 [country]).

Excluded from the list are most Japanese-made subject-predicate compounds, due to the fact that since such compounds are also used as the subject and predicate of a sentence, their meaning can be easily discerned. For example, 芽生え (めばえ budding) can be easily understood from the corresponding common phrase 芽が生える (めがはえる sprout). A few Japanese-made compounds that have no phrasal equivalents, such as 背広 (せびろ business suit), are, however, included.

The list is arranged according to the stroke count of the first kanji in the compounds.

2 strokes 人 人為 (ジンイ artificial)
人造 (ジンゾウ man-made)
人望 (ジンボウ popularity)
人選 (ジンセン selection [of a suitable person])

4 strokes 公 公示 (コウジ public announcement)
公布 (コウフ promulgation)
公立 (コウリツ public [institution])
公定 (コウテイ officially fixed)
公営 (コウエイ public management)
公認 (コウニン official recognition)
幻 幻滅 (ゲンメツ disillusionment)
水 水洗 (スイセン washing, flushing)
天 天分 (テンブン natural gift)
天変地異 (テンペンチイ natural calamities)
天賦 (テンプ inherent)
日 日没 (ニチボツ sunset)
日長 (ひなが long day)
日限 (ニチゲン fixed time)
日食 (ニッショク eclipse of the sun)
日照 (ニッショウ shining of the sun)
日暮 (ひぐれ nightfall)

5 strokes 世 世襲 (セシュウ transmission by heredity)
氷 氷解 (ヒョウカイ thaw)
民 民有 (ミンユウ private ownership)
民営 (ミンエイ private operation)
民選 (ミンセン popular election)
目 目撃 (モクゲキ witness)

6 strokes 州 州立 (シュウリツ state-built)
地 地震 (ジシン earthquake)
年 年少 (ネンショウ tender age)

年長 (ネンチョウ seniority)

耳 耳鳴 (みみなり ringing in the ears)

両 両立 (リョウリツ compatibility)

7 strokes 我 我慢 (ガマン patience)

私 私立 (シリツ private)

私有 (シユウ private ownership)

私設 (シセツ private)

私営 (シエイ private operation)

体 体育 (タイイク physical culture)

体得 (タイトク master)

体験 (タイケン personal experience)

豆 豆腐 (トウフ bean curd, *tōfu*)

8 strokes 炎 炎上 (エンジョウ flame up)

国 国立 (コクリツ national)

国有 (コクユウ state ownership)

国定 (コクテイ state-authorized)

国連 (コクレン United Nations)

国産 (コクサン national production)

国営 (コクエイ state operation)

国際 (コクサイ international)

毒 毒殺 (ドクサツ killing by poison)

林 林立 (リンリツ stand close together)

9 strokes 皆 皆無 (カイム none)

神 神出鬼没 (シンシュツキボツ appearing in unexpected places and at unexpected moments)

背 背広 (せびろ business suit)

点 点在 (テンザイ be scattered)

点滴 (テンテキ drops)

10 strokes 格 格別 (カクベツ special)

骨 骨折 (コッセツ fracture of a bone; ほねおり trouble)

師 師走 (シわす/シはす December)

11 strokes 蛇 蛇行 (ダコウ meander)

鳥 鳥居 (とりい *torii*)

都 都立 (トリツ metropolitan)

都営 (トエイ operated by Tokyo Metropolis)

雪 雪崩 (なだれ snowslide)

符 符合 (フゴウ coincide)

12 strokes 雲 雲散霧消 (ウンサンムショウ vanish like mist)

景 景勝 (ケイショウ scenic beauty)

歯 歯痛 (シツウ toothache)

13 strokes 腹 腹痛 (フクツウ stomach-ache)

腰 腰痛 (ヨウツウ lumbago)

雷 雷鳴 (ライメイ thunder)

雷撃 (ライゲキ striking by lightning/by torpedo)

14 strokes 銃 銃殺 (ジュウサツ shooting to death)

15 strokes 縁 縁起 (エンギ omen)
　　　　　樹 樹立 (ジュリツ establishment)

16 strokes 頭 頭痛 (ズツウ headache)

17 strokes 霜 霜降 (しもふり pepper-and-salt)
　　　　　優 優勝 (ユウショウ victory)

Verb-Object

An example of a verb-object compound word in English is "cutthroat," someone who literally "cuts throats" or an adjective describing merciless competition and the like. There seem to be relatively few such words in English, but many in Japanese. Specific types are the following:

1. Verb+object: 造船 (ぞうせん [lit., make boat], shipbuilding). The majority of the compound words in this section are of this type.
2. Verb+locative: 在日 (ざいにち [lit., be at Japan], be in Japan)
3. Verb+predicate nominative: 成人 (せいじん [lit., become person], adult)

A large number of Jōyō Kanji act as the first, verbal, element in such compounds. Since not all such kanji and their compounds can be listed here, only the most frequently used verbal kanji are. These kanji make up the headings below; the compounds within each list are arranged in order of increasing stroke count of the second kanji.

有　**have**
有力 (ユウリョク　powerful)
有功 (ユウコウ　merit)
有史 (ユウシ　historic)
有用 (ユウヨウ　useful)
有色 (ユウショク　colored)
有名 (ユウメイ　famous)
有形 (ユウケイ　tangible)
有志 (ユウシ　interested)
有声 (ユウセイ　voiced)
有余 (ユウヨ　more than)
有利 (ユウリ　profitable)
有価 (ユウカ　valuable)
有効 (ユウコウ　validity)
有毒 (ユウドク　poisonous)
有限 (ユウゲン　limited)
有益 (ユウエキ　useful)
有害 (ユウガイ　harmful)
有能 (ユウノウ　able)
有料 (ユウリョウ　charged)
有望 (ユウボウ　promising)
有閑 (ユウカン　leisure)

有期 (ユウキ　terminable)
有給 (ユウキュウ　paid)
有産 (ユウサン　propertied)
有終 (ユウシュウ　conclusion)
有税 (ユウゼイ　taxable)
有罪 (ユウザイ　guiltiness)
有数 (ユウスウ　prominent)
有償 (ユウショウ　conpensation)
有線 (ユウセン　[by] wire; cable [TV])
有機 (ユウキ　organic)
有識 (ユウシキ　intelligent)

出　put out; come out

出力 (シュツリョク　generating power)
出火 (シュッカ　fire)
出水 (シュッスイ　flood)
出札 (シュッサツ　issue a ticket)
出世 (シュッセ　success in life)
出血 (シュッケツ　bleeding)
出社 (シュッシャ　go to work)
出身 (シュッシン　native)
出廷 (シュッテイ　appear in court)
出兵 (シュッペイ　dispatch of troops)
出金 (シュッキン　payment)
出品 (シュッピン　exhibit)
出荷 (シュッカ　shipment)
出家 (シュッケ　priest)
出校 (シュッコウ　report for duty at school)
出陣 (シュツジン　take the field)
出席 (シュッセキ　attendance)
出馬 (シュツバ　offer oneself as a candidate)
出猟 (シュツリョウ　go out hunting)
出棺 (シュッカン　[funeral procession] leaves)
出勤 (シュッキン　go to work)
出港 (シュッコウ　leave port)
出場 (シュツジョウ　participation)
出資 (シュッシ　investment)
出演 (シュツエン　appearance)
出獄 (シュツゴク　be released from prison)
出漁 (シュツリョウ　go fishing at sea)
出頭 (シュットウ　presence)
出講 (シュッコウ　give lectures)
出願 (シュツガン　application)

入　enter; put in

入札 (ニュウサツ　tender [a bid])
入会 (ニュウカイ　admission)
入社 (ニュウシャ　enter a company)

入学 (ニュウガク admission to school)
入京 (ニュウキョウ arrive in Tokyo)
入金 (ニュウキン payment/receipt of money)
入国 (ニュウコク entry into a country)
入所 (ニュウショ entering)
入念 (ニュウネン careful)
入門 (ニュウモン become a pupil)
入城 (ニュウジョウ enter a castle)
入荷 (ニュウカ arrival of goods)
入庫 (ニュウコ warehousing)
入党 (ニュウトウ join a political party)
入梅 (ニュウバイ rainy season)
入浴 (ニュウヨク bathing)
入港 (ニュウコウ enter port)
入場 (ニュウジョウ admission)
入隊 (ニュウタイ enlistment)
入道 (ニュウドウ lay priest)
入閣 (ニュウカク enter the Cabinet)
入獄 (ニュウゴク imprisonment)
入賞 (ニュウショウ win a prize)
入選 (ニュウセン be selected)
入籍 (ニュウセキ entry into the family register)

開　open

開口 (カイコウ opening of a speech)
開会 (カイカイ opening of a meeting)
開花 (カイカ come into bloom)
開廷 (カイテイ hold court)
開国 (カイコク opening of a country)
開店 (カイテン open a shop)
開門 (カイモン open a gate)
開巻 (カイカン on the first page)
開城 (カイジョウ surrender)
開封 (カイフウ break the seal)
開院 (カイイン opening of the Diet)
開校 (カイコウ opening of a school)
開眼 (カイガン initiation; カイゲン enlightenment)
開基 (カイキ founding of a temple)
開帳 (カイチョウ unveiling of a Buddhist image)
開票 (カイヒョウ counting of votes)
開運 (カイウン improvement of fortune)
開港 (カイコウ opening of a port)
開業 (カイギョウ open for business)
開場 (カイジョウ open)
開腹 (カイフク perform laparotomy)
開幕 (カイマク the curtain rises)
開演 (カイエン start a performance)

開館 (カイカン   opening of a hall)
開講 (カイコウ   begin a series of lectures)

発   let out; send

発火 (ハッカ   outbreak of fire)
発心 (ホッシン   religious awakening)
発令 (ハツレイ   gazetting)
発汗 (ハッカン   perspiration)
発光 (ハッコウ   radiation)
発狂 (ハッキョウ   insanity)
発言 (ハツゲン   speech)
発車 (ハッシャ   departure [of a car])
発声 (ハッセイ   utterance)
発売 (ハツバイ   sale)
発芽 (ハツガ   germination)
発効 (ハッコウ   coming into effect)
発音 (ハツオン   pronunciation)
発信 (ハッシン   post)
発案 (ハツアン   suggestion)
発祥 (ハッショウ   cradle)
発病 (ハツビョウ   fall ill)
発砲 (ハッポウ   discharge a gun)
発情 (ハツジョウ   sexual excitement)
発電 (ハツデン   generation of electric power)
発端 (ホッタン   origin)
発熱 (ハツネツ   fever)

在   exist

在中 (ザイチュウ   containing)
在天 (ザイテン   in heaven)
在日 (ザイニチ   be in Japan)
在外 (ザイガイ   overseas)
在世 (ザイセイ   during life)
在宅 (ザイタク   at home)
在任 (ザイニン   in office)
在米 (ザイベイ   be in America)
在位 (ザイイ   on the throne)
在学 (ザイガク   be in school)
在京 (ザイキョウ   be in Tokyo)
在室 (ザイシツ   be in the room)
在庫 (ザイコ   in stock)
在郷 (ザイゴウ   in the countryside)
在勤 (ザイキン   in office)
在野 (ザイヤ   out of power)
在獄 (ザイゴク   in prison)
在職 (ザイショク   in office)
在籍 (ザイセキ   on the school register)

脱　**remove**

脱水 (ダッスイ　dehydration)
脱毛 (ダツモウ　hair loss)
脱皮 (ダッピ　shed skin)
脱衣 (ダツイ　undress)
脱会 (ダッカイ　withdrawal from membership)
脱字 (ダツジ　omission of word)
脱色 (ダッショク　decoloration)
脱法 (ダッポウ　evasion of law)
脱臭 (ダッシュウ　deodorization)
脱俗 (ダツゾク　unworldliness)
脱脂 (ダッシ　remove grease)
脱党 (ダットウ　secession)
脱税 (ダツゼイ　tax dodging)
脱腸 (ダッチョウ　hernia)
脱穀 (ダッコク　threshing)
脱獄 (ダツゴク　jail-breaking)
脱線 (ダッセン　derailment; digression)

製　**manufacture**

製氷 (セイヒョウ　ice manufacture)
製本 (セイホン　bookbinding)
製糸 (セイシ　spinning)
製材 (セイザイ　lumbering)
製油 (セイユ　oil manufacture)
製茶 (セイチャ　tea manufacture)
製紙 (セイシ　paper making)
製粉 (セイフン　milling)
製菓 (セイカ　confectionery)
製陶 (セイトウ　pottery manufacture)
製麻 (セイマ　hemp dressing)
製塩 (セイエン　salt manufacture)
製靴 (セイカ　shoe making)
製鉄 (セイテツ　iron manufacture)
製鋼 (セイコウ　steel manufacture)
製糖 (セイトウ　sugar production)
製薬 (セイヤク　drug manufacture)

失　**lose**

失心 (シッシン　swoon)
失礼 (シツレイ　rudeness)
失言 (シツゲン　slip of the tongue)
失効 (シッコウ　lose effect)
失念 (シツネン　forget)
失明 (シツメイ　loss of eyesight)
失格 (シッカク　disqualification)
失笑 (シッショウ　burst of laughter)

失恋 (シツレン disappointed love)
失脚 (シッキャク fall from power)
失望 (シツボウ disappointment)
失敬 (シッケイ impertinence)
失意 (シツイ disappointment)
失業 (シツギョウ unemployment)
失権 (シッケン loss of rights)

防 prevent

防火 (ボウカ fire prevention)
防水 (ボウスイ waterproof)
防共 (ボウキョウ defense against communism)
防虫 (ボウチュウ insect-proof)
防犯 (ボウハン crime prevention)
防疫 (ボウエキ prevention of epidemics)
防音 (ボウオン soundproof)
防臭 (ボウシュウ deodorization)
防風 (ボウフウ protection against storms)
防雪 (ボウセツ protection against snow)
防寒 (ボウカン protection against the cold)
防湿 (ボウシツ moisture-proof)
防弾 (ボウダン bullet-proof)
防腐 (ボウフ prevention against putrefaction)
防縮 (ボウシュク shrink-proofing)

退 leave

退庁 (タイチョウ leave government office)
退会 (タイカイ withdrawal of membership)
退任 (タイニン retire from office)
退位 (タイイ abdication)
退役 (タイエキ retire from the service)
退社 (タイシャ leave office; leave one's company)
退廷 (タイテイ leave the court)
退学 (タイガク withdrawal from school)
退院 (タイイン discharge from hospital)
退校 (タイコウ withdrawal from school)
退陣 (タイジン decamp)
退席 (タイセキ leave one's seat)
退場 (タイジョウ exit)
退職 (タイショク retirement)

結 bind; end

結石 (ケッセキ a calculus [physiological])
結氷 (ケッピョウ freezing over)
結局 (ケッキョク finally)
結社 (ケッシャ form an association)
結果 (ケッカ result)
結実 (ケツジツ bear fruit)

結核 (ケッカク   tuberculosis)
結党 (ケットウ   formation of a party)
結球 (ケッキュウ   a head)
結晶 (ケッショウ   crystallization)
結構 (ケッコウ   structure; fine; well enough)
結膜 (ケツマク   conjunctiva)
結審 (ケッシン   conclude a hearing)
結論 (ケツロン   conclusion)

減   decrease

減水 (ゲンスイ   decrease of water)
減収 (ゲンシュウ   decrease in income)
減刑 (ゲンケイ   commutation of sentence)
減価 (ゲンカ   price reduction)
減食 (ゲンショク   to diet)
減点 (ゲンテン   demerit)
減員 (ゲンイン   reduction of staff)
減配 (ゲンパイ   reduction of dividend)
減俸 (ゲンポウ   salary reduction)
減産 (ゲンサン   curtailment of production)
減給 (ゲンキュウ   reduction of pay)
減税 (ゲンゼイ   tax reduction)
減量 (ゲンリョウ   loss in quantity)
減額 (ゲンガク   reduction)

対   face

対人 (タイジン   personal)
対日 (タイニチ   toward Japan)
対外 (タイガイ   foreign)
対米 (タイベイ   toward America)
対角 (タイカク   opposite angle)
対局 (タイキョク   play a game of *go*, etc.)
対価 (タイカ   equivalent)
対岸 (タイガン   opposite bank)
対物 (タイブツ   object)
対面 (タイメン   meeting)
対校 (タイコウ   interschool)
対陣 (タイジン   be encamped facing each other)
対象 (タイショウ   object)

Adjective-Noun

In many Japanese compound words the first component has an adjectival relationship to the second component. (An example of this sort of word in English is "grandmother," a combination of the adjective "grand" and the noun "mother.") The various possibilities are as follows:

1. First component is essentially adjectival: About 180 of the Jōyō Kanji are used independently as adjectives ending in *i* (高い[たかい tall]) or *na* (妙な[ミョウな

strange]. About 60 more are not used as as independent adjectives, but have an essentially adjectival meaning, for example, 巨 (キョ huge). These kanji are also commonly used in adjective-noun compounds.

2. First component is essentially verbal: Kanji with a basically verbal nature are often used with an adjectival sense as the first element in compounds. For example, 教 (teach), appears in 教室(キョウシツ[lit., teach room], classroom).

3. First component is essentially nominal: Most first kanji in compounds of the "adjective-noun" type are actually basically nouns themselves. An example is 国政(コクセイ [lit., country administration], national administration). The most commonly used first kanji in this category are numerals (一, 二, 三, etc.), temporal or locative kanji(e.g., 前 [ゼン/まえ front; former]), and kanji for the seasons (夏, 冬, etc.).

Not listed in this section are numeral-classifier combinations(e.g., 三人 [サンニン three people] and 一箱 [ひとはこ one box]), which are limitless in number. Limited listings are given for such first kanji as 新(new), which continue to be used to make new compound words.

Some adjectival first kanji are often added to compounds to form three-or-more-kanji combinations, for example, 新国際空港(シンコクサイクウコウ new international airport). Such compounds are not listed here.

The first, adjectival kanji make up the headings below; the compounds within each list are arranged in order of increasing stroke count of the second kanji. Because of the vast number of words, only a few important first kanji are listed.

新　new
新人 (シンジン　new face)
新月 (シンゲツ　new moon)
新手 (シンて　new way)
新仏 (シンほとけ　newly departed soul)
新本 (シンポン　new book)
新曲 (シンキョク　new musical composition)
新式 (シンシキ　new style)
新宅 (シンタク　new house)
新年 (シンネン　new year)
新米 (シンマイ　new rice)
新作 (シンサク　new piece of work)
新居 (シンキョ　new home)
新制 (シンセイ　new system)
新版 (シンパン　new edition)
新法 (シンポウ　new law/method)
新味 (シンミ　freshness)
新店 (シンみせ　new store)
新芽 (シンめ　bud)
新妻 (にいづま　new wife)
新型 (シンがた　new model)
新柄 (シンがら　new pattern)
新春 (シンシュン　New Year)
新星 (シンセイ　nova; new film star)

新茶 (シンチャ   new tea)
新派 (シンパ   new school)
新品 (シンピン   new article)
新風 (シンプウ   new phase)
新郎 (シンロウ   bridegroom)
新盆 (にいボン   first Bon festival)
新案 (シンアン   new idea)
新株 (シンかぶ   new stock)
新酒 (シンシュ   new brew of the year)
新教 (シンキョウ   Protestantism)
新雪 (シンセツ   fresh snow)
新婦 (シンプ   bride)
新訳 (シンヤク   new translation)
新装 (シンソウ   refurbishment)
新語 (シンゴ   new word)
新種 (シンシュ   new variety)
新説 (シンセツ   new theory)
新緑 (シンリョク   fresh verdure)
新暦 (シンレキ   solar calendar)
新劇 (シンゲキ   new drama)
新穀 (シンコク   new crop of rice)
新編 (シンペン   new edition)
新館 (シンカン   new building)
新薬 (シンヤク   new medicine)
新顔 (シンがお   newcomer)

外   outside

外人 (ガイジン   foreigner)
外皮 (ガイヒ   integument)
外用 (ガイヨウ   external use [of a medicine])
外気 (ガイキ   open air)
外交 (ガイコウ   diplomacy)
外耳 (ガイジ   auricle)
外出 (ガイシュツ   go out)
外地 (ガイチ   overseas land)
外米 (ガイマイ   foreign rice)
外角 (ガイカク   external angle)
外形 (ガイケイ   external form)
外見 (ガイケン   external appearance)
外車 (ガイシャ   foreign car)
外来 (ガイライ   foreign; outpatient)
外国 (ガイコク   foreign country)
外注 (ガイチュウ   outside order)
外泊 (ガイハク   sleep away from home)
外界 (ガイカイ   outside world)
外海 (ガイカイ/そとうみ   open sea)
外相 (ガイショウ   Foreign Minister)
外食 (ガイショク   eating out)

外面 (ガイメン/そとづら outward appearance)
外洋 (ガイヨウ open sea)
外科 (ゲカ surgery)
外孫 (そとまご/ガイソン child of a daughter married into another family)
外貨 (ガイカ foreign currency/goods)
外商 (ガイショウ foreign merchant)
外部 (ガイブ outside)
外務 (ガイム foreign affairs)
外野 (ガイヤ outfield)
外側 (そとがわ outside)
外堀 (そとぼり outer moat)
外勤 (ガイキン outside duty)
外港 (ガイコウ outer port)
外装 (ガイソウ wrapping; facing)
外報 (ガイホウ foreign news)
外遊 (ガイユウ foreign travel)
外道 (ゲドウ heresy)
外債 (ガイサイ foreign loan)
外資 (ガイシ foreign capital)
外傷 (ガイショウ external injury)
外電 (ガイデン foreign dispatch)
外聞 (ガイブン reputation)
外線 (ガイセン outside line/call)
外敵 (ガイテキ foreign enemy)
外輪 (ガイリン tire; paddle wheel)
外観 (ガイカン external appearance)
外題 (ゲダイ title of a book/play)

国   **country, nation**

国力 (コクリョク national power)
国土 (コクド country)
国王 (コクオウ king)
国文 (コクブン Japanese language/literature)
国外 (コクガイ outside the country)
国号 (コクゴウ name of a country)
国史 (コクシ national/Japanese history)
国内 (コクナイ inside the country)
国民 (コクミン nation)
国字 (コクジ Japanese characters/script)
国技 (コクギ national sport)
国体 (コクタイ national polity)
国防 (コクボウ national defense)
国利 (コクリ national welfare)
国学 (コクガク study of Japanese classics)
国法 (コウホウ laws of the country)
国宝 (コクホウ national treasure)
国威 (コクイ national prestige)

国事 (コクジ　affairs of state)
国是 (コクゼ　national policy)
国政 (コクセイ　national administration)
国風 (コクフウ　national customs)
国書 (コクショ　Seal of the State)
国辱 (コクジョク　national disgrace)
国粋 (コクスイ　national virtues)
国情 (コクジョウ　conditions of a country)
国務 (コクム　state affairs)
国運 (コクウン　national destinies)
国策 (コクサク　national policy)
国税 (コクゼイ　state tax)
国葬 (コクソウ　state funeral)
国道 (コクドウ　national road)
国費 (コクヒ　national expenditure)
国富 (コクフ　national wealth)
国債 (コクサイ　national debt)
国勢 (コクセイ　national conditions)
国賊 (コクゾク　traitor to the country)
国鉄 (コクテツ　national railways)
国語 (コクゴ　national/Japanese language)
国賓 (コクヒン　guest of the nation)
国難 (コクナン　national crisis)
国璽 (コクジ　Seal of the State)
国籍 (コクセキ　nationality)

高　**high**
高山 (コウザン　high mountain)
高圧 (コウアツ　high pressure/voltage)
高台 (たかダイ　high ground)
高地 (コウチ　high ground)
高年 (コウネン　advanced age)
高名 (コウメイ　fame)
高位 (コウイ　high rank)
高見 (コウケン　excellent views)
高弟 (コウテイ　chief disciple)
高利 (コウリ　high interest)
高価 (コウカ　high price)
高官 (コウカン　high official)
高所 (コウショ　high ground)
高音 (コウオン　loud sound)
高架 (コウカ　elevated)
高段 (コウダン　high grade)
高度 (コウド　altitude; height)
高級 (コウキュウ　high class)
高原 (コウゲン　plateau)
高座 (コウザ　platform)

高速 (コウソク   high speed)
高値 (たかね   high price)
高進 (コウシン   acceleration)
高率 (コウリツ   high rate)
高温 (コウオン   high temperature)
高給 (コウキュウ   high salary)
高等 (コウトウ   high; advanced)
高評 (コウヒョウ   great reputation)
高僧 (コウソウ   high priest)
高楼 (コウロウ   tall building)
高説 (コウセツ   excellent opinion)
高層 (コウソウ   lofty; high storied)
高調 (コウチョウ   high pitch/spirit)
高熱 (コウネツ   high heat; fever)
高論 (コウロン   excellent opinion)
高潮 (たかしお/コウチョウ   high tide)
高齢 (コウレイ   advanced age)
高額 (コウガク   large sum)

英   superb; English
英才 (エイサイ   talent)
英文 (エイブン   English)
英気 (エイキ   vigor)
英字 (エイジ   English letter)
英学 (エイガク   study of English)
英国 (エイコク   Britain)
英知 (エイチ   wisdom)
英法 (エイホウ   English law)
英姿 (エイシ   gallant figure)
英貨 (エイカ   British money)
英断 (エイダン   decisive)
英訳 (エイヤク   English translation)
英略 (エイリャク   good plan)
英雄 (エイユウ   hero)
英傑 (エイケツ   great man)
英詩 (エイシ   English poem)
英資 (エイシ   brilliant qualities)
英語 (エイゴ   English)
英領 (エイリョウ   British territory)
英霊 (エイレイ   spirit of departed)

食   eat
食用 (ショクヨウ   table use)
食事 (ショクジ   meal)
食卓 (ショクタク   dinner table)
食物 (ショクモツ   food)
食後 (ショクゴ   after a meal)
食指 (ショクシ   index finger)

食前 (ショクゼン   before a meal)
食品 (ショクヒン   food)
食紅 (ショクべに   red food coloring)
食通 (ショクツウ   gourmet)
食料 (ショクリョウ   food)
食堂 (ショクドウ   dining room)
食欲 (ショクヨク   appetite)
食道 (ショクドウ   gullet)
食費 (ショクヒ   food costs)
食塩 (ショクエン   table salt)
食傷 (ショクショウ   food poisoning)
食糧 (ショクリョウ   rations)

東   east

東天 (トウテン   eastern sky at dawn)
東方 (トウホウ/ひがしかた   east)
東北 (トウホク   northeast)
東亜 (トウア   East Asia)
東邦 (トウホウ   Eastern country)
東岸 (トウガン   eastern coast)
東国 (トウゴク   eastern country/province)
東海 (トウカイ   eastern sea)
東南 (トウナン   southeast)
東風 (ひがしかぜ/トウフウ   east wind)
東洋 (トウヨウ   Orient)
東宮 (トウグウ   Crown Prince)
東経 (トウケイ   east longitude)
東部 (トウブ   eastern part)
東端 (トウタン   eastern end)

春   spring

春分 (シュンブン   spring equinox)
春本 (シュンポン   pornography)
春色 (シュンショク   spring scenery; glamorous)
春先 (はるさき   early spring)
春作 (はるサク   spring crop)
春画 (シュンガ   pornographic picture)
春季 (シュンキ   springtime)
春雨 (はるさめ   spring rain)
春物 (はるもの   spring goods)
春風 (シュンプウ/はるかぜ   spring breeze)
春眠 (シュンミン   spring sleep)
春雪 (シュンセツ   spring   snow)
春暖 (シュンダン   warm spring weather)
春闘 (シュントウ   spring labor-management negotiations)

Adverbial First Kanji

There are several kinds of kanji compounds in which the first element has essentially an adverbial function. Some first kanji are used exclusively or primarily in one of these categories, as noted below:

1. Adverbial kanji modifying adjectival kanji: Examples are 最大 (サイダイ [lit., most large], largest) and 不快 (フカイ [lit., not pleasant], unpleasant). 最 is mostly used to modify an adjectival kanji, while 不 may be used to modify adjectival kanji and verbal kanji (next category).
2. Adverbial kanji modifying verbal kanji: Examples are 未完 (ミカン [lit., not yet finish], unfinished) and 不滅 (フメツ [lit., not die], immortality). 未 almost always modifies verbal kanji.
3. Nominal kanji (used as adverbs) modifying verbal kanji: 三拝九拝 (サンパイキュウハイ [lit., three bow nine bow], repeated obeisances).
4. Adjectival or verbal kanji modifying verbal kanji: 黙座 (モクザ [lit., keep silent+sit], sit silently).

Such first kanji as 不 and 未 may be added as prefixes to kanji compounds, forming more complex compounds, e.g., 不可能 (フカノウ impossible) and 未成年者 (ミセイネンシャ minor [underage person]).

The first, adverbial, kanji make up the headings below; the compounds within each list are arranged in order of increasing stroke count of the second kanji. Because of the vast number of words, only a few important first kanji are listed.

不　not
不毛 (フモウ　barren)
不可 (フカ　bad)
不正 (フセイ　injustice)
不払い (ふばらい　nonpayment)
不平 (フヘイ　discontent)
不用 (フヨウ　useless)
不安 (フアン　uneasiness)
不吉 (フキツ　ill luck)
不朽 (フキュウ　immortality)
不在 (フザイ　absence)
不死 (フシ　immortality)
不当 (フトウ　unjust)
不同 (フドウ　difference)
不向き (ふむき　unsuitable)
不老 (フロウ　eternal youth)
不快 (フカイ　unpleasant)
不具 (フグ　deformity)
不孝 (フコウ　undutifulness)
不作 (フサク　poor crop)
不肖 (フショウ　unlike one's father)
不足 (フソク　shortage)
不妊 (フニン　sterility)
不抜 (フバツ　firm)

不利 (フリ disadvantage)
不良 (フリョウ bad)
不況 (フキョウ economic depression)
不屈 (フクツ indomitability)
不幸 (フコウ unhappiness)
不治 (フジ/フチ incurable)
不定 (フテイ unfixed)
不届き (フとどき insolent)
不服 (フフク dissatisfaction)
不法 (フホウ unlawfulness)
不明 (フメイ obscurity)
不和 (フワ discord)
不急 (フキュウ not urgent)
不浄 (フジョウ uncleanness)
不信 (フシン distrust)
不貞 (フテイ infidelity)
不発 (フハツ misfire)
不変 (フヘン constant)
不便 (フベン inconvenient)
不帰 (フキ die)
不時 (フジ unexpectedness)
不純 (フジュン impure)
不祥 (フショウ ill-omened)
不振 (フシン slump)
不通 (フツウ interruption)
不納 (フノウ nonpayment)
不能 (フノウ incapacity)
不倫 (フリン immorality)
不断 (フダン constant)
不動 (フドウ immovable)
不敗 (フハイ invincible)
不偏 (フヘン independent)
不問 (フモン disregard)
不猟 (フリョウ unsuccessful hunting)
不運 (フウン bad luck)
不覚 (フカク failure)
不遇 (フグウ misfortune)
不敬 (フケイ disrespect)
不順 (フジュン unseasonable)
不善 (フゼン evil)
不測 (フソク unforeseen)
不評 (フヒョウ unpopularity)
不満 (フマン dissatisfaction)
不惑 (フワク age free from vacillation)
不渡り (フわたり dishonor)
不意 (フイ unexpected)
不義 (フギ immorality)

不詳 （フショウ　unknown）
不戦 （フセン　no fight）
不滅 （フメツ　immortality）
不徳 （フトク　vice）
不慣れ （フなれ　unaccustomed）
不漁 （フリョウ　poor catch）
不縁 （フエン　divorce）
不潔 （フケツ　uncleanness）
不審 （フシン　doubt）
不随 （フズイ　paralysis）
不確か （ふたしか　uncertainty）
不調 （フチョウ　failure; bad condition）
不敵 （フテキ　bold）
不慮 （フリョ　unforeseen）
不穏 （フオン　unrest）
不興 （フキョウ　displeasure）

最　**most**

最下 （サイカ　lowest）
最小 （サイショウ　smallest）
最上 （サイジョウ　best）
最大 （サイダイ　largest）
最少 （サイショウ　youngest; fewest）
最中 （サイチュウ　in the middle）
最古 （サイコ　oldest）
最北 （サイホク　northernmost）
最多 （サイタ　greatest）
最近 （サイキン　recent）
最初 （サイショ　beginning）
最低 （サイテイ　lowest）
最良 （サイリョウ　best）
最長 （サイチョウ　longest; oldest）
最後 （サイゴ　last）
最前 （サイゼン　foremost; little while ago）
最南 （サイナン　southernmost）
最高 （サイコウ　highest）
最悪 （サイアク　worst）
最強 （サイキョウ　strongest）
最終 （サイシュウ　last）
最善 （サイゼン　best）
最短 （サイタン　shortest）
最愛 （サイアイ　dearest）
最新 （サイシン　newest）
最適 （サイテキ　best）

未　**not yet**

未刊 （ミカン　unpublished）
未払い （みばらい　unpaid）

未完 （ミカン　unfinished）
未決 （ミケツ　unsettled）
未見 （ミケン　unacquainted）
未来 （ミライ　future）
未知 （ミチ　unknown）
未定 （ミテイ　undecided）
未明 （ミメイ　early dawn）
未納 （ミノウ　unpaid）
未婚 （ミコン　unmarried）
未済 （ミサイ　unsettled）
未設 （ミセツ　unestablished）
未遂 （ミスイ　attempted）
未着 （ミチャク　not yet arrived）
未満 （ミマン　under, less than）
未詳 （ミショウ　unknown）
未熟 （ミジュク　unripe; unskilled）
未練 （ミレン　regret; cowardice）
未踏 （ミトウ　unprecedented）

独　**alone**

独占 （ドクセン　monopoly）
独白 （ドクハク　monologue）
独立 （ドクリツ　independence）
独行 （ドッコウ　self-reliance; traveling alone）
独座 （ドクザ　sitting alone）
独走 （ドクソウ　running alone; runaway）
独学 （ドクガク　self-education）
独居 （ドッキョ　solitude）
独歩 （ドッポ　ambulatory patient; matchless）
独奏 （ドクソウ　solo）
独酌 （ドクシャク　drinking alone）
独修 （ドクシュウ　self-study）
独習 （ドクシュウ　self-study）
独唱 （ドクショウ　vocal solo）
独断 （ドクダン　arbitrary decision）
独得 （ドクトク　peculiarity）
独裁 （ドクサイ　dictatorship）
独善 （ドクゼン　self-righteousness）
独創 （ドクソウ　originality）

予　**beforehand**

予見 （ヨケン　foreknowledge）
予言 （ヨゲン　prophecy, prediction）
予告 （ヨコク　advance notice）
予防 （ヨボウ　prevention）
予知 （ヨチ　foreknowledge）
予定 （ヨテイ　plan）
予約 （ヨヤク　preengagement, reservation）

予習 (ヨシュウ preparation [of lessons])
予断 (ヨダン   prediction)
予期 (ヨキ   expectation)
予測 (ヨソク   estimate; forecast)
予備 (ヨビ   preparation; reserve)
予報 (ヨホウ   forecast)
予感 (ヨカン   premonition)
予想 (ヨソウ   anticipation)
予算 (ヨサン   estimated cost, budget)
予審 (ヨシン   preliminary investigation)
予震 (ヨシン   foreshock)
予選 (ヨセン   preliminary match/contest)

Auxiliary Kanji

A number of compounds include one kanji in an auxiliary function, either in the first or final position. For instance, 被 (ヒ) indicates the passive voice of the meaning of the second kanji, as in 被爆 (ヒバク be bombed), while 然 (ゼン/ネン) indicates the "state of" the meaning of the first kanji, as in 冷然(レイゼン[lit., cold state], cold).

Although the number of such auxiliary kanji is small, a few of them are highly productive. For instance, 的 (テキ) is used widely after two-kanji combinations to add the meaning "-ic, -ical," as in 科学的 (カガクテキ scientific). 的 is also itself the second element of some two-kanji compounds; only these, and not the three-kanji type, are shown below. Similarly, 化 (カ change; -ization) and 性 (セイ nature; -ity; -ness), not originally auxiliary kanji, are now used as such to form three-kanji compounds, such as 機械化 (キカイカ mechanization) and 可能性 (カノウセイ possibility). New words, including such loan words as ドラマ化 (ドラマカ dramatization) and インテリ性 (インテリセイ intellectuality), continue to be made. Compounds with 化 and 性 are not shown below.

然 state
公然 (コウゼン open)
天然 (テンネン nature)
必然 (ヒツゼン inevitability)
平然 (ヘイゼン calm)
本然 (ホンゼン natural)
未然 (ミゼン beforehand)
自然 (シゼン/ジネン nature)
全然 (ゼンゼン entirely)
当然 (トウゼン rightly)
同然 (ドウゼン similar)
決然 (ケツゼン resolute)
判然 (ハンゼン clear)
冷然 (レイゼン cold)
依然 (イゼン as ever)
卒然 (ソツゼン suddenly)
突然 (トツゼン suddenly)

純然 (ジュンゼン pure)
泰然 (タイゼン calm)
偶然 (グウゼン happenstance)
悠然 (ユウゼン calm)
断然 (ダンゼン decisively)
陶然 (トウゼン mellow)
猛然 (モウゼン fiercely)
敢然 (カンゼン boldly)
粛然 (シュクゼン silently)
超然 (チョウゼン detached)
漠然 (バクゼン vague)
雑然 (ザツゼン in disorder)
端然 (タンゼン upright)
漂然 (ヒョウゼン casually)
確然 (カクゼン definite)
憤然 (フンゼン indignantly)
整然 (セイゼン orderly)
厳然 (ゲンゼン stern)
騒然 (ソウゼン noisy)
翻然 (ホンゼン with a sudden turn)

所 nominalization

所用 (ショヨウ business)
所見 (ショケン one's view)
所存 (ショゾン intention)
所有 (ショユウ possession)
所定 (ショテイ fixed)
所持 (ショジ possession)
所信 (ショシン conviction)
所要 (ショヨウ necessary)
所産 (ショサン product)
所得 (ショトク income)
所望 (ショモウ desire)
所期 (ショキ expectation)
所属 (ショゾク belong to)
所感 (ショカン impression)
所載 (ショサイ printed)
所管 (ショカン jurisdiction)
所説 (ショセツ opinion)
所領 (ショリョウ fief)
所蔵 (ショゾウ colletion)
所懐 (ショカイ view)
所轄 (ショカツ jurisdiction)

的 -ic, -ical

公的 (コウテキ public)
人的 (ジンテキ human)
心的 (シンテキ mental)

外的 (ガイテキ   outward)
私的 (シテキ   private)
性的 (セイテキ   sexual)
知的 (チテキ   intellectual)
物的 (ブッテキ   material)
法的 (ホウテキ   legal)
美的 (ビテキ   aesthetic)
病的 (ビョウテキ   morbid)
動的 (ドウテキ   dynamic)
量的 (リョウテキ   quantitative)
詩的 (シテキ   poetic)
静的 (セイテキ   static)
劇的 (ゲキテキ   dramatic)
質的 (シツテキ   qualitative)

以   **than, from**

以下 (イカ   less than)
以上 (イジョウ   not less than)
以内 (イナイ   within)
以外 (イガイ   except)
以来 (イライ   since then)
以後 (イゴ   thereafter)
以前 (イゼン   ago, before)
以降 (イコウ   on and after)

子   **thing**

金子 (キンス   money)
格子 (コウシ   lattice)
骨子 (コッシ   gist)
扇子 (センス   folding fan)
帽子 (ボウシ   hat)
障子 (ショウジ   *shōji*, sliding door)

被   **passive marker**

被告 (ヒコク   defendant)
被災 (ヒサイ   suffer from a disaster)
被害 (ヒガイ   injury; damage)
被爆 (ヒバク   be bombed)

Two Kanji in a Nonsyntactic Relationship

Reduplication of Kanji

Forming kanji compounds by using the same kanji twice has two main functions:

1. pluralization of nouns: 人々 (ひとびと people), 山々 (やまやま mountains)
2. Intensification of the kanji's meaning: 黙々 (モクモク silence), 騒々しい (ソウゾウしい noisy)

Note that the kanji repetition symbol, 々, is typically used for this sort of compound kanji. As seen in the last example, adjectives have been formed by adding しい to reduplicatons, whether the reduplications are independent words or not.

In modern Japanese approximately eighty such compounds with *on-yomi* and seventy compounds with *kun-yomi* are used. Some kanji are used with both their *on-* and *kun-yomi* for either similar or distinct meanings. Additionally there are about ten compounds of two two-kanji reduplications, such as 明々白々 (メイメイハクハク as clear as day).

In the following list, plural-noun reduplicated compounds are excluded. Other compounds, including four-kanji ones and those ending in しい, are included. The compounds are arranged by stroke count of the kanji; within the same count they are listed in Japanese syllabary order.

1 stroke   一々 (イチイチ one by one)

3 strokes   口々 (くちぐち every mouth)
            下々 (しもじも the lower classes)
            上々 (ジョウジョウ best)
            丸々 (まるまる plump; entirely)

4 strokes   少々 (ショウショウ a little; a few)
            切々 (セツセツ earnest)
            月々 (つきづき every month)
            内々 (ナイナイ secretly; うちうち private)
            中々 (なかなか quite; not easily)
            日々 (ひび daily)
            方々 (ホウボウ everywhere)
            元々 (もともと originally)

5 strokes   白々 (しらじら transparent; whitely)
            末々 (すえずえ the future)
            代々 (ダイダイ from generation to generation)
            半々 (ハンハン half-and-half)
            広々 (ひろびろ spacious)
            由々しい (ユユしい grave)

6 strokes   色々 (いろいろ various)
            仰々しい (ギョウギョウしい exaggerated)
            再々 (サイサイ again and again)
            先々 (さきざき the future)
            早々 (ソウソウ/はやばや early; right away)
            共々 (ともども together)
            年々 (ネンネン year after year)
            安々 (やすやす easily)

7 strokes   初々しい (ういういしい naive)
            折々 (おりおり from time to time)
            近々 (キンキン/ちかぢか before long)

8 strokes   青々 (あおあお verdant)
            明々 (あかあか brightly)

炎々 (エンエン blazing)
刻々 (コッコク every moment)
直々 (ジキジキ direct)
空々しい (そらぞらしい false)
毒々しい (ドクドクしい spiteful)
所々 (ところどころ/ショショ in places)
苦々しい (にがにがしい disgusting)
物々しい (ものものしい showy)
若々しい (わかわかしい youthful)

9 strokes　　荒々しい (あらあらしい rough)
重々しい (おもおもしい grave)
神々しい (こうごうしい heavenly)
重々 (ジュウジュウ repeatedly)
津々 (シンシン full to overflowing)
草々 (ソウソウ in haste)
度々 (たびたび often)
段々 (ダンダン stairs; gradually)
点々 (テンテン here and there)
便々 (ベンベン idly)
面々 (メンメン every one)
洋々 (ヨウヨウ vast; great)

10 strokes　恐々 (キョウキョウ panic-stricken)
個々 (ココ individual)
徐々 (ジョジョ gradually)
時々 (ときどき sometimes)
華々しい (はなばなしい brilliant)
紛々 (フンプン confusedly)
脈々 (ミャクミャク continously)
弱々しい (よわよわしい weak-looking)
朗々 (ロウロウ ringing)

11 strokes　細々 (こまごま minutely)
渋々 (しぶしぶ reluctantly)
深々 (シンシン/ふかぶか deeply)
淡々 (タンタン disinterested)
転々 (テンテン wandering)
堂々 (ドウドウ dignified)
得々 (トクトク triumphantly)
粘々 (ねばねば sticky)
悠々 (ユウユウ composed)
粒々 (リュウリュウ painstakingly)
累々 (ルイルイ in heaps)

12 strokes　痛々しい (いたいたしい pitiful)
営々 (エイエイ strenuously)
軽々 (かるがる easily)
軽々しい (かるがるしい careless)

寒々　(さむざむ　cold-looking)
順々　(ジュンジュン　in turn)
遅々　(チチ　slowly)
着々　(チャクチャク　steadily)
程々　(ほどほど　moderately)
満々　(マンマン　full)
道々　(みちみち　on the way)
揚々　(ヨウヨウ　in triumph)
隆々　(リュウリュウ　rising)

13 strokes　数々　(かずかず　many)
続々　(ゾクゾク　one after another)
微々　(ビビ　small)
福々しい　(フクブクしい　happy-looking)

14 strokes　様々　(さまざま　various)
静々　(しずしず　quietly)
種々　(シュジュ　all sorts)
精々　(セイゼイ　as much as possible, at most)
銘々　(メイメイ　each one)
綿々　(メンメン　continously)
歴々　(レキレキ　distinguished)

15 strokes　黙々　(モクモク　in silence)

16 strokes　薄々　(うすうす　dimly)

17 strokes　懇々　(コンコン　earnestly)
頻々　(ヒンピン　frequently)

18 strokes　騒々しい　(ソウゾウしい　noisy)

19 strokes　麗々しい　(レイレイしい　conspicuous)

Commonly used four-kanji compounds

子々孫々　(シシソンソン　posterity)
正々堂々　(セイセイドウドウ　fair and square)
平々凡々　(ヘイヘイボンボン　commonplace)
年々歳々　(ネンネンサイサイ　year after year)
奇々怪々　(キキカイカイ　most strange)
明々白々　(メイメイハクハク　as clear as day)
津々浦々　(つづうらうら　all over the country)
戦々恐々　(センセンキョウキョウ　panic-stricken)

Combinations of Two Kanji of Similar Meaning

A compound of two kanji of similar meaning has one of two resultant senses:

1. A sense common to both kanji: 身体　(シンタイ〔lit., body body〕, body)
2. A meaning combining the two senses of the component Kanji: 強大　(キョウダイ〔lit., strong big〕, mighty)

The combination often results in compounds having an abstract meaning.

The following lists are headed by kanji frequently used in making such compounds. The first section of each list gives words with that kanji as the first component; the second section gives compounds with the kanji as second component. Each "half-list" is arranged by the stroke count of the other kanji.

発 bring out; emit

発生 (ハッセイ appearance)
発布 (ハップ promulgation)
発行 (ハッコウ issue)
発見 (ハッケン discovery)
発作 (ホッサ paroxysm)
発育 (ハツイク growth)
発明 (ハツメイ invention)
発送 (ハッソウ dispatch)
発射 (ハッシャ firing)
発展 (ハッテン development; expansion)
発起 (ホッキ proposal)
発掘 (ハックツ unearthing)
発現 (ハツゲン manifestation)
発覚 (ハッカク detection)
発揮 (ハッキ display)
発散 (ハッサン diffusion)
発達 (ハッタツ development)
発露 (ハツロ expression)

出発 (シュッパツ departure)
告発 (コクハツ prosecution; complaint)
啓発 (ケイハツ improvement)
開発 (カイハツ development; exploitation)
揮発 (キハツ volatilization)
摘発 (テキハツ disclosure)
奮発 (フンパツ exertion)
爆発 (バクハツ explosion)

感 feel

感心 (カンシン admiration)
感受 (カンジュ receive an impression)
感応 (カンノウ induction)
感染 (カンセン infection)
感情 (カンジョウ feeling)
感動 (カンドウ impression; excitement)
感覚 (カンカク sense)
感謝 (カンシャ gratitude)
感傷 (カンショウ sentimentality)
感触 (カンショク sense of touch)
感想 (カンソウ impression)
感嘆 (カンタン admiration)

感慨 (カンガイ deep emotion)
感激 (カンゲキ deep emotion)

情感 (ジョウカン feeling)

平　flat; even; calm
平凡 (ヘイボン commonplace)
平安 (ヘイアン peace)
平均 (ヘイキン average)
平易 (ヘイイ easy)
平定 (ヘイテイ suppression)
平明 (ヘイメイ easy)
平和 (ヘイワ peace)
平常 (ヘイジョウ normal)
平等 (ビョウドウ equality)
平静 (ヘイセイ quiet; calm)
平穏 (ヘイオン quiet; peace)
平衡 (ヘイコウ balance)

公平 (コウヘイ fairness)
和平 (ワヘイ peace)

明　light; plain; clear
明白 (メイハク clear)
明快 (メイカイ plain)
明朗 (メイロウ bright and cheerful)
明細 (メイサイ details)
明確 (メイカク clearness)

公明 (コウメイ fairness)
灯明 (トウミョウ sacred light)
平明 (ヘイメイ easy)
光明 (コウミョウ light)
判明 (ハンメイ become clear)
発明 (ハツメイ invention)
透明 (トウメイ transparency)
賢明 (ケンメイ wisdom)
鮮明 (センメイ clearness)

分　distribution
分与 (ブンヨ distribution)
分岐 (ブンキ branch off)
分別 (フンベツ judgment)
分析 (ブンセキ analysis)
分派 (ブンパ branch)
分配 (ブンパイ division)
分割 (ブンカツ partition)
分散 (ブンサン dispersion)
分裂 (ブンレツ disruption)
分解 (ブンカイ analysis; dissolving)

分離 (ブンリ　separation)

配分 (ハイブン　distribution)

節分 (セツブン　the day before the calendrical beginning of spring)

出　put out; come out
出生 (シュッショウ/シュッセイ　birth)
出奔 (シュッポン　abscondence)
出発 (シュッパツ　departure)
出現 (シュツゲン　appearance)
出産 (シュッサン　childbirth)

退出 (タイシュツ　leave)
傑出 (ケッシュツ　stand out)
現出 (ゲンシュツ　appearance)
産出 (サンシュツ　production)
脱出 (ダッシュツ　escape)
転出 (テンシュツ　move out)
輸出 (ユシュツ　exportation)

作　make; act
作用 (サヨウ　action)
作成 (サクセイ　draw up)
作為 (サクイ　intention)

制作 (セイサク　create)
発作 (ホッサ　paroxysm)
耕作 (コウサク　cultivation)
造作 (ゾウサク　fixture)
著作 (チョサク　writing)
動作 (ドウサ　action)
創作 (ソウサク　original work)
製作 (セイサク　manufacture)
操作 (ソウサ　operation)

生　live; birth
生存 (セイゾン　life, existence)
生命 (セイメイ　life)
生活 (セイカツ　life, living)
生息 (セイソク　live)
生産 (セイサン　production)
生殖 (セイショク　reproduction)
生誕 (セイタン　birth)
生鮮 (セイセン　fresh)

出生 (シュッショウ/シュッセイ　birth)
発生 (ハッセイ　appearance)
誕生 (タンジョウ　birth)

変　change; disturbance
変化 (ヘンカ　change)

変更 (ヘンコウ   alteration)
変革 (ヘンカク   reform)
変異 (ヘンイ   variation; mutation)
変転 (ヘンテン   change; turn)
変動 (ヘンドウ   fluctuation)
変換 (ヘンカン   conversion)
変遷 (ヘンセン   transition)

改変 (カイヘン   alter)
異変 (イヘン   change; disaster)
転変 (テンペン   change; turn)

通   **pass through; communication**
通行 (ツウコウ   passage; traffic)
通告 (ツウコク   notification)
通知 (ツウチ   notice)
通航 (ツウコウ   navigate)
通運 (ツウウン   transportation)
通過 (ツウカ   passage)
通報 (ツウホウ   report)

交通 (コウツウ   traffic)
流通 (リュウツウ   circulation)
貫通 (カンツウ   penetration)
開通 (カイツウ   open 〔to traffic〕)

Combinations of Two Kanji with Contrastive Meanings

Compound words made up of kanji having contrastive or opposite senses often express one on the other (or both) of these types of meanings:

1. The meanings of both components together: 日夜 (ニチヤ day and night, all the time),   子女 (シジョ sons and daughters, children)
2. The meanings of the components taken alternately: 真偽 (シンギ true or false, truth, authenticity), 可否 (カヒ okay or not, propriety, advisability)

Some such compounds, such as 大小 (ダイショウ large and small, both/all sizes; large or small, size), can be taken either way, as context dictates.

A new type of compound that has become quite common is an abbreviation formed from the first kanji of each of two two-kanji compounds, e.g., 収支(シュウシ income and expenditure), from 収入(シュウニュウ income) and 支出(シシュツ expenditure), and 日米(Japan and the U. S. A.), from 日本(ニホン/ニッポン Japan) and 米国 (ベイコク U. S. A.).

The following compounds are arranged by stroke count of the first kanji; kanji having the same count are listed in Japanese syllabary order.

2 strokes   人畜 (ジンチク   humans and animals)

3 strokes   才知 (サイチ   talent)
山河 (サンガ   mountains and rivers)
山海 (サンカイ   all sorts of)

山水 (サンスイ　hills and rivers)
山野 (サンヤ　fields and mountains)
山林 (サンリン　mountains and forests)
子女 (シジョ　sons and daughters, children)
子孫 (シソン　descendants)
上下 (ジョウゲ　up and down, high and low)
大小 (ダイショウ　large and small ones; size)
土砂 (ドシャ　earth and sand)
土木 (ドボク　engineering works)
山川 (やまかわ/サンセン　mountains and rivers)

4 strokes 　公私 (コウシ　public and/or private)
今昔 (コンジャク　past and present)
心身 (身心) (シンシン　mind and body)
月日 (つきひ　months and days)
手足 (てあし　hands and feet)
天地 (テンチ　heaven and earth; earth and sky)
内外 (ナイガイ　the inside and the outside)
日時 (ニチジ　the time)
日夜 (ニチヤ　day and night)
夫婦 (フウフ　man and wife, married couple)
父兄 (フケイ　guardians)
夫妻 (フサイ　husband and wife)
父母 (フボ　father and mother, parents)
文武 (ブンブ　civil and military)
木石 (ボクセキ　wood and stones)

5 strokes 　凹凸 (オウトツ　unevenness)
加減 (カゲン　degree)
可否 (カヒ　right or wrong)
兄弟 (キョウダイ　brothers and sisters)
去来 (キョライ　come and go)
甲乙 (コウオツ　difference)
古今 (ココン　ancient and modern)
左右 (サユウ　right and left)
主客 (シュカク　host and guest)
主従 (シュジュウ　master and servant)
生滅 (ショウメツ　birth and death; appearance and disappearance)
白黒 (しろくろ　right and wrong)
生死 (セイシ　life and death)
出入 (でいり/シュツニュウ　going in and out)
皮肉 (ヒニク　sarcasm)
母子 (ボシ　mother and child)
本末 (ホンマツ　cause and effect)
右左 (みぎひだり　right and left)
矛盾 (ムジュン　contradiction)

6 strokes 　衣鉢 (イハツ　mantle)

紅白 (コウハク red and white)
死活 (シカツ life and/or death)
自他 (ジタ oneself and others)
多少 (タショウ large and/or small, more or less)
年月 (ネンゲツ years and months)
名実 (メイジツ name and fact)

7 strokes 肝心 (カンジン essential)
肝要 (カンヨウ importance)
言行 (ゲンコウ words and/or action)
言動 (ゲンドウ speech and action)
見聞 (ケンブン observation)
伸縮 (シンシュク elasticity)
男女 (ダンジョ man and woman)
売買 (バイバイ buying and selling)
利害 (リガイ interests)

8 strokes 往来 (オウライ traffic)
学問 (ガクモン learning)
金銀 (キンギン gold and silver; money)
金品 (キンピン money and other articles)
苦楽 (クラク pleasure and pain)
呼応 (コオウ act in concert with)
呼吸 (コキュウ breath)
妻子 (サイシ wife and children; one's family)
事物 (ジブツ things)
姉妹 (シマイ sisters)
始末 (シマツ circumstances)
取捨 (シュシャ selection)
姓名 (セイメイ full name)
知能 (チノウ intellect)
長短 (チョウタン length; merits and demerits)
長幼 (チョウヨウ young and old)
東西 (トウザイ the east and the west)
波風 (なみかぜ wind and waves; discord)
表裏 (ヒョウリ right and wrong side)
明暗 (メイアン light and shade)
明滅 (メイメツ flicker)
物事 (ものごと things, matter)
和英 (ワエイ Japanese and English)
和漢 (ワカン Japanese and Chinese)

9 strokes 後先 (あとさき before and behind; order)
胃腸 (イチョウ stomach and bowels)
草木 (くさき plant)
昨今 (サッコン recently)
春秋 (シュンジュウ spring and autumn; years)
是非 (ゼヒ right and wrong; by all means)

前後 (ゼンゴ　front and rear, order)
昼夜 (チュウヤ　day and night)
動静 (ドウセイ　movements)
南北 (ナンボク　north and south)
発着 (ハッチャク　arrival and departure)
美醜 (ビシュウ　beauty and ugliness)
風雨 (フウウ　wind and rain)
風雪 (フウセツ　wind and snow)
風潮 (フウチョウ　trend)
風波 (フウハ　wind and waves; discord)
面目 (メンボク　face, honor)
要領 (ヨウリョウ　essential points)

10 strokes　家庭 (カテイ　home, family)
高低 (コウテイ　height; unevenness)
師弟 (シテイ　master and pupil)
消息 (ショウソク　news)
書画 (ショガ　painting and writings)
真偽 (シンギ　truth, true or false)

11 strokes　異同 (イドウ　difference)
陰陽 (インヨウ　positive and negative)
強弱 (キョウジャク　strength and/or weakness)
虚実 (キョジツ　fact and fiction)
黒白 (コクビャク　black and white)
始終 (シジュウ　always)
情理 (ジョウリ　reason and sentiment)
野山 (のやま　hills and fields)
貧富 (ヒンプ　wealth and poverty)
問答 (モンドウ　questions and answers)
理知 (リチ　intellect)

12 strokes　朝晩 (あさバン　morning and evening)
朝夕 (あさゆう　morning and evening)
飲食 (インショク　eating and drinking)
開閉 (カイヘイ　open and shut)
軽重 (ケイチョウ/ケイジュウ　relative importance, weight)
勝敗 (ショウハイ　victory and/or defeat)
勝負 (ショウブ　game)
晴雨 (セイウ　rain or shine)
善悪 (ゼンアク　good and/or evil)

13 strokes　意識 (イシキ　consciousness)
遠近 (エンキン　distance)
雌雄 (シユウ　male and female; victory or defeat)
新旧 (シンキュウ　old and new)
損得 (ソントク　loss and gain)
腹心 (フクシン　trusted)
福利 (フクリ　welfare)

雷雨 (ライウ   thunderstorm)

14 strokes 増減 (ゾウゲン   increase and/or decrease)

15 strokes 賞罰 (ショウバツ   reward and punishment)

16 strokes 親子 (おやこ   parent and child)
　　　　　縦横 (ジュウオウ   in all directions; たてよこ   length and breadth)

17 strokes 優劣 (ユウレツ   superiority and/or inferiority)

Index by Stroke Count

Note: Within each stroke-count grouping, the entries are grouped by classifier, shown on the left. The symbol "c" indicates that the entry is itself a classifier.

12 strokes

Index by Reading

コ/こ，ゴ/ご